Relational Reality

Relational Reality

New Discoveries of Interrelatedness
That Are Transforming the Modern World

by

Charlene Spretnak

Green Horizon Books
2011

For the Earth Community

Green Horizon Books are published in association with

Green Horizon Foundation
P.O. Box 476
Topsham, ME 04086

www.green-horizon.org

Library of Congress Control Number: 2011924855

ISBN-13: 978-0615461274
ISBN-10: 0615461271

Cover Photograph: photos8.com

Cover Design: David Moses

Other Books by Charlene Spretnak

The Resurgence of the Real:
Body, Nature, and Place in a Hypermodern World

States of Grace:
The Recovery of Meaning in the Postmodern Age

Green Politics: The Global Promise (coauthor)

The Spiritual Dimension of Green Politics

Missing Mary:
The Queen of Heaven and Her Re-Emergence
in the Modern Church

The Politics of Women's Spirituality (editor)

Lost Goddesses of Early Greece:
A Collection of Pre-Hellenic Myths

Contents

Relational Reality

I

RELATIONAL REVELATIONS

Discovery and Emergence in the 21st Century

Our hypermodern societies currently possess only a kindergarten-level understanding of the deeply relational nature of reality. It may seem unlikely that such advanced cultures could have missed "the way the world works," but it was simply a matter of habit. Our cultural tendency has been to perceive the physical world as an aggregate of separate entities. We noticed some relationships between and among things, of course, but those seemed of marginal significance compared to what things are made of and how they function.

The failure to notice that reality is inherently dynamic and interrelated at all levels – including substance and functioning – has caused a vast range of suffering: our medical system designed treatments as if our bodies were biomachines with independently functioning parts; our education systems regarded students as essentially isolate units into which learning can be implanted; our psychologists authoritatively conveyed to patients the Freudian notion that separating from core family relationships is the key to healthy maturation; and our workplaces and dwellings were designed with no inkling of the relationship between human health and natural light. Moreover, our communities have become fragmented and alienating, as the focus of modern life has largely contracted to the sphere of the Individual Consumer, a disintegration that has not been countered by support for the social fabric. Even more tragically, the entire planet is now imperiled by climate destabilization and ecological degradation, resulting from the modern assumption that highly advanced societies could throw toxic substances "away" somewhere and could exude staggeringly unnatural levels of carbon dioxide and other greenhouse gases into our atmosphere without ill effect.

In recent years, however, the medical profession's general advice about staying healthy – eat nutritious food, get sufficient exercise, get a full night's sleep, avoid smoking, and wash hands often during cold and flu season – was joined by an incongruous addition: have friends and socialize often with them. *Friends?* This amended list seemed to me at first like one of those children's puzzles that ask "Which of these does not belong?" We were accustomed to hearing medical experts explain that illness results from quantifiable physical conditions, such as the malfunction of, say, the heart or the endocrine system, or the presence of a nasty bacteria or virus – but personal relationships? Moreover, we were assured that this new finding is now firmly established in 21st-century medical knowledge because it has been replicated in numerous well-designed scientific studies and published in prestigious medical journals. All of which left me wondering, "How is possible that the vast analytical powers of modern medical research had missed this crucial fact for hundreds of years? And what else, by the way, have they missed?"

The answers to that question continue to unfold. As soon as it became respectable for medical researchers to study relational effects on human health and mental capabilities, a flood of discoveries and new basic knowledge emerged and entered the medical journals. For instance, it was found in 2002 that the presence of a small circle of good relationships in an elderly person's life is far more likely to prevent dementia than is the practice of doing mental calisthenics such as crossword puzzles. In fact, researchers ascertained in 2007 that for people of all ages ten minutes of talking with someone, in person or even by phone, boosts mental performance and memory as much as doing crossword puzzles for the same amount of time. Moreover, it was found that the more social contact people have, the higher their level of mental functioning. In 2009 a study of older adults found that those with fewer social interactions experienced a more rapid rate of decline in motor function such as walking, gripping, and balancing. Several studies have found that if one's social contact includes being of service to others, such as volunteering weekly, the volunteer experiences improved physical health and longevity.[1]

Perhaps the most surprising discovery in what might be called "relational physiology," however, is that even our IQ, long held to be a measure of innate, fixed intelligence, is partially a malleable, relational matter. Earlier studies had found that one's IQ is influenced by one's place in the birth order, in that the eldest child generally scores a few IQ points higher on a standardized intelligence test. The startling finding of a study conducted in 2007, however, was that becoming the eldest because of the early death of an older sibling, or even two older siblings, still yields the additional IQ points at age 19 commonly seen in the scores earned by eldest children.[2] In short, the development and expression of intelligence (at least on a standardized test) is significantly affected by relational dynamics in the family. Is this because parents relate differently to their eldest child, giving her or him more responsibility (such as watching over the younger ones on occasion), which might cause the child to feel more capable and confident? Is it because the eldest child tends to identify more with the adult world (and being tested by it) than do the younger siblings? The researchers did not speculate, yet their findings are remarkable.

Even more surprisingly, a study in 2009 found that IQ scores within the United States, as well as cross-culturally, are influenced detrimentally by whether a child was spanked and how often. The more spanking the slower the mental development of the child, and even a small amount of spanking made a difference.[3] Apparently, corporal punishment is such a relational violation of a child's being that it is a trauma to the entire bodymind, which causes lasting damage to his or her capabilities of intelligence.[4]

Any one of these discoveries would have been dismissed out of hand only a decade ago by nearly all physiologists. The evidence of the centrality of relational dynamics had always been right under the noses of the experts, but it did not fit into the frame of reference with which they had been trained to practice medicine, focusing solely on physical matter and quantifiable processes. In fact, it clashed directly with the foundational assumption that had shaped the entire body of modern medical knowledge since its beginnings in the 17th century: humans are essentially self-contained biomachines that operate on biomechanical principles. From the biomechanistic perspective, whether or not a patient had a number of enjoyable friends could not have been more irrelevant to physical health.

Less dramatic than the discoveries in "relational physiology," but also unexpected, have been the recent findings in studies of what could be called "relational behavior": aspects of our behavior, such as overeating or not and feeling happy or not, are apparently influenced by the behavior of others situated near us in our network of social interactions. Researchers in the social sciences call this phenomenon "connectivity" (or sometimes "social contagion"). In September 2009 *The New York Times Magazine* featured a cover story about the new studies in connectivity, "Is Happiness Catching?" – or, as the journalist put is, "The Way the World Works."[5]

Well, certainly relational behavior is a part of the emerging sense of how inherently relational reality actually is, but it merely one example of a far larger phenomenon.

A growing stream of discoveries in recent years has begun to dislodge assumptions that have been in place for nearly four centuries about how we humans and the rest of the natural world function. With each new finding, it is becoming apparent that the established view was quite wrong about us in many respects, overlooking significant evidence that would have led to far more accurate systems of knowledge. Yet nearly all of us were schooled in the modern, mechanistic perspective, and those of us who have gone on to invest their entire professional lives in a field that is tightly bound by that frame of reference have been understandably resistant to acknowledging the mounting evidence to the contrary. Nonetheless, reality is far more relational and dynamic than various experts thought, though they have been able to deny the obvious throughout their career, just as the modern West has done for centuries. It is somewhat amusing, actually, to watch the medical profession, for instance, try to casually absorb the startling new relational findings by merely tacking them on to their usual way of regarding the human body – *Oh, yes, here's one more prescription: socialize with friends to stay healthy* – when, in fact, that single relational discovery alone challenges the most basic assumptions of modern medical science.

One simple idea underlies the systems of knowledge that have shaped modernity: that all entities in the natural world, including us, are essentially separate and that they function through mechanistic ways of interacting. In contrast, a very different, yet elegantly simple, idea is now emerging and correcting the extremely limited mechanistic view: that all entities in the natural world, including us, are *thoroughly relational beings of great complexity, who are both composed of and nested within contextual networks of dynamic and reciprocal relationships.* We are made entirely of relationships, as is the whole of the natural world. Both the mechanistic and the relational modes of perceptions are ways of seeing the world. They are each a foundational frame of reference, which results in a particular worldview, or paradigm. The relational worldview, however, is a close fit with the relational nature of reality, while the mechanistic worldview is not.

The most widely acknowledged example of the relational shift in thinking is the recognition that our health is determined to a significant extent by creative, dynamic relationships within the bodymind[6] as well as relationships among people and with other forms of life. However, numerous examples in fields other than physiology and medicine are also surfacing with increasing frequency. For instance, Malcolm Gladwell made the case in *The Tipping Point* that collective change is best understood by paying attention to the relational "power of context," and he next demonstrated, in *Outliers*, that the full expression and cultivation of one's talents is very much situated in a web of either challenging or supportive relationships. That is, the long-standing assumption of the born genius, or the entirely self-made successful person, is being corrected by the relational perspective. Similarly, David Brooks analyzed recent discoveries in cognitive science and concluded in his book *The Social Animal: The Hidden Sources of Love, Character, and Achievement* that we emerge out of relationships and live to bond with each other and connect to larger ideas.

In a related vein, Oxford University Press published a book in 2009 titled *Relational Being: Beyond Self and Community* by Kenneth Gergen, which they described as presenting the "radical and potentially exciting landscape of relational thought and practice" that is sweeping through the field of psychology. Around the same time *The Empathic Civilization* by Jeremy Rifkin was published, making the case that we are "hardwired" for empathy, which he defines as the ability to show solidarity with others. Several other recent books have analyzed a particular current event, crisis, or situation by focusing on the relational dynamics, a perspective that yields a far more accurate sense of what is going on. Each of these works explores a significant aspect of the overview I propose here. Certainly there will be many such books in the future explicating "the growing understanding in many disciplines about all things being fundamentally relational," as the British magazine *Resurgence* observed in 2009.[7]

For my part, I have long been intrigued with the emergent perception of relational reality, though my focus has not been limited to its effect on interhuman connections. All of reality is relational. I was puzzled – and still am – by the fact that it took only about 100 years for the mechanistic worldview to spread through nearly all social institutions and systems of knowledge in 18th-century Britain and France (beginning with the culmination of the Scientific Revolution in the late 17th century) yet it has now been more than 100 years since Einstein's first two articles established that the universe is best understood as highly relational, rather than mechanistic. Wouldn't one expect a (post-mechanistic) worldview to spread from science into society at a far more rapid pace in the 20th century than did the previous, comparable shift? Instead, the implications of the new physics have hardly affected society's ways of thinking, perhaps because people find them too abstract to be relevant to daily life. In the 1980s and 1990s complexity studies in biology and other areas of science discovered that dynamic interrelatedness is the key to understanding living systems. The implications of those discoveries, too, had some impact beyond science but did not really have a significant impact on the mainstream. Similarly, the emergence of alternative medicine (now called integral, or integrated, medicine) made some waves as it was grudgingly, but increasingly, accepted by the medical system. (Many of the recent discoveries of relational physiology, however, are surprising even to practitioners of integral medicine.)

Because of this partial progress, I was able to gather some examples of the relational perspective for my book *The Resurgence of the Real* (1997), although that book was focused mainly on cultural history. After finishing that project, my attention was drawn elsewhere. Perhaps, I thought, the Relational Shift would not become widespread in my lifetime. So I was surprised to begin noticing in mainstream media, around 2004, a growing stream of references to discoveries of the relational nature of reality in various fields, nearly all of which had successful applications. Moreover, I was often amazed by the findings in many of the recent studies, even though I was no stranger to the phenomenon. Evidently, reality is far more deeply interrelated than even relational thinkers had previously supposed.

It seems to me that a coherence exists among the numerous, yet seemingly disparate relational discoveries and innovations. Taken together, the discoveries, new perspectives, and innovative applications can be seen to have engendered the Relational Shift. In my view, they can be recognized as one coherent phenomenon, with myriad versions, which is transforming the modern world. We are profoundly relational beings who have been living – with some difficulty – in anti-relational (mechanistic) systems of thought and ways of doing things. Finally, all that has begun to change.

In this book I seek to illuminate the largely unrecognized common ground among the relational discoveries within various fields – and also among various fields. My goal is to map the territory and present the Big Picture of this vast development. My hope is that readers of this book will emerge with a well grounded sense that we are now living through a transformation of a grand scale, as many of the most basic assumptions of the centuries-old modern worldview are being radically corrected, expanded, or replaced entirely. In many respects, it feels as if the blinders are coming off that had conditioned modern societies to overlook the profound significance of the relational dimension of life and living. Of course, modernity did not so much "overlook" the relational worldview as aggressively replace it. Hence the often difficult, and sometimes forced, transition to modernity from indigenous or traditional societies involved at its core the abandoning of a relational perception of the world for a more "sophisticated," mechanistic perspective.

Rather than try for an encyclopedic account of the extent of the relational transformation, I focus on four major areas as examples: education and parenting, health and healthcare, community design and architecture, and the economy. There are, however, many more. For instance, some of the old assumptions about criminal justice are yielding to the success of a relational approach called "restorative justice": communities across the country have found that arrested offenders, when given the chance to take responsibility for their actions in a relational manner and repair the harm they have done (such as apologizing, returning stolen money, or doing community service) in exchange for having the charges dropped, tend to avoid engaging in any further criminal activity in the future. That is, their rate of recidivism is only 10 percent, compared to 70 percent among those who go through the traditional criminal justice system.[8]

In truth, no field of human endeavor lies beyond the revitalizing influence of this rising phenomenon. Having touched on some of the changes in physiology and medicine at the beginning of this chapter, I will now cite a few of the manifestations of the Relational Shift in three others fields, each of which is covered in one of the following chapters.

First, in the related areas of education and parenting, efforts to teach and learn have been severely compromised in recent decades by the detrimental effects on children's formative years of electronic immersion, vapid but mesmerizing media content, non-nutritive "food," lack of physical exercise, and a widespread condition that psychologists call "attachment displacement disorder," which orients many children away from their parents and leaves them hardened and "cool" but seriously adrift, as they struggle with deficits in their development. The frightening groundlessness that results in high levels of alienation and depression in so many adolescents is being addressed by several new approaches that cultivate the student's relational capabilities. In the younger grades, school gardens are one means by which a connection with nature, for instance, is nurtured. Additionally, young children learn about basic relationships (between plants and the sun, for instance) and gradually increase their knowledge of the network of relationships that constitute arithmetic, literature, science, social studies, art, and all other areas of human accomplishment. At the university level, relational thinking is rippling through all the disciplines, replacing the mechanistic assumptions underlying many foundational concepts with more realistic perspectives that pay attention to interrelatedness and dynamic context. Relational analysis quickly crosses the boundaries of traditional academic disciplines, as well, so it is increasingly evident in the mushrooming growth of interdisciplinary programs at universities. As various fields of knowledge have begun to adopt the relational perspective, the new thinking has begun to spread throughout society and to reshape our institutions.

Second, in architecture and city planning the ways in which we build houses and buildings and design our cities has shifted significantly because of relational insights and remarkable innovations with regard to various ecosocial realities. For example, not only are structures now built to meet standards of ecological efficiency but we have discovered that people remain healthier if the buildings in which they work allow natural light to come in. In the past, designers would have dismissed such a distinction on the grounds that "Light is light – as long as it illuminates the employee's desk sufficiently." That was an incorrect assumption. Our bodymind thrives in organic relationship with that which is vital and life-giving, such as the light of the sun.

Third, the science of modern economics, which has long been enthroned at the center of all industrialized societies regardless of their form of government, holds as a underlying premise that the expansion of material production and economic growth automatically brings in its wake solutions to social problems and personal well-being for citizens. Yet even that foundational slab of modern economic theory – which drives governments to strive for continuous growth of their Gross Domestic Product and per capita income – has been challenged in recent years by various Quality of Life Indicators and by the new field of "happiness economics," or "happiness studies."

Combining the analytical tools of economics and psychological surveys, many of these socio-economic studies have found that in much of Europe in recent decades, happiness (or "contentment") has decreased while material prosperity has increased. What factors correlate with people's happiness in the high-scoring countries? The European Social Survey of thirty countries found in 2007 that high levels of trust in their governments, the police, and the justice system, as well as those around them were consistent factors in the happy societies, in addition to having plenty of friends and acquaintances and at least one very close friend, or "significant other." Denmark was the happiest country, followed by Sweden, Finland, and the Netherlands. Women generally classed themselves as happier than did men, while the old and the young tended to be happier than people in mid-life.[9] On the global level the World Database of Happiness, which compiles the findings of several surveys in 148 nations, found that in 2009 the happiest countries were Costa Rica, Denmark, Iceland, Switzerland, and Canada, with the United States ranking 20th.[10] (When sustainability is also considered – via life enjoyment, life expectancy, and the country's "ecological footprint" on the environment – the Happy Planet Index of 143 countries found in 2009 that Costa Rica comes in first and the United States ranks 114th.[11])

In general, such studies have found that beyond a basic level of material comfort and security, happiness does not appear to be a matter of having conspicuous material possessions of the latest design. Rather, happiness is largely a result of having a network of good relationships – with family, friends, co-workers, community, and with nature, as well as cultivating the mental qualities of gratitude, hope, and zest for life. In fact, we are significantly happier when we spend money on gifts or give to charity than when we spend it in ourselves.[12] Moreover, although most people experience loss as having a more intense and lasting effect in their lives than does gain, they are better able to adapt to loss in their finances than in the relational sphere, including family bonds, romantic relationships, and the social fabric of community.[13] Beyond a certain level of security, per capita income is not, after all, the key to happiness and well-being, yet classical economic theory was oblivious to this relational reality.

Is a relational analysis useful when considering the causes of the economic collapse that began in the oversized banks and trading firms of New York in 2008 and led to a global economic crisis? It was a horrifying lesson in what can go wrong when all economies are entangled in a tightly integrated but insufficiently regulated and highly reckless, credit-driven globalized finance market that is skewed by countless new forms of speculation and dominated by a relatively few gargantuan banks, investment firms, and corporations. In the collective process of rethinking the operative assumptions of our financial system, which was the most gripping topic in late 2008, the relational perspective was brought to the fore by the financier George Soros in his book *The New Paradigm for Financial Markets*, on the role of the relational factor he calls "reflexivity" in the dynamics by which market value is actually set.[14] He presents an analysis of self-deceiving assumptions that are injected into the spiraling feedback loops of information, which influence the perception of value (see Chapter 5, The Economy).

Prior to the collapse of international markets and credit flow, the newly globalized system of investment and trade, under the World Trade Organization (WTO), was already experiencing failure in several areas. It had been designed in the early 1990s to allow the free movement of capital in and out of countries (with no regulatory say from the countries affected). Within only a few years, the actual results of the new system proved to be highly problematic. When the American financial sector imploded in fall 2008, the WTO had already been faced with several failed rounds of negotiations, numerous disillusioned member states, and the increasing impoverishment of vast populations. While the grand scheme for untethered "liberated capital" with no attachment to any place or people was foundering, however, local, regional, and even some national governments around the world were trying new, more wisely relational approaches to structuring economic activity for the well-being of society. Such approaches have been applied to regional trade, development, energy, food security, local economies, water, waste, carbon dioxide emissions and other toxins, and transport. Simultaneously, a basic rethinking of how we manufacture products has been transforming modes of production, as well.

Almost every day we read or hear about significant changes in the ways things are done within a field or the way problems are analyzed, yet these bits of news tend to dissolve in our awareness as disparate, isolated droplets in the relentless stream of info-glut. New things are always popping up here and there but are soon forgotten in the onrushing flow. Even through that blur, though, it is possible to make out the contours of common ground among these seemingly disparate events: *Why do so many of these new solutions to very different sorts of problems seem to be moving in the same direction? And why is so much "remodeling" of foundational perceptions and concepts happening simultaneously?*

Throughout the modern and hypermodern countries of the world, a shift is occurring in habits of perception – a profound shift comparable to the one that ushered in the modern era roughly 400 years ago, when Europeans learned to see reality through the lens of the mechanistic worldview. Under the influence of that perspective, we moderns have been socialized to see the world as an aggregate of separate objects and persons who may, or may not, have some interactions or relationships. In the hypermodern version of this condition, which is familiar to nearly everyone in the United States today, the underlying assumptions are exaggerated: activity becomes speeded up in the name of efficiency, existence becomes somewhat disembodied as virtual reality engulfs the human psyche of our young people, and psychological habits of reflection give way to gazing at a stream of fleeting images on a screen for several hours daily.

In the 21st century, however, both the modern habit of perceiving fragmentation and fundamental separateness, as well as the hypermodern artificial merging of fragments into streams of electronic visual images, are gradually yielding to a larger, deeper truth of existence: every aspect of human life, as well as the life of every species and ecosystem on Earth, is literally *composed* of interactive, organic relationships, which are always changing creatively and are alive with responsiveness. These are far more complex and vital than are the electronic versions of connectedness. Inherent relationships within our bodymind, with other people, with animals, and with the rest of nature all interact and infuse each other, making us what we are. It is not merely a matter of *having* relationships but *being* relationships. As the interactive relationships that constitute the world respond to what is happening from moment to moment, a dynamic state of emergence brings into being new patterns of relationship. This is the relational reality in and around us. Nothing in the entire universe is completely static or exists outside of this vast web of creative, responsive relationship.

Yet the abstract worldview of strict separation and fragmentation has long stood confidently – and tragically – in exile from The Real, by which I mean the dynamic, interrelated reality of everything on this Earth. Because the mechanistic worldview conditioned us to perceive the world as if it were an aggregate of discrete, fundamentally separate, largely self-contained entities, whether animate or inanimate, relationships were seen as extraneous to the characteristics and capabilities of a being or an object. The Western tendency to focus far more on substance and category than on process and dynamic relationship was intensified with the emergence of the modern era. A child born today, however, will grow up with a decidedly different perception of reality.

The Relational Shift, then, is deeply personal at the same time it is revamping the thinking that underlies all our institutions and social systems. Rather than regarding ourselves as isolate individuals enclosed in a bag of skin, we can see that each of us is a constellation of vital relationships within our bodymind and beyond it. The insights of the Relational Shift reveal ways in which we can stay healthier, feel happier, and create more wisely relational homes, offices, and communities. It can help our schools to educate and guide our children in ways that connect with their inherently relational selves. Cultivating the habit of thinking relationally – because reality is more profoundly relational than we can even grasp – changes the way in which we experience and shape life in the modern world. Alive to the relational, dynamic nature of life, we are newly aware of possibilities. Moreover, we are each an agent of this historic corrective effort to move beyond the limiting assumptions of the past.

Ecological = Organically Interrelated = Relational

To think relationally is to open our minds to the revitalizing experience of organic thought. "Organic" here means not only living, as opposed to inert (in the sense of organic chemistry as distinct from inorganic chemistry) but also, and primarily, connotes the word's further definition as "integral, fundamental, constitutional, structural" and "likened to an organism in organization and function." In keeping with the latest biological sense of the life and times of an organism, then, the organic perspective involves the perception and conscious awareness of the contextual, dynamically interrelated nature of reality. This is different from saying "Everything is connected." Beads on a string, for instance, are connected, but interrelatedness denotes the constitutional nature of inherent relationships. All forms of life are composed of relationships and function in dynamic relationship with everything else. The fields of interaction include the vast stretches of the universe, the minute dance of subatomic particles, and the familiar level of perception we know as life on Earth. It is all in play, zinging with creativity every fraction of a second. Nothing exists in isolation.

One of the major sources of the emergence of the organic perspective has been the key findings of the relatively new field called ecology, though it was not until recent years that such thinking moved beyond green circles into the mainstream. The delay perhaps resulted from a strange divergence within ecological activism in our country. On one hand, mainstream environmentalism has tended to focus almost entirely on (admirably) identifying serious problems in "the environment" and on advocating accountability and solutions – a simple cause-and-effect approach that you might have thought would be convincing and effective in no time. It was a streamlined focus that seemed politically expedient, yet it did not challenge our received way of perceiving and thinking about the natural world. Since Western cultures tend to perceive the world as being composed of discrete, essentially unrelated entities that may or may not interact at times with other entities, we tend to end up with a simple cause-and-effect understanding of interactions among different life forms. Hence it is understandable that this view often informed the campaigns mounted by mainstream environmental organizations.

On the other hand, what might be called the ecological approach focused on the intriguing patterns and interconnections that shape the natural world, what came to be called the "ecological worldview." The more ecological activists studied the new science of ecology in the 1970s and after – aided by the perceptive, deeply moving ecological writings of such sages as John Muir, Rachel Carson, Aldo Leopold, and Gregory Bateson – the more we began to grasp that interrelationships shape the physical form of every organism and also continuously affect its life. We began to realize that the ways in which the natural world operates offer clues about the ways in which the human body and human interactions work. We saw that modern society's received notions about the nature of the human are essentially mechanistic assumptions, which miss entirely the profound dynamics of interrelatedness.

So ecological activists in the 1970s, myself included, began to think about John Muir's observation in the 1890s that everything in the universe turns out to be "hitched to everything else." As contemporary scientists working in the fields of ecology and systems theory would later put it, everything exists in a network, or system, of relationships, rather than in isolation. Moreover, every entity is literally constituted by its relationships, both internal and external. This was pretty much the opposite of what we'd been taught in our modern education. With the insights of the ecological worldview, The Real – the dynamic, relational nature of the physical world – had finally burst through the mechanistic assumptions that had shaped the modern worldview for centuries.

Still, it took decades for ecological thought to be embraced by the American public, to the extent that it has. After thirty-five years of environmental efforts following the first Earth Day in 1970, the actual condition of our planet was, in many respects, worse than ever. Year after year even the most alarming scientific findings about environmental destruction and toxic dangers in our country were successfully batted off the table by the American corporate sector and its representatives in government and the media. Exasperated citizens in grassroots organizations tried to figure out what words, what photos, what scientific data might succeed in convincing the American people to take the situation seriously and to "green" their thinking and their voting. Aside from some partial successes, however, the goal remained out of reach, even as the ecological crises intensified.

Then, in 2006, everything seemed to shift, partially because of grassroots showings of Al Gore's film, An Inconvenient Truth. Politicians at all levels began to declare that reducing the level of carbon dioxide emissions in our country was a top priority for America, and several corporate leaders insisted that the Bush administration institute mandatory caps on allowable carbon emissions for all companies. In September Business Week launched a new section titled "Green Biz," and the following month Fortune added a 16-page supplement titled "It's Good to Be Green." Even Thomas Friedman, an aggressive cheerleader for the dynamics of economic globalization, with scant attention previously to ecological concerns, changed course onto a green trajectory, suddenly declaring that America's future depends on going green as "a national security imperative."15 America's major cities began competing to become the "greenest," while our large institutions pledged to reduce their consumption of resources and production of wastes. The relational connection between individual actions, as well as institutional practices, and the health of the Earth was suddenly foremost in the consciousness of millions of Americans. In the November elections the Democrats gained control of Congress, promising to cut our country's carbon emissions. By late spring of 2007, it was unusual to come across a corporation or small business, a municipal or state government, an architectural firm, or a school or college that was not focused on trying to green their operations, realizing – at last – that money could be saved through reduced energy bills.[16]

As someone who had been involved in the ecology movement for some thirty years at that point, I was gratified – not to say dumbfounded – to see the green awakening finally going mainstream, and so quickly, in the fall of 2006.[17] However, in terms of actually changing policy to correct various destructive patterns, that burst of ecological-relational analysis and vision was, once again, largely deemphasized and ignored in the following years by both major parties.

But this is not a book about the environmental crises or the eco-designs that have arisen in response. It is not even a book about the green awakening, such as it is, except insofar as the spread of ecological awareness is one, highly significant part of a larger dynamic that is emerging: the Relational Shift. This book maps the emergence of a massive correction of the limited, inaccurate, and habitually damaging ways of thinking about life that have led to the current crises we face in the modern world.

Should we laugh or cry, though, that extremely basic facts about the relational nature of human existence are being "discovered" only now, in the 21st century? Is it not pathetic that so many of our modern systems of knowledge have been distanced from reality for so long by anti-relational theories based on mechanistic premises? How did this come about?

Our Checkered Past

Did it ever really feel right to anyone? That the body is separate from the mind? That humans are completely separate from nature? That there is a fundamental separation between self and the rest of the world? That we have no biological interconnection with other humans or other species because, after all, everything is an unconnected fragment, a discrete entity? That any information we gain from sensations of emotion is entirely separate from rational thought, being lower in value and having no part to play in accurate reasoning? That properly objective thinking makes all of this self-evident?

These assumptions about the nature of reality, which we inherit in Western cultures, came to dominance partially because of the influence of the mechanistic conclusions in the field of science during the Scientific Revolution in the 16th and 17th centuries. It followed in the 18th century that the new mechanistic way of looking at the world (called the "new mechanical philosophy") was then applied to all our institutions: everything was seen to resemble a machine, or a clockworks, and every institution was redesigned to function like an efficient machine.

Actually, the West had taken a fateful turn away from the relational worldview long before the culminating emergence of the modern, mechanistic orientation. The earliest Greek philosophers, the pre-Socratics had seen the world in a holistic, interrelated way, much as the residents of the neolithic, preGreek settlements in southeastern Europe had, judging from their holistic sculptures. Their art seems to express a sense of embeddedness in nature, such as figurines that are incised with symbols of water or are half bird and half woman. The leading philosophers of classical Greece, however, subsequently steered the West from holism onto a course of perceiving radical discontinuities – what today might be called major "disconnects": between the body and the mind, between humans and nature, between self and the rest of the world, and between immanence (the physical world) and transcendence (divine creativity and presence). The rest of the world at that time – that is, indigenous societies and various cultures in Asia – continued to develop an engagement with the world centered on extensive attention to relationship, process, and change.

The Greek philosophical focus on the supposed discontinuities shaped European thought for centuries and, eventually, provided the foundational perspective underlying the values of modernity. Consequently, what we have regarded as rational thought in the West is rational within a limited frame of reference but is quite lacking in a more comprehensive grasp of reality. Our Aristotelian focus divided the natural world into distinct categories according to differing forms and functions. The main focus was on entities and how to categorize them, far less on process or interrelatedness.

In addition, the theory of atomism (that the physical world is composed of tiny, invisible, indivisible bits of matter that ricochet around, colliding and combining) was proposed by the Greek philosopher Democritus. This idea was revived during the Renaissance, embraced by the Scientific Revolution, and then applied to social theory in the 18th century. According to "the new mechanical philosophy," individuals are to society as the tiny particles are to the physical world. That is, society was thought to be atomized, such that people ricochet around like billiard balls, sometimes colliding or combining into a group, or setting near one another. People, however, have no inherent interrelationships with one another in this view.

As the worldview of modernity – built on what could be called the "worldview of the four disconnects" – continued to coalesce during the 18th century, the concept of the Autonomous Individual arose in Britain and France. This projection of an ideal figure, still familiar to us, is a free-wheeling player thoroughly liberated from all premodern "constraints" – nature, tradition, religion, community ties, and the extended family. Unleashing the Autonomous Individual's power to make money, govern, and shape culture was considered essential to the greatness of Western progress and thought.

The Aristotelian foundation, the mechanistic worldview derived from the Scientific Revolution (including atomism), and the ideal of an unbounded Autonomous Individual, then, set the course for the modern era. No doubt it seemed like a good idea at the time, but this orientation caused Western cultures to subsequently miss a lot of what was actually going on in human life and its interactions. Perception in nearly every sector of public life was informed by the core assertion of "the new mechanical philosophy": that everything in nature is essentially like a machine. Consequently, our institutions in the 18th century were made machine-like in their design and functioning. Through this mechanistic lens, modern medicine saw the body largely as a bio-machine with parts that break down and can be repaired, or not. The major fields of human endeavor were conceptualized as separate wheels (science, the economy, and government) whose cogs intermeshed with each other in certain places. Modern (American) democracy was modeled on a well-wrought machine with "checks and balances" in its mechanisms. Most importantly, modern socialization taught us that material reality – such as our bodies and the innate intelligence with which we were born – is far more significant than anything as inconsequential as "mere" relationships or relational dynamics. In the mechanistic worldview, value and importance are accorded only to things that can be measured and quantified.

Understanding modernity – its interlocking mechanistic assumptions and their pervasive presence in every field – is the key to understanding the grand transition that is occurring today. The Relational Shift is springing up in every field all over the modern world because the abstract, limited, mechanistic perspective it challenges and broadens underlies every area of modern life. That is, *the Relational Shift is the antidote to those assumptions of modernity that have turned out to be wrong.*

Although the West passed through more then two and a half centuries with the modern, mechanistic lens strapped firmly in place and continues to do so, in the last three decades of the 20th century researchers in the new fields in science -- such as systems theory, chaos theory, and especially complexity studies in biology -- discovered that knowing the material properties of an entity does not tell you the ways it will react and change and behave. Creative and unpredictable responses arise from the emergent dynamic relationships within the entity and from its dynamic relationships with its surroundings. The new focus became the *contextual dynamic systems* (or *complex adaptive systems*) in which an entity exists, as well as the internal dynamic systems that constitute the entity itself. The compelling new subject is interaction and interrelationship, which bring about the emergence of new properties of a system and new conditions for its parts, or sub-systems. The grand discovery was that nature is actually composed of zillions of dynamic relationships embedded within one another! Moreover, the human species is probably not an exception to all this.

The Relational Imperative

If the rise of relational awareness today were "merely" about revolutionizing modern systems of knowledge in order to address the long-standing faulty, mechanistic assumptions and to arrive at a more accurate perception of reality, that surely would be reason enough to pursue the grand correction. The historic moment in which this organic perspective is arising, however, is one of extreme urgency. In recent years we have witnessed the alarming increase of environmental crises and have watched as one after another of our institutions reeled from scandals, corruption, and near-collapse, causing bruising disruptions that have rippled through millions of American lives and billions more abroad. Since it is probably true that a society cannot work its way out of crises with the same kind of thinking that created the problems, it is most fortunate that we do not now have to start from square one to try to figure out – extremely quickly – some sort of alternative to the mechanistic worldview and other wrong assumptions. For several years surprising discoveries, new ideas, and successful innovations have been quietly accumulating and gaining acceptance. This new relational thinking – taking different forms in various sectors – is now surging into the mainstream. In many quarters – but, alas, not all – the panoply of institutional failures has resulted in a new willingness to adopt new thinking, new methods, and new vision.

Yet making only isolated changes here and there, even large ones, is not going to be enough to successfully avoid full-scale catastrophe unless we master a different way of thinking about being humans on this Earth that is more closely grounded in the Real, the actual interrelated nature of life. This utterly crucial rethinking depends on our grasping the coherence of the myriad examples of the Relational Shift now taking place in very different areas: *if we miss the common ground underlying many of the changes – a shift from a mechanistic way of seeing the world to relational ways of seeing the world – we will fail to tap the power and potential of this vast and historic turning.*

The state of the planet calls on modern humans to radically – and relationally –rethink the way we do things. The way we feed ourselves in modern societies, for instance, seems to assume that we live on top of nature, rather than depending for our very lives on nature's health and well-being. Building up a local, nontoxic food economy, instead of buying from the industrial food distribution system, brings fresh, healthy food into our bodies in seasonal cycles, reduces energy consumption needed for long-distance transport, creates local and regional jobs, and strengthens the sense of community as well as its literal vitality. It allows us to make relational choices with beneficial effects that multiply, rather than disengaged choices that accumulate and damage us.

The many relationships that emanate from decisions about how we feed ourselves, though, are merely one cluster among many. Far from being isolate units of consumption, we are profoundly related to everything in our food chain, our watershed, and our blue-green garden planet. We are even related at the molecular level to everything on Earth and in the entire universe. Our lineage, along with that of all everything else, stretches back through time to our common ancestor, which is actually a dynamic event: the cosmic birthing forth of the universe at the beginning of time. Everyone and everything – the grass, the rivers, the galaxies – are our relations.

We are very far from living in a culture that reflects that fact of nature – but we are closer now than we modern humans have ever been. Our best hope is that we can "get" reality – grasp its actual relational nature – and then "get real" by bringing human endeavors into sync with the relational nature of the world. The many discoveries I present in this book that are correcting the mechanistic assumptions about life will no doubt multiply in the coming years. Yet the new findings and the disparate examples of successfully applying the new thinking, even as they have entered the mainstream, will not be enough in themselves to effect the needed transformation.

Haven't we all had the experience of noticing something beneficial and desired in the world, something that seemed to signal a new way of doing things, only to see that early blossoming of a correction be dissolved back into the status quo? I am convinced that the key to the success of the Relational Shift is that the myriad changes based in relational awareness not be seen in isolation but as part of a coherent planetary phenomenon affecting the entire Earth Community (a term coined by the cultural historian Thomas Berry to denote the relational totality of all species and all ecosystems). I hope to provide a lens with which readers can "connect the dots" so as to perceive the Big Picture: the vast interrelated network of human actions that are creating the historic relational turn. This is the larger meaning of Green. [In activist circles "green" (lower-case) has always denoted an environmental, or ecological, focus, while "Green" (with an upper-case G) denotes a more encompassing ecosocial analysis and worldview, as in a Green political perspective, which unites an ecological and a social frame of reference.]

The Relational Shift is truly reshaping every area of human endeavor and our own sense of ourselves, but I have focused in the following chapters on four major areas as examples – education and parenting, health and healthcare, architecture and community design, and the economy. In each area I begin with a snapshot of the current crises we face (though the structure of the chapter on architecture is an exception). Although I realize that this composite picture of the serious problems may be dismaying, as most people generally find it more comfortable to ignore worrisome developments, I believe that we cannot correct the problems unless we are willing to look directly at them, to look into the face of the hardship and suffering and to name what is happening. The second reason I begin the chapters with an overview of the problems we face is so that readers will begin to notice how many of those problems and crises are the result of erroneously anti-relational assumptions and thinking, or at least the absence of relational wisdom. Only then can we grasp the significance of the relational breakthroughs and solutions that are emerging.

The snapshot of the current crises in human health, at the beginning of chapter 3, Health and Healthcare, is perhaps the most sobering of any of the areas because so many families and individuals are struggling with various damaging effects of our hypermodern condition as a society. It is not sufficient that we happen to be aware of examples of this suffering in the lives of people around us, as well as in our own lives, though. We are all called upon to make an effort to grasp the vast scope of these problems and the interrelated dynamics that cause them – as well as to be aware of the many recent and extremely effective developments that are part of a rising, healing culture of relatedness.

Without doubt, this is a time of historic transformation. The massive Relational Shift is yielding fecund possibilities, previously unimagined, as it brings us into right relationship with nature, society, human effort, and our inner selves. May this book aid the spread of relational perception and thought, which is truly our saving grace.

II

THE RELATIONAL SHIFT IN
EDUCATION AND PARENTING

A Snapshot of the Current Crises

From the moment of birth a child takes in sensory impressions, clues, and relational information about the society into which it has been born. The infant's initiation into the world begins with a mother's caress and loving smile and continues to unfold within the parents' and the family's sphere, which, as the child gradually discovers, exists within a much larger context – the neighborhood, the town or city, the country, the planet, the cosmos. Each life brings to this learning process its unique cosmological inheritance, intertwined from the maternal and paternal lines of its forebears through all the past generations, back through the emergence of our species and, long before that, back to the emergence of our planet and even to the birth of the universe. Such is the miracle of the child emerging into life.

It is often observed that a society can be judged by how well it attends to its children in their formative years. In that most crucial of responsibilities we adults in the hypermodern societies seem to have become recklessly distracted or callously uncaring, or both. Many of the children, psychologically, are adrift.

The Growing Gaps in Education

The graduation rate of urban American high schools is alarmingly low. Every year a stream of functionally illiterate young people is sent out into our society to try to fend as best they can. Although the United States ranks near the top of Western industrialized countries in terms of highly literate adults (21 percent), we also rank near the top in the portion regarding those who are functionally illiterate (also 21 percent).[18] The national high school graduation rate, which peaked at approximately 80 percent in the late 1960s, is now about 75 percent. Although nationally approximately 65 percent of both African Americans and Latinos graduate, the national graduation rate for (often dilapidated) urban schools is only *52 percent*. Those drop-outs who return to earn a General Equivalency Degree do not fare much better over time, in terms of employment and earnings, than do drop-outs.[19]

Other gaps continue to widen as well. Annual test scores gathered internationally track the descent of American students in their levels of knowledge and capabilities when compared with their counterparts in other countries. However, when asked to rate themselves in science and math, American students tend to place themselves at the top with their better-educated peers, blithely unaware of their lack. As most older adults have noticed, our young people seem to know less and less with each graduating class. One study in 2007 concluded that American high school students are taking more Advanced Placement classes, getting better grades, and apparently learning less than their counterparts of 15 years ago. That is, grade inflation and diminished standards have plumped up students' grade point averages (and their ego), while their scores on standardized tests generally have not improved.

Sadly, the teaching of literature – which allows children to enter the lives of other people and learn empathy – and even the ability to read well are steadily disappearing from most high schools. With them go the ability to write well. Perhaps because only *25 percent* of high school seniors are proficient writers, according to a study in 2008,[20] a growing number of high schools are giving up entirely on written end-of-the-year exams. They opt instead for "performance-based assessment" (including PowerPoint or other oral presentations or exhibits by the students) to determine whether a student is ready to proceed to the next grade or to graduate. No doubt parents and educators who support this trend are trying to escape the tyranny of the standardized tests – and the distortion in the learning process caused by overemphasis on those scores – but to demote writing skills (which comprise a wide range of thinking skills) to being all but unnecessary is an alarming turn further into a very wrong direction.

When high school graduates go on to college today, they often find that they are ill prepared for the work expected of them. Moreover, they generally do not have a sense of higher education as a process enabling them to enter into the historical stream of culture and learning that shapes society. Rather than looking up to learned persons, they tend to regard their peers as their role models and as the source of the only approval that matters. Because their childhoods most likely were overly programmed with lessons, extracurricular classes, and other structured activities, today's students often experience difficulty working independently, engaging in original thought processes, or showing initiative. They may well have had "helicopter parents," who did the child's homework, argued with teachers over grades, and even filled out the applications for admission to college. Not only are the freshmen suddenly on their own, which can be far more jarring psychologically than it was for past generations, but, for many of them, no course of study is as interesting as their own peer group. Consequently, their academic work is generally regarded as an onslaught of tiresome, irrelevant tasks one must perform to get credentialed. These students are disengaged from the exciting process that learning can be – as well as the attendant deep immersion and inner growth it can entail.

A study of 2,300 college students between 2005 and 2009 found that the average amount of time spent studying had dropped by more than 50 percent from the 1960s. Yet their collective grade point average is 3.16, even for the 31 percent who spend only five hours per week studying alone.[21] Because of the falling level of interest in their studies and the accommodation in grading standards, the level of literacy among our college graduates is dropping significantly (as reflected in the National Assessment of Adult Literacy).[22] In 2007 it was found that, on average, Americans ages 15 to 24 spend only seven minutes of their daily leisure time reading. The decline in reading correlates with a decline in writing skills, reading ability, school grades, graduation rates, workplace performance, volunteer work, attending cultural and sports events, exercising, and voting.[23]

A common complaint among employers is that many young adults enter the workplace with a sense of entitlement (feeling they deserve big salaries and prestigious assignments) even though their skill levels are mediocre or worse and their work habits are often disengaged and careless. An even more worrisome gap yawns perilously between the responsibilities of citizenship and the capabilities of most citizens. A study released in 2011 found that most college students make little improvement over four years with regard to critical thinking skills (even the simple task of distinguishing fact from opinion); complex reasoning; communicating; and effective problem-solving.[24] In addition, numerous studies have found that Americans have scant knowledge of history, geography, science, or politics. Moreover, young adults tend not to perceive current events in a developmental, historical context because neither history nor context seems to have much relevance for them. Instead, immersion in an electronic childhood has conditioned them to perceive the world as a thoroughly wired, constantly shifting manifestation of "stuff happening."

The Venal and Vapid Socialization of Our Youth via the Media

The quality of the relationship between parent and child in the United States has been damaged by parents' having to work longer hours and experiencing greater financial insecurity and stress than a few decades ago. The weakening of family relationships leaves a painful void in the child's inner life, into which rush the new primacy of peer relationships ... and the marketers. The guidance and direction that modern children do receive from their families and their teachers are overshadowed by the constant barrage of messages, images, and behavioral cues and modeling they receive from the media in various modes of delivery. Habitual patterns of superficial communication via electronic devices diminish children's ability to read social cues and converse comfortably in person. By 2010, only a third of children age 12 through 17 talked to their friends face-to-face on a daily basis.[25]

Moreover, each of the 40,000 commercials the average American child watches on television annually is designed to make the viewers feel inadequate if they do not own the product. Susan Douglas, a professor of communications at the University of Michigan, observes that advertising has afflicted Americans with a perpetual unease that can be appeased but never quite satisfied with new purchases: "Advertising is designed to sell us envy, and the person we envy is the future self we will become if we use the product."[26] Along with millions of parents and teachers, she concludes that the media has "colonized the minds" of our youth. Relentless upscale consumption also figures largely, along with plots of backstabbing and destructive gossip in popular novels written for teenage girls and then made into movies or television series in recent years.

What specialists in child development call the "culture of childhood" – the unprogramed play time in which children traditionally learned how to settle their own arguments, make and break rules, and respect the rights of others – has all but disappeared. The diminished peer socialization has been replaced by the rise of self-absorption, bullying, teasing, and discrimination that has poisoned the school experience. Recess has become such an arena of meanness and aggression that many elementary schools have had to hire "recess coaches" to oversee the playground. Similar problems manifest themselves in middle school.[27]

Adolescents have always had to deal with peer pressure, but today it comes at them amid the epidemic of mean and callous behavior, habitual prevarication, routinely cutting corners (cheating or otherwise taking the easy way out), and feeling protectively disengaged from all but a small group of friends. The girls feel they must put themselves on display from an early age (cleavage in eighth-grade, Lolita garb on preteens, and sexy Halloween costumes on second-graders), although weariness over being so exposed has finally led many girls to opt for more coverage. Still, girls as young as age seven commonly tell their mothers that they feel worthless unless they look sexy enough to attract a boyfriend, and they turn in desperation to beauty products and spa treatments while still in elementary school. This same sentiment now holds for many girls all the way through high school, college, and beyond: "hotness" is considered the most important factor in their self-worth. By high school the boys, too, feel pressure to look like young men in ads and films so they often ingest bodybuilding supplements and engage in other efforts to bulk up. For both sexes their sense of worth is heavily dependent on their clothing, accessories, and electronic devices. The notion of developing their capabilities through education is far less compelling to most children and adolescents today than obsessively addressing their supposed physical inadequacies, as gauged against the daily deluge of air-brushed advertising fantasies, or flaunting whatever they consider to be their power of physical allure and cool demeanor.

Amid all the posturing and flaunting run tendencies that are worrisome. Why do so many of today's teenagers and young adults love to watch contestants being humiliated on televised reality shows or competitions involving scathing rejections? Why do they love to follow the gossip reports about young celebrities who are revealed to have "flaws"? Why do they enjoy hearing about a young celebrity who got caught doing something embarrassing? *Because it makes them feel better about themselves.* When I first heard of that explanation from college students, I found the pathos to be daunting. All their ego-inflation and pride in their sexy clothes, cool demeanor, and well-wired lifestyle are stretched thin over deep feelings of insecurity, ungroundedness, and even self-loathing?

The coarse content in much of the mass media is part of the problem, but another is the nature of our children's immersion throughout their formative years in electronic stimulation – videos and video games, computers, television, movies, DVDs, and "loaded" cell phones with cameras, internet access, instant messaging, and text messaging. By 2010, half of all American teenagers were sending at least 50 text messages a day, while one-third were sending more than 100 a day; two-thirds of teens preferred texting their friends to speaking with them on the phone.[28] Even very young children are eagerly supplied with videos, video games, and e-books by their parents, and few parents follow the recommendation of the American Academy of Pediatrics that children younger than age two should watch no television at all. Children with a television in their bedroom score lower on school tests than do children without one, as do children who watch television or play video games on school nights.[29] Later, teenage girls who habitually watch televisions programs in which a lot of sexual activity is portrayed are twice as likely to become pregnant while in high school as girls who watch few such shows.[30]

One result of electronic immersion is that children come to perceive reality as contingent and ever-shifting. Over time, the fast pace of fleeting images apparently compromises their attention span and damages their capacity for the "duration experience," in which one is able to pause and reflect deeply on a subject, or an event, or a character in a book, as myriad teachers and professors have noted in recent years. "Incomplete comprehension" is a problem encountered routinely by educators at all levels. The thought processes of most adolescents have become more superficial, at the same time that their written use of language is becoming corrupted by the abbreviated, bare-bones style of text messaging. Mark Bauerlein, a professor at Emory University and author of *The Dumbest Generation*, notes that when adolescents spend their coming-of-age years in the online world where no one ever has to stick with anything that bores or challenges them, the addictive online time habituates them to juvenile mental habits.[31] The result is not only disengagement and self-absorption but also juvenile stances on ethics and morality. Lying seems to come easily, as does finding seemingly innumerable ways to cheat other kids when playing avatar games at "virtual world" sites, as a study in 2008 found. The veil of online anonymity enables children at such websites to indulge in dominating and upsetting others, which they seem to find satisfying and even addictive, according to studies of the phenomenon.[32]

Moreover, receiving an education, both informal as well as formal, in which much of the information is limited to that which can be expressed through a computer or video screen makes the non-electronic world, for most teens, seem slow and rather dumb, something one has to put up with. Rules, values, and standards bore or annoy them. As one 21-year-old college student put it in December 2007 when describing her generation to a gathering of corporate marketers eager to reach "the Millennials": "My generation is always trying to find the easy way out, not the right way. We have a different idea of what passes as a work ethic. We freak out if we make mistakes."[33]

Spending years focused on a screen of one sort or another with quickly changing images not only flattens young people's sense of historic time and complexity, leaving them with little sense of contextual dynamics in current situations. It also shrinks their focus to the personal sphere, which is experienced as being highly contingent and vulnerable to the extremely unstable "now." In a continuous state of anxiety, they check their text messages, incoming tweets, and the social media sites frequently to see if they are missing anything or are being trashed and written off. They live in fear that they have not posted enough or have failed to post the right thing that will make others perceive them the way they want. This self-absorption – which for many of them must feel like a survival mode – is one reason that students today have the highest scores on the Narcissistic Personality Inventory since it was first given in 1982. Fully two-thirds of the American college students who took the survey in 2006 scored above average on narcissism.[34] This development has perhaps furthered the popularity of Twitter, which has become a personal broadcast medium that makes users the star of their own reality show.[35]

All of the above influences on adolescents leave most of them feeling somewhat scattered and psychologically frail, which is why psychotherapists on campuses often refer to today's college students as "the tea cups." Moreover, among the psychologically vulnerable stalk the predators. Dating has become a dangerous pastime for many adolescent girls because so many boys have come of age playing violent video games with abundant violation of the female characters and because, lacking the socialization that dating provided for them in past generations, many adolescent boys today tend to conflate sexual desire with the acting out of a macho role of dominance and control. This often includes nearly constant surveillance of their girlfriend via cell phones and texting. Such boys will text-message the girl more than 100 times a day, demanding an immediate accounting of where she is and what she is doing. At first the girl often finds the attention flattering, but she eventually sees that it is all about controlling her in every way. The boy calls the girl repeatedly in the middle of the night, while her parents are asleep, to berate, ridicule, and weaken her psychologically. Not taking his call or not responding immediately to a text message brings a punitive response. For the girl to try to leave such a relationship can be extremely dangerous, having resulted in the murder of numerous high school and college girls in recent years. "Dating abuse and violence" is now so widespread a problem that many high schools have preventative programs, and law enforcement officials regard such acts as a category of domestic violence.[36]

School Life: In Class, Online, and Texting

We like to think of our schools as safe spaces where children gather amid cheerful décor to learn about the world and the many areas of knowledge we value. In truth, most of our inner-city schools are neither safe nor cheery because they are badly in need of extensive repairs and because many of the students struggle with learning since they lack access to medical treatment for chronic ailments or emotional stress. In addition, many schools at all socio-economic levels have become health hazards because of toxic pesticides applied to landscaping; or exhaust fumes in classrooms because of nearby idling trucks, buses, and cars; or classroom supplies that contain lead, mercury, asbestos, solvents, or formaldehyde; or mold growing in various parts of the building. At the same time, school cafeterias have increasingly become sites of outbreaks of food-borne illnesses.[37]

Even more difficult to address than physical toxins in many schools is the toxic atmosphere caused by rising levels of bullying and harassing, both on school grounds and online. Though many school psychologists have long assumed that bullying was caused by patterns in the home environment, a study published in 2011 of middle and high school students in North Carolina found that bullying is used most often as a tactic for advancing one's social position at school and that the acquiring of status increases acts of aggression toward students who are "below" one.[38] A study of eighth-graders in eleven states who had been identified as "gifted" by their school system found that two-thirds of them had been bullied at school. Other frequent targets are boys who are taunted as being "gay" because they may be of slight build or exhibit mannerisms considered less than macho. Several studies have found that some 80 percent of students have encountered sexual abuse, often with daily taunts of coarse and sexually explicit language. Most alarming to educators has been the increasing number of incidents of sexual assault by boys at very young ages, in middle school and even in elementary school.

As for online attacks, fully 90 percent of middle-school students have had their feelings hurt online, where anonymity (the use of invented cyber-names) enables tormentors to harass, threaten, or seek to humiliate others – simply because, as one attacker expressed it in a message, "ugly girls like you deserve to be put in their place." Ugly is the key word here, certainly, but it pertains to the mind of the attacker. Patterns of cyber-bullying include websites created for posting destructive rumors to a large audience. Because such harassment can make it impossible for a targeted student to concentrate, some school districts have prevailed upon state legislators to pass laws that allow them to intervene in incidents that occur away from school if the activity in question causes an impact on the learning environment.[39]

The absolute anonymity afforded online users, by the way, is the result of design decisions made in the formative years of the Internet by the young, male software engineers of Silicon Valley, who vigorously embraced the cultural ideal of the Thoroughly Autonomous Individual. By making it possible for online users to sever all relational responsibility to others and be completely "free" to say whatever they wished with no consequences, those designers of the Internet helped to enable, in the view of Jaron Lanier, the dark side of human nature to manifest itself in myriad ways. Lanier notes in his book *You Are Not a Gadget* (2010) that those design choices have resulted in a flood of nasty, anonymous attacks and "a culture of sadism" that has gone mainstream.[40] As a researcher at Harvard University observed in 2010, "Increasingly, today's 'social web' doesn't empower people. It empowers hate, exclusion, and polarization."[41] Anonymous interaction has also provided free range for predators.

Internet safety was the subject of a report commissioned in 2009 by the nation's attorneys general. A Harvard-led task force found that, while relatively few older sexual predators cruise the social networking sites designed for young people (although they do so in adult chat rooms), the most frequent threats that minors face on those sites are bullying, meanness, exclusion, and harassment, often from peers; moreover, minors routinely proposition other minors for sex on those sites. In response to the report, the communications director for the National Association of School Psychologists concurred: "The most common problem is kids being mean to each other and 13-year-old girls posting nude pictures of themselves."[42] A national survey of participating teenagers in 2009 found that fully 21 percent of the girls and 18 percent of the boys had sent or posted nude or semi-nude pictures of themselves, a texting practice known as "sexting."[43] The combination of anonymity and meanness – and, for many girls, a desperate need to be considered "hot" -- results in a frequently wounding online youth culture that most parents are not really aware of. As one mother told a school psychologist, "What do you mean my daughter's depressed and isolated? She has 900 friends on MySpace!"[44]

The nature of acquiring "friends" and communicating with strangers on the social networking sites is, of course, an oddly skewed version of being in relationships with others in embodied, embedded reality. A young person who gets drawn into one of these sites tends to develop a degraded sense of relationships (in that "friends" are entities useful for increasing your total number). More importantly, habitual patterns of narcissism, exhibitionism, and voyeurism are encouraged. To a certain extent, users experience a fragmented identity because they create a carefully edited version of themselves to present and operate online. This sort of "impression management" intensifies a young person's feeling that there are inadequate aspects to themselves that they must keep hidden. Use of social networking sites – especially sharing personal information with strangers – has been correlated with mood disorders such as depression, loneliness, and anxiety.[45] Obsessive engagement among young people with virtual "friends" also results in a lack of exercise and sunlight (which can worsen depression), as well as denying them the possibility of experiencing actual relationships with complexity and intimacy in the young person's physical context, or actual place. Instead, an entire generation has become inclined toward experiences of isolation and alienation from the Real, their off-line surroundings. Moreover, they tend to shy away from intimacy and to expect quick fixes and quick results when perturbed.

Many universities today warn their incoming freshmen not to reveal personal information on the social networking sites and remind them that all postings are archived by those sites, that is, available forever to data-miners who may be hired by prospective employers or others. Such caution, though, will not protect students from the ubiquitous online treachery of peers who relish posting a nude photo of someone (taken with a cell phone camera in the showers or dressing room of a gymnasium, for instance); who decide to post about their roommate's secret drug use or eating disorder or abortion on a gossip site; or who forward to a large distribution list some embarrassing academic error made in a class or study session. For example, an Ivy League gossip site receives a daily deluge of what the editors describe as "vicious gossip culled from forwarded e-mails, MySpace screen shots, and candid pictures snapped by students' camera phones." The editors explained in 2008 that they select only about one in six submissions to publish on the blog site – but they added that they archive all of the "vicious gossip" in case any of the targeted students might become prominent someday.[46]

Freshman orientation today must also cover such non-electronic concerns as drugs and date rape, binge drinking and violence, bulimia and anorexia, and depression and suicide. One institution, New York University, presents that heads-up in an informative – not to say hair-raising – play for incoming students titled *The Reality Show: NYU.* In a less dire sign of the times, a professor at that same university has found it necessary to offer a well-attended workshop for incoming freshmen that offers tips on how to initiate a conversation and talk with people in real time!

Peer-Oriented "Attachment Displacement" Disorder

Many of the problems encountered by educators today – the increasing levels of disrespect, hostility, and even violence in the classroom; the growing numbers of sullen students who are disengaged from learning; the resultant "dumbing down" of academic effort and achievement; the narcissism and shallow values; and the climate of meanness and callous disregard among students for anyone outside their group of peers – stem from a pervasive dynamic in modern cultures that is not widely understood. In fact, this baffling and worrisome syndrome comes into clear focus only when a relational analysis is brought to bear.

Like the young of many species, our children require the care and guidance of a primary adult or two, or more, throughout their process of maturation. Our species is unusual, though, in the extended length of the juvenile phase of life: physical growth is not complete until around age 23. During that long period of development, children and adolescents depend on their parents, grandparents, aunts, and uncles. Psychologists, beginning with the work of John Bowlby, call this primary connection the "attachment relationship," the tendency in a child to seek closeness to another person (usually the mother and/or father) and to feel secure when that person is near. "Attachment" is a mutual instinct through which the child is nurtured, guided, and oriented in the world. However, a particular context is necessary: a child must be receptive to parenting, and the extent to which there is receptivity depends on *the quality of the relationship.* All else – praise and encouragement, hugs and kisses, gifts and rewards – count for little with the child if she perceives the attachment relationship to be inadequate, half-hearted, or not really there at all. As this aspect of child development is better understood, the traditional sense of parenting as a role is being enhanced by attentiveness to the relationship itself.

Children are much more strongly driven by their need for attachment than are adults, so they are more sensitive to compromised versions of it. Unfortunately, economic pressures on parents today often require them to work long hours or take a second job, which causes them not only to be absent from the child much of the time but also to feel overloaded and be distracted, to multitask, or to feel exhausted when they are together at home. Unbeknownst to the parent, who probably loves the child deeply and is merely trying to cope with the weight of modern life, children in such circumstances usually feel emotionally rejected or abandoned. For instance, a study in 2009 found that teenagers who eat dinner with their families fewer than three times a week are more likely to turn to alcohol, tobacco, and drugs than are peers who take part in family dinners daily or almost so.[47] If a child's instinctual need for a loving primary attachment is (in his or her mind) repeatedly given short shrift, he or she will cease to feel oriented and will experience the highly uncomfortable mental state psychologists call an "orientation void," which the human mind finds intolerable. That is when the child begins to turn to peers for primary attachment and primary orientation. To the extent that the child transfers both of those interlocked instinctual needs to a group of other juveniles, who use each other as their compass points, she or he will reach adulthood with her or his psychological, emotional, intellectual, ethical, and social maturation distorted and arrested at levels substantially below those of normal development.

One of the most astute analysts of the effects of primary peer-orientation (or "reactive attachment disorder") is the Canadian psychologist Gordon Neufeld, whose observations I will summarize here. Peer-oriented children (by which he means those who have transferred their *primary* attachment and orientation relationship from their parents to a group of their peers) live in a universe of severely limited and superficial attachments. They attach to their peers via sameness (striving to resemble one another in look, demeanor, thought, tastes, and values), but they find that the peer society is extremely contingent, ever shifting, and insecure. Safety is sought by being in a group and expressing negativity toward everyone outside the group – yet the daily gossip and put-downs can be turned against anyone at any time. Bullies are often cheered on by peers because their targeting of someone brings structure in the ever-shifting social landscape.

Peer-oriented children learn to achieve a measure of invulnerability in their unstable world by cultivating emotional hardening. One result is that they become desensitized to the cruel treatment of other children. They also have fewer mixed feelings about attacking people than do children who are not primarily peer-oriented. The ultimate ethic in the peer culture is "cool," the complete absence of emotional openness or sharing of feelings. Instead, bonding occurs by putting down other people through gossip, verbal attacks, or rejection. Difference in other children causes feelings of revulsion and antipathy in peer-oriented children; they seek to distance themselves from such vulnerability, often by ridiculing the child who is different. Their emotional hardening can make peer-oriented children and adolescents seem older than they are and seem very sure of themselves, sophisticated, and fearless – although underneath it all, they feel very insecure.

Peer-oriented children are unable to feel fulfilled, and this insatiability comes to dominate their emotional functioning, primarily taking the form of an obsession with peer connection. This obsession results in a state of "attachment frustration," by which psychologists mean that no matter how much such children hide their true personality or feelings and how much they display sameness, their attachment with peers falls short of what they crave – because what they are really seeking is the unconditional love, guidance, and protection that only a mature adult can give. The peer-oriented child feels as if she or he can never really get enough from the peer group. As a result of this yearning and frustration, attention from parents and instruction from teachers are regarded as annoying, barely tolerated interference that keeps them from hanging out with their friends. Many peer-oriented children and adolescents can barely stand to speak with their parents at all and openly display disgust and hostility.

Peer-oriented children tend to tune out during class time, or they listen to the teacher only enough to figure out how to do the minimal amount of work to get by in their studies, which they deem irrelevant. Peer-orientation tends to extinguish curiosity and jeopardizes adaptive trial-and-error learning. The only learning these children really desire occurs at recess, lunch time, and after school when they can connect through proximity with their peers, bond through small talk, and learn which way the winds are blowing that day regarding gossip and put-downs. Because of these obsessive patterns, peer-oriented children are generally unable to let go when a particular pursuit is clearly futile and are less able to adapt in various situations.

By the time they reach high school, or even middle school, they have erected a wall of low-level contempt toward their teachers – and have accepted the peer culture's conviction that the entire adult world (schools, churches, elections, etc.) is one big effort to manipulate and lie to them. Consequently, they distrust all teachers and feel they must stiff-arm them and remain loyal to the collective peer antipathy toward the adult world. (Oddly, they seem to give a pass to those adult endeavors that actually *are* fully focused on targeting them for manipulation: the pop media, the myriad advertisers and marketers fixed on their demographic group, and the publicists for celebrities.)

Sex among emotionally hardened peer-oriented teenagers is usually considered by the girls, as young as 12 or 13, to be something necessary to be accepted by the group. It is regarded as a task for the girls and a subject of bragging and "cool" achievement among the boys. Needless to say, feelings, caring, and tenderness are absent, and a loving commitment is literally unthinkable. In fact, "personal subjects" are never raised with temporary sex partners anymore than they would be with other "friends" in the peer group.

Finally, peer-oriented adolescents often exhibit impulsiveness, aimlessness, and a lack of long-term aspirations. (When these males move into adulthood, they often pride themselves on their insensitivity and crass comments about women.[48]) Even well into adolescence, their minds have not matured to the stage of "integrative functioning" – the ability to hold different perceptions, senses, thoughts, feelings, and impulses all at the same time without becoming confused or paralyzed in action. Also, they generally lack the ability to conceive and hold to a goal beyond immediate satisfaction.

Fortunately, Dr. Neufeld has written an extremely helpful book, *Hold On to Your Kids*, in which he not only presents the above observations, with plenty of case histories, but ends with a substantial section of proven approaches for parents who want to rescue their children from the damage of "peer-oriented attachment disorder," including his own experience as a parent of five children. This book has become popular with the "attachment parenting" movement.[49] In it, he wisely suggests ways to assure that children feel lovingly attached, including expressing affection spontaneously (not solely in response to test scores or other performance, which the child interprets as conditional, insecure love that is not worth much) as well as taking time to reconnect after an absence (a week-long business trip or just eight hours at the office). Neufeld also explains how parents can "re-create the Attachment Village," which includes interfamilial and intergenerational friendships.

He speaks from an organic perspective when he assures parents, "The good news is that nature is on our side": children do want a deep connection with their parents (even if they have hardened themselves against the loss of it), and once the quality of the parent-child relationship is repaired and nurtured, our natural parenting instincts emerge in various situations and are far more valuable than any prescribed techniques for getting children to do what they should. Children's friendships are then enjoyable and healthy but supplemental. Moreover, nature's way for juveniles to achieve maturation, he reminds us, is a story of paradox: it is dependence and attachment that foster independence and genuine, healthy separation. The book opens with an epigraph from the teachings of J. Krishnamurti: "Action has meaning only in relationship and without understanding relationship, action on any level will only breed conflict. The understanding of relationship is infinitely more important than the search for any plan of action."[50]

The relational frame of reference Gordon Neufeld provides has direct relevance to parenting and education, but it also demystifies the characteristics of so many young adults today that are puzzling to most older people. Why, for instance, do so many "millennials" regard the concept of a "work ethic" as such a joke, activating in them the habitual responses of defiantly tuning out, cutting corners, and doing the minimum to get by? Because growing up with primary peer-orientation renders adults, in the minds of those adolescents, tiresome obstacles who force you to do things (or try to) and are to be ignored, lied to, or outfoxed whenever possible. Similarly, the lasting effects of primary peer orientation explain why so many entry-level employees regard the managers and senior members of their firm, institute, or corporation as uncool old fools to be manipulated, ignored, and used.

That attitude of superiority was abundant among the young whiz kids on Wall Street in the late 1980s and the 1990s who dreamed up various schemes in the finance sector and then arrogantly sought out a corporate home that would essentially leave them alone while they ran the (extremely reckless) "game," which the old guys upstairs didn't really understand and were not welcome to question. It is also the attitude of the hot-shot marketing boys in Hollywood when they take pride in lying to and manipulating the older, accomplished directors and producers about what sort of advertising campaign their movies will be getting. It is the widespread attitude of young journalists who routinely write snide, disparaging profiles of older, accomplished people (or reviews of their art) but rave over the coolness of a subject who is a member of their own generation. It even explains the baffling experience nearly every middle-aged or older patron has had in stores in recent decades: two young sales clerks will continue chatting with each other while the customer stands waiting, and not until it is absolutely necessary to break away from their peer conversation does one of the clerks, with an air of boredom and resentment, wait on the customer.

Understanding the damaging effects of primary peer-orientation explains why that college student who addressed the audience of marketers, which I cited a few pages back, explained that the Millennials opt for "not the right way but the easy way" and also that "we freak out if we make mistakes." I suppose she means that making mistakes results in sudden feelings of vulnerability, which they are psychologically "defended against" elsewhere in their lives by displaying a persona of "cool." No doubt the sexual patterns established during an adolescence shaped by primary peer-orientation also inform their adult life. Those patterns certainly seem to figure largely in the fact that so many young adult males today will not "commit" in a romantic relationship; a deep, complex feeling such as love might well seem not only scary and unnecessary but literally unimaginable to them if they have opted for primary peer-orientation during their coming of age.

As for the young women who came of age with primary peer-orientation, their formative habits of bonding through putting down others day after day turn out to be hard to shake. As one Millennial woman told a middle-aged journalist from the *Los Angeles Times* in 2009, "It's hard to find a community of girls who are not ego-driven to criticize and critique. We are trying to eliminate the cattiness, the gossiping, the inauthenticity. We've got so much going for us, but we're our own worst enemy." Asked why so few young women consider themselves "feminist," she explained, "Your generation was 'Us against Them.' Our biggest problem is 'Us against Us.' Your brand of feminism can't solve that for us."[51]

Even more poignantly, the "attachment disorder" of primary peer-orientation, which is endemic in our hypermodern society, must surely be a major factor in the very large portion of young adults who currently seek out psychotherapy because they feel there is "something wrong with me." Many of them experience serious levels of depression and get through each day only with a dose of one or more anti-depressant medications. The modern condition has both interfered with the parental relationship they experienced and also drawn them elsewhere, into the media-saturated, consumption-dazed, self-obsessed peer culture with its extremely damaging developmental pitfalls.

This erosion and partial replacement of the parent-child relationship has been building since the early 1950s, when advertisers began to identify a "youth culture" that functioned as its own world. Several factors then converged to intensify the phenomenon with each passing decade. Foremost, marketers continually presented American youth not as apprentices to adulthood but as a separate group with a special need to purchase specific products and clothing. Second, the modern ideal of the Autonomous Individual, intensified by the grip of Freudian theory on psychology in the 1950s, was applied here to sanction adolescent separation from families as an important developmental step. Third, the modern worldview always honors the new, the up and coming, so within modern societies the "youth culture" has a cachet it would not garner in more traditional societies, where respect for elders is central. Fourth, for most Americans the nuclear family became the norm, replacing the earlier model of an extended family of "attachment relations" nearby. Fifth, television sit-coms and movies usually portrayed family members with highly problematic and antagonistic "attachment relationships" with each other, which young viewers came to see as normal. Sixth, children began to pass their formative years indoors, missing the benefits of communion with nature, which enhances child development in many ways. Seventh, the modern condition expanded the demands of the workplace on parents, often requiring electronic engagement with work at all hours and leaving them to cope with their children as best they could during "spare time." Eighth, since modern, mechanistic worldview socializes everyone not to notice the deeply relational nature of how humans actually function, it did not occur to modern parents that cultivating *the quality of their relationship* with their children was the most important aspect of "correct parenting." Ninth, "peer-oriented attachment disorder" became so widespread by the mid-1990s that adults began to mistake it as normal development in children and adolescents (with responses such as "Students seem to prefer to learn from each other"), so they devised peer-teaching options that further the entrenchment of this orientation. Tenth, the invention of the social media sites, e-blast e-mails to a large list of recipients, and text messaging intensified an already highly stressful situation for adolescents, from which many of them feel they dare not turn away, even for the length of a family holiday dinner at grandmother's house.

One need only consider the example of friends, relations, and acquaintances who came of age at various times during the past six decades to realize that the influence of "peer-orientation attachment disorder" has intensified with each generation and half-generation, causing ever more serious problems, frailty, and suffering with regard to psychological and emotion development. The grip of this syndrome also begins at increasingly young ages, often by third grade, and continues well into adulthood and their own try at parenting. Moreover, this ever-worsening condition is common to all modern societies. It results from an anti-organic model of the human as a container into which we pour knowledge for twelve or more years and whom we encourage to separate (from the family) as soon as possible so that autonomy and independence will be assured. This process, bereft of relational wisdom, results instead in deeply wounded feelings of having been insufficiently loved and understood. Feelings of inadequacy and insecurity then shape their lives as young adults. They managed to fledge (though many return to the nest), but nature was thwarted in its efforts to bestow maturation.

Parenting, like teaching, is a sacred calling. Each entails gradually evoking and nurturing the child's unique gifts and deep interiority and providing a sound orientation in this world. We as a society must do better at protecting and supporting these delicate processes of maturation – and at comprehending that relationship is the heart of it all.

The Emerging Relational, Green Culture in Education

Biological needs are inherent in childhood development. The unfolding of the child takes place in a biological, relational continuum between the child's bodymind – its perceptions and sensations – and the life-forms around her or him (including stuffed animals, of course, because very young children are liberal thinkers in their embrace of both living animals and fabric versions). Their sense of wonder pulls them further and further into exploring the world beyond, but not severed from, the maternal presence, so pillowy, warm, and welcoming. The astute theorist of childhood imagination Edith Cobb called this process "bioaesthetic striving," which she saw as a matrix of cultural evolution because the intensified moments of perception in childhood often spark an interest much later, in adulthood, that leads to artistic creativity and scientific discoveries. Cobb considered the "spirit of childhood," with its "biosynthesis of body (perception) and cosmos (nature)," to be the source of the creative principle in the adult.[52]

Similarly, Rachel Carson published an essay titled "Help Your Child to Wonder" in *Woman's Home Companion* magazine in 1956, a few years before her ground-breaking book *Silent Spring*. Carson urged parents to nurture a child's "inborn sense of wonder" so that it might last a lifetime as "an unfailing antidote against the boredom and disenchantments of later years, the sterile preoccupation with things that are artificial, the alienation from the sources of our strength." She advised that feelings and sense experience are of utmost importance for a child because they are the fertile soil in which seeds of knowledge and wisdom will later grow.[53] American society, so caught up in the post-World War II burst of modernity and its grand promises of technology, could not imagine then how prescient Carson's warning would prove to be.

The deeply relational connection between a young child and her world can be expanded through various experiences and types of play with her parents and then through educational activities when the child enters pre-school, kindergarten, and the elementary grades of school – or it can be gradually suppressed by a dominant projection of hypermodern societies: that every student is in training to create his own reality, to be empowered as the Autonomous Individual who lives on top of nature, to utilize the powers of cyberspace to actuate his will. Like the Earth itself, our children have been damaged by these distortions so favored by modernity. Far too many of our young people feel like islands unto themselves, experiencing little felt connection with others and even less with the world beyond humans, which is their source of life and living. In response, the Relational Shift is beginning to reshape the form and content of education at all levels so that children can thrive with a healthy sense of themselves and the world. A more relational, comprehensive sense of "accountability in the post-No-Child-Left-Behind era," for instance, was advocated in a report issued in June 2009 by a bi-partisan team that included three former Assistant Secretaries of Education who are involved in the Broader, Bolder Approach to Education Campaign. Asserting that the fixation on test scores must be broadened, they advocate a concept of relational assessment that includes "qualitative evaluation of schools and districts to ensure the presence of a supportive school climate."[54]

Relational Factors in Learning

A study of schools in Chicago in 2000-01 found that a relational ambiance – that is, the presence of "relational trust" among teachers, students, the administration, and parents – was a far more significant indicator of academic success than were material indicators such as money or class size.[55] Although class size is important, especially during the first several years of elementary school,[56] that factor, along with the other quantifiable "inputs" in modern schooling, are best understood as elements in a richly complex, unquantifiable web of relationships. I would add to "relational trust" the importance of relational warmth, especially in the early years of elementary school. The really memorable teachers in one's early schooling – there may have been one or two – are those who wisely and skillfully created a relational attachment with each student. Amid the clamor for school reform, the mentality that seeks modern efficiency through an emphasis on that which can be measured tends to dismiss attention to the quality of relationships within an institution as inconsequential and sentimental clap-trap. Cultivating relational trust, though, turns out to be a secret of success.

Another relational quality that affects students' capacity to learn is happiness. Research in the new field of positive psychology shows that emotional well-being enables better learning: happy children learn more, earn more (later on), and have more satisfying lives.[57] Students, like the rest of us, can become happier by trying. That is, cognitive neuroscience has found that habitual thoughts influence the development of neural pathways in the brain. These thought patterns become strengthened over time and amount to our "automatic" moods or responses to events. To help children cultivate thought patterns of happiness and well-being, some schools teach ways to develop mental "happiness habits." These are essentially relational. Examples include the habit of gratitude (starting the day by thinking about someone or something in your life for whom you have a deep appreciation, repeating the practice just before lunch, and ending the day by thinking about something that happened that day that you appreciate). Two other "happiness patterns" are the habit of thoughtfulness (do something for someone every day) and the habit of optimism (curbing negative self-talk and focusing on possibilities).

Of course, inner skills of happiness cannot be cultivated successfully if a student delights in destroying the happiness of others, that is, in participating in the plague of meanness that now undermines our schools. This is because much of the tormentor's mind is agitated with negative thoughts about others, which poison the quality of her or his own mind. Traditionally, it might have been effective for parents and teachers to explain to children that mean behavior, including going along with it in a group, exposes the tormentor's inhumanity and base sensibilities to all who witness it. The entrenched dynamics of "peer-orientation attachment disorder," however, call for a more ambitious effort.

Moreover, for reasons that are not well understood by researchers, levels of empathy in American adolescents took a nosedive after 2000. A meta-analysis conducted at the University of Michigan of data from 72 studies involving nearly 14,000 college students over the past thirty years found that students in 2009 scored nearly 40 percent lower in "dispositional empathy" (or "interpersonal sensitivity") than their counterparts twenty or thirty years earlier. Specifically, the students in 2009 scored 48 percent lower in empathic concern and 34 percent lower in "perspective taking" (imagining how things look from the perspective of others). The researchers surmise that multiple causes may include the combination of violent video games, social media (where one can tune out of conversations), reality television shows, and highly competitive situations. The director of the meta-study, Sara Konrath, noted that many people have observed the current wave of college students to be "the most self-centered, narcissistic, competitive, confident, and individualistic in recent history."[58]

To counter this type of behavioral drift before the habits of mind harden into lifelong patterns, many school systems across the country have added "empathy workshops" to their middle-school curriculum. The good effects resulting from these relational exercises and programs would no doubt be multiplied and could have a truly transformative outcome if they were regarded by parents and middle-school educators as part of a larger, concerted effort to de-center students' obsession with primary peer attachment by healing and revitalizing what should be their primary attachments. (In such an effort, parents and teachers might find helpful the suggestions offered by Dr. Neufeld and others.) Admittedly, it is difficult to imagine how successful such remedial programs could be at a large, impersonal high school where the adolescents with primary peer attachment disorder had already erected a personal wall of aggressive indifference.

Of course, some degree of meanness and insensitivity has always been present among school children. When children are not gripped by an obsession with peer attachment as their primary orientation, however, insults and taunts do not result in a complete psychological collapse and a wave of teenage suicides. Still, people of all ages tend to hurt each other's feelings at times, and this behavioral pattern is ever with us to greater or lesser extents. A problematic aspect of our evolutionary inheritance is that we are all acutely aware of hurtful things that others do to us, but we are largely oblivious to our hurtful effects on others. No doubt our paleo-ancestors' chances for survival were improved by acutely remembering forever the scorpion's sting or someone's life-threatening gesture, yet this mental tendency means that every slight we suffer is registered more deeply in our minds than is useful in modern times. Worse still, we seem to lack a parallel awareness of how we may sting others inadvertently, not only by what we do and say but also by what we fail to do and say. Humans, in short, are rather self-absorbed.

Children deserve an education that provides them with skills to correct this tendency and thereby become happier and more morally accomplished. Some schools have introduced units on cultivating "emotional intelligence" and "social intelligence," based on the insightful books by Daniel Goleman on each of those subjects.[59] Another approach is to teach habits of communication that express a child's preferences and needs, yet do not hurt others, as demonstrated in the technique designed by Marshall Rosenberg called Nonviolent Communication.[60] This is a wisely relational method that identifies and honors inner needs. The approach has been used successfully by an extremely wide range of practitioners from kindergartners in various societies to mediators in intensely charged international political situations.

An even more comprehensive way to map the relational factors necessary for learning is to focus on helping children develop resilience, understood simply as the ability to spring back from and successfully adapt to adversity. Just as our bodymind is able to regain homeostasis after perturbations hundreds of times a day, so our conscious mind tends to self-right itself after a disturbance, unless it is thwarted by an accumulation of negative habits of thought. Research in the psychology of learning has found that efforts to bounce back from intense stress, trauma, low self-esteem, and "at risk" behavior are far more likely to be successful if the student has certain conditions in her or his life. One widely used program for helping children cultivate resilience is based on the book *Resiliency in Action* by Nan Henderson. Her "Resiliency Route to Academic Success" presents teachers and counselors with four steps (such as "Use strengths to overcome weaknesses" and "Build resiliency-fostering conditions around each student"). Nearly all the recommendations are relational, that is, about relationships in the school and elsewhere in the child's life. This program has proven so effective that it is used in the public school systems in New York City and Los Angeles, as well as in Pennsylvania, where the Secretary of Education recommended in 2008 that all schools in the state should adopt it. Perhaps the results are best summarized by the definition of resiliency submitted by a sophomore in high school after taking a semester of resiliency training: "Bouncing back from problems and stuff with more power and more smarts."[61]

Another new relational method employed to build a sense of connectedness and trust among students in school is the practice of the talking circle, or "council." Used successfully from elementary classrooms to special high schools for "delinquent" students, participants abide by council guidelines: to speak from and listen with the heart and to remain silent when the person with the talking stick, or object, is speaking. Social and emotional development ensue, as well as a sense of bonding and caring about others.[62]

While feelings of trust, happiness, and resilience are important to learning, several studies have also found a relationship between high scores on tests and being physically fit.[63] The benefits were demonstrated in all academic areas but were most evident in math scores, at three selected grade levels. In addition, the correlation was particularly strong for girls. To get children moving again, even in neighborhoods where parents do not feel safe sending them off alone all the way to school, "walking buses" have been established by parents who take turns, usually in pairs, "picking up" children at "walking-bus stops" throughout the neighborhood and walking with them to school in the morning and back home in the afternoon. Disallowing television after school usually results in better fitness (and less weight gain) in children, as well.[64] While many schools still have physical education classes, far too many others have eliminated them (and even recess!), along with music and art classes, in order to pay for thousands of laptops or for computer labs (whose equipment is soon obsolete and must be continually updated – all the while damaging the young children's formative process). It would be well to reverse those priorities in school budgets. In a related vein, it follows that since physical fitness correlates so strongly with high test scores, the cultivation of wellness plays a role, too. Several states, notably New York State, have invested in establishing a health clinic in more than 185 schools so that students with ailments and chronic conditions but little access to medical treatment can simply walk in and be seen by a medical professional.

Many of our schools, then, are becoming places where children can experience relationships of trust and can learn skills and attitudes that will serve them well in their ongoing development. Several high schools in Georgia, for instance, have been able to increase graduation rates dramatically since 2006 when they began matching a graduation coach with high-risk students; "a strong relationship with a caring adult" made all the difference in the academic life of those students.[65] In a growing number of elementary schools, roles and relationships are being shifted to transform the annual parent-teacher conference. Children are included not only to listen but to lead the meeting with a presentation of their work and their progress. The principle of an elementary school in a working-class neighborhood northwest of Chicago that adopted this relational shift explained their decision: "The old conferences were such a negative thing, so we turned it around by removing all the barriers and obstacles." Once they opted for the more relational model, 525 parents attended the conferences, compared with a turn-out of 75 parents previously. A parent at the school observed, "At the student-led conferences, our children are learning to be organized and capable adults someday.... My daughter is learning that the teacher is not responsible for her learning. She knows that she is responsible for her own success."[66]

Yet the bombardment of messages children and adolescents also receive relentlessly from the media and the electronic world tends to destabilize their sense of self-worth and their budding values and competence with extremely clever ways to make them feel inadequate if they do not own the product being advertized or to act, dress, and think in certain ways that serve the purposes of advertisers. So it is not sufficient to focus on teaching children to cultivate positive attitudes and relational skills without also paying attention to protecting them from influences that would negate all that is being created. This dual focus is badly needed throughout the K-12 range of students. For instance, verbally and physically violent behavior has been found to decline significantly among elementary-school students if they reduce the amount of time they spend watching television or videos and playing videogames.[67]

By 2007 several school districts around the country began to phase out one-to-one computer-based teaching programs (involving a laptop for every student in high school and sometimes middle school), which they had eagerly begun at least five years earlier. The programs were found to be "educationally empty – and worse."[68] Knowing facts and data does not constitute a coherent sense of a subject, and watching a hodge-podge of fleeting images does not teach students how to think systemically. Computers offer a certain kind of learning experience, but other kinds are devalued and crowded out by the lure of the power to control options in the virtual world. One of the most astute critics of computer-based education I have encountered is Lowell Monke, who reflects in the essay "Charlotte's Webpage" on his experience in the classroom:

> During the two decades I taught young people about digital technology I came to realize that the power of computers can lead children into deadened, alienated, and manipulative relationships with the world.... The influence of the computer is so compelling that it lures children away from the kind of activities through which they have always most effectively discovered themselves and their place in the world.... I repeatedly found that after engaging in internet projects, students came back down to the Earth of their immediate surroundings with boredom and disinterest – and a desire to get back online.... The child becomes less animated and less capable of appreciating what it means to be alive, what it means to belong in the world as a biological, social being.... The dependence on computers encourages a manipulative, "whatever works" attitude toward others.... Our children are likely to sustain this process of alienation – in which they treat themselves, other people, and Earth instrumentally – in a vain attempt to materially fill up lives crippled by internal emptiness.[69]

Never heard any of this in the clever, hip advertising from the computer industry? Our children have been the guinea pigs in a vast experiment in what would happen to childhood development if permeated by an electronic immersion. A stream of new devices continually seeks to mesmerize them, a recent example being e-books for young children! Since most American children spend five hours a day of recreational time staring at a screen of some sort,[70] the last thing they need in school is more computer time. Fortunately, as we shall see, a rising tide of wise and creative pedagogy is reengaging young minds with the Real.

Ecoliterate, Relational K-12 Education

Of all the areas being revitalized by the Relational Shift, the education of our children may well be the most poignant. While the relational perspective is, as yet, more influential in the academic disciplines at universities than it is in elementary and secondary schools, this is a moment of tremendous potential for reshaping the educational experience of young children starting out on their journey from kindergarten to high school graduation – and beyond. For the first time in the modern era, they are increasingly likely to be taught not the misleading mechanistic worldview but, rather, a coherent presentation of the relational nature of reality, a study of the fundamental relationships of the physical world and the cultures of the human family.

An organic progression would begin for very young children with a focus on the internal relationships that allow their own bodies to work so well (that is, a version for 5- and 6-year-olds of the recent discoveries in relational physiology that reveal how creative and smart our internal bodymind relationships are). This would lead into a focus on the relationships between their bodies and the sun, the weather, and water – and subsequently to relationships between oxygen and breathing, between sunlight and photosynthesis for plants, between bees and pollination, and between juveniles and their parents in all animal and human families. From the early years of elementary education the children would enter into an understanding that the various areas of study are specific ways of grasping the relationships that constitute the world. They would learn about relationships among numbers (arithmetic); relationships among letters and words (reading, writing, and storytelling); relationships among the sun, the Earth, the moon, and the other planets (science); relationships among people who constitute a culture (social studies), and so on. As the children mature, through high school, their understanding of the dynamic, creative relationships that constitute life becomes increasingly advanced, in areas such as literature, mathematics, science, history, art, music, social studies, and political science (what used to be called civics). These would no longer be viewed as isolated fields, from which students readily disengage. They would comprise ways for students to grasp the relationships in which they themselves exist. In each area, understanding one level of relational analysis opens students' eyes to the presence of further levels and developments.

Surely the shaping of a child's consciousness would be enhanced by learning from the very beginning that she or he exists as an inherent part of more richly complex relationships – physical and mental, organic and cultural, creative and open-ended – than anyone could ever map. Along the way, children would also be taught the relational keys to happiness, resilience, responsibility, and what Edith Cobb called "compassionate intelligence." By that Cobb meant a "generous worldview and process of understanding" involving a sense of relational identity that transcends a narrow focus on the self and that benefits from "humility as the creative tool." She observed that a child's development is "regulated by the meanings of nature imparted to him by the culture of his particular period in history." In modern Western culture, she noted that a very young child "perceives preverbally *the logic of relationships* that are overlooked in later, more formally fixed and intellectualized systems of knowledge."[71] Cobb made that observation long before the (relational) critique of modernity illuminated the problem: the relational aspect of reality is not simply "overlooked" but brusquely shoved aside by the inculcation of the mechanistic worldview into the minds of children once they enter modern schooling.

The exciting potential in K-12 education today is not only that we might finally *get it right* in terms of accurately bringing our (mechanistic) knowledge systems up to date with the myriad recent discoveries in science about the deeply relational nature of the physical world. The relational orientation, in fact, contains all the best of several recently proposed educational reforms, including a focus on getting our children more interested in math and science so that they will not be shut out of 21st-century jobs – but this overarching approach also offers much more. For our children to come of age securely situated in the understanding of organic and cultural interconnectedness might, just might, rescue them from the contagion of narcissism, aimlessness, and alienation that plagues so many of our young adults. It might well give them back their birthright as human organisms fully engaged with the embodied, embedded, organic interconnections needed to be healthy and to thrive, no longer isolate units of "coolness" and consumption but linked in their very cells with the dynamics of the entire Earth community (all the generations!) and the entire universe (from the beginning!).

For thousands of elementary, middle, and high schools across the country that are moving toward an ecologically based, relational approach to teaching and learning, the school garden has been the starting point. A well-designed curricular engagement with a school garden, usually designed with the relational principles of permaculture, can provide lessons in botany, the hydrologic cycle, soil science, biology, history, mathematics, poetry, group work, and the felicitous results of attentive caring about living plants. Often the school garden has walking paths and a place for children to eat their lunch. Whether in suburbia or the inner city, the testimonials of students who have become involved with a school garden express multiple benefits that far exceeded their expectations. As numerous teachers have noticed, in the garden anger dissolves and tensions ease among children who are considered problems in the classroom. A sixth-grader at a predominantly low-income school in St. Petersburg, Florida, for instance, explained the effect of the school garden to a journalist in 2009 as follows: "Before, we were all mean to each other, but now if you have a watering can and somebody wants it, you say, 'Here!'"[72]

One comprehensive K-12 curricular approach to ecologically informed education is called "ecoliteracy." Developed by a range of relational educators through the Center for Ecoliteracy since 1994, this orientation is "situated at the confluence of several powerful streams": the study of living systems, place-based pedagogy, sustainability as a community practice, and real-world learning. Emphasizing systems thinking and what they call the "four competencies" (skills associated with Head, Heart, Hands, and Spirit), the Center has developed the initiative "Smart by Nature: Schooling for Sustainability." While their focus on sustainability is only one part of the relational perspective on the academic subjects in the K-12 curriculum, they have made significant contributions to shifting thinking in a Green, relational direction, not only in the United States but also through several schools that participate in their informal international network. The Center for Ecoliteracy's website presents a wealth of information for educators and parents alike.[73] They were also instrumental helping the restaurateur Alice Waters found the Edible Schoolyards program, which she began in 1996 at a middle school in Berkeley, California. Students not only learn, cooperatively, how to raise food in a school garden but also how to cook it.

As numerous local pioneers of relational, ecoliterate education have discovered in their neighborhood schools, children love learning the logic of how the Earth community works and learning the names for the various parts and processes. They love place-based education, through which they learn about the immediate world around them. While it is not uncommon for media-raised students, especially those in middle or high school, to be disappointed by their first look at a pond or a stream because it looks less dramatic than the on-screen versions, they gradually begin to see and hear and smell and feel various aspects of the complex vitality there. What happens eventually is whole bodymind engagement with the more-than-human world that revitalizes the modern person of any age. Very young children seem to experience the extensive diversity and dynamism of nature via a permeability sensibility, such that they strongly feel oneness with the thrilling display they are observing. This immersion evokes the development of a plasticity of mind that leads to a deeper sense of creativity and meaning, which is always with them.[74]

Even one immersive experience in nature can have a transformative effect on students who have been shaped by an electronic childhood. In Richard Louv's book *Last Child in the Woods: Saving Our Children from Nature-Deficit Disorder,* he coined the phrase "nature-deficit disorder" and included this testimony from an adolescent about nature's healing effects: "For the past few months, I've found myself unmotivated. I almost felt a disconnection from myself because I couldn't take the time to think. When I sat down in nature to write this weekend, I found myself reconnected, my insides and outsides."[75]

Building on the allurement that nature studies and ecoliteracy evoke in students, a relational curriculum can then not only introduce the teaching of progressively more complex relationships but also make tangible the need for cultivating those relationships that have been discarded in many schools in recent years, principally in respect to the arts. For instance, what is the nature of the relationship between humans and music? It transcends our frenetic interior monologues, carries us to a bodily engaged type of listening, and even improves our health. Our languages are thought by some to have first emerged in response to the music of birdsong and other Earth sounds around us (including the sounds of human mothers soothing babies). Indeed, our musical response to birdsong may have evoked stages of development in the evolution of the human brain and may well have predated the emergence of language systems. Certainly, humans have been fashioning musical instruments since the Upper Paleolithic era, a recently discovered example being a flute from 30,000 BCE unearthed by archaeologists in the sediment in a cave near Ulm, Germany in 2009; it was created by making a row of holes in a narrow, 9-inch-long wing bone of a vulture.

The act of making music regularly in our formative years affects humans deeply. Learning to play a musical instrument before age 10 seems to influence brain plasticity and usually correlates with doing well in mathematics and other subjects. That is, for students who are motivated and creative, learning about the relationships in a musical score and creating music seem to facilitate better understanding of other relational systems of knowing, such as mathematics.[76] Similarly, when children learn about painting and sculpture, their engagement with form and beauty correlates with improved scores in various categories of literacy and critical thinking skills.[77] In fact, middle and high school students might well demand the reinstatement of the study of literature if they realized that reading lots of good-quality fiction in one's formative years correlates with increased empathy, interpersonal perception, and social skills: the reader is drawn beyond his or her limited life experience to understand more about the lives of other people, from the inside of characters' minds.[78] The arts help us to become more relationally knowing. Without them, our development is diminished.

One of the founders of the science of ecology, Eugene Odum, observed that every ecosystem has a strategy for development. So should every child and adolescent! The strategy for a student who understands the centrality of relationships is the passionate desire to take in everything from every source that tells her more than she knew the day before – a grandmother's tales of growing Victory Gardens during World War II, a flower struggling because is requires more sun, a shadow that hits a wall in a slightly different spot at the same time every day, an article about war refugees who have no chance of ever going home, a poem that suddenly dislodges the habitual patterns of thought. With every experience and every learning exercise, we grow relationally. Moreover, like an ecosystem we have the ability to design solutions to various situations that arise. If we get hungry, we may design a sandwich and go to the kitchen to assemble the ingredients. If we have a disagreement with a friend, we can design a resolution and try it out. If we have a lot of homework or a heavy workload, we design an order in which we will be most likely to achieve completion successfully. The more we know about relational possibilities, the more apt our designs are likely to be.

Knowledge is, indeed, knowledge of relationships – visible or invisible, subtle or gross, complex or even more complex. Therefore, the quality of our knowing depends on the quality of our relationships and the quality of our awareness of relationships. Not that relationships are static. At the subtle level, everything is always in vibratory flux, for nature proceeds with novelty as well as continuity. Yet when a new form or situation suddenly arises, it exists in new relationships arising from those already present. Nothing exists outside of relationships. The knowing about relationships, then, is itself a relationship. What kind of knowledgeable relationship do we have with body, nature, and place? With other people? With other cultures? Isn't that what education is about – or could be?

By the time the relational perspective trickles down from the college disciplines to their high school counterparts, including the Advanced Placement courses, educators will realize that the historically irreversible process we have entered with the Relational Shift involves a rethinking of the very nature of intelligence. It requires that we set aside the Cartesian sense of the detached spectator and manipulator for a more realistic perspective: knowing involves an interactive engagement with the relational dynamics that constitute any situation or subject. If the students regard, and experience, learning as the continuation of the organic process of knowing ever more about the relational nature of the world, which they began in kindergarten, high school will seem less like irrelevant busy work and more like the threshold to relationally savvy adulthood and citizenship.

Moreover, the organic perspective will shift all the areas of study back into the grand framing story of human engagement with the Earth community: the planetary context of human endeavor. During the modern era, our focus on economism made it the framing story into which science, mathematics, economics, sociology, and psychology were placed – but the Relational Shift opens that box. Instead, the larger context of the relationships of the Earth community intrigue and enrich our thinking. Then, too, with attention to "relational literacy" informing not only students' academic classes but their interactive perspective on the world, graduates will be far better equipped to see the trivial in modern life for what it is – and to seek that which is truly necessary and vital in their ongoing engagement with the world.

Finally, it should be mentioned that numerous K-12 schools have acted to "green" both the cafeteria offerings and the school environment. Nearly everywhere, the content of vending machines and school cafeterias has shifted in recent years to healthier snacks and lunch food. Moreover, schools with subsidized breakfast programs that changed from sugar-laden, white-flour cereals to cereals with complex carbohydrates saw an improvement in students' test scores. In several parts of the country, a shift in thinking about subsidized school lunches may well succeed in rechanneling the federal money to buying food produced within 100 miles of each school by family-run farms, which would provide the opportunity for the children to learn about the regional food economy – and to eat well. Some school districts have switched entirely to organic food, covering the additional cost by eliminating dessert. In addition, most K-12 schools have "gone green" by switching to non-toxic cleaning products, reducing energy consumption, and improving their recycling and conservation efforts.

A College Education in Relational Knowledge

The evolution of a liberal arts education in England and the United States was strongly influenced by the ideas of John Henry Newman as expressed in *The Idea of a University* (1854), in particular, by his distinction between "liberal" learning and "practical" learning. With the former, nothing accrues of consequence other than the academic activities themselves, for liberal education and liberal pursuits were seen as exercises of mind, reason, and reflection. Practical learning had no place in a liberal education.[79] Of course, this theory of education is built on the Cartesian assertion, and that of the Greeks as well, that an inherent dualism separates human consciousness from the rest of the world. That is, mind is set apart and is best educated by treating it as such. Therefore, the study of our biological and ecological reality was considered distant from the humanities, merely a specialized niche within the science departments.

After 75 years of this model's influence on higher education, however, the philosopher Alfred North Whitehead asserted that the "exclusive association of learning with book-learning" and the accompanying fixation on "second-hand scraps of information" have resulted the "mediocrity" of the learned world. A truly successful education results in a cultured mind that is not only more abstract but also more concrete, more interested in "the facts," or what I call the Real. Thought, Whitehead asserted, should be based on first-hand observation and "material creative activity."[80] He saw that our theories and mechanistic assumptions about the physical world completely missed our profoundly organic embeddedness in it and, even worse, that those misperceptions had become reified. That is, the (mechanistic) concepts and theoretical premises of Western science had been accorded the weight of realities themselves. The theoretical assumptions, in fact, had become by far the most important reality – at least, for academics and other intellectuals. The accumulation of conceptual frameworks had clattered on, with no real experiential knowledge or immersion into the rich, vital, organic complexity of the natural world in which our human thinking fills a small space. This situation is characterized, Whitehead warned, by the error of "misplaced concreteness," the investing of all our attention and powers of engagement in the concepts and theories of the day instead of regarding them as partial forays into apprehending, as best the human mind can, the complex process and relational wonder of it all. Therein lies true discovery.

As for what students find when they initially arrive at university campuses today, they may notice bicycles available at discounted prices or for rent, along with miles of bike lanes and parking stalls. The campus cafeterias probably serve (at least some) fresh, local produce and other locally produced food whenever possible. In addition, the campus facilities managers have most likely switched to greener procurement criteria for a range of cleaning supplies and other materials, as well as non-toxic paints and fabrics for dormitories and classrooms. Moreover, a Presidents Climate Commitment has been signed by over 600 presidents of American colleges and universities who have pledged to initiate a campus-wide plan to reduce emissions and energy usage to the point of being "climate neutral" in the near future. According to the 2009 College Sustainability Report Card, two-thirds of the universities surveyed had improved their efforts to "go green" in the previous year.[81] But since colleges and universities now compete to attract students by advertising how ecosocially advanced they have become, a well greened campus probably comes as no surprise to the entering freshmen.

Whether they concentrate their studies in the sciences or the humanities, college students today are likely to encounter a very different perspective and frame of reference from the ones that were taught to their parents' generation. The curriculum in earlier decades offered a range of subject areas that all viewed the world through the mechanistic lens: things are fundamentally separative (separate or separable) and are neither interdependent nor inherently interrelated. There was no need to teach this perspective explicitly, as it had shaped the students' thinking since elementary school. Working within that orientation, the various disciplines in both the physical and the social sciences focused on protocols for prediction and control. Foremost, the professors taught analytic approaches that were based on a belief in reductionism: if you break down a subject, whether an entity or situation or circumstance, so as to isolate simple, single parts and causes (even when great complexity is involved), you will understand the system, situation, or entity. When a complex system had been taken apart, literally or conceptually, an isolated part or cause was then declared to be the key to understanding the subject, such as "Single-mother households cause juvenile delinquency." This belief system then influenced numerous professions, even though single-cause analyses (as well as the bundling of single causes as "multiple causality") miss the dynamic relational nature of problems, crises, and concerns. Consequently, the widespread application of predictability-and-control methods – through reductionist, single-cause or multiple-cause intervention – was almost always thwarted by that which lay outside the analytical frame of reference: complex, dynamic interrelationships.

Today, in contrast, the new emphasis on a relational analysis and awareness can be found increasingly throughout the disciplines. Rather than studying entities in isolation, the relational perspective requires attention to inherent, dynamic, causal interrelatedness. In biology, for instance, it is now understood that order in natural systems is "context-sensitive": order and form emerge from relationships and maintain themselves through relationships of biocomplexity. The key is the pattern of interactions. This is true at the level of genes, cells, organs, organisms, ecosystems, the entire biosphere, and even the whole universe. In fact, life on Earth began through the relational process called symbiosis, a system in which organisms of different species live in close physical contact. Initially prokaryote bacteria moved into other prokaryote bacteria, eventually forming eukaryote bacteria; from a symbiotic relationship, then, resulted in a more complex cell with mitochondria, choroplast, and a nucleus. Nucleated cells are far more like a dynamic, closely knit community than a single entity. From those complex cells, the entire range of organisms of fungi, plants, and animals eventually evolved. Moreover, it may well be that the major dynamic in the formation of new species is neither gradual change through genetic mutations nor "genetic drift" but, rather, "symbiogenesis" (for example, the interaction of a bacteria with a more complex organism that causes a change in the offspring, which becomes the beginning of a new species). This is the influential theory of the biologist Lynn Margulis. She points out that symbiosis is a more likely explanation than is genetic mutation for the sudden and rapid change (called "punctuated equilibrium") that occasionally appears in the evolutionary fossil record. Margulis is gradually convincing scientists schooled in mechanistic thinking to consider relational causality, reminding them that "we are symbionts on a symbiotic planet."[82]

During this period of transition, many of the scientists and other academics who are deeply immersed in the implications of the Relational Shift have realized that our mechanistic terminology does not fit the relational dynamics being described. That the pioneering physicists of the 1920s explained the extremely relational, nonmechanistic quantum level of reality through terms like "quantum *mechanics*" is one illustration of the problem. More recently, the terms "intricacy" (for order arising from the "interweaving" that forms and affects all entities) and "web dynamics" have been proposed by Sally Goerner in her insightful book *After the Clockwork*

Universe.[83] Like "network dynamics," all these terms can work if they are understood to mean something more process-centered than the weaving of things, or webs of things, or networks of things – even things that function dynamically.

The stunning vitality of (relational) reality is hard to capture in a simple phrase, especially since the West's Indo-European languages favor nominalization, an emphasis on the naming of things (nouns) rather than on process-oriented ways to express aspects of subtle, dynamic states of being, which are themselves composed of vital, dynamic relationships. Even though we must take into account our culture's linguistic handicap as we move further into the relational perspective, many of the sciences, and nearly all of the life sciences, have entered an exciting state of transition focused on the discovery of relational complexity. Clearly we have reached the end of what has lately been called in hindsight "the Age of Categories."[84]

In the humanities, familiar subjects are being seen anew with the relational perspective. For example, relational sociology (which focuses on the formation of meaning and identities in social networks) has been called "probably the most important and innovative research perspective in American sociology in the past two decades."[85] Nor is that emergent focus singular. Throughout the social sciences the very methodology by which research is conducted has made room for a range of relational approaches known variously as organic inquiry, participatory inquiry, and action research – all of which take into account the relationship between the researcher and the subjects, as well as the ongoing, changing relationship between the researcher and the research findings being revealed.

In the field of philosophy, relational ontology (the realization that interrelations between entities are ontologically more fundamental than the entities themselves and are also causal) has influenced several areas. Any theory of being must engage with the fact that to be a living presence is more a matter of dynamic, creative responses in webs of relationship than it is a matter of categories and substances. As such, relational ontology is now a factor in such fields as psychology, political theory, educational theory, and even information science.[86] Today philosophy students take courses with such titles as Relational Philosophy (or Philosophy of Relations); Relational Ontology (including the new concept of "relational autonomy"); Relational Epistemology; and Relational Ethics.

Other examples of courses on the relational perspective at various universities in recent years have included Relational History; Relational

Linguistics; Relational Geography; Relational Economics (and Relational Economic Geography!); Relational Models for Literary Criticism; Relational Art (a phenomenon that emerged in the 1990s); Relational Rights and Responsibilities in Political and Legal Theory; and Relational Theory for Social Work. Numerous breakthrough works of scholarship have illuminated previously unrecognized interrelationships between two subjects or areas; these studies are often called "comparative" (an old term originally coined to cover studies that compare separate entities).[87] Many sub-fields have been born of relational realizations across disciplinary dividing lines, such as Environmental History and also Ecological Literary Criticism (EcoLitCrit for short).

An ambitious and relational planetary project, the Forum on Religion and Ecology, housed at Yale University, has helped to nurture what is now a rapidly expanding area of scholarship and activism within ecologically engaged religions.[88] Several graduate institutes and research centers also emphasize a relational perspective, such as the California Institute of Integral Studies. The Claremont Graduate School of Theology houses the Center for Process Studies, whose motto is "A Relational Worldview for the Common Good" and whose focus is the implications of the profoundly relational philosophy delineated by Alfred North Whitehead.[89] Elsewhere in the field of religious studies, the 20-year debate over whether spiritual experience is merely a projection of culture (a "linguistic construction") or is a subset of a particular "revealed" religion is giving way to various relational insights on the nature of spirituality, which are sometimes referred to as "the participatory turn" in scholarly perspectives.[90]

In the field of psychology, the hugely influential, 100-year-long dominance accorded the Freudian model of separation as the hallmark of mental health has finally been relegated to the margins as a specialty called "classical psychoanalysis." Instead, the relational perspective on the human psyche, often called Psychodynamic Theory, has become the mainstream orientation within the field. A major research focus is on "attachment theory" and the implications of how "secure," "ambivalent," or "avoidant" a person is in his or her intimate relationships. Mental health is seen primarily, but not entirely, as a matter of how "securely" one is able to attach to, rely on, and relate to another person – which is nearly a 180-degree shift away from the assumptions of Freudian theory (with its resignation that essential separation was continually threatened and compromised throughout one's lifetime by the expectations and demands of various relationships). New concepts such as "father hunger" and "mother hunger" are seen as quite understandable responses to inadequate core relationships, whereas Freud probably would have viewed them as pathological. Moreover, students are now taught that the successful psychotherapist is not opaque and distant but, rather, that the quality of the therapeutic relationship with the client is key to the healing process.

One of the sources of this gradual but profound shift in the field of psychology was the relational-cultural model of mental health that was developed in the late 1970s and early 1980s by theorists at the Stone Center at Wellesley College (especially Jean Baker Miller) and through kindred work by numerous feminist psychologists and researchers elsewhere, including Carol Gilligan at Harvard University and, later, Shelley Taylor at UCLA. Looking back, the psychologist Mihaly Csikszentmihalyi observed that this work "finally incorporated women's experiences and sensibilities into the scientific model of the ideal self" (which was previously delineated, he recalls, as "hard, independent, detached, autonomous, capable of distancing itself from other people and from its own emotions, motivated by a fierce need to survive and prevail – something like a ferret hiding in its hole, ready to pounce on any moving thing it can kill and drag into its lair"). The relational-cultural perspective, he notes, established a fuller model of the self as responsive, responsible, and interdependent with others.[91] Although the women who initially articulated this correction to the (Freudian) assumptions dominating psychology were called "unscientific" in the 1970s, cognitive science in the subsequent decades has validated the relational model they pioneered. In addition, Catherine Keller's *From a Broken Web: Separation, Sexism, and Self* (1986) was an influential work on "the separative self" and "the connective self."

For an overview of the research findings that relationships are central to human life, psychology students are often referred to two recent works: *Relational Being: Beyond Self and Community* by Kenneth J. Gergen (2009) and *The Neuroscience of Human Relationships* by Louis Cozolino (2006). Gergen, in particular, presents an expansive analysis in which he contrasts the culture of "bound being" (abusive, constraining, and undermining of the self, resulting in feelings of isolation, unrelenting self-evaluation, and thwarted self-esteem) with his sense of a culture of "relational being" (a liberating, bonding, co-creative reconceptualization of self and life). In addition, numerous studies in relational psychology are available from the Jean Baker Miller Training Institute, located at Wellesley College. In recent years, field studies in a wide range of areas have continued to illuminate the relational grounding of mental health, which was obfuscated in most quarters of 20th-century psychology. For instance, a recent study of which factors predict psychological stress or its absence in college students found that the protective factors are entirely relational, not separative (as Freud would have asserted as predictors of success): "secure parental attachment; authentic, empowered, and engaged community relationships; and, for the women especially, peer relational quality."[92]

Because students are increasingly concerned about the ecological crises, foremost global climate disruption, a new subject area known as sustainability literacy is becoming one of the goals of an education at "green" colleges and universities. Courses have been developed in recent years that present the pragmatic ramifications of relational awareness with regard to the natural world and the built world. On many campuses, such programs have been organized by the students themselves and then absorbed into the curriculum. The students cultivate ecological and ecosocial intelligence, competence, and imagination with regard to new possibilities. They also learn that thinking, no matter what style of thought, is often a matter of the human impulse to design – we constantly design meaning, coherence, and solutions to difficult situations. As a generation, the "millennials" have volunteered in activist organizations (often as a peer activity) at a much higher rate than has the "Gen X" generation before them. They often do so because they feel a personal connection with a cause, such as an aunt who has breast cancer, and they tend to be attracted to pragmatic solutions rather than philosophical or moral motivations for action.

Yet the increase in activist students and the appearance of courses on sustainability is not nearly sufficient to draw higher education out of its fragmented, human-centered status quo into the realization that teaching about human endeavors as if we lived on top of nature is irrational and is destructive of our possibilities for cultivating an ecosocial culture. We exist only in profound relationship with the rest of the natural world – and all human systems are derivative of it, not the other way around. As the sage and "geologian" Thomas Berry declared, the Earth is the great university, the great economy, the great cathedral, the great art gallery, the great history museum, the great engineering system, the great hospital, the great theater, and the great font of all our stories and song. It is toward this deeper context that the Relational Shift has begun to move our colleges and universities, and there is no going back to the mechanistic worldview. The transition will be furthered if courses on the history of ideas, for instance, present the great organic, relational thinkers of Western culture, such as Leonardo da Vinci, Goethe, John Ruskin, Charles Darwin, Catherine Beecher, Charles

Sanders Pierce, John Muir, Maria Montessori, Alfred North Whitehead, Jean Gebser, David Bohm, Thomas Berry, and so many others.[93] As we are beginning to learn, the recovery of relational knowledge and wisdom has deep roots and abundant flowering.

Life-Long Learning and the Relational Shift

In many instances the Relational Shift has moved more quickly into venues of adult education – local lecture series, weekend and summer workshops, conferences, and other programs – than into the calcified curricula at many universities. Annual conferences around the country, such as the Bioneers and a wide variety of Green gatherings, present ecosocial, relational analyses and pragmatic solutions to the challenges facing people in their communities today and in the world at large. Networks of local discussion groups have grown out of such conferences and frequently sow seeds of the ecosocial, relational perspective with regard to current problems and situations.

More in-depth offerings are available through numerous institutes – such as the Whidbey Institute, the Omega Institute for Holistic Studies, and the New York Open Center. Many of these organizations employ a descriptive label similar to that of Schumacher College in England: "Transformative Learning for Sustainable Living."[94] The courses offered present the relational shift in health and healing, new ways of doing business, green building, community revitalization, and other topics. They often introduce books and other materials, but more importantly, the adult education workshops, courses, and gatherings serve to present the relational perspective on multivalent levels because friendships and collegial ties emerge among the participants, which they carry on into the work. When the participants return home, they do not feel that they are striving in isolation to nudge the new thinking forward in their town. Rather, they are always in relationship, always carried. For that reason, these venues have played a significant role in moving relational thought from the level of insight and analysis to actual applications in the world.

III

THE RELATIONAL SHIFT IN HEALTH AND HEALTHCARE

A Snapshot of the Crises

What is happening to us, to our species?

We modern humans live longer than ever before, yet we now carry in our blood and tissue scores of industrial chemicals, many of which are toxic and did not even exist sixty years ago. Bisphenol-A, for instance, is a toxic compound found in numerous consumer products, plastic bottles, and linings of cans used for canned food. Because it is an endocrine disruptor, it has been found to be a causal factor in erectile dysfunction and other conditions.[95] It has not yet been banned nationally; instead, men are sold the supposed solution of Viagra, which can cause health problems. How are we doing on reproduction? Sadly, most of us are aware that couples among our family and friends are struggling with infertility, usually because the average sperm count in Western industrialized countries is less than half of what it was in 1950. Even when conception is achieved, the reproductive cells of both parents frequently have sustained some impairment from the toxins in and around us.[96] Moreover, the combination of compromised immune systems plus the ubiquitous environmental toxins has led to substantially increased rates of several types of cancer and other diseases. We do not like to think about these developments because Americans generally consider our nation the most fortunate on Earth. In truth, our life expectancy is now shorter than that of almost every other industrialized country.[97]

As we have seen in recent years, the spreading obesity epidemic now claims not only middle-aged and young adults but also children as young as preschoolers. It came about largely because Americans eat too much comfort food of little nutritive value (lots of fat, salt, and ubiquitous fructose sugar). Additionally, millions of people thought they were making a healthy dietary choice by opting for artificially sweetened "diet sodas," but they were actually damaging their health: it turns out that drinking even one can of that stuff per day significantly increases your risk of developing obesity, high levels of blood sugar, low levels of good cholesterol, and metabolic syndrome.[98] Even more tragically, children are at high risk for developing serious disease when they are raised on far too much junk food, fast food, and processed food. At the same time, exposure to endocrine-disrupting chemicals known as phthalates, which are common in pliable plastics and in personal care products, has been linked to obesity in children and to increased risk of their becoming diabetic.[99] By 2008 hundreds of thousands of children in the United States were taking adult medications for Type 2 diabetes, high blood pressure, high cholesterol, and acid reflux – all problems linked to obesity that were practically unheard of in juveniles twenty years ago and that spiked in incidence between 2001 and 2007.[100]

Even when we seek to improve our health by eating more (conventionally grown) fruits and vegetables, things are not what they seem: numerous studies have found that industrially grown produce today has far lower levels of nutrients than did produce in the past. For instance, a study in 1988 found that the nutrient value of broccoli, carrots, cauliflower, kale, onions, and five other vegetables had, on average, 27 percent less calcium (53 percent less in broccoli), 37 percent less iron, 21 percent less vitamin A, and 30 percent less vitamin C than the levels of nutrients in 1975.[101] Moreover, it was discovered in 2010 that the excess amounts of carbon dioxide in the atmosphere block crops' ability to pull nitrogen-based nutrients from the soil, making them less nutritious.[102] Though we don't realize it, most of us are consuming wan substitutes for what fruits and vegetables used to be, leaving our bodies without the nutrition they need to resist the mounting environmental stresses (including the synergistic "cocktail effect" of daily exposure to toxins) and to successfully stave off the development of illness. The supposed solution offered is a multi-billion-dollar industry in vitamin supplements to compensate for the degraded, industrialized condition of our food. Fortunately, there is an alternative: more than 75 studies, as of March 2009, have found that organically grown produce has far higher levels of nutrients than does produce grown with synthetic fertilizers and pesticides.[103] As yet, though, most Americans are consuming merely "lite produce," and they are also eating meat and dairy products that are laced with antibiotics and synthetic hormones, which further compromise the natural resilience of our bodies.

How about our nervous systems and general mental condition?

Three-quarters of Americans have trouble sleeping at night. During the work day, the common immersion in ringing telephones and incoming e-mail results in diminished mental functioning (registered in one study as a 10 point drop in IQ).[104] Checking for e-mail messages frequently is admittedly an addiction for 62 percent of adults.[105] In addition, our eyes have been compromised by computer use: computer users tend to blink less often, an average of seven times per minute rather than the normal rate of 22 times per minute, which results in eye dryness and fatigue.[106] Even worse, the National Eye Institute announced in 2009 that the rate of myopia among Americans had jumped 41.6 percent between 1999 and 2004. Hours of computer use combined with a lack of outdoor distance vision are suspected as probable causes. This deterioration in vision is worrisome because myopia increases the risk of other eye diseases, including glaucoma, retinal detachment, and blindness.[107]

Many of us live in a state of sustained or recurring stress, which causes premature aging, brain deterioration, and diminishes our immune system. This results because our potent human stress responses (such as fight or flight) evolved to meet short-term emergencies that occurred intermittently, such as spotting a snake near our footfall. At such moments our bodies are flooded with up to six times the normal amount of the adrenal hormones ACTH, cortisone, and cortisol – not a healthy condition if extended habitually because of noise pollution and other ongoing stressful situations. Although many people, especially urban dwellers, regard habitual stress as the price one pays for enjoying the benefits of modernity, it can cause metabolic disruption and nutritional deficiencies, a diminished immune system, and early aging.[108]

Are we happy? Not according to reported rates of depression, which are often called "epidemic" in the 21st century. A study of women begun by the National Institute for Mental Health in the 1970s found that although prosperity increased in the decades since World War I, rates of depression increased as well. The NIMH research team had expected depression to be linked with periods of hardship, particularly the Great Depression of the 1930s or World War II, but they found the opposite: among women born around World War I, only 1 percent had experienced depression; for those born around World War II, the percentage was 3; among those born around the time of the Korean War, it was 7 percent; for those born during the Vietnam War era, the rate was 10 percent; and for those born in the post-Vietnam War era, between 12 and 15 percent had had a serious episode of depression by the time they had completed high school.[109] As the relational web of community ties and extended family connections diminished over the course of the 20th century, so, too, did the women's sense of well-being.[110] An additional factor that correlates with depression, in both sexes, is too much television viewing.[111]

We might well finally ask – now that so many Americans born after 1970 are on daily anti-depression medication – whether our hypermodern way of life is inherently unsettling, undermining, and downright debilitating for the human bodymind, unless counterweighted with ways to stay grounded, connected, and vital. Might there be cumulative effects of having to drive too much, grab fast food on the go, and have too little time for our relationships with our families and friends? Millions of people struggle with financial loss and continuous insecurity – enduring first a "restructured" domestic economy that "downsized" their jobs or "off-shored" them and then the economic meltdown of 2008. Those who have lost their jobs strive to cope with mounting debt, stress, and isolation. Those still in the American workplace frequently feel time-starved, exploited, and somewhat ill as they struggle under severely increased workloads.

But perhaps I merely have a bad attitude toward the dynamism of 21st-century life in America because my formative years unfolded in a slower, less artificial, and largely pre-electronic world (in a tree-lined suburb of Columbus, Ohio, in the 1950s). To get a better sense of how humans who are more fully adapted are doing, let's take a look instead at the state of the children of our species, who are born into a hypermodern wonderworld and are unburdened by any temptations of nostalgia for less frenetic times.

Lucky the baby who is breastfed, as it boosts IQ and provides numerous benefits such as immunity to various diseases. But wait! The breastmilk of all mothers now contains industrial chemicals, and in many parts of the United States it would, if bottled, be too toxic to gain FDA approval to be sold. Tragically, mothers' milk has become a stew of PCBs, DDT, dioxin, flame retardants, and other toxins. *Mothers' milk!* As for the alternative, most plastic baby bottles were, until recently, toxic as well; they contained bisphenol A, which is demonstrably linked to a range of serious reproductive disorders and diseases of the reproductive organs in both sexes.[112] Moreover, synthetic formula, whether conveyed in plastic or glass bottles, falls far short of matching the nutritional value of mothers' milk and, worse still, is usually loaded with fructose, which has ill effects on the body's metabolic functions.[113]

Breastfed or not, today's newborns emerge into the world with a body burden of industrial chemicals they have absorbed through their mother's umbilical cord. A study of umbilical cord blood from babies born in U.S. hospitals in August and September 2004 found *an average of 200 synthetic chemicals and pollutants*, including mercury, flame retardants, pesticides, and PFOA, which is used to make Teflon. In total, the babies' umbilical blood contained 297 chemicals, 209 of which had never been detected in cord blood before.[114] (Even so, those babies are the lucky ones. Some industrial chemical compounds, such as certain solvents and the pesticide methoxychlor, prevent embryonic implantation in the uterus, while polycyclic aromatic hydrocarbons in air pollution can kill eggs in the ovary.[115])

It is likely that the synergistic interaction of the inborn toxins along with subsequent environmental stress (ongoing exposure to additional toxins, dietary deficiencies, and other stresses to the bodymind) explain why so many young adults are manifesting diseases previously seen only among the middle-aged, such as diverticulosis, metabolic syndrome, and a range of "adult" cancers. Even more shocking is the effect of endocrine-disrupting chemical compounds, ubiquitous today in industrial agriculture and consumer products, on the development of male fetuses: as of 2009 up to 7 percent annually of newborn American boys had undescended testicles (though this condition often self-corrects over time), and up to 1 percent of boys in the United States are now born with hypospadias, in which the urethra exits the penis improperly, such as at the base rather than at the tip.[116]

The synergistic effects of environmental assaults are also thought to play a role in the high rates of learning disorders, Attention Deficit and Hyperactivity Disorder (ADHD), autism, Asperger's Syndrome, and a range of symptoms related to faulty cognitive development, all of which are common childhood afflictions today. A study in 2002 found that an estimated 2.5 million American children were taking anti-psychotic prescriptions drugs for ADHD, a nonpsychotic disorder, even though the effectiveness of those drugs (which were designed for adults) has not been proven in treating ADHD and even though there are serious "side" effects.[117] The number of children and adolescents given these anti-psychotic drugs for problems like aggression and mood swings increased fivefold between 1993 and 2002.[118] Hundreds of thousands of American preschoolers have now been diagnosed with ADHD and are being given the prescription drug Ritalin (approved only for children age 6 and older), even though the drug causes far more pronounced "side" effects in young children than in older children.[119]

As for autism, the U.S. Department of Education reported a 1700 percent increase in the number of schoolchildren diagnosed with it between 1992 and 2002. Though high concentrations occur in certain areas, such as California,[120] the American public was shocked when the Centers for Disease Control announced in 2006 that one in every 150 American children has an Autism Spectrum Disorder, or ASD (autism, Asperger's syndrome, or another pervasive developmental problem). By 2011 the rate was one in every 110 American children. Even worse, in 2009 the CDC found that the rate of incidence of ASD was one in every 100 eight-year-olds in the United States.[121] The cause is still unclear, though there seem to be several contributing factors. A major candidate is exposure to environmental toxins while in the womb (that is, while the brain is forming) or shortly after birth.[122] In some cases, genetic defects are also are involved, though sometimes they are not inherited but were caused by a mutation sometime after fertilization, possibly due to environmental influences. Children born to mothers who live close to the air pollution of freeways, for instance, have twice the risk of autism as children who do not.[123] In addition, higher rates of autism correlate with premature births with low birth weight; close birth spacing (being born less then two years after a sibling); paternity by men over age 40 (which, by the way, also correlates with lower IQ in the child); and/or serious depression or personality disorders in the mother.[124] A causal hypothesis is further complicated by a study in 2008 that found significantly higher rates of autism in children who had lived in a rainy climate between the ages of one and three.[125]

Pediatricians are also baffled by the sharp increase of children manifesting allergies to foods, particularly peanuts. American children are much more likely to be allergic to peanuts, sometimes fatally so, than are children in less industrialized countries; the rate is estimated to have doubled in the United States in the past decade. (About 4 percent of the American public is now allergic to peanuts, tree nuts, fish, or shellfish, but a decade ago only 1 percent were so afflicted.[126])

Less puzzling but equally life-threatening to our children is the combination of "junk food" and inactivity. More than 5.3 million adolescents, nearly 4 million children under 12, and even 10 percent of children under age five are now overweight or obese. (In adults, obesity increased by 75 percent between 1991 and 2004; by 2009, two-thirds of American adults were obese or overweight.) Rates of childhood obesity tripled between 1980 and 2009, by which point 30 percent of the children in 30 states were obese.[127] Two million American adolescents – one out of every fourteen – has a pre-diabetic condition; one million adolescents have metabolic syndrome, putting them at risk for heart disease.[128] A national survey in 2005 found that 34 percent of adolescents have poor cardiovascular fitness.[129] The high salt content in most American diets, along with large dollops of sucrose and fructose in sodas and other processed foods, has resulted in a steep increase in the incidents of kidney stones in children, even as young as five or six.

Let's return to their neurological development in a hypermodern childhood. Unlike in the thousands of generations who preceded them, our children's brains and nervous systems today are saturated with electronic stimulation throughout their formative years. Hardly anyone gave serious thought to whether such modern "advancements" might cause developmental problems. For the past two decades, though, teachers have noticed that students, in general, have a shorter attention span, less capacity for reflection (or the "duration experience"), less patience, less empathy, more shyness and constricted body language, and – increasingly among the older students – a sense of alienation such that they feel as if they are closed in on themselves and detached from the world. From an early age (pre-schoolers and even infants are the "target market" for an array of computer programs, e-books, and television shows), our children spend hours every day staring at a glowing screen, moving their eyes and their bodies far less frequently than did earlier generations at any given age. A Nielsen survey in 2009 found that most American children between ages two and five now spend 32 hours per week watching television.[130] Not only are their eyes fixed on the screen but what they are seeing is flat, so it involves no varying depth perception.

Moreover, the normal developmental sequence for young toddlers is disrupted in those who watch hours of television nearly every day. The natural sequence of development involves an aural phase in young toddlers during which hearing family stories around a table or camp fire had, for eons, sparked imaginative visualization in the child's mind, creating synaptic growth in the brain that becomes the foundation for subsequent synaptic growth. When "electronic babies" at that age receive both the aural and the visual information simultaneously, however, the brain reacts by making a quick, efficient connection between the two, diminishing the usual process of imaginative stimulation and synaptic development.[131]

Worse still, our children's imaginative range shrinks to match the canned reality on the screen, as their desires become shaped by the commercial and noncommercial messages they watch continuously. Not only do young children's cognitive patterns adapt to the relentlessly zippy pace of the moving images, but their ability to see the Real – to distinguish among the vast range of colors in nature, for instance – seems to atrophy. They are accustomed to seeing only synthetic color, for they rarely play outdoors. They are cut off from the aesthetic richness with which nature and various interactions with family members have always evoked the cognitive powers of the very young. Instead, they are mesmerized by an electronic screen … almost from birth.

A study released in 2010 by the Kaiser Family Foundation found that the average young American spends practically every waking minute – except for time in school – using a smart phone, computer, television, or other electronic device. Those who are ages eight through eighteen spend about 7.6 hours a day with such devices (more than 53 hours per week), compared to 6.5 hours per day five years earlier. Because so many of them are multitasking – surfing the Internet, for instance, while listening to music – they are actually taking in nearly 11 hours of media content during those 7.6 hours. The study also found that more than 70 percent of the children have a television in their bedrooms, and about 33 percent have a computer with Internet access in their room. The heaviest media users are the "tweens" (those ages 11 to 14) and minority youth.[132]

An earlier study by the Kaiser Family Foundation, in 2005, also focused on the media habits of very young children in the United States and found that more than 25 percent of children from birth to age 3 had a television set in their own room; on average, babies from 6 months old to age 3 spent an hour every day watching television and 47 minutes a day on other screen media, such as videos, computers, and video games.[133] Although most parents of young children assume that early exposure to television is helpful to a child's brain development, children from "television-heavy" homes are less likely to be able to read before age 6, and in later grades they score lower than their peers on tests in mathematics and language arts.[134] A typical American child watches 28 hours of television a week, has seen 8,000 murders enacted by the time she or he finishes elementary school, and has received the core message from advertisers in myriad ways that You Are What You Buy. When additional hours are spent playing video games and using the computer during the formative years, the daily compulsion of media immersion results in children who miss out on running and jumping and playing outdoors. They also miss out on the socialization process that psychologists call the "culture of childhood" – the dynamics of self-organizing play among children through which they learn to settle their own quarrels, to establish the rules for a game, and to respect the rights of others. The lack of those developmental skills has resulted in the need for a new staff position at many elementary schools nationwide: specially trained "recess coaches."

When children begin to play team sports in the upper grades of elementary school, they seem to many youth coaches today to be oddly unphysical, as if they are not acquainted with the physical possibilities of their bodies. They lack bodily confidence and are frequently afraid to take a chance at executing a play during a game. When they do take a tumble, in play or sports, children today experience 42 percent more arm fractures, caused by poor bone density, than thirty years ago. Their bones are weak because of a lack of load-bearing exercise such as running, skipping, and jumping. In fact, a study of 447 children under age fourteen who suffered repeat bone fractures found that 67 percent already had osteoporosis![135]

Increasingly our children suffer from sleep disorders, as well. This problem results in headaches, irritability, impaired concentration, and sometimes agitated behavior that is akin to ADHD (which has been linked in many studies to exposure to organophosphate pesticides).[136] Perhaps due to the relentless marketing and sales efforts by the pharmaceutical corporations, most pediatricians readily put the sleep-deprived child on a prescription drug. A study in 2007 of 18.6 million sleep disorder patients under age 18 found that only 7 percent had received dietary counseling (such as the advice to avoid caffeinated soft drinks and too much sugar) and that only 22 percent had received treatment through behavioral therapies (such as relaxation techniques, along with staying off electronic stimulation for at least a half-hour before bedtime). Eighty-one percent of the young patients were simply put on a prescription drug, often one that was not specifically designed to aid sleep (but causes drowsiness as a "side effect") and that has not be studied for effectiveness or safety when taken by youth. This particular niche of prescription drug sales increased 14.6 percent in 2006 alone, more than any other category. From 2001 to 2006, the rate of usage for children from age 10 to 19 increased 80 percent for girls and 64 percent for boys.[137] What are these drugs doing to the neurological development of these millions of children?

As they grow up, our teenagers eschew interactions with a range of people they may encounter throughout the day, preferring to stay on their cell phones, speaking, or text-messaging obsessively to a very small circle of friends. In recent decades, high school dating in many areas was largely replaced by more detached patterns of "hooking up," which generally entails sex without emotional involvement or an ongoing relationship. Without the experience of dating, high school boys forfeit much needed socialization (adolescent girls are developmentally about four years ahead in emotional maturity, a pattern that is not new). Meanwhile, the boys see plenty of sexually violent videos and video games, which feature coarse plots of dominance and forcing one's will on others. Is this progress? While adolescents are generally adept at putting up a good front and being "cool with it all," many of them today complain privately of being too pressured, misunderstood, anxious, bitter, angry, sad, and always feeling empty.[138]

At the college level, the cumulative effects of the electronic childhood and other undermining influences are plain to see. A typical undergraduate classroom today usually contains an assemblage of young people almost eerily drained of vitality, protectively withdrawn from nearly everyone (except their small core of friends) and everything, much too self-conscious to risk raising a hand or joining a public discussion, and lacking the enthusiasm that had always been common to their age group. A large part of their self-identity is invested in the brands of clothing they wear. Many of the young women adopt little-girl voices so that they will be perceived as *very* nonthreatening to young men, and both sexes often speak very fast, running their words together in an electronic-like blur.

Tragically, rising numbers of college students are afflicted with more complex and serious psychological problems than campus counseling centers have seen in the past. At Kansas State University, for instance, the percentage of students treated for depression, as well as the number of suicidal students, both doubled between 1989 and 2001. A study in 2006 of the responses to a mental health survey sent to 2875 randomly selected undergraduate and graduate students at Cornell University and Princeton University found that fully 20 percent had purposely injured themselves by cutting, burning, or other means.[139] Between 1996 and 2002 at Columbia University, there was a 40 percent increase in the use of the psychotherapy counseling center, requiring extended hours and the addition of psychotherapists' offices in dormitories. In 2009 a study by the American College Counseling Association found that 93 percent of schools surveyed had seen increasing numbers of students "with severe psychological problems."[140] The director of counseling and psychological services at the University of Nebraska has observed, "People just don't seem to have the resources to draw upon emotionally to the degree that they used to. What would once have been a difficult patch for someone in the past is now a full-blown crisis."[141]

Our species is being altered fundamentally.

How could three hundred years of modern progress have delivered us to such an increasingly impaired version of *Homo sapiens*? Moreover, how could the unraveling of our collective physical and mental well-being have gone largely unnoticed? Our attention is continually directed elsewhere – to the vacillations of the stock market and other portents of an economic recession, to the management of household debt, to the insecurity of the globalized economy and related political developments, to the current trends and styles, to the depressingly crass pop culture, and once in a while to the degraded state of our democracy and the State of the Union. Too bad we never get a State of the Human report. Or a State of the Earth report either. Or, rather, one combined report on the thoroughly interrelated fates of the human and the Earth, the EcoSocial Index.

We lost sight of that connection, missed it entirely, throughout the modern era. All our impressive inventions and scientific discoveries seemed to elevate modern societies to an advanced plane of existence on which we hovered confidently above nature. We could dump massive quantities of toxic chemical compounds into the environment and not feel it had any relationship to us. We could replace young children's tactile exploration of the natural world with hours of television time and not have a clue that their cognitive development was being diminished, rather than enhanced. We could construct vast economies, either capitalist or socialist, that considered the destruction of nature by industrialization to be a "mere externality," which should logically be set aside from the important numbers on the balance sheets. It all seemed self-evident.

The modern era was blind to other relational realities as well that contributed to the accumulating impairment of the human. Remarkably, the cultural power of two concepts – the mechanistic model of the body (which was seen to be essentially unrelated to people or things around it) and the dualistic separation of body from mind – blocked modern medicine from perceiving the unified dynamics of the bodymind for centuries. Even when Freud finally proposed in the late 19th century that physical ailments can be caused by turmoil in the (unconscious) mind, his extrapolations remained within the mechanistic assumptions of modern science. After World War II, modern medicine slowly began to acknowledge some mind-body connections, but this was done largely through the pejorative label "psychosomatic symptoms," meaning that in certain cases the patient's faulty mental processes were actually causing real, or imagined, effects in the body.

The more closely modern physiology clung to the (mechanistic) "medical model" of the bodymind, the more things just didn't make sense. For instance, medical science discovered "germ theory" (the causal connection between certain bacteria and certain diseases), but it could not explain why myriad people can carry a harmful type of bacteria for decades and never develop the disease that it causes. The answer is that our immune system, as it turns out, is highly relational. Whether it is robust or impaired depends not only on heredity, diet, and lifestyle choices (or opportunities) but also on the condition of the relationships in our lives.

The Emerging Relational Perspective in Physiology and Medicine

So many postmechanistic discoveries about the bodymind have been made in recent years that it is almost as if we are getting to know ourselves anew, as if the Real were a distant relation returning after a long exile. Our bodymind, rather than being a complicated contraption that tends to malfunction now and then, is increasingly understood to be a highly perceptive, resourceful, and creative organism, one that is constituted of myriad dynamic relationships operating both internally and with its surroundings. For the past several years, physiology and medicine have been undergoing a profound transformation, a gradual opening to a more complex and subtle understanding of the bodymind – how it reacts to stress and other perturbations, how it heals and restores balance, and how intricately relational and creatively responsive are its inner workings. This shift has occurred partly because of successful clinical tests of several alternative, or complementary, therapies that support the bodymind's healing capacities in gentle and subtle ways. These therapeutic techniques are being interwoven with the best of conventional, modern medicine to arrive at what is called integral, or integrated, medicine.

The new sense of the human that is emerging from physiological studies is based on three areas of discovery that were formerly unthinkable in the mechanistic model: that our health is strongly affected by our relationships with other people; that body and mind are so intricately interrelated that processes of perception, memory, and decision-making take place throughout the body; and that we exist in a continuous process of responding to subtle changes in the environment around us. That is, to be alive is to be in dynamic relationship at every moment. I'll present a sampling of these revolutionary findings in the following three subsections: (1) interpersonal relationships and human health, (2) dynamic physiological relationships within the human bodymind, and (3) interrelatedness between the human bodymind and its environmental context.

Interpersonal Relationships and Human Health

The biomechanical model was never able to explain why some people catch cold far more often than others, even if they eat well, exercise, and take vitamin C. In 1997, though, researchers at Carnegie Mellon University designed a postmechanistic experiment – and discovered the elusive answer. They sprayed a cold virus directly into the noses of subjects and then correlated the connection between those who had a rich social network and those who developed a cold. They found that those people with more friends were four times less likely to come down with a cold after they received the virus.[142]

We are all exposed to countless viruses and bacterial infections. In addition, we all experience minor internal inflammation and imbalances, of which we are generally unaware. Yet some of us develop heart disease, cancer, and other illnesses, while others of us do not. The causes of any disease are now known to be complex and usually include the strain on one's bodymind from a lifetime of exposure to a synergistic mix of environmental toxins. Yet a person's probability of developing various diseases is now irrefutably linked in clinical data with the physical effects of the quality and abundance of one's relationships.

To begin with, the robustness of our immune system is formed in childhood through love. A 35-year follow-up study of Harvard alumni who had participated in the Harvard Mastery of Stress survey when they were students in the mid-1950s found a strikingly significant correlation between whether a boy had felt well loved by his parents and whether he later developed a chronic disease in mid-life. The students had been asked to rate each of their parents on characteristics associated with positive perceptions of parental caring (such as "loving," "just," "fair," "hardworking"). The participants were also asked, "Does your father love you enough?" and "Does your mother love you enough?" Of those mid-life alumni who had rated both their parents high in parental caring, only 25 percent had developed a chronic disease such as cardiovascular disease, ulcers, alcoholism, and others. Of those men who had rated both their parents low in parental caring, 87 percent had developed a chronic disease by mid-life. The remaining subjects, who rated one parent high and one parent low in parental caring had rates of sickness in mid-life that fell between those of the high-high and the low-low groups.[143] (Of course, those Harvard men who had felt insufficiently loved by one or both parents may have gone on to lead a life with few friends, thereby compounding the relational deficit and its detrimental effects on their health.)

It may be that those mothers of the Harvard boys who were less loving and emotionally engaged with their children had suffered through an alienating experience of giving birth: two recent studies have found that whether a woman in delivery is treated in an emotionally off-putting manner (as is often the case in modern obstetrics) or, conversely, in a supportively relational manner affects the extent to which she bonds with the baby. Women who were encouraged and reassured in delivery by a *doula* (a woman trained to give emotional support to the mother, not a midwife who delivers the baby) were less likely to request anesthesia in the hours after birth (which is hard on the baby, who thrives on contact with the mother's body) and were more affectionate with their babies at two months of age, as well as more supportive and emotionally involved with them at six months of age, than were a control group of women who delivered without a *doula*.[144]

On a related note, feeding a newborn only breast milk for the first six months results in a healthier respiratory system and helps to protect the baby from stomach viruses, ear infections, asthma, juvenile diabetes, sudden infant death syndrome, and childhood leukemia, yet only 12 percent of American mothers do so.[145] Moreover, breastfeeding has a beneficial effect on a baby's intelligence. Overturning the mechanistic assumption that we arrive in this world with a fixed level of inherited mental ability, researchers hypothesize that, while breast milk itself contains several neurosugars that are highly beneficial for the developing brain, the hours of interaction between the mother and the nursing infant in which numerous types of relational information are exchanged through the eyes, voice, and other body language stimulate brain development in ways that a baby bottle with a plastic nipple does not.[146] Because breastfeeding causes the release of the "bonding hormone" oxytocin in the mother's bodymind, she and then the infant become relaxed as the communication, verbal and nonverbal, is given by the mother – her lovingly embodied gift of enhanced intelligence, which has been measured as up to 7.5 additional IQ points![147]

Equally remarkable was a finding in 2003 that many premature babies who are born weighing less than two pounds and who subsequently test as "borderline retarded" on IQ tests at age three can develop, with caring relational guidance and encouragement, a surprising amount of mental capacity during early childhood. In fact, children in the study developed so much brain function by age eight that they tested in the "nearly normal" range of intelligence. If they were in a caring relationship with parents or other adults, they had gained an average of six points overall on the IQ test and 11 points on the verbal section.[148] In a similar vein, a recent breakthrough in the treatment of children with Autism Spectrum Disorder depends on a relational approach involving the parents: the Developmental, Individual Difference, Relationship-based Model (also known as DIR Floortime therapy) created by Dr. Stanley Greenspan.

Whatever the quality of parental love and caring attention in one's childhood, it seems that cultivating friendships as an adult can do much to improve the resilience of our immune system and our physical ability to fend off the beginnings of disease. In fact, the research on the relational aspect of health is so solid that Edward M. Hallowell, M.D., an instructor of psychiatry at Harvard University, has stated, "Connectedness is as much a protective factor – probably more – than lowering your blood pressure, losing weight, quitting smoking, or wearing your seatbelt. It's the unacknowledged key to emotional and physical health – and that's a medical fact." Without healthy levels of relationship at home, at work, and in the community, he observes, we are more likely to get sick, flood our bodymind with damaging chemicals, and die prematurely.[149] Even thinking about times in our lives that were particularly characterized by connectedness and happiness – a mental habit often denigrated in modern life as "nostalgia" – is therapeutic, as it can buffer people from feeling severe loneliness during difficult, isolating times.[150] On the other hand, merely thinking about rejection makes us feel physically cold, as if the room suddenly became chillier.[151] (The relationship works in the opposite direction as well: holding a cup of a warm beverage inclines us to have a more favorable impression of others than would otherwise be the case.[152])

A recent study found that feelings of loneliness (even when there are people around) have been found to precede dementia and the onset of Alzheimer's disease in elderly people.[153] In fact, a remarkable approach to treating Alzheimer's patients was developed in recent years at the Beatitudes nursing home in Phoenix by creating a cooperative, relational environment (the patients are allowed to eat whenever they wish, to have favorite foods such as chocolate or even a shot of whiskey) and by conducing one-to-one therapy to discover what objects, activities, or places brought the person happiness earlier in life. The therapist then offers an object or activity that transports the person to the happy relational associations. The result is a dramatically reduced need for psychiatric drugs and restraints, plus the complete disappearance of "sundowning" (agitated, delusional behavior that generally starts around dusk). As of early 2011, hundreds of medical personnel in Arizona and Illinois had taken the Beatitudes training and now apply the method.[154]

Another detrimental effect of feelings of isolation is the physiological connection between loneliness and high blood pressure and/or the onset of illness. Clearly, this causal dynamic presents one of the most significant challenges of relational physiology to the mechanistic assumption that the simple presence of various genes cause disease: rather, it is now known that whether we feel lonely or socially isolated affects the way our genetic make-up is expressed. That is, in socially isolated people, genes that express higher inflammatory responses are "turned on" (that is, not squeezed or covered over by surrounding protein in the epigenome), and the genes that express anti-inflammatory responses are suppressed (that is, squeezed or covered over), or "turned off."[155] Other studies have found that "psychosocial stress" causes the release of hormones such as glucocorticoids, which further the growth of breast tumors (at least in laboratory rats).[156] These are among the reasons that by 2007 some twenty large-scale epidemiologic studies had all found that the more "socially integrated" we are the longer – and better – we live.[157]

Unfortunately, the number of confidants Americans have dropped from three, which was the most common response in a survey in 1985, to zero, which was the most common response (by one-quarter of respondents) in a follow-up survey in 2004.[158] One of the reasons this is a significant loss is that feelings of well-being and happiness have been linked to having conversationally deep connections with friends, rather than passing every day in superficial small talk.[159] The realization that feelings of loneliness and isolation can result in social pain, though, has led some researchers to regard it as a built-in warning system telling people to become more socially connected before physical damage takes its toll. This relational key to health and well-being apparently applies for all age groups. Teenagers, for instance, who have regular meals with their parents experience less depression and earn better grades than do adolescents lacking the relational ritual of family meals.[160]

The pioneering study on health and relationships was published in 1979 after tracking 7,000 people in Alameda County (part of the San

Francisco Bay Area) in California over nine years. Whether people smoked, drank, or lived on bacon cheeseburgers, those with the fewest connections to family, friends, community, and religious institutions were three times more likely to die during the course of the study.[161] The results of the Alameda County study have since been replicated not only in this country but in many societies around the world. In 2004 a ten-year study that had tracked 12,000 male employees of a French gas and electricity company, all in their 40s and 50s, found that those men who felt the least socially integrated (in a network of social ties) were three times more likely to die during the period of the study.[162] A similar study of middle-aged Swedish men found that levels of emotional support from both close relationships and friends were significantly lower in men who subsequently developed coronary disease.[163]

As for the health benefits of belonging to a religious institution, Dr. Hallowell asserts, "Even if you don't have a lot of faith, even if you're sort of wishy-washy about it, just sitting in church and thinking big thoughts for an hour a week is good for you. There are even studies now that show that people who do that live longer."[164] I suspect that the group singing during that hour benefits one's health as well. In any event, numerous studies have found a correlation between religious involvement and better levels of healing and health. In addition, the act of "emotional forgiveness" (internally forgiving a transgressor, as distinct from "decisional forgiveness," an external effort to reconcile with a transgressor) has been found to bring a range of healing results, both physically and mentally, as well as in improved levels of social interaction.[165] In therapeutic forgiveness and letting go of anger, it is important that self-blame is not a motivation. Psychotherapists assert that it is just as important to forgive ourselves as others.

Parts of the human brain atrophy in conditions of isolation. Clearly, our bodymind functions best in relationship and, even more so, in a state of giving and receiving love – including the love between humans and pets. Older people who have a pet have been found to develop fewer minor medical problems, to have shorter hospital stays, and to cope better with stressful life events. People of all ages who have a pet have better mental and physical health than is the norm and, on days when they take their pet to work with them, have lower blood pressure than usual.[166]

People also experience better health and live longer if they feel that their lives are meaningful and that they can make a difference, often spending some time helping other people either through regular volunteering commitments or informal connections. By 2005 more than a dozen physiological studies had found significant links between mental and physical well-being and the act of helping others.[167] Apparently a "helpers' high" occurs in the internal dynamics of our bodymind when we reach out and connect in such ways as to benefit others. Specifically, a spike occurs in the level of dopamine, the neurochemical associated with feelings of pleasure, followed by a second stage, which researchers have called the "healthy-helper syndrome," in which a longer lasting sense of calm and heightened emotional well-being occurs, countering stress and feelings of alienation or depression. This bodymind reaction must be what Gandhi was referring to when he answered a journalist who had demanded to know what his real reason was for devoting so much time and energy to helping poor villages to initiate self-help projects; Gandhi replied that he did it for a purely selfish reason: it made him feel good. The new relational physiology has now proven his seemingly quaint line of reasoning to be quite literally true.

There seems to be a neurological dimension to empathy because when we witness someone suffering the same part of our brain becomes activated as if we ourselves were suffering.[168] In addition, it has been discovered that the primitive part of our brain, associated with pleasurable responses to food and sex, is activated when we opt to put the interests of others above our own.[169] Overall, the health benefits of helping others, especially volunteering regularly, include lower rates of incidence for ulcers, diabetes, depression, and other diseases. A study in 1995 of 2,025 older Californians found that those who volunteered for two or more organizations had a 63 percent lower likelihood of dying during the period of the study, even factoring out the status of their health when compared to the control group.[170]

As one might expect, the new research has also found that unpleasant relationships can harm our health. Even a social slight, or snub, registers in the same part of the brain that registers physical pain, the anterior cingulated cortex. (That same part of the cortex, though, also contains lots of optoids, painkillers that are released when we are touched or hugged.) Moreover, the emotional stress that induces depression can set off serious physical symptoms, such as irregular or rapid heartbeat, high blood pressure, elevated levels of insulin and cholesterol, and faster blood clotting.[171] Depression also impairs our entire immune system, changing the activity of natural "killer" cells and T-cells, which help protect the bodymind against early stages of a wide range of threatening developments.

In a related finding, a study in 2007 that tracked over 6,000 British civil servants over nearly eleven years found that those who indicated that they had been treated unfairly and suffered an injustice were more likely to develop coronary problems, and the more egregious was the experience of unfair treatment the stronger likelihood of suffering a heart attack.[172] Clearly, discrimination is a violation of respectful treatment, and such interpersonal violation pains our relational bodymind. Callousness can literally break a heart – and given all the injustice that plagues this world, the amount of bodily suffering from this one dynamic is incalculable.

Imagine the effect on our bodymind when we are ill and have go to a doctor only to find that he or she does not convey respect (registering, instead, boredom, condescension, or disapproval); does not give any importance to our sense of what sort of relational dynamic might be causing or exacerbating the problem; and does not encourage or support us in our efforts to heal, preferring impatiently to move directly to a prescription drug or an invasive procedure. Or the doctor may silently resent a patient's own detection of diagnostic information, which was demonstrated in the findings of a study in 2002: a woman who approached her doctor about a lump in her breast was three times more likely to have it diagnosed as a false negative than a woman whose cancer was discovered by the doctor during an examination.[173] Here again, we see medical care distorted by the cultural attitude that women are essentially complainers whose words can well be ignored. (This is why women have commonly been undermedicated for pain in hospitals: their calls for relief were commonly dismissed as mere whining.)

In recognition of the studies demonstrating the importance of a positive relationship between doctor and patient, the association that accredits medical schools now requires that medical students be taught and assessed on their interpersonal skills and communication.[174] In a related example, Columbia University began in 2009 offering a Master of Science degree in Narrative Medicine, based on the realization that "The care of the sick unfolds in stories. The effective practice of healthcare requires the narrative competence to recognize, absorb, interpret, and act on the stories and experiences of others." Further, "narrative skills" are taught in this program so that the relational quality of the "intimate, interpersonal experiences of the clinical encounter" can be improved. [175] Given the complex causal dynamics of illness and chronic conditions, the move to cultivate a healing partnership between doctor and patient, in which the doctor actually listens to the information and insights the patient contributes, constitutes a significant shift. At last, awareness is growing in the medical community that disempowering the patient undermines the healing process.

The nursing profession has been addressing the need for relationally informed healthcare since the 1970s, thanks largely to the pioneering work of Martha Rogers, developed further by Janet Quinn and others in the 1990s. They see the nurse as not merely being *in* the patient's environment but as part of it, as understanding her or his "nurse-self" as an energetic, vibratory field, integral with the environmental energy field in the room and with the patient's energy field. The nurse is to concentrate on how to become "a sacred healing vessel" for the patient in every moment during treatment, involving the voice, presence, and often a technique called Therapeutic Touch.[176]

It is not possible to accurately assess the ways in which negativity and stress in interhuman relations affect the human, though, without noting the other major revolution in physiology in recent years: the discovery that the female bodymind functions differently from that of the male not only at the level of systems and organs but even at the cellular and molecular levels. These discoveries are situated in a new field of research: the physiology of the female. Throughout the centuries of modern physiology, the male bodymind was considered the norm (as in culture and society). Nearly all major studies of the human body were done on male bodyminds, except for studies on female organs that are related to reproduction, or the "female sex organs" (which has been called in hindsight "bikini medicine"). Once enough women were elected to Congress, however, they forced a major change in policy at the National Institutes of Health and related agencies in the early 1990s such that funding was finally made available to study – for the first time in the 350-year history of modern medicine – female physiology and health in its entirety.[177]

With regard to studies of stress reactions, until around 2002 almost all the scientific findings had been gathered by studying solely males, resulting in the conclusion that "fight or flight" is the "human" reaction to highly stressful situations of threat. While that is true for men, the response pattern for women, on average, is different. Stressful situations cause both sexes to release a hormone in their systems called oxytocin, but the flood of testosterone released then in male bodies tends to suppress the effect of oxytocin, while the presence of estrogen in women's bodies tends to enhance it. The effect of the release of oxytocin in females buffers the "fight or flight" response and tends to make a woman want to gather with other women and tend to children. Once a woman who is under stress connects with her women friends, more oxytocin is released, which counters the (potentially damaging) stress reactions in her body and produces a calming, healing effect. The pattern has been called women's "tend and befriend" physiological response to stress.[178] This scientific discovery certainly makes "girl talk" look far less frivolous than society has considered it. Moreover, the more loving touch there is in a woman's life, such as hugging and massage, the higher her levels of oxytocin (so the lower her levels of anxiety) and the lower her blood pressure, even when faced with a stressful task or situation.[179]

Numerous studies have found that the immune system in both sexes becomes suppressed during a stressful situation, such as taking exams at college, but if the cause of the stress was an interpersonal event, such as a serious "lovers' quarrel," the immune system of the woman will be far more suppressed than that of the man. How women handle such quarrels have a great impact on their health: married women who keep silent during marital disputes have a greater chance of dying from heart disease and other conditions than women who speak their minds. No such correlation has been found among men.[180] Similarly, intense feelings of loneliness have a high correlation with the onset of coronary heart disease in women, but not in men.[181] On the other hand, men seem to suffer more devastating effects of a suppressed immune system, such as developing higher rates of cancer than do women. Sex differences also figure largely in what sort of symptoms of depression one might express and what sort of relationships are most effective in preventing a deeply depressed person from slipping into suicide: being in a marriage protects a depressed male from suicide more than it protects a depressed female, while being a parent of a young child protects a depressed mother from suicide more than it protects a depressed father. In general, researchers have found that a man's health is somewhat protected from heart disease by being in a marriage of any quality, while the health of a woman's heart usually suffers from being in a bad marriage.

From all this new research on the health effects of interpersonal relationships, we can better grasp why rates of diseases and ailments are on the rise: who has time in this crunched economy and our overloaded lives to spend as much time with friends and loved ones as we would like? And when we do spend time with them, are we too preoccupied to be able to listen well and to be fully present? If so, we undergo a double loss, for the relational skill of active listening has been found to bring significantly more health benefits than does talking.[182]

We are starving at a banquet. There are people all around us, and we profoundly need to connect with them, but we hope there will be more time for that ... later. Perhaps we would do better to realize that for every hour that might have been spent with friends but wasn't we have moved ourselves further into the risk category for disease. This may strike many as an overly utilitarian motivation for developing friendships, but it might be enough of an incentive to convince people to rebalance their lives. Besides, the art of being a friend curbs the human tendency toward narcissistic self-absorption.

In short, enhancing our health by goofing off and hanging out with friends and loved ones turns out to be a potent prescription.

Dynamic Physiological Relationships
Within the Human Bodymind

Do you remember the science films and books that taught children about the body by showing separate systems that worked with efficient one-way commands, usually from "command central" (the brain) to various organs? It is clear now that that was largely a mechanistic projection, a seemingly logical but factually incorrect application of the concept of the human organism as a biomachine. Regrettably, that perspective, which was dominant for 350 years and is the foundation of modern medicine, missed most of the relational reality of the bodymind. The various "systems" might better be called "biosystems" to connote the dynamic complexity with which they interact. Had this basic fact been recognized by modern medicine a few hundred years ago, we would not have witnessed contemporary medical researchers proudly declaring in the *New York Times* and elsewhere as recently as 2009 that they had just discovered a piece of utterly elementary knowledge about the highly relational human organism, such as the following: "No organ is an island, and the skeleton is connected functionally to many more organs than we had anticipated."[183]

Because the bodymind was thought to function largely like a biological machine, illness or disease was regarded as a localized problem within a discrete system of the body, for which doctors could provide an external solution. One of the most remarkable projections was the belief that if a prescription drug was designed to address a particular organ, system, or disease, the specific interaction with the "target goal" would constitute the body's primary response to the drug. There was, admittedly, the stubborn problem of "side effects," but these were continually played down. Actually, there is no such thing as "side effects" with prescription drugs, merely a range of effects; the one you desire may not be stronger than those that are unwanted.

Even when significant "side effects" were admitted, the traditional, mechanistic belief in the separation of mind and body caused medical researchers and clinicians to identify solely bodily "side effects" with drugs designed to affect the body. It was not until the 21st century that the U.S. Federal Drug Administration, as well as several pharmaceutical companies, were forced by mounting evidence to issue warnings about psychiatric "side effects," such as depression and suicidal thoughts, reported by patients taking certain drugs that had been designed to treat physical conditions such as asthma, influenza, convulsive seizures, and addiction to tobacco.[184] For decades, this sort of synergistic, whole-bodymind response was simply beyond the realm of possibility for experts who were trained in the mechanistic model. (Of course, researchers working in the big pharmaceutical corporations were disinclined to name these problems, as were the myriad physicians who were receiving gifts and paid vacations from pharmaceutical representatives in exchange for prescribing the drugs.)

In accordance with the mechanistic model, whenever a "part" within the biomachine ceased to function properly it was simply taken out, if possible. This logic of modern medicine was applied in particularly brutal ways in the lives of women. Scores of thousands of depressed housewives in the 1940s and 1950s had part of their brain sliced away in frontal lobotomies (or "jump started" via electroshock treatments). Millions of women in the 1960s and 1970s had to suffer the trauma of having their womb cut out because of minor conditions that usually resolve themselves (such as fibroids) or because their gynecologist assured them that, if they had already had children, the uterus and ovaries were merely a nonfunctional "part," which might possibly cause trouble later. (That was a thoroughly ignorant assertion: it has recently been established that routine removal of the ovaries before age 50 increases the woman's risk of heart disease and premature death later on.[185]) Millions of breast cancer patients in recent decades had an entire breast cut off before doctors realized that a lumpectomy is usually equally as effective. All of these aggressive, devastating, and (for the doctors) lucrative procedures were performed far more often in the United States than in a comparison society such as Britain.[186]

In short, there are countless reasons why the contemporary

superceding of the mechanistic model of the body is perhaps the greatest advance ever achieved in Western physiology and medicine. Not only is the foundational error that has dogged the West since the Greeks – that the mind and the body are two discrete entities – now yielding to an accumulation of evidence to the contrary, but current physiology demonstrates that body and mind are not even two entities with more sites of connection than were supposed earlier. Rather, "mind" (intelligence of several sorts) exists throughout the body, and information travels in both directions (between the organs and the brain) as well as between nested levels of organization from individual cells to whole-body systems, such as the immune system.

The overarching concept of interrelatedness that is replacing the mechanistic model of the body (and mind) is what scientists call "dynamical systems." This new focus on dynamic processes is attentive to all the ways in which elements within the bodymind act and interact in context, that is, the ways in which they perceive and respond to information, energy, and perturbations; influence other subsystems and systems; and creatively alter their interconnections and their own (relational) state of being from moment to moment. Each of us is continuously *happening* – with emergent options at each moment throughout our entire life. Moreover, the mechanistic assumption that the presence and amount of a substance in our bodymind, such as sodium or potassium, was the simple cause of, say, cardiovascular disease is yielding to the discovery that it is the relationship, or proportion, between the two substances that either furthers health or predicts illness.[187] In health, as elsewhere, all is relational.

The new understanding of the bodymind has emerged from discoveries over the past twenty-five years. Initial studies in biochemistry on the way in which mood-altering drugs work on the brain via neuropeptides (molecules that deliver or receive a neurochemical that affects emotions) eventually broadened to the realization that neuropeptides, neurohormones, and ligand proteins flow throughout the bodymind, finding their respective receptors, and are not limited to passing along hard-wired channels of neurotransmission, as had been thought; rather, they have the ability to travel across alleged "barriers" between biological systems. Moreover, neuropeptides are not merely dispensed from the brain, acting as a central control station; instead, neuropeptides are also produced, stored, and secreted by the cells of our immune system, affecting our emotional states.[188]

Emotions, then, exist throughout our bodymind. For instance, when you are becoming ill, the message from your activated immune system to your brain causes you to feel lethargic, unmotivated, and perhaps "down." Similarly, what we call "gut reactions" are actually the effects of the ongoing two-way communication between our intestinal tract and our brain, now known as "the brain-gut connection" – and also the workings of the enteric nervous system itself, which is located in the sheaths of tissue lining our digestive organs and is packed with neurons, neurotransmitters, and proteins that send messages between neurons or support cells like those found in the brain. This neural ecology within the digestive tract can act independently, learn, and remember.[189] Throughout the bodymind, messenger molecules can pass into a cell and even enter the nucleus (if the extremely discriminating, decision-making cell membrane allows it entry). We are composed of communication!

Further, all our lives we continue to create new brain cells that join all that sociable communication occurring within us. It was discovered in 2001 that neuropathways, which were previously assumed to be completely independent (that favorite projection of the mechanistic worldview), actually "cross-talk" with each other and influence, or "regulate," each other.[190] Most importantly, our brains are not merely an inert clump of tissue, a sort of biological "hardware" that hosts neurological events. Instead, our brain is always being relationally redesigned in response to changes in the conditions in our lives and our reactions to them. It was discovered in 1986 that relational dynamics continuously resculpt our brains at the synaptic level. This process is called neurogenesis, the generative activity of brain cells whereby new synaptic pathways are created in response to new needs or new learning and habits of thought. This is why children with autism spectrum disorders respond well to linguistic, behavioral, and "occupational" therapies (for example, how to unscrew the cap on a tube of toothpaste) if the intervention is begun when they are very young (age two or three) when their brains are even more conducive to neural resculpting than later on.

Entire neural pathways, it was proven in 2004, can regrow after the brain has been damaged by a stroke if the undamaged side of the body is restrained (such as putting the arm on the undamaged side into a restraining sling) so that the damaged side becomes the sole active receptor of "motor" messages from the brain and gradually reacquires much of its functioning.[191] Unfortunately, this particular discovery of neural plasticity and capability – that regrowth and recovery occur if simple "constraint-induced movement therapy" is used – came too late for the millions of stroke victims who had tragically been left to "veg" in their chair all day for years because mechanistic medicine failed to grasp the full range of innate healing capabilities of the dynamic bodymind.

Am I being too hard on mechanistic medicine? I do not deny that it has been effective in numerous and highly significant ways. Yet it was imposed aggressively and arrogantly on everyone in the West for hundreds of years, nearly always with a condescending, and sometimes violent, dismissal of anyone or any group who had a pretty good hunch that the bodymind is less a biomachine and more a resourceful, relational life form with its own internal healing system. So much arrogance about such constricted knowledge. We would do well to remember that our human systems of knowledge are always partial, for the complexity and creativity of the Earth Community and the universe exceed our grasp.

I am confident that the Relational Shift will continue to challenge the medical field to acknowledge that which the mechanistic model utterly lacks: recognition that the bodymind has powerful self-healing capacities, which can be either supported or thwarted. Is not the fact that approximately 30 percent of any test group given a placebo pill will experience improved health a striking indication of the profound relationality of our bodymind? Oddly, this neon sign pointing to the deeply relational nature of our body and mind was roundly ignored by modern medicine for decades, until recently, because it did not fit into the biomechanistic model. Now that it is a hot topic in medical research, it has been found that patients experience better results from a placebo pill they are told costs $2.50 than one that they are told costs 10 cents![192]

As the relational orientation becomes increasingly accepted, medical practice may well recover the perspective expressed by the third-century Roman physician Galen: "The physician is only nature's assistant." Toward that end, some of the pioneering holistic physicians today say that the bodymind "has a healing system," but it is more accurate to say that the remarkably astute and effective internal relations within the bodymind have a healing *function* among the many other types of responses made to events and perturbations from moment to moment. Admittedly, a large portion of the scientific community still cling to a non-dynamic, non-complex explanation of illness based on fixed causes, such as the simple presence of certain genes or certain bacteria. Yet evidence is rapidly accumulating that counters this blindered view of our physical reality.

For instance, the short but sassy dominance of genetic determinism in the field of biology was based on the assertion that our individual nature and our psychosomatic fate are predetermined by the presence or absence of particular genes. Initially it was estimated that there must be 180,000 genes in the human genome. A collective *Ooooops* went up from the Human Genome Project, however, when they had to announce in 2001 that there are far fewer genes in the human than they had supposed: specifically, it was determined in 2003 that there are only about 23,000 genes in the human, about the same number as in a chicken but fewer than in a grape or an ear of corn. What, then, accounts for the complexity of the human organism? Quickly the action switched to a hunt for particular proteins and enzymes that might be the "master controllers," which led to the emergence of the field of studies called epigenetics.

The epigenome is the dynamic, embedding system through which each gene is expressed or blocked. One's epigenome consists of two types of "bobbles" that are attached to our chromosomes: methyl groups and histones, which are enzymes and proteins. These "bobbles" act so as to "hug" the genes in each cell, making each gene either accessible to the cell ("turned on," according to the mechanistic metaphor commonly used by geneticists) or inaccessible to the cell ("turned off").[193] That is, in the early stages of the development of an embryo, the matter of whether or not a gene is expressed and when that activation occurs is controlled by regulator material (genetic "switches") in the DNA, but in the later stages of fetal development and throughout life, it is the epigenetic dynamics (epigenetic "switches") that control which genes are expressed. At all stages of life, exposure to environmental toxins and pollutants can disrupt normal epigenetic regulation of genes. If such exposure occurs during the early months of pregnancy, the normal processes of differentiation in the fetus can be affected, leading to chromosomal instability and, hence, increased risk of several kinds of disease.

Other than exposure to toxins early on, however, what causes changes in the epigenome itself? The answer, once again, is dynamic relationships. Apparently, whether or not the histones "hug" a gene so tightly that it is rendered inactive is a response to environmental events and relationships, both physical and emotional. Epigeneticists have found, for instance, that although various genes in laboratory rats do control how reactive they are to stressful situations, those rats that received post-natal nurturing from their mothers are less reactive to stress than are their counterparts who did not experience a nurturing relationship with their mother. The relational influences on our epigenome explain why identical human twins who are raised apart, in different types of circumstances, look less alike in their later years than do identical twins who were raised in the same home and family. This phenomenon is known as "epigenetic drift."[194]

One of the surprising discoveries in epigenetics is that babies who had a grandparent who had suffered through a period of malnutrition, from famine or other causes, were likely to be born with low birth weight – even if their own mothers ate well during pregnancy.[195] That is, the patterned reactions in the epigenome – caused not only by fetal exposure to toxins but also by severe trauma and stress as children or adults – are passed on to future generations. (All of which means that poor Jean-Baptiste de Lamarck, the early-19th-century French invertebrate zoologist who has long been scorned by modern biologists for asserting that acquired traits can be inherited, might now garner respect as a pioneer of post-mechanistic, dynamic, relational biology. In light of contemporary epigenetics, Lamarckian theory is being dusted off and reconsidered.)

More importantly, neither genes nor their embedding epigenome constitute the whole of our bodymind's complex responsiveness to life's events and conditions. Our remarkable self-rebalancing processes have evolved from the morphological dynamics among the following: form (involving such forces as gravity, adhesion, and electricity); relational interconnections, both internal and with environmental events; and various types of energy and memory. While it is true that genes play an important role, influences from "the environment," such as fetal conditions and, later, the addition of breastfeeding for an infant, are often just as important. Moreover, the tendency in mechanistic medicine to see only fixed causes and supposedly irreversible symptoms of illness and chronic conditions is increasingly challenged by myriad cases in which heart disease, diabetes, and even cancer, as well as disorders of the circulatory system, the nervous system, the endocrine system, the musculosketetal system, and the reproductive system, have been significantly lessened in intensity or entirely healed by the bodymind's own complex of healing dynamics, once healthy changes in lifestyle were made.[196] Quite possibly, the natural healing processes include corrective changes in the epigenome, which render protective genes accessible to their cells.

In general, the multidimensional ways in which our cells, tissues, and organs register damaging external events is not well understood. A cell can actually remember and recognize a virus that it encountered twenty years earlier. Less well known is the is the fact that an organ involved in but not physically damaged by the trauma of sexual assault, for instance, seems to hold some sort of memory of the trauma because it often will malfunction later in life. (One of the physical results of this sort of traumatic "relational damage," though not the sole result, may be impairment of the epigenome such that a protective gene is made inaccessible, resulting eventually in cellular malfunction or disease.) Adults who experienced traumatic sexual or other abuse as children, for instance, have a far greater than usual incidence of developing ischemic heart disease.[197] In addition, women who were raped as girls often experience physical problems with their ovaries or their womb and during the process of giving birth.

Do our cells remember all the dynamical energy-information exchanges that occurred during all the traumas that have ever affected them, in the way that they remember all viruses? Does the heart, which seems to be involved in a vital way with processing emotions, "remember" strong emotions or habitual patterns? About 15 percent of heart-transplant recipients, usually female, are "cardiac-sensitive" to some extent, in that they often experience new cravings for certain foods, new moods (different from their previous personalities), new memories of unfamiliar events, or an emotional charge associated with a name that had meant nothing to them previously. Later, when contact is made with the family of the heart donor, the new emotional tendencies experienced by a "cardiac-sensitive" recipient often turn out to have been prominent features of the donor's life.[198] Does the heart process (via relational dynamics with parts of the brain and the entire bodymind) and store emotional memories in some way? If so, it is far more than a mechanistic pumping muscle. (By the way, heart transplant recipients are 25 percent more likely to survive, and with fewer post-operative complications, if the sex of the donor is the same as the recipient.[199])

Certainly those memories that result from a traumatic experience seem to be held in the tissues and organs of the bodymind, not merely in the brain, which can cause lifelong post-traumatic distress in either sex. (Women exposed to trauma are, however, 2.5 times more likely to develop post-traumatic stress disorder than are men; if the trauma was sexual, the women's PTSD rates are even higher.[200]) Fortunately, several therapeutic approaches have proven effective in treating the lingering effects of trauma. The psychotherapeutic technique called "guided imagery intervention," for instance, verbally resculpts the neurological patterns that are causing nightmares and anxiety attacks. Even more remarkable is the therapeutic finding that having patients write about pain, either physical or emotional, seems to transfer it from inside to outside: out through their fingertips and onto a piece of paper or a journal, a new location that is quite separate from the self. In one study, of patients suffering from rheumatoid arthritis or asthma, they were divided into two groups and asked to write regularly for four months. In the group who were instructed to write about traumatic events or the stress in their lives, 47 percent experienced significant clinical improvement, compared to 24 percent in the control group who were asked to write about neutral subjects.[201] Somehow, this quiet but powerful expulsion of the charged emotional field around a tormenting memory seems to effect a deep resolution of a negative relational hold.

The new focus on dynamical energy systems throughout the bodymind, like the growing attention to bodily memory and to epigenetics, expands the scope of research inquiry beyond attention to neurochemical and mechanical processes to include patterned energetic dynamics within and across systems. The big question is what provides the unity among the trillions of cells that make up our bodymind. The "cardiac synchronized energy patterns" generated by the heart throughout the cardiac system, and probably beyond, have been proposed as a possible answer to the mystery.[202] The heart is undisputedly the largest generator of rhythmic energy patterns in the bodymind, but it is likely that they function in multidirectional, systemic, and subtle ways that exceed the modern model of one-way cause and effect. If there is a "master regulator" – although the top-down connotation of that term is an ill fit – it is more likely our heart than our brain.

From moment to moment and over longer arcs of years, our bodymind is exquisitely skillful at recovering from perturbations and restoring its harmony and balance, usually without any conscious awareness on our part. One condition that throws it off, sometimes fatally, is the ongoing presence of stress. A state of chronic stress, in which one finds him- or herself in a negative situation that one is unable to control, stop, or resolve, makes wounds heal more slowly, suppresses our entire immune system, and seems to contribute significantly to the manifesting of problems during and after the bodily trauma of surgery. Banishing stress before surgery, via a 15-minute hypnosis session in which breast cancer patients were urged to think of a relaxed scene such as a beach, resulted in their experiencing less pain during the procedure (that is, less anesthesia was needed during surgery) and also less pain afterward.[203] Another effective pre-op technique used by many anesthesiologists is simply to joke with the patient to encourage him or her to laugh and thereby relax the bodymind.[204] After surgery, stress-dissolving techniques have also been found to lower the incidence of post-operative complications. For example, a medical insurance company found that the surgery and hospitalization bills for each surgery patient to whom it gave a half-hour tape on guided imagery (a relaxing mental practice) were, on average, 4.5 percent lower than usual because none or fewer of the common post-op problems developed.[205]

The perception of pain within the bodymind can also be lessened through the practice of mindfulness meditation, which gently builds the mental habit of greater balance and less reactivity to negative experiences. So many clinical studies have found that people who practice mindfulness meditation report a lessening of pain and an increase in mobility, as well as lowered blood pressure, that mindfulness programs are now offered to pain patients at many of the leading medical centers in the United States. Around the world there are more than 250 "mindfulness-based stress reduction" programs at clinics and hospitals.[206]

Over time the effects of mindfulness meditation (also called insight meditation, or *vipassana* meditation) include a shift of habitual responses from agitation, fear, anger, confusion, anxiety, craving, or hatred to less reactive states characterized by equanimity. Neuroscientists have now discovered that this shift in the minds of mindfulness meditators can be observed empirically as a shift, or resetting, of what is sometimes called "the brain's emotional set point." That is, studies using functional Magnetic Resonance Imaging (fMRI) show that when we are angry or scared, the right prefrontal area and the amygdala (the key area of emotional reactions) become activated, but when we are feeling content or upbeat, those two areas are quiet, and the left prefrontal area is more active. Studies using fMRI have found that established meditators tend to experience a higher proportion of left prefrontal area reactions (balanced, content, positive) to various stimuli than do nonmeditators.[207] Not only does our bodymind allow this shift in our habitual patterns of reaction but, as many meditators have noticed, it seems to support our efforts to attain greater balance and inner poise. That is, if we are willing to do the mental work of establishing a practice of mindfulness meditation, however imperfectly, we eventually feel "carried" by the process such that we experience the benefits at unexpected times.[208]

Our efforts to achieve greater equanimity, though, are often thwarted in this culture by the stress that results from functioning with a "sleep deficit," which throws the normally fine-tuned relationships within our bodymind out of whack. Sleep deficit has been linked to weight gain and to depression in both adults and children, as well as to the development of Type 2 diabetes in adults. It was recently identified as part of the reason for the baffling rise in childhood obesity. A study conducted in 2007 found that sixth-graders who averaged less than 8.5 hours of sleep a night had a 23 percent rate of obesity, compared with the 12 percent obesity rate among their peers who got 9.75 hours of sleep. In addition, no matter what their weight as third-graders, getting too little sleep at that age correlated with being obese by the sixth grade. Researchers concluded that, while sleep deficit may well cause tired children to forego exercise and irritable children to reach for snack food, we clearly do not yet understand the relationship between sleep deficit and a disruption in the expression of certain hormones, appetite, and metabolism itself.[209] To make matters worse, fewer than a quarter of the adolescents who go to their doctor with a sleep problem receive instruction in behavioral therapies that can "reprogram" habits and bedtime routines to cure insomnia naturally.[210] Although insomniacs are usually advised not to nap during the day, most people are well advised to do so because your heart likes it: a significant drop in blood pressure occurs during those deeply drowsy moments right before we fall asleep, so a short nap is all that is needed to generate the full benefit.[211]

If only a daily nap were all it takes to keep our bodymind happy. Alas, exercise is also necessary. All of our bodymind's complex inner relationships seem to optimize when we perform some sort of physical exertion, perhaps because our systems evolved over eons in physically active lives in the forests and on the savannahs of Africa. Children who are physically fit have been found to score higher on academic tests and have much better memories, reaction times, and problem-solving skills than control groups.[212] Exercise was also found, in placebo-controlled clinical trial in 2007, to have nearly the same level of beneficial results in depression patients as did Zoloft: after sixteen weeks, 47 percent of the people taking Zoloft experienced improvement, but so did 45 percent of those who exercised in supervised groups, as did 40 percent of those who exercised on their own. About 30 percent of the group taking a placebo pill and not exercising improved, which is "a finding consistent with the placebo effect."[213]

Exercise combined with other factors in the Therapeutic Lifestyle Change for Depression has achieved even more dramatic results: of 64 patients completing the program in 2007 in Lawrence, Kansas, 76.6 percent experienced a favorable response, compared with 27.3 in the control group, which received medication and/or traditional psychotherapy. The 14-week TLC regimen includes group therapy, increased sleep, aerobic exercise, taking 1000 milligrams of omega-3 fatty acids daily, bright-light exposure (time spent outdoors), social interaction, and replacing rumination (dwelling on negative thoughts) with activity. The program's originator, Stephen Ilardi, an associate professor of psychology at the University of Kansas, notes, "We feel perpetually stressed. And the more we learn about depression neurologically, the more we learn that it represents the brain's runaway stress response." Moreover, he adds, "There's increasing evidence that we were never designed for our sedentary, socially isolated, indoor, sleep-deprived, poorly nourished lifestyle." The successful TLC program is all about "moving, interacting, and doing" -- supporting the bodymind to correct without drugs.[214]

Physical exercise in mid-life has also been found to help ward off the development of Alzheimer's disease or dementia later on,[215] and adding mental exercises has been shown to help older people's brain functions remain sharp for years afterward.[216] Ah, but the best discovery comes from Italy: in 2006 research physicians reported that people who waltz had better oxygen uptake and less muscle fatigue than did a group doing traditional exercises and a control group who neither exercised nor danced.[217] In addition, the waltzers reported a better quality of life.

This overview of the relational, dynamical constitution of our bodyminds would be seriously lacking without some further attention to the significant differences between the sexes. Those differences extend from the basic cellular biochemistry to the entire organism. Three-quarters of genetic diseases are found in boys, and males are far more likely to develop learning disabilities, autism, and attention deficit hyperactivity disorder (but in 75 percent of cases, ADHD appears to be largely a temporary condition caused by a developmental delay in the maturation processes of the brain).[218] Women, on the other hand, are far more likely than men to develop autoimmune diseases. The sexes have different brain structures, process information differently (in different parts of the brain), and react to sense stimuli differently (women have higher levels of perception of sound, touch, and pain). Women are better able to perceive and remember emotions. Men are quicker than women to hear and grasp words about sex, while women are quicker to recognize words about romance. Male brains produce more serotonin, so men are less susceptible to depression. The sexes' immune systems react differently to stress. In addition, each sex tends to exhibit different symptoms during a heart attack and also different personality changes during advanced stages of Alzheimer's disease. Tobacco and alcohol have more detrimental effects on females than on males. Finally, here is a crucial discovery from the new field of sexuate physiology that female readers will want to make sure their anesthesiologist is aware of should they ever need surgery (because anesthesiologists traditionally gauge the amount of painkiller that an unconscious patient needs after surgery by monitoring blood pressure): although elevated blood pressure accurately reflects discomfort in male bodies, female bodies in pain tend to have an accelerated heart rate instead.[219]

No matter the sex, though, each bodymind is relational and dynamical in its own unique way. In recent years it has been discovered that diabetes, characterized by the failure of the bodymind to regulate the amount of glucose in the blood, was not merely a problem involving the pancreas, liver, muscle, and fat. Instead, the regulating of our blood sugar levels is a far more complex process involving hormones secreted by the skeletal system, as well as signals from the immune system, the brain, and the small intestine. Moreover, there are many causes of impaired glucose regulation, and they differ significantly from one patient to the next.[220] This is why pharmaceutical drugs for diabetes work for one person but not another. In fact, with regard to all prescription drugs, your doctor cannot predict what reactions your body will manifest.

The unique patterns, experiences, and responses of each patient, however, are at the center of all diagnoses in a new branch of medicine called Functional Medicine. It seeks to broaden the types of information that are typically gathered in standard clinical medicine, which have been selected by clinicians over time so as to narrow down the patient's information and data as quickly as possible to a streamlined model by which the doctor efficiently arrives at a short list of possible diagnoses. The speed and efficiency of this model are often appropriate in settings where acute conditions require immediate attention, but this common diagnostic model negates the possibility of a comprehensive response to chronic and complex illness.

In addition to the traditional "review of the systems" (organ systems of the body), a physician practicing Functional Medicine then conducts a "review of the dynamics (or mechanisms)" of the particular bodymind, which are charted as a circular matrix that includes any environmental inputs (diet, nutrition, supplements, exercise, exposure to toxins); structural imbalance; gastrointestinal imbalance; hormonal and neurotransmitter imbalance; immune and inflammatory imbalance; energy production / oxidative stress; detox and biotransformation; and relational dynamics (with people, pets, nature, and spirituality or religion). Through medically interpretive "knowledge-coupling" of the antecedents, triggers, and mediators in this comprehensive history, plus observations during a comprehensive examination and relevant laboratory results, the doctor selects particular therapies to correct the imbalance(s). The therapies are chosen for their potential impact, or functionality, at five levels: whole body, organ system, metabolic or cellular, subcellular/mitrochondrial, or subcellular/gene expression. A key focus of Functional Medicine is a review of the underlying mechanisms, or dynamics, of illness.[221] Because this more relational, multidimensional type of medicine takes more time, it has not been widely accepted by the current medical insurance system, but that will no doubt change with the increase in incidences of chronic, complex illnesses, which often baffle doctors who use the narrower, "fast-track" version of diagnosis. After all, how "efficient" is a modern diagnostic method that cannot tell you why you are ill?

An influential factor in the complex of reasons why we become ill or remain well seems to be our ability to achieve a state of happiness. We cannot control everything that happens to us, but we can control our reactions. We can embrace either healthy or unhealthy perspectives in any situation. People who live long and have generally good health tend to have not only a positive, optimistic attitude about life but also a firm belief in the resilience of their own bodymind. They choose not to stew endlessly in negative thoughts, which apparently have toxic effects on our bodymind. Instead, they find aspects of life to enjoy and treasure.

Toward that end, the dynamics of the bodymind present us with a precious gift in our older years: greater happiness and emotional stability than is typically experienced in one's earlier decades. Many elderly people report that their happiest years were between their late 50s and late 70s. The interrelated reasons for this felicitous condition have recently come to light through studies using fMRI scans, electroencephalograms (EEGs), and various psychological tests. Our amygdala (the deep center in the brain where raw feelings such as fear are processed) becomes less reactive to fearful and other negative stimuli between our middle and later years, while our medial prefrontal cortex (a "higher" center in our brain in which discernment, judgment, and planning take place) becomes more active, causing us to be more discerning about the import of occurrences and to feel less bothered by bothersome people and events.[222] We become more adept after age 60 or so not only at weighing the significance of negative developments but also at transcending bad memories and forgiving others.

Moreover, almost every type of happiness tends to increase with age, whether it is good moods, feeling satisfied, or having a sense of well-being.

In tandem with changes in our brain and neurochemistry, our years of experience yield a sense of perspective about life's unpleasant surprises. Older people, in general, tend to feel more drawn to positive emotions than to the negative, experiencing a deeper richness of emotional satisfaction.[223] In addition, older people have a different sense of time, inclining them to appreciate the present and to enjoy an inner glow of gratitude for many things in their life.

Interrelatedness Between the Human Bodymind and Its Environmental Context

How did it come to pass, though, that we experience ourselves as discrete beings thoroughly separated from the rest of the natural world by our sack of skin? We tend to feel that we are self-contained beings whose physical surroundings are of no great consequence, being merely the "backdrop" of human endeavors. This particular perception was not our original cultural orientation in the West. Like early societies the world over, the settlements of neolithic Europe, judging from the art and artifacts that have been excavated, appear to have felt embedded in the ecological and cosmological processes in and around them. And so they were, as are we. The Western notion of the self, however, underwent a gradual contraction to an imagined isolate self, a thoroughly independent Autonomous Individual who is unrelated to his or her "mere" surroundings.

After some 2,000 years of trying to conform ourselves to this cultural projection in the West, the Relational Shift is bringing a reality check to bear. In many instances, the new findings support what we have often thought and felt about our personal experiences with the rest of the natural world, though we may well have kept those perceptions to ourselves, as they would receive no cultural support. The many new findings on dynamical context and interrelationships draw us out of our seemingly enclosed selves, inviting us to realize the larger grandeur of existence. Our lives are embedded in our larger context – in ways we can barely imagine but perhaps have always known at a precognitive level.

As we ride around the solar system on our spinning orb, our bodyminds respond to the cyclical patterns. The daily solar cycle of light, for instance, deeply affects our health, our consciousness, and our behavior. Many of our internal processes have innate circadian rhythms that are set by light-sensors, found on 2 percent of the retinal cells in the eye, to be in sync with the appearance and disappearance of natural light.[224] Being exposed to artificial light all night, as are workers on the night shift, has been found to correlate with the growth of cancerous tumors in women; even though they were getting plenty of sleep during the day, their production of a vital sleep hormone had dropped. Until recently, epidemiologists were reluctant to acknowledge this causal connection because light of any sort was thought to be inconsequential.[225] It is now recognized, however, that night workers are also more prone to develop heart disease, digestive difficulties, and sleep disorders. Once the bodymind's circadian rhythms are thrown off, the endocrine system malfunctions, causing the balance of hormones to slip: levels of cortisol (a stress-related hormone) climb, while levels of prolactin (produced by the pituitary gland) and growth hormone dip; levels of adrenaline increase, while levels of testosterone decrease. All of these hormonal changes, by the way, are more pronounced in those night-workers who hate their jobs.[226]

Our sleep patterns, degrees of hunger, and ability to ward off disease are all related to the type and amount of light that our bodyminds experience. Perhaps the most widely acknowledged effect of light is the vicissitudes in our moods. Up to 5 percent of the American public suffer significant blue moods on cloudy days and feel better in the sunlight. Even artificial exposure to ultraviolet rays of light in a tanning salon has been found to bring on feelings of contentment and relaxation.[227]

When seasons bring long stretches of overcast weather, depression becomes common, a syndrome called Seasonal Affective Disorder, in which the level of serotonin in the brain drops because it is adjusted via a protein that requires sunshine to be activated. Seasonal changes also affect our cholesterol levels, causing a rise in the winter months; this is more pronounced in women than men and much more pronounced in people of both sexes who already have high levels.[228] The activating effects of sunlight on the bodymind's processes of healing have been found to yield significant improvement in at least 21 diseases, injuries, and conditions.[229] Moreover, an analysis of cancer statistics from 107 countries in a database maintained by the UN World Health Organization found that the more sunlight a population is exposed to the lower the rates of breast cancer. That is, the risk of breast cancer is lower in the sunny tropics than in countries far from the equator.[230]

Sufficient exposure to sunlight has recently been identified as a partial antidote to the rise of myopia around the world. In the United States, for instance, the incidence of myopia increased 66 percent between 1970 and 2000. Yet 12-year-olds who spent more than 2.8 hours per day outdoors were found in 2008 to be less likely to develop myopia than those who spent less time outside, regardless of the amount of time they spent doing close-focus tasks. (Researchers did not determine whether the protective effect may have been caused by the combination of sunlight plus the habit of continually focusing on the distance when playing outdoors.)[231]

Seasonal changes, including the amount of sunlight, also affect levels of libido, as has long been noted in the folk observation that in spring a man's fancy turns to erotic activity. Indeed, studies have found a significant springtime spike in the number of gay men's sexual encounters, for example. Within the seasonal cycles, our libido is also influenced by the lunar cycles, which also affect not only the tides of the oceans but our metabolism and sleep patterns. In short, we are cosmological beings right down to our cellular level, innately attuned to the grand passages of our Earth and moon on our spiral arm of the Milky Way galaxy.

Because we are unaccustomed to thinking of ourselves as inherent parts of the Earth community and the cosmos, the Relational Shift in physiology has thus far reached only an elementary understanding all the subtle interactions that occur within us in response to light, color, sound, air pressure and humidity, as well as proximity to other people and mammals (even in zoos) and to nature. It's odd that so many young scientists bemoan the fact that all the significant discoveries have already been made when, in fact, we are probably on the threshold of a comprehensive make-over for science.

How does the bodymind heal, for instance? The complex process is not well understood and is not at all predictable. Yet an intriguing aspect of healing, demonstrated in numerous studies, is that gazing at nature – or even at a photograph of nature – helps us to heal. Hence you may have encountered, on your most recent visit to a hospital, this intersection between relational medical science and hospital décor: a wall-size photographic mural of a mountain scene, or a meadow in bloom, or a forest glade may well have been installed in the patient's room – or you may have noticed a pattern depicting leaves in the partitioning curtains in the emergency room. If you have had an MRI recently, perhaps the ceiling panels above the rolling bed on which you waited had been replaced with a photographic mural such that the last thing you saw as you were rolled into the machine was an expanse of blue sky with a few while clouds and some tree tops around the edges. In some hospitals a "bedscape" curtain wrapping around a patient's bed is combined with sounds of gurgling water and birdsong and is used during various scoping procedures, resulting in a significant drop in reported pain. Even the sight of trees outside the hospital window of surgery patients has been found to shorten the healing time and to lessen the amount of painkillers needed, compared to patients whose window faced a brick wall. The UCLA Health System combined a number of relational considerations when designing its new Ronald Reagan UCLA Medical Center. A full-page ad in the *Los Angeles Times* in September 2008 touted the features of the new hospital: "All rooms are private, have pull-out beds for visiting guests, and have windows with views to the outside. Green spaces and water features create a soothing, more peaceful environment, which has been shown to be conducive to faster healing."[232]

Proximity to trees not only speeds our process of healing but seems to improve our interpersonal attitudes, as well. A series of studies in a huge and dreary public housing project in Chicago found that residents who live close to trees are more likely to interact with one another. Those residents feel safer and more hopeful about life and exhibit less procrastination and aggression when dealing with life issues.[233] An urban tree-planting program in our large cities, then, would apparently achieve even more benefits than "merely" the absorption of carbon dioxide emissions and the aesthetic appeal.

When we were living closer to nature, our sense perceptions were no doubt more acute. In the modern era, how many of us register, for instance, the twenty-nine variations of moonlight each month? Perhaps we do, though – because other relational sense perceptions are still with us even though we are unaware of them. For instance, when we hear a sound, consciously or not, receptors in every cell become aware of the vibration and frequency of the sound. When the sound is music, both the ancient part of our brain, which deals with basic drives, and the higher thinking centers in the cortex are activated, as is every cognitive part of the entire brain. Because the note scales of music evolved in proximity to birdsong and share several aspects in common, something very ancient in the human, even preceding speech, is activated when we hear music. Its therapeutic value has been demonstrated in many studies with stroke patients, premature babies, and children with cancer or with Autism Spectrum Disorder.[234] In addition, listening to music aids in managing pain, reducing the amount of painkillers requested after surgery; improves mood and mobility of people with Parkinson's disease; decreases nausea during chemotherapy; relieves anxiety; lowers blood pressure; eases creativity; and enhances concentration and creativity.[235] A German study of 120,000 patients in 2000 found that music produced a significant health benefit in 95 percent of the subjects.[236]

The psychophysiological benefits are so extensive that listening to music – or, better still, making music or singing – should probably be one of those minimum daily recommendations, like eating at least five servings of fruits and vegetables.

Our sense of smell also connects us bodily with our environmental context, even when we are not consciously aware of perceiving a scent, and it activates extremely ancient associations. For instance, a whiff of a familiar scent, such as roses, can help a slumbering brain to better remember things that it learned the evening before, improving the subject's performance on a memory test by about 13 percent. Extensive research has documented the effects on health and moods after subjects inhaled various essential oils of plants, trees, and flowers.[237] Even when a subject has lost the sense of smell, the sensory effects and benefits still take place within the bodymind. In addition, after people have fallen asleep, studies have found that putting a pleasant or unpleasant aroma under their nose affects whether they have pleasant or unpleasant dreams.[238] We definitely respond nonconsciously throughout the day and night to various scents we encounter. This is one of the many examples of the vast and complex web of relationships in which we exist, which far exceeds our conscious awareness.

And flowers! There is a biological reason a woman enjoys having flowers in the room: more than a green plant without flowers, the proximity of a vase of colorful flowers and/or a flowering potted plant has been found to aid relaxation, diminish the awareness of pain, and increase creativity among female subjects in experiments.[239] It is theorized that this resilient connection comes from our evolutionary history, as women were the gatherers of plants and roots, that is, they were closely observing botanical experts. (By the way, the gatherers brought in 80 percent of the caloric "income" in most hunter-gatherer societies, which more accurately should be called gatherer-hunter societies.) In addition, a study of 450 office workers of both sexes in Texas, Kansas, and Missouri in 2008 found that those who had at least one plant in their office rated themselves as happier in their work and more satisfied with life in general than did those without a plant.[240]

We spent so much of our evolutionary past out of doors that our being out in nature seems to have more restorative benefits than can be analyzed. No one ever seems to come home from hiking, bird-watching, or gardening in a bad mood. Numerous developmental benefits result from the communion young children experience with nature if they are blessed with that opportunity. Moreover, various types of eco-therapy and daily "green time" have been found to calm anxious children, to relieve the symptoms of ADHD, and to result in numerous physical benefits to ailing people of all ages. In addition, traumatized children have experienced healing breakthroughs after weeks of patient psychotherapeutic work in a garden setting.[241] Simply living near green, open spaces has been found to decrease the incidence in urban residents of depression, anxiety, and a range of diseases such as asthma, diabetes, intestinal problems, and back and neck pains.[242]

Gardening itself, as horticultural therapy, also yields beneficial results. For patients with Alzheimer's disease, it is particularly effective because it stimulates memory, recalling gardening experiences they had earlier in life.[243] In several European countries, hundreds of Green Care farms and gardens provide the opportunity for the physical activity of gardening to patients with a range of illnesses.[244] A national survey of Medicare beneficiaries in 2000 found that the monthly healthcare expenditures of people who garden regularly were 17.2 percent lower that those of nongardeners over a twelve-month period.[245] Planting and nurturing a garden instills a sense of accomplishment and self-esteem, while improving moods, lowering blood pressure and cholesterol levels, and slowing the progress of several diseases.

I still recall a conversation I had years ago on a visit to an urban community garden founded by Catherine Sneed in a double lot behind a store in San Francisco. My guide through the garden was a young man who, like most of the gardeners there, had formerly been incarcerated in the county jail. He was particularly keen on showing me the series of four large compost bins, which were open wooden boxes. As he pointed to the first bin, his friendly expression faded a bit, as if he were recalling unpleasant times, and he explained, "This is where it all starts, with this garbage. It's just nothing. Nobody even wants to look at." At the second bin, his face brightened a bit: "After it starts to break down a little and change, I move it over here and mix it up." At the third bin, I began to grasp the subtext, his own transformation: "Here you can see it's not nasty and disgusting anymore. It's coming along, and I keep mixing it and watching it." At the fourth bin: "Over here, look at it now. It's soil! It's fine. It's ready to grow things. It's beautiful," he beamed. I agreed wholeheartedly and instantly realized the genius of Ms. Sneed's Garden Project.

Like gardening, we are beginning to realize that food itself has a complex relationship with our bodymind, even though modernity has tended to regard food as merely efficient fuel for our biomachine, hardly powerful enough to be considered seriously medicinal. As we have learned from numerous studies in recent years, food is a powerful preventive medicine, yielding benefits that often cannot be duplicated by nutritional supplements. The Mediterranean diet, for instance, not only cuts the risk of heart disease and cancer but also seems to protect against Alzheimer's disease. Risk for the latter is also reduced by drinking fruit or vegetable juice, as well as coffee and tea.[246] The drink our bodymind enjoys the most, however, is water. We think better after drinking water because its presence allows the hemoglobin molecule in our neural system and elsewhere to absorb up to four times more oxygen.[247] That's why sipping water is a good idea during test-taking (as is chewing gum), before giving a presentation, or anytime we encounter a problem.

Food has not only preventative powers but curative effects as well, which are increasingly being accepted by mainstream medicine. Particularly for certain diseases, specialized diet has been found to reduce symptoms significantly. A ketogenic diet (a 4:1 or 3:1 ratio of fat to protein and carbohydrates) controls seizures in patients with medication-resistant epilepsy. Anti-inflammation diets can control symptoms in a range of chronic diseases of mid-life and old age. A low-glycemic diet is now used to treat macular degeneration, while a low-fat weight-loss diet has been found to reduce by 58 percent the chance that people with pre-diabetic syndrome will develop Type 2 diabetes. Mood disorders, especially those involving sugar cravings, often respond to dietary changes, such as the one advocated in *Potatoes Not Prozac*. Some depression responds to an increased intake of omega-3 oils (fatty acids).[248]

Still, special diets are far less likely to be prescribed than pharmaceutical drugs. Sadly, it has taken several decades, as mentioned earlier, with millions of patients taking various prescription drugs before the detrimental "side-effects" have been identified – and admitted to. Once the Federal Food and Drug Administration initiated a system in 1998 that (at last) makes it easier to report significant side-effects, the number of deaths attributed to prescription medications nearly tripled by mid-2007. Twenty percent of drugs account for 87% of adverse effects, with the biggest offenders being painkillers and drugs that modify the immune system.[249] It is now established that prescription digestive acid-inhibiters, which are big sellers for the pharmaceutical corporations, increase the risk by 2.5 times in elderly people of developing dementia![250] Chemotherapy, too, causes complex, unscripted results: patients have long reported to skeptical oncologists that they had begun to experience mental fuzziness, memory loss, and cognitive impairment. Indeed, the syndrome is now known as "chemo brain," caused by chemotherapy's killing of brain cells and the subsequent shrinking of parts of the brain.[251] It is astounding, really, to realize how many drugs have been designed on a mechanistic model that assumes only a simple, not complex, bodily reaction to the substance – and equally astounding that doctors clung to that false assumption for years in the face of patients' experience to the contrary. Moreover, the bodymind's dynamic complexity is unique to each person, so the assumption by doctors of predictable reactions to any drug is partly wishful thinking.

In fact, many experts have concluded that most drugs, whatever the disease, work for only about half the people who take them.[252] One response to this largely unacknowledged but critical problem is a new clinical discipline called pharmacogenetics, which aims to tailor-make drugs for each patient by striving for a closer match with the patient's genetic profile.[253] One hopes that the designers factor in sexuate difference: aspirin therapy, for instance, affects the sexes very differently, giving males more protection against heart attack while giving females more protection against stroke.[254] A second caveat is that too close a focus on a patient's genetic make-up alone would miss the ongoing relational dynamic between one's genes and the particular bodymind's epigenetic response to various toxic assaults from polluted environments and to myriad other relational realities in the person's life, which at the subtle levels are always changing.

Males with damage to the DNA in their sperm, for instance, have been found to have high levels of polychlorinated biphenyls (PCBs) in their blood, and male births have declined by as much as 10 percent in populations adjacent to petrochemical, polymer, and other industrial plants.[255] In addition, increased probability of criminal activity by male populations has been correlated with exposure to lead poisoning when they were young children.[256] On the other hand, many toxins have an even stronger physical effect on women, especially lead, pesticides, and a range of estrogen-mimicking, endocrine-disrupting chemical compounds. That last group – especially parabens and phthalates, which are found in food, cosmetics, toys, and paint and which have increased sharply in children's blood samples in recent years – are thought to play a role in the alarming drop in age for the onset of female puberty.[257] So many girls as young as eight are experiencing breast development (though they may not reach menarche for three more years) that many pediatric endocrinologists now urge that the definition of what is considered medically normal be redefined: age eight would simply be accepted as the new normal for onset of female puberty!

While the obesity epidemic and other factors may well play a role in early puberty, researchers in public health are increasingly focusing on estrogen-mimicking chemical compounds in the modern environment. These are ubiquitous, unfortunately, making it impossible to find a control group for a study. Still, evidence has accumulated from industrial accidents, such as the inadvertent mixing of estrogenic chemicals in cattle feed in Michigan in 1973. The daughters of pregnant women and nursing mothers who ate meat and dairy products from the cows began menstruating up to a year earlier than girls not exposed to the chemicals. Even so, there is not enough data to make the case for a direct causal influence of estrogenic chemicals, a situation that has caused the biologist Sandra Steingraber, author of the book *We All Live Downstream*, to express exasperation. In a report titled "The Falling Age of Puberty in U.S. Girls" (2007), she observes: "As a mother I say, 'They've introduced all these chemicals into the environment, and they have no idea what it's doing. What are they, nuts?' I want data demonstrating safety, not data demonstrating ignorance."[258]

One large step out of ignorance and into relational wisdom is the new recognition in fetal physiology and medicine that a pregnant woman is not an isolate organism whose body and fetus pass through the various biological stages of pregnancy while not impinged upon by unimportant "background" factors such as air, food, and stress. Instead, a new research focus on the origins of disease has shed light on a number of relational dynamics involving the environment of the mother and the fetus. Regrettably, this organizing concept has been given the mechanistic label "fetal programming," as if we were computers. Still, this new focus includes relational findings involving both the food that a pregnant woman eats and the environmental toxins to which she is exposed. The inheritance of genes is only part of the dynamic regarding our lifelong tendencies to develop illness and chronic conditions – or not.

As most pregnant women have long intuited, what they eat while their body is growing a baby directly affects it. This influence, however, is far more extensive than they might have guessed, as the following findings from various studies demonstrate. Women who ate more than seven servings of beef a week during pregnancy gave birth to sons who were more likely to have poor sperm quality as adults – possibly because of the synthetic hormones fed to American cattle. Women who ate lots of apples during pregnancy gave birth to children who had less asthma later in life than did children of women who ate few apples while pregnant.

Women who ate diets high in fat and sugar during pregnancy gave birth to children who were more likely to become obese and to develop diabetes, heart disease, and hypertension later in life. Women whose diet provided insufficient levels of folate (a B vitamin) or excessive levels of the amino acid homocysteine gave birth to babies with an increased risk of schizophrenia. Even consuming seemingly harmless doses of ubiquitous substances at the wrong stage of development can produce deleterious effects – such as eating half a dozen cans of (mercury-laden) tuna fish at a sensitive stage of development.[259] Moreover, eating too little food during pregnancy can result in low birth weight, which can affect the baby's "emotional set-point" later on: if weighing less than 5.5 pounds at birth, a child is far more likely to develop adolescent depression than is a child of normal birth weight.[260]

Environmental toxins have been found to have the following effects on a fetus. Several types of pesticide residue on industrially grown produce, as well as pesticide drift from agricultural fields, increase the risk of damage to the fetal nervous system and reproductive organs and can contribute to the likelihood of childhood asthma. More than a dozen studies worldwide have linked air pollution to low birth weight (which usually results in serious health risks), reduced intrauterine growth, and stillbirth, as well as impaired functioning of the lungs of the fetus. Exposure to lead (often from old paint, water pipes, or other products) affects the brain of the fetus and mental functioning throughout childhood. The chemical compound phthalate DBP, which has been found in animal studies to harm the testes of the male fetus, is found not only in nail polish but also in substances more difficult for a pregnant woman to avoid, such as shower curtains, car seats, wall coverings, and vinyl floor tiles.[261] In addition, women whose mothers were exposed to the pesticide DDT, widespread in the United States throughout the 1950s and 1960s until it was banned in 1972, are five times more likely to develop breast cancer.[262]

It is now well established that both women, whether pregnant or not, and children are more susceptible to various toxins than are men. For instance, the endocrine-mimicking chemical compounds (toxins that replace natural estrogen in cells) can cause a range of disorders in the female bodymind, including impairing the epigenetic dynamics that govern the expression of genes. Nonetheless, our country's standards of "risk assessment" and allowable levels of toxins were all developed from studies done over decades on male workers. Why not make the most vulnerable bodyminds in society the standard so that everyone would be protected? Why not realize, as the Mohawk midwife and environmental health researcher Katsi Cook has put it, "Women are the first environment"?[263]

Finally, a third area that influences "fetal programming" is the level of stress to which the pregnant woman is exposed.[264] Emotional trauma from such events as job loss, divorce, or the death of a loved one has been found to increase the risk of birth defects and autism. As a researcher in this area concluded, "Stress is probably really important…. Any kind of environmental influence could perturb programming."[265] It follows that stress-reducing practices and relaxing pastimes are important. Moreover, for the pregnant woman's mate the extrapolation here should be obvious: your job for nine months is to maximize your baby's health by keeping the mother unstressed, happy, and content. Therefore, if she asks you to do something, give her a big hug and *just do it*. Love, appreciation, healthy food, mild exercise, and the careful avoidance of toxic substances will allow myriad right relationships to support the prenatal growth of the fetus.

While many physicians are doing their best to incorporate the new knowledge of relational reality into their practices and into courses they teach in medical schools, the medical profession in general and the practice of medicine are so thoroughly permeated by foundational mechanistic assumptions that one group of holistic doctors decided to simply declare a new, interdisciplinary field: Ecological Medicine. After a meeting at the Commonweal center in Bolinas, California, in 2002, they issued "a call for inquiry and action," which includes the following relational concepts and values: interdependence (our bodymind's profound interconnection with Earth's ecosystems); resilience (the innate ability of biological systems to recover); "First, do no harm" (healthcare should not undermine public health or the environment); appropriateness (maximal health with minimal intervention); diversity (health is served by diverse approaches and healing traditions); cooperation (between patients and practitioners, between the medical profession and ecologists); and reconciliation (healthcare services should be sustainable, equitable, modest in scale, of high quality, noncommercial, readily available to all, and harmonious with the health of the Earth).[266] Here at last is a prescription for the healthcare profession that brings together relational wisdom and ecological imperatives. Poignantly it brings into focus the dismaying chasm between conventional medicine and where we need to be. Yet it suggests a path for getting there.

Preserving Our Deepest Relationship

For the first time in the history of our species, the lineage of our cosmological inheritance may be severed forever in the coming decades. The integrity of the ongoing process spanning eons that resulted in each of us emerging into life as a unique expression of biological processes that are themselves expressions of the creativity of the universe is threatened by genetic engineering of the human. Genetic researchers assure us that humanity (at least those with sufficient funds) will soon have the capability to replace nature's design of their offspring by designing humans according to their whim of the moment. Enthusiasts of germline genetic engineering assure us that all the worrisome mental and physical health problems I cited in the opening section of this chapter can be engineered right out of humans. Those physiological vulnerabilities would be replaced, instead, by designer minds, looks, and abilities in post-human beings, who would be a better fit with the technological world and who "could really turn society upside down," in the words of one of the more exuberant prophets of the post-human future, Lee Silver, a biologist at Princeton University.[267]

That's for sure. Children would no longer be born with an intact cosmological inheritance, linking them through their parents and grandparents all the way back to the beginnings of the universe. Instead, they would be post-human engineered devices, designed by their parents' choices to have certain preselected tendencies, talents, and traits. Their younger siblings, and all younger people in society, would have the next technological "generation" of even further improved, flashier genetic enhancement and so would be bionically superior to all older persons. As Gregory Stock, another prominent booster of the post-human future, puts it, the continual upgrades in genetic enhancement that would be available are not unlike software: "You'll want the new release" for every child you decide to have.[268]

Most of us feel revulsion at the looming possibility of human cloning and designer babies, but an entire profit-driven scientific-industrial complex is coming together and pushing hard for the "inevitable" next step in our evolution: post-humans who (or that) are a blend of bionic engineering and human biology. Earlier promises that science was interested solely in somatic genetic engineering (curing diseases by implanting healthy DNA into existing cells in a body) are melting away, as the technological capabilities emerge to actually select the DNA that would be part of a baby's conception, as well as building in various computer chips or other bionic elements. What should worry us most is historical precedent: when has a technological leap ever been held back from development if it promised untold power and control, even if it was certain to add more misery to the world? Moreover, how many times have human tastes and preferences been seen later to be a profound error?

One example of the push into a post-human future is Singularity University, a Silicon Valley offshoot devoted to bringing about "the Singularity – a time, possibly just a couple of decades from now, when a superior intelligence will dominate and life will take on an altered form that we cannot predict or comprehend in our current, limited state."[269] A leading founder of Singularity University, Raymond Kurzweil, and its director, Peter Diamondis, both state that their "target is to live 700 years."[270] Their thoroughly instrumental view of body and nature is displayed in a belief expressed by Kurzweil: "Ultimately, the entire universe will become saturated with our intelligence. This is the destiny of the universe." The school and think tank is funded by venture capitalists and such tech-millionaires as both founders of Google and the founder of PayPal. Part of the Singularity group's next phase is "an education and protection framework." As Kurzweil puts it, they seek to "put analytical clothing on the concept [of post-humans] so that people can think more clearly about the future."[271] Define "clearly." Their own view is tragically blindered, embarrassingly juvenile, profoundly reckless, and propelled by an alarming hubris.

The massive inertial thrust by the well-funded boosters of techno-humans versus our queasiness and sense of foreboding is a dangerously lopsided match-up. The academic institutes on the ethical concerns regarding genetic engineering and bionics are largely ineffectual. Only the few vulnerable laws now on the books are forcing a holding pattern, which is widely regarded by prominent scientists engaged in this endeavor as a constricting boundary to be broken through. When we witness their macho bravado at press conferences as they position themselves as the "boundary-pushers of science," surely red alarms should go off in our minds. Excessive swagger combined with insufficient wisdom generally results in a disastrous course of action.

It might help if the public grasped that those scientists and their supporters often reveal in their statements a loathing of the human and an adolescent-male urge to escape all limits, to have more and ever more – more brains, more sex, an endless life span, total freedom from any biological limits, and so on. Perhaps, as Bill McKibben has suggested in *Enough: Staying Human in an Engineered World*, only an argument from meaning can help us see clearly enough into the dystopic future that is being urged upon us by those who are determined to produce souped-up post-humans. The specialness and the meaning of our lives, created with the play of both capabilities and limits, would be gone. We would simply do whatever our programming directs us to do, McKibben notes, and probably rage at our parents for having made the wrong design choices for us. Human consciousness would become extinct ... except in the lowly "unenhanced" classes. If a genetically engineered post-human future descends upon us – with waves of (quickly obsolete) techno-humans – the effect will be irreversible. We will have allowed the end of the human species, and there can be no going back to recover what we will have lost.

Yet this ghastly future is no more inevitable than any other set of tragic choices we might allow. The reason we have drifted so close to entering a post-human future is largely a result of our not understanding the relational needs, dynamic capabilities, and organic integrity of the bodymind. As a result of our being acculturated in the mechanistic worldview, we tend to have a more distant, less intimate knowledge of the integrity of our own bodymind than do people in nonmodern societies. With the relational lens in place, though, we can see the larger perspective and preserve our birthright if enough people stand up to the increasingly powerful subculture of bionic dystopia peopled by technological experts, boosters, and investors. Only a strong moral and political will that is *ecologically grounded in relational wisdom* will be able to draw the line before the human is discontinued.

Desires of the Bodymind

We have seen from this overview of the Relational Shift in physiology – focused on the central role played by social relations, internal relations, and environmental relations – that the optimal functioning of the bodymind is one of those aspects of life in which simple means yield remarkable ends. Truly, our bodymind asks so little of our conscious decision-making: we need only refrain from placing obstacles in the way of its abilities. We thwart those intricately balanced dynamics by not bothering to eat a healthy diet, not making the effort to cultivate skillful reactions to stressful situations, not devoting any part of our day to exercise, becoming socially isolated because of overwork or other reasons, or wallowing in negative thoughts. Must we? Even though modern life piles on obstacles to our health and even though modern medicine has been somewhat oblivious to what the bodymind actually requires for healing and health, the Relational Shift is now providing the knowledge we need to make wise decisions that support our capacity for vitality and well-being.

Besides a healthy diet and some exercise, we need some socializing every day and some solitude. The latter is a time to replenish ourselves with meditation, contemplative practices, prayer, guided imagery, journal entries, gentle music, or simply a whole-body feeling of gratitude to our bodymind for all it has done and continues to do for us, all its powers of recuperation, protection, and daily maintenance. Gratitude, too, is due for the abundant generosity of nature and for all that is good and precious in our lives. The processes of our bodymind flourish when we cultivate a zest for life and a light-hearted spirit that seeks to honor the good in others and ourselves. Communion with the natural world nourishes us and reconnects us with our matrix, the Earth community and the universe. Situated in these webs of support, the stunningly effective design of the human organism allows each of us to cultivate our potential and shape a unique life.

There is one thing more – the biological and ecological key to human happiness. One of the great gifts of Eastern spiritual teachings is the realization that we experience unhappy states of mind, even utter misery, when our mind bounces constantly between replaying the past or worrying about the future. Back and forth, back and forth goes our "monkey mind" for endless repetitions, giving our actual present moment the quality of an unoccupied void. The antidote is to gently steer one's consciousness back to the present moment, to be fully present to the present. Various versions of this insight have been retailed in the West, such as "Be here now" or "the power of now" – but why does cultivating the ability to be fully aware of the present moment bring relief from the compulsive nature of our "monkey mind" jumping between past and future? Why does it feel so qualitatively different to be grounded in the present moment than not, as we experience the currents of daily life swirling through and around us?

I believe it is because our addictive visits to the past or future are merely mental. In contrast, when we really alight in the present and pay attention to the physicality of the present moment, our mental processes suddenly take part in – and are infused with – the vast grounding constituted by the myriad dynamic biological and ecological relationships that have brought forth our body-in-nature. We feel more alive, more free, and less reactive when we pay attention – even very quickly in the heat of an agitating situation – to the feel of our body, the sensations arising and passing away within it, the fact that this evanescent moment of life envelopes and vitalizes us through nature's gifts of sun, water, and food.

You – your bodymind, in a chair, around a table with others, just now, in a room, in a city, all linked with the whole of the Earth Community and with all universe life.

If it is possible to glance out at nature during challenging moments and to focus, even fleetingly, on the simple but potent fact of our body in the web of life – *as* the web of life – a change will come over the mind. Powers of wonder and awe arise in the mind. Existence is a wonder, every moment. Who knew? Not the supposedly Autonomous Individual with his biomachine of a body. It is time to retire that sorry Western projection of the 18th century so that we can come into our full, gloriously interrelated humanity.

Human consciousness when situated in the present moment is both anchored and expanded by embodiment and embeddedness. Yet our mind when darting around outside of the present moment is unmoored, ungrounded, and compromised in its capabilities. It has lost conscious contact with the Real, our bodies in their vast embeddedness. How different those ungrounded mindstates are from the generative well-being we feel, the lightness and grace, when we immerse our bodymind in nature on a long walk or in quiet time in a garden. That lightness and expansiveness, which both guards and guides us through reactions to life's events, is ours whenever we settle into a bodily awareness of the amplitude of our existence. We are each a luminous presence in the bountiful web of life, related inherently to all else.

IV

THE RELATIONAL SHIFT IN COMMUNITY DESIGN AND ARCHITECTURE

The Emerging Relational Perspective in Our Built Environment

Dwellings orient us. They can bring us into deeper relationship with our bioregion and with the nourishing presence of sunlight – or not. They can be designed to welcome light and to frame views of nature, whether a backyard garden or a far vista, such that we are continually fed by our visual communion with its multiplicity of forms and changing colors. Throughout the day we are buoyed whenever we take a moment to gaze out at nature's intricate patterns, the original art in our species' formative experience. To realize that our lives are situated in this vitality, its processes and abundance, is to feel blessed beyond measure.

Most urban and suburban buildings, however, orient us solely within their walls toward human endeavors, reinforcing modernity's premise that an advanced society properly lives apart from nature. Moreover, those buildings are usually clustered in a rigid grid pattern of city streets bereft of trees or other botanical life. Walking through a modern city is, in general, a harsh experience in a sterile habitat. We have become accustomed to it but at what inner cost? (Once again, sexuate difference figures largely in the human response: a study in Denmark found that living in a modern urban area seems to decrease the risk of suicide in men but to increase it in women.[272])

How did we end up with city planning and design that is so oblivious to nature and is composed of such anti-organic architecture? The answer runs through our architectural history. It is best that we take a brief "detour" here into that history before we consider the various contemporary developments, for I have witnessed several times the disappointing results that occur over time when a new movement proceeds in ignorance of, or disengagement from, a knowledge of its antecedents. Therefore, the following section presents the historical context of the new direction in thinking in order to demonstrate that the Relational Shift in community design and architecture is not merely a quirky new fad because "green" is temporarily "in." Rather, the rising relational culture carries forth – in ways more potently expressed and widely accepted than ever before – an organic lineage that is deeply rooted in our history. Certainly its antecedents long predate the dominant geometric and mechanistic style, from neoclassical to high-tech and contemporary "Late Modern." Moreover, organic design has been intermittently embraced throughout the history of architecture in the West as a grand correction to the geometric styles, even though each wave of organic manifestations was eventually overrun by the relentless march of mechanistic styles in their many guises.

Then, too, the current organic florescence has more than deep roots. It is a child of urgency, which seeks to deliver us to a deep healing we can barely imagine. Unlike the usual sort of urgent action that seeks to restore the status quo – such as rebuilding a neighborhood after a tornado, flood, or fire the way it was – our situation is entirely different. We are summoned by the urgency of the ecological crises to realize at last that we have been building and dwelling in wrong relationship to nature. In re-engaging with the rest of the natural world so as to leave a smaller footprint of ecological damage, to restore and enhance the habitats of our and other species, and to ecologize our thinking in every area, we experience an unexpected benefit: we are collectively healed of the corrosive, distorting effects of a modernity that had cut us off from the web of life. We are called by the urgency of the escalating ecological crises to turn away from trivial, soul-deadening endeavors on our mechanistic treadmills of daily modern life, to draw deeply from the well-springs of our creativity, and to discover, in the area of our built environment, how communities and buildings can be rethought so that we live differently, no longer slogging along feeling off kilter and disconnected.

In this historic process of reconnecting, we have begun to reconsider core assumptions and seek new possibilities in which ecosocial values are held central: what are the actual, relational needs of human beings in their communities and dwellings? In their home ecosystem? The new Green thinking strives to cultivate sensibilities that inform those design values that make a city, a neighborhood, or a building not merely efficient but vital. The resulting greened, relational projects and structures often feel deeply resonant – and literally delightful. They are revitalizing, even just to read about. To get a sense of this vast turning toward a Green vision of the built world, we will take a look at several examples of community revitalization. We will then take in some of the most insightful ideas in organic architecture, the sort that are attentive to our bodily relationship to buildings, nature, and each other. Finally, we will pay a visit to an imaginary city called Relationton to see what they have achieved in the relational make-over of their built environment in recent years. First, though, we will situate this organic florescence in the continuity of its lineage.

Geometric Dominance and Organic Rebellions

Historians of Western architecture like to begin with classical Greece. The Greek dedication to rational design based on fixed proportions, which they felt reflected harmony mathematically, was expressed in massive geometric temples and civic buildings. These usually took the shape of a huge rectilinear orthogonal hall, a post-and-lintel structure with a long row of columns on each side. They eschewed the more organic elements of surviving pre-Greek structures, while pumping up and codifying only the geometric elements from those earlier eras, such as the charming palace of Knossos on Crete. The result was public buildings on steroids, triumphant and awe-inspiring expressions of the confident Greek worldview. Three aesthetic orders informed the prominent columns in these behemoths: the Doric (the plainest); the Ionic (featuring moldings, scrolled volutes at the top of the columns, and fancier fluting on the columns); and the Corinthian (fancier still). Decorated or not, the columns in each style had a fixed proportion: the diameter of the base of a Doric column to its height was 5.2:1; in an Ionic column it was 9:1.

The Romans subsequently adopted the Greek fondness for imposing rectilinear orthogonal buildings of fixed proportions, as was evidenced in the Imperial Forums of Rome. As their empire expanded into North Africa, the Near East, and Europe, the Romans established new military settlements based on an adaptation of the geometric grid plan that had been used in Etruscan and later Greek cities. (The grid had also been used in laying out the quarters of the slaves who built the Egyptian pyramids and had been used by the Assyrian Empire when designing garrisons and detention centers in conquered territories.) Throughout the Roman occupation, though, most European towns were able to maintain their organic patterns of streets that had developed, for instance, around the bend in a river or on the rise of small hills and bluffs. During the Middle

Ages, the ancient towns and cities were often encircled by a high stone wall for protection. These medieval walls survived in many European cities until the mid-19th century, when they were torn down to make room for a more "rational," geometric lay-out of the streets, such as the Ringstrasse in Vienna. In Barcelona, the demolition in the 1850s of the stone walls (which were not medieval but dated from 1714) was accompanied by the construction of a vast grid of new streets, a city plan that was imposed in the name of modern, neoclassical rationalism – but caused a brilliantly organic rebellion only a few decades later, as we shall see.

During the Middle Ages two architectural styles of churches emerged in contrast to the straight and narrow dictates of classical geometric structures. The earlier, the Romanesque, featured low-pitched arching ceilings and massive pillars that almost seem to have grown from the earth. The later, the Gothic, inspired elegant cathedrals and churches with high walls, slender spires, and exuberant stone carvings that celebrated the profusion of life forms in God's creation, as well as the communion of saints and angels. The proportions of the archaic Golden Mean were used to lay out the main rectangle of the nave in Gothic cathedrals, but beyond that fixity, the alluring curves, stunning creativity, and aesthetic abundance held sway. Exuberantly carved arching rows bearing a small multitude of figures spread over the tympanum above the entrance, while an arching sweep of the flying buttresses supports the outer walls. Inside the Gothic cathedral still more curves create the vaulted ceiling high above and the choir wall behind the altar. To the medieval pilgrim stepping through the great wooden doors, it must have felt like entering a parcel of heaven.

As the beginnings of the modern worldview began to emerge with the dominance of neoclassical thought in 15th- and 16th-century Italy, a new architecture emerged to reflect the new values. The neoclassical architecture of the Renaissance signaled a radical break from the aesthetics of both the Romanesque and the Gothic by adopting the design principles that had guided the creation of the great structures of the classical age in Greece and later in Rome: the application of mathematical proportions to arrive at geometrically ordered buildings, which are nearly always an imposing rectilinear orthogonal shape that incorporates long rows of columns and which have very little ornamentation. While not lacking in elegance when done well, neoclassical buildings arose as power-laden expressions of the new, rationalist age. Not only did neoclassical architecture become the hallmark of the early modern era but it was considered doubly apropos for governmental buildings in the new democracy of the United States, connoting both rational thought and continuity with the birthplace of democracy, Greece. The results were uneven: although the elegant arching verticals in the dome of our nation's capitol are always a delight to behold, many of our state capitols are a regrettable mishmash of attempted neoclassical logic that sorely lacks all grace.

Neoclassical logic was attacked in 1836 in England by a young architect named Augustus W. N. Pugin, who successfully called for a Gothic Revival. In his book *Contrasts* he praised the elegance of Gothic design (such as medieval English universities) and criticized the "present decay of taste" that had allowed what he considered a philistine aggregate of modern buildings in Victorian London, designed according to rigid neoclassical dictates. In contrast, Pugin saw the principles of Gothic design as being flexible and responsive to the particular purpose of a building.

The cause was subsequently taken up by John Ruskin, whose famous chapter "The Nature of the Gothic" in *The Stones of Venice* (1853) asserted that the Gothic soul embraces imperfection, irregularity, and change. While he considered neoclassical architectural ornamentation to be "servile" to fixed convention, he praised Gothic ornament as "revolutionary" because Christian culture recognized the value of every soul and so gave freedom to the medieval workman's imagination to respond to the divine glory of the natural world. Earlier he had observed that the essential forms of Gothic design are to be found in leaves and plants, being beautiful in ways that elude utilitarian explanations because they were traced "by the finger of God."

Several architects who had been influenced by the Gothic Revival in their youth later created a related departure from the neoclassical: the Arts and Crafts movement, which was extremely influential in Britain, Central Europe, Scandinavia, and the United States from the late-1870s until the first few years following World War I. In this country, the Arts and Crafts influence resulted in "organic architecture," a term coined by Louis Sullivan, who asserted that it could cast off the shackles of neoclassicism and reunite culture with nature. A group of young architects in Sullivan's office formed the Chicago Society of Arts and Crafts, among whose members was Frank Lloyd Wright. Examples of organic architecture include Wright's prairie houses (designed with a bold horizontal baseline to "associate with the ground"); the Craftsman bungalows on the West Coast; and grander versions of the organic design principles, such as the Biltmore Hotel in Ashville, North Carolina, and the Gamble House in Pasadena, California.

Nowhere did the interest in the Gothic Revival and the desire to reconnect with nature yield more brilliant architecture than in Barcelona during the late 19th and early 20th centuries. Of the half dozen major architects associated with this reaction against the neoclassical and the massive grid plan that had been imposed on their beloved city, the two most organic designers were Antoni Gaudí and Josep Maria Jujol. Gaudí was the great master of a new form that was inspired by a spiritual desire to situate his work in the colors and contours of God's creation (but, truly, even God didn't think of what Gaudí came up with). He admired much about the Gothic structures in Catalonia, yet he felt, "Gothic art is imperfect ... it is geometric, formulaic, with endless repetition."[273]

The year 1903 was particularly significant in Gaudí's creative unfolding, for it was then that he read Ruskin, in translation, and found a soul mate who recognized nature as the ultimate aesthetic guide. It is deeply moving to consider even one of Ruskin's well-known assertions from *The Seven Lamps of Architecture* – "All perfectly beautiful forms must be composed of curves; since there is hardly any common natural form in which it is possible to discover a straight line" – and to reflect on all that followed from the meeting of these two questing hearts and minds. Through Gaudí's seemingly inexhaustible well of creativity, Ruskin's powerful ideas were transformed into a brilliantly organic reality that he himself had never imagined.

In addition, Gaudí had long been drawn to the study of botanical forms and also drew inspiration from geological surroundings. The undulating, curvilinear façade of his Casa Milá, for instance, reminds many visitors of the sea, but Gaudí stated that the curves of the façade relate to the curves of the Collcerola and Tibidabo Mountains, which can be seen from the building. Gaudí built with locally quarried stone and insisted that every architectonic element must have at least some color because "nature presents us with no object that is not colored."

Gaudí's work is sometimes associated with the organicism of Art Nouveau, but his designs are less tame and never predictable. He was continually engaged in research to learn more about the non-Euclidean forms found in nature, such as his studies on the strength of the parabolic arch. Josep Maria Jujol, who was 27 years younger and worked with Gaudí for many years, brought a less theoretical (but no less spiritual) engagement with nature to his work, arriving at remarkably energetic organic decoration, from wall paintings to iron banisters. Each of them liberated not only the exterior form but also every interior room from the confines of the geometric box, creating high-swirling ceilings, parabolic walls, and eccentric curves. Gaudí and Jujol each designed public spaces, schools, churches, and homes, sometimes remodeling a rectilinear townhouse, sometimes creating an entirely new structure.

The *modernisto* style of architecture in Barcelona was the most creative and most organic version that modernism was ever to achieve.[274] Had this particular organic expression of the post-neoclassical, post-Gothic-Revival, modernist style – instead of the more geometric, machine-inspired version – carried the day and spread around the world in the first decades of the 20th century, imagine how spectacular our modern cities would look today. Imagine what it would be like to live and work in organically shaped rooms and buildings born of continually unfolding creativity that is deeply relational with nature. Walking through the rooms would be like walking through the mind of nature conveyed via the imaginative powers of the human. Imagine the effect it would have on our consciousness. Would our thinking have become more organic, less shaped by the mechanistic metaphors we inherited with our language? Would our science, art, and literature have evolved toward organic perspectives? Would our bodyminds have felt more at home? Would we have recovered some of our felt relationship with nature, even when indoors?

We cannot know – because those organic styles were batted out of the way, beginning around the time of World War I. In Germany the architect Walter Gropius, who would later head the Bauhaus school of modern design, was inspired partially by certain American factory buildings to champion a new reductive, but idealistic, architecture that would eliminate color and all ornamentation, which was felt in those circles to be dishonest because it disguised the building. All socioeconomic classes would be equal in the new puritan buildings, in line with socialist ideals. In France in the early 1920s the architect Le Corbusier declared a "new spirit" expressed via his theory of "Purism," which furthered a novel iteration of geometric buildings: stark white slab walls with flat roofs and no ornamentation. Oddly, this swing back to a baldly geometric architecture – so mechanistic that Le Corbusier called a building "a machine for living in" – was declared to be courageously new. It was, however, drastic reductionism from which we still suffer visually.

Skyscrapers followed in the 1930s, huge rectangular expanses patterned only by a rigid grid formed by the windows and minimal trim in what became known as the International style because it had been "liberated" from all references to place, culture, and nature and could be situated anywhere. Modern cities the world over soon surrendered their character to the dominance of these triumphalist towers, eventually referred to by some architects after thousands of replications as the "dumb box." Since then, we have remained largely in the grip of the spare, rectangular building, whether stood on its side vertically as a skyscraper or set on the ground horizontally as tract houses, schools, and modern buildings designed for myriad purposes.

In a parallel trajectory, the design profession between the two World Wars rejected the organic motifs of the Arts and Crafts decades in order to follow the new "machine aesthetic" called Art Deco, mimicking the lines of a streamlined locomotive engine on everything from toasters to picture frames to building facades. In the sixty years since World War II – with the striking exception of Frank Lloyd Wright's spiral-shaped Guggenheim Museum in New York (1942) – the "dumb box" has demonstrated dismaying resilience, prevailing through various postmodern and deconstructionist architectural challenges, after which it always comes roaring back with a renewed celebration of its "seriousness" and sleek power.

And yet – in 1997 Frank Gehry's design of the Guggenheim Museum in Bilbao, (Basque) Spain, blew open the dumb box into a profusion of arching curves, which some people see as a giant, titanium-clad rose. It was agreed by most architectural critics to be the most important building of the last quarter of the 20th century. Since then many prominent architects have labored to slip a curve or two into their geometric or deconstructionist designs, sometimes to pathetic effect because it is difficult for someone who has devoted an entire professional life to the geometric – or to the trendy hard angles of "exploded" deconstructionist architecture – to suddenly acquire a truly organic aesthetic. Still, one hopes that the engagingly organic cladding on the 82-story Aqua building in Chicago (designed by Jeanne Gang, 2010) and that on the 72-story building at 8 Spruce Street in New York (designed by Frank Gehry, 2011) will inspire further escapes from the ubiquitous grid patterning.

Just as our foundational public buildings in the United States adopted the values and aesthetic of neoclassical geometrics, so too was our sense of land use and planning influenced. The neoclassical grid, prized in the 18th century for its pristine rationality, was embraced as the guiding principle of urban design and land use when our country was born. In 1785 the Continental Congress passed the National Land Ordinance, which laid a Roman colonial grid over all lands "west of the Ohio River" (surely they meant northwest of the Ohio because it flows from northeast to west), instituting the platting of land into square townships, sections, and quarter-sections across the Midwest. Our towns and cities – most dramatically, Washington, DC – also followed the grid pattern to some extent. What's my gripe about the grid? Although it was prized by the Roman Empire for the efficient standardization and control it affords, the grid lay-out imposes a geometric template onto the urban area that bears no relation to land forms, rivers, or the organic integrity of place. Moreover, the sort of neighborhood places for gathering and visiting that develop naturally in non-grid cities are generally missing in grid cities.

In the second half of the 20th century, the dumb box marched out from our cities and towns in boxcar-like progressions that formed endless rows of strip malls. Our cities were gutted to make room for the "urban renewal" that followed Le Corbusier's rationalist Radiant City plan, which called for superhighways and close groupings of high-rise apartment buildings separated by space that soon became a wasteland. To the geometric, reductionist, "disciplined" mentality of the modernist movement, the organic, relational connections of community that nurtured the residents of the inner city counted for nothing. Those haphazard meeting spots and walkways through yards were seen merely as unmodern untidiness that had to be replaced.

Yet, as Mindy Thompson Fullilove reports in *Root Shock: How Tearing Up City Neighborhoods Hurts America, and What We Can Do about It* (2004), residents of those neighborhoods experienced the situation quite differently. Fullilove conducted research with residents of the Hill District in Pittsburgh, where Corbusian "urban renewal" had displaced 15,000-20,000 people by demolishing entire blocks, which often stood vacant for decades until high-rise "projects" were erected. Prior to that modern catastrophe, Fullilove was told, "a field of kindness" had held the community. Gardeners planted crops in small backyards and had food to share; men of various occupations managed the streets and minded the wild children, to limit as much as possible their descent into harm; and "musicians and dancers and athletes gave content to consciousness," providing ideas and "access to the tools of creation." Fullilove learned that kindness had "worked through the collective as both buffer and glue." It was possible to learn quickly about someone's pain or glory and to respond as needed. Urban renewal shattered that field of community, creating "a downward trend in kindness over the ensuing decades" in the shattered neighborhood.[275] "Blighted" urban areas could well have been "renewed" in ways that would have preserved and enhanced the precious connectedness of community and human scale of the buildings – if only the ideological blinders of modernity had not obscured the value of the relational social fabric that was in place.

"The projects" of the inner city, the depressing strip malls, and the replacement of unique character by the grim grid and geometric sameness in block after block amounted to a barren urban environment by the final quarter of the 20th century. It was not the case that the architects who designed the high-rise "projects" hated nature and cared little about the relational needs of people who would occupy their buildings; rather, their intensely modern education had emphasized the rational application of abstract ideas and geometric forms, with efficiency and a highly constrained sense of logic as their design guides. Unfortunately, the "tough-minded," (narrowly) rational design process prized during the post-war period placed people and nature off to the side somewhere as largely peripheral concerns, mere components who would automatically benefit by living in such rational buildings.

During those closing decades of the 20th century, major cities were further whacked by postmodern buildings designed to be a "strike against context," to purposely clash with their surroundings, making a "statement" for the architect's portfolio. While a few of the leading postmodern architects courted beauty, most shunned it. The gradual uglification of our towns and cities was simultaneously compounded by suburban sprawl that had devoured prime farm land, beginning during the great build-out of the post-World War II population boom.

In the "rationalized" cities that replaced so much of our earlier, somewhat more organic urban forms, we have little considered the effects of such regimented surroundings on our own well-being. How have our imaginative capacities, which evolved in concert with the vibrant complexity of nature's patterns and cycles, atrophied to match urban surroundings characterized by sameness or visual busyness? What costs do our sprawling, rapacious cities impose on the integrity of the soil, water, and air, as well as our animal neighbors? What about future generations who will inherit a degraded state of nature wherever we built? In response to those haunting questions of the modern age, the Relational Shift is unfurling the possible with bold strokes of organic thought that restore optimism and even happiness.

Dreaming up new "sustainable cities" and eco-villages is not difficult, especially with all the talented ecosocial designers now at work, but the real challenge is to regenerate our existing neighborhoods, towns, and cities. What can be done about run-down areas or grim urban residential neighborhoods? Is there any way to enliven the acres of tract housing that stretch across suburbia? Can we create community not only with our neighbors but with the more-than-human world as well?

Community Revitalization

A sense of community is intangible, but it is situated in the sights and sounds and scents of the *lived world* of our everyday experiences. The sensuous and the relational, then, are central in the new organic approaches to community renewal. These values are far different from the mainly formal concerns (how a building relates formally – in terms of line, volume, pattern, and color – to the building forms around it) of most architects and city planners in the modern past. By reweaving the interrelationships, the community modality that has largely dissolved in most modern lives is gradually being nurtured and recovered. Moreover, the greening of our urban neighborhoods, the retrofitting of our suburban tracts, and the building or remodeling of structures that enhance rather than degrade the ecosystem are springing up all over the country.

The ideal of dwelling "in place" means paying attention to the dynamics of the ecosystem in which one lives, but it also entails rethinking our built environment. With the dual goals of "greening" the neighborhood and creating community, even dreary intersections in urban neighborhoods have been transformed in recent years. When this sort of transformation is achieved through neighborhood participation, two problems of modernity are eased at once: the relentless grim regularity of the grid as well as the feeling of partial isolation and lack of connection among most urban dwellers.

A pioneering model of volunteer efforts to beautify and enliven urban neighborhoods is the City Repair movement, which began in Portland, Oregon, and has spread nationally. Examples of the "repair" include painting a large, dazzling sunflower mandala in the intersection as the first step in creating a partial piazza (a small plaza area in which neighbors can socialize); installing half-tub planters so that cars cannot park in the piazza; building a trellis on each of the corners and planting it with a honeysuckle vine; devising a solar-powered fountain that flows with rainwater from a nearby roof; and adding sculptural benches made of cob (an adobe-like material made of earth, sand, straw, and water that dries to the strength of concrete). Other projects tend to follow from the revitalizing of the intersection, such as converting a garage into a neighborhood sauna. Houses suddenly get repainted and otherwise spruced up. Window-boxes and other plantings appear. Cars move more slowly through "repaired" intersections, and neighbors tend to congregate on the corner areas with benches and other amenities.

In the process of brainstorming about possible designs and eventually arriving at a collectively pleasing design plan, people get to know their neighbors in a new way. Participants also realize along the way that they must sort out their personal preferences from other things they want more – to be part of moving the project forward, to blend their ideas with those of others, to be more than a person who is living in the neighborhood in a detached, self-focused way. Working together, the residents in various neighborhoods have created enduring physical spaces that are a vibrant social commons.

Through the City Repair process, co-founded by the architect Mark Lakeman, residents arrive at a new sense of themselves as people who are making a difference. Another co-founder, Charla Chamberlain, explains that the process involves each person's figuring out what it means to be a citizen: "Somehow we have to unlearn our conditioning of fear and isolation and relearn a new way of being."[276] A professor of public health in Portland, Jan Semenza, who suspects that modern urban planning may contribute to the contemporary epidemics of obesity, diabetes, and depression, assigned his students the task of comparing statistics for crime and other factors for an improved intersection (the Sunnyside Piazza) and an unimproved intersection in a demographically parallel neighborhood. After 700 interviews, they found that 65 percent of the Sunnyside residents considered their neighborhood an excellent place to live, as compared to only 35 percent of the residents near the unimproved intersection. In addition, 86 percent of the Sunnyside residents reported excellent or very good health, compared with 70 percent in the comparison neighborhood, and 57 percent of the Sunnyside residents were "hardly ever depressed," as compared to only 40 percent making that statement in the comparison neighborhood.[277]

None of these benefits, however, was initially apparent to city officials in charge of the streets, so when the first intersection in Portland was "repaired" by community members without city approval (and named Share-It Square, being located at Sherrett Street and SE 9th Street), the municipal Department of Transportation threatened to sandblast the painting off the intersection. Fortunately, Mayor Vera Katz and the city council recognized the transformative possibilities for the neighborhoods so intervened to create a municipal ordinance that permits City Repair projects and serves as a model legislative response for other cities. Once a design is arrived at, 80 percent of the residences within a one-mile radius, plus the property owners on all four corners, must approve it. Also, neighborhoods are required to apply to City Repair for technical assistance at the outset of the project to help achieve an effective process. The thriving City Repair movement has taken as its motto "A public square in every neighborhood!"

We are paying more attention to the needs of other neighbors beyond our own species as well. Most residential blocks with facing backyards create a greenway for wildlife, including a flyway for birds. To green our cities and make them hospitable to the more-than-human world, though, it is not sufficient that such block-long greenways exist in isolation. By connecting strips of existing greenery, including tree-lined urban streets, by situating small parks and ponds as links, and by designing new streets and blocks such that one greenway flows into another, an unbroken habitat can stretch for miles throughout a city so that other species can flourish among us. Indeed, they can even flourish directly above us now as we work, for many new office and manufacturing buildings are topped with a green roof system of soil, grasses, and plants. These rooftop gardens provide insulation for the building and a nature preserve that birds love. Under our feet as we walk through modern cities, urban creeks rush beneath the streets, confined in large culverts, yet this walling off of nature is also yielding: sections of many urban creeks are now being uncovered, or "liberated," thereby enhancing the vitality of our surroundings as the natural stream beds and riparian habitat are restored.

Such Green considerations enhance and extend the principles of "New Urbanism," a movement started two decades ago in land use and planning that calls for mixed-use zoning (residential and small-business, for instance); transit and shops to be within walking distance of residences; houses with porches (instead of garages in front) from which visitors and neighbors can be greeted; alleys behind residential streets on which the garages are located; "in-law units" above garages; live-work units; narrow, "calmed" (curved or irregular) streets; and bicycle paths. This type of planning, inspired by workers' cooperatives and the "garden cities" movement in Europe, had once flourished in the United States for almost a decade, beginning around the time of the outbreak of World War I. In the early and mid-1920s, however, the atmosphere of the Red Scare resulted in the abandonment of well-planned government-sponsored housing developments because any government-related urban planning was suddenly considered too socialist and acutely unAmerican.

Only after seventy years of constructing subsidized apartment buildings – "the projects" – as if they were isolated blocks of cement did we begin to regain the level of urban planning that was common in the 1920s: the U.S. Department of Health and Urban Development (HUD) officially adopted the principles of New Urbanism in 1996, emphasizing that the complete neighborhood should be the basic unit of urban development. Adopting formal principles of *Green* New Ubanism would be even better – and may be coming soon. A related set of design goals is known as "Smart Growth," which seeks to locate denser development at an urban core with less dense zones radiating out from the core to "reserve areas" (a greenbelt that might some day be developed) and then to "preserve areas" (never to be developed; often held by a non-profit land trust). A method by which municipal governments can analyze proposed development projects within a particular area, or zone, is the Smart Growth Criteria Matrix, in which points are given for such relational aspects as having a downtown location; being within one or two blocks of a mass transit stop; having mixed residential, office, and retail use; encouraging street-level pedestrian uses; being bicycle-friendly and traffic-calming; having greenways and affordable housing; using local architects and contractors; being water- and energy-efficient; incorporating a neighborhood food market and other retailers needed by residents; re-using existing buildings and preserving heritage structures; including good landscaping and streetscaping; being consistent with any existing neighborhood plan; and having local participation and support.[278]

But what to do with our endless acres of suburban sprawl? Smart Growth planners are among those who have taken on the problem of how to transform the existing sprawl of tract houses into more convivial and less energy-intensive neighborhoods. Having ascertained that a ten-minute, quarter-mile walk is the most that Americans are willing to undertake in order to get to shops or restaurants, Smart Growth planners often seek changes in the zoning laws governing the suburbs such that they be allowed to insert small commercial clusters every half mile. Suddenly there's a café or ice cream parlor where people can gather, joined by a few small businesses that offer frequently used services. Neighbors encounter one another not only in the mini-hub but also on the quarter-mile walk to and from it. (As for new housing developments, "Smart neighborhood development" is now required in many building codes, such as the Smart Code Program in the State of Maryland's Department of Housing and

Community Development.)

Combining the principles of New Urbanism with the conviction that "a city's inspiration draws from spirit and history, human and nature, imagination and fellowship," John Knott, a builder in Charleston, South Carolina, has developed a process of sustainable urban renewal he calls CityCrafting.[279] His firm has undertaken the largest sustainable urban renewal project of its time in the United States: the re-crafting of 2700 acres in North Charleston, a district called Noisette, which is home to 130,000 residents. The area includes 300 acres of a defunct Navy base, a riverfront area, and several distinct neighborhoods, some of which have been in existence since before the Civil War. Following Knott's concept of "a place for everything, without everything being displaced," 5000 housing units are being renovated, and 4000 new units are being built. Neighborhoods, business districts, and school centers will be connected by a network of parks and green spaces that will reconnect the community with the Cooper River waterway, with its web of marsh-lined creeks that wind through the district. These natural areas will be held by a local land trust and conservancy, which are part of an institutional framework of non-profit organizations collaborating on the re-crafting. Knott's design team strives to create urban areas that celebrate their role as ecosystem as well as community and marketplace. Their vision includes preserving what's beautiful, restoring what's natural, and building a sustainable future such that the resulting neighborhoods are places people are proud to share through art, discovery, and friendship. In short, relational values prevail.

Like other Green firms, Knott's team of designers involve the community through a charette, a process of brainstorming leading to tentative designs that are then brought back to a subsequent meeting with the residents. As the last stage of Knott's version of the charette, his designers offer the marking pens to anyone in the audience who wants to change anything in the design. Offering veto power on any part of the plan to all the co-participants is an act of trust and relational connection. Through all his Green re-crafting projects – the entire huge make-over for Noisette will take more than twenty years – Knott is guided by his belief that we each have a responsibility to see the inner, sacred fire within everyone we meet and to help it burn brighter.[280]

A related development to help low-income families is non-profit public housing trusts, such as the pioneering public-private trust formed in 1999 in Santa Clara, California. Within only a few years it had launched a First-Time Homeowner Assistance program; a Multifamily Rental Housing program (which had created 1,249 units by 2005); and a program to build special-needs housing units (630 units by 2005).[281] Increasingly, such public-private trusts, as well as local agencies overseeing public housing projects, have committed themselves to building not only low-income housing but "green" buildings designed to facilitate a sense of community as well as an enhanced relationship to nature.

Whether revitalizing a neighborhood, renovating a house, or building something entirely new, the emergent relational, Green culture has arrived at some basic practices of ecological design. One version, created by the Ecological Design Institute in Sausalito, California, consists of the following five principles: (1) Solutions grow from place (via intimate knowledge of and sensitivity to the local human and more-than-human conditions, that is, nature); (2) ecological accounting informs design (via sophisticated attention to a wide range of ecological impacts over the entire life-cycle of the building or project); (3) design should be created to harmonize with nature (to work with living processes so as to regenerate rather than deplete); (4) design should enhance the visibility of nature (avoiding a denatured environment by making natural cycles and processes visible); and (5) everyone is a designer (healing both their place and themselves when participating in ecosocial design work). [282] These Green principles have roots in the values of "organic architecture" – the concept framed by Louis Sullivan more than 100 years ago to express his vision of uniting nature and culture in the built environment of American cities. I think he would be pleased to see that the philosophical and spiritual dimension of the organic orientation in architecture, along with the new capabilities in design and construction, have grown far beyond his pioneering insights.

Organic Architecture

Buildings that are no longer set in opposition to nature evoke an immediate physical response from the human organism. For example, once workplaces began to be "daylighted" (designed with lots of natural light), we discovered that our bodyminds love to be reunited with the cosmological gift of the sun while we work. Indeed, studies have found that "daylighted" buildings result in lower absenteeism, higher productivity, and less depression. Multiple benefits occur when we escape the "dumb box" and spend our days in well-designed buildings (with some curved lines!) that fit wisely into the natural world and contribute to its beauty. We feel nourished when we look out the window from our workplace at a nature preserve that is itself nourished by the wisely channeled run-off water from the building. We are once again living *within* nature rather than on top of it.

Relational Building for Bodies in Nature

The ways in which natural light and the elements of physical space affect our creativity, cognition, and mood are now being studied by teams of architects and cognitive scientists through the Academy of Neuroscience for Architecture, in San Diego. Many of their findings were gathered in 2009 in the book *Healing Spaces: The Science of Place and Well-Being*.[283] Such econometric measurements of our bodymind's responses to buildings (their forms, colors, and siting) will no doubt increase our knowledge about these dynamics, but to cultivate wisdom we might well also turn to the work of architectural theorists who have been incorporating the insights of phenomenology into their observations about organic architecture.

Phenomenology is the branch of philosophy, founded in the early 20th century, that reflects on the felt immediacy of the world, that is, on the dynamics of our experiential processes. It focuses close attention on the ways in which the world becomes evident to our awareness, the ways in which things first arise in our direct sensorial perceptions. It could be said that phenomenologists study the ways in which our embodiment (our sense experiences and non-discursive ways of sensing and knowing) relates to our embeddedness (in the subtle processes of the natural world). An example of a phenomenological study of the effects of postwar "urban renewal" is the book mentioned earlier on the felt character of Pittsburgh's Hill neighborhood, according to the lived experiences of its residents, before and after the "renewal."

Another example of a phenomenological consideration of architecture, and also the teaching of architecture, is a prize-winning essay by Rachel McCann, "On the Hither Side of Depth," in which she warns her profession that the gravest problem facing the field of architecture is lack of engagement with the surrounding world. "Following a general trend of the Enlightenment" to design educational programs emphasizing logic, clarity, and dispassionate manipulation of ideas and elements, McCann observes, we have become insular. She finds regrettable all architecture that is designed to "present itself compositionally to the gaze," to be taken up as images – rather than taken in spatially and materially over time. Instead of continuing the "domestication of the senses" ensconced in Western socialization, McCann advocates an architecture that celebrates multi-sensory involvement ("embodied context"); offers different amounts of detail to the view at different distances; gives careful attention to evanescent qualities of light, shadow, and color ("sensuous entanglement"); stresses bodily engagement; and recognizes the primacy of our connections with the material world ("architecture as carnal echo").[284]

What is it about some buildings, then, that causes our senses to feel engaged and our entire bodymind to feel a sense of allurement? Perhaps the most ambitious formalist analysis of why some buildings feel far more satisfying than others was offered by Christopher Alexander in his four-volume study, *The Nature of Order* (2003-04). He asserts that a building, or any other artifact, that seems to have life, or "aliveness," is constituted by a field of interrelated, strong centers (each composed of other centers). He also identified fourteen additional qualities that are found to a greater degree in "alive" artifacts and buildings and to a far lesser degree in dead, sterile, "image-laden" artifacts and buildings: levels of scale, boundaries, alternating repetition, positive space, good shape, local symmetries, deep interlock and ambiguity, contrast, gradients, roughness, echoes, the void, simplicity and inner calm, and non-separateness. An architect who reviewed the book observed, "Alexander gently educates the eye to see how modern architecture often bulges with ego, technological prowess, and form-making cleverness but is short on soul, heart, and understanding what makes some buildings and places more alive than others."[285]

I appreciate Alexander's decades of analytical research into the relational qualities of buildings with "aliveness," but my own response to architecture is more bodily. In a recent visit to a city where I had lived twenty years earlier, for instance, I was simply walking on the sidewalk of a main street, idly registering with part of my awareness, I suppose, the colors and textures of the buildings I was passing, when suddenly the diffused range of my perceptual attention must have picked up some distinctive colors and forms to my right because my head turned in that direction without any instruction from my conscious thoughts. I saw that the subtle, intriguing earth tones were accompanied by elegant, harmonious shapes and openings in and on the façade and that the entire building had a stately yet unique and compelling presence. I felt a visceral response, a whole-body meeting with a charming massive beauty that quietly displayed a powerful visual intelligence that seemed to hold me in its field of aesthetic existence. As I stepped back, I could see that, far from being the usual block of cement, its stucco façade held at center, high up, an alluring tower with Venetian-style arcades, recessed balconies, graceful arches, and some decorative tiles; large and small details echoed each other throughout its surprises. The city was Berkeley, which, it seemed to me, had suffered several regrettable new buildings, either boring or too busy or both – but this fascinating building skillfully blended references to the Mediterranean climate (through Italianate and other influences) as well as continuity with the city's history as an architectural center of the Arts and Crafts movement around the time of World War I. The building might well have been there for 100 years – except that nothing like it had been seen before. I noticed that a brass plaque was set into the wall on the far left side. Along with the structure's name, the Bachenheimer Building, and that of the architect, the polished surface of the plaque was etched with a quotation from the great Jane Jacobs, an insightful scholar of the vitality of cities: "Possibilities to add convenience, intensity, and cheer in cities ... are limitless."[286] Ah, just as I suspected: buildings like this do not spring from air – or from frenetic hypermodern design fads; they are rooted in the grand tradition of relational thought, fondness for the best of the past, and attentive creativity that seeks to evoke revitalizing pleasure in all who dwell within and all whose gaze alights upon it. It was, to me, as much a benediction as a building.

Eco-Effective Architecture

Numerous Green architects are creating designs that successfully reengage with the natural world. In this fast-growing area of architecture, I find the ideas of William McDonough to be among the most interesting because he pushes our thinking beyond compromised terms such as "eco-efficiency" and "sustainable" to more ambitiously and deeply Green perspectives. McDonough, who believes that the human impact on the environment can be "positive, vital, and good -- even regenerative," heads an architectural and community design firm located in Charlottesville, Virginia. He suggests that a Green design protocol should seek to answer this fundamental question: How do we love all the children of all species for all time? He proposes that we need the imagination adequate to engage with the notion of legacy, a legacy of abundance and hope that respects the right of all living things to exist within a healthy and prospering world. Rather than "sustainable" designs and operations that are merely able to keep functioning, McDonough asserts that good Green design should be deeply "sustaining," or nurturing, for all those affected, the human and the more-than-human sphere. Rather than "eco-efficient" architectural practices, which merely slow down the destructive dynamics, McDonough advocates architecture that is "eco-effective" in its capabilities to regenerate urban ecosystems and play a positive role in the flow of energy and materials.

His vision of a deeply sustain*ing* architecture includes "cradle-to-cradle" building materials, a concept he developed in partnership with Michael Braungart, a Green industrial chemist, at their process and design firm, MBDC. Rather than the usual quick-throughput building materials that go from their initial function in a building to the landfill, cradle-to-cradle materials are environmentally intelligently designed to meet a broader definition of quality. The MBDC firm's Cradle-to-Cradle (C2C) Certification program assesses building products with a number of criteria: the use of safe and healthy materials; design for material reuse and recycling; use of renewable energy and energy efficiency; efficient use of water and maximal water quality throughout production; and the instituting of strategies for social responsibility.

Cradle-to-cradle architectural materials realize their full potential when used within cradle-to-cradle building design, which is the process of discovering fitting, beneficial ways for humans to inhabit the landscape. In every landscape, nature is the guide. McDonough explains,

> We study landforms, hydrology, vegetation, and climate, trying to understand all the natural systems at play.... We investigate environmental and cultural history; study local energy flows; and explore the cycles of the sunlight, shade, and water. Out of these investigations comes an "essay of clues," a map for developing healthy and creatively interactive relationships between our designs and the natural world. The sun is the key to the whole show.[287]

McDonough and his associates – who were awarded the "2004 National Design Award – Environment,"[288] – have created buildings that not only fit into but enhance their natural surroundings, for such clients as Ford Motor Company, The Gap, IBM, Nike, and Herman Miller, plus various city governments and institutions. In their redesign of the Ford Motor Company's Rouge River plant in Detroit, the building and its surroundings (including tarmac with a porous, filtering surface; an adjacent restored wetlands preserve; and a 12-acre rooftop habitat) store carbon;

purify water; provide habitat and food (seeds and berries from the plants) for other species; and offer employees a workplace that celebrates sunlight, air, and the beauty of the changing seasons. McDonough's sustain*ing* architectural design seeks to help modern humans become "native to place" once again, to "celebrate the abundance of the world and the generosity of spirit." Sustaining design, he notes, honors ecological realities, social equity, and economic endeavor by creating "affordable, profitable things that build diversity and mixed use and connect to the natural world in ways that are fecund and healthy."[289] Ecologically wise design can result in buildings and factories like trees, that purify their own wastewater, accrue solar income, and produce oxygen and food.

The building industry responded when McDonough and several other Green architects and builders initiated, in 1993, the formation of the U.S. Green Building Council, a coalition of leaders from that field dedicated to promoting the construction of buildings that are ecologically responsible, profitable, and healthy places to live and work. Noting that buildings in the United States account for 65 percent of total electricity consumption, 36 percent of total energy use, 30 percent of greenhouse gas emissions, 30 percent of raw materials use, 30 percent of waste output, and 12 percent of potable water consumption, the U.S. Green Building Council has developed a rating system for high-performance, ecological design in the following categories: proposed commercial buildings and major renovations, existing building operations, commercial interior projects, homes, and neighborhood development. This standard is called LEED (Leadership in Energy and Environmental Design). Building projects that qualify are awarded one of four levels of LEED certification: Platinum, Gold, Silver, or Certified. The U.S. Green Building Council emphasizes state-of-the-art strategies for sustainable site development, water savings, energy-efficiency, materials selection, and indoor environmental quality.[290] In one of the LEED categories of assessment, Innovation in Design, the U.S. Green Building Council, as of 2007, awards a point to a project if its choice of building materials has successfully completed the MBDC firm's Cradle-to-Cradle Certification process.

Clearly, these developments are changing the ways buildings are being designed and built in our country. Not only is the LEED evaluation and certification sought for projects in major architectural and design firms but, as of fall 2010 more than 384 municipal governments require or recommend LEED certification.[291] In the initial stage, it is often required only for any proposed public-sector building; eventually the requirement is extended to structures in the private sector, beginning with large-scale buildings. The director of environmental services for the city of San Jose, California, Carl Mosher, was a leader in pushing for the adoption of LEED certification and other green building practices: "We reduce operating and maintenance costs by saving energy, water, and other natural resources, in addition to reusing certain materials."[292] By early 2005, over 58 green public building projects were underway in San Jose.

Today the American Institute of Architects hosts a very active Committee on the Environment (COTE), which has chapters all over the country and features on its website a wealth of information as well as photos of the annual "Top Ten Green Projects."[293] It should be noted that white roofs may even edge out "living roofs" in our efforts to reduce the amount of electricity needed to cool buildings: a study conducted at the Lawrence Berkeley National Laboratory in 2008 found that if the roofs and pavement in 100 major urban areas were changed to white, or a reflective near-white color, it would offset 44 metric gigatons of greenhouse gases, which is more than all the countries on Earth emit in a single year.[294] In Europe over 6,000 houses have been built to Passivhaus specifications, which result in a 95 percent reduction in energy use for heating and cooling. In Spain all new buildings must get at least 30 percent of their hot water from solar panels. Inspired by the range of innovations, the Architecture 2030 initiative is pressing to have all new buildings and major renovations in the United States be 100 percent carbon-neutral by 2030.[295]

Several architectural firms are designing not only ecological buildings but new Green developments and industrial parks in the United States. In fact, the William McDonough + Partners firm is designing several entire towns and cities in China. But what about our towns and cities here that were built and rebuilt with a pre-ecological consciousness? They often fail to relate to the natural world wisely and leave residents feeling stranded from the sustenance of nature. To see what might be done, let's take a tour through an imaginary American city that has incorporated many ideas that have worked elsewhere. It's all about rethinking relationships – among people and buildings and with the embedding ecosystem. It's called Relationton, USA.

A Visit to Relationton

Although the citizenry of the imaginary city Relationton have incorporated the new relational ways of thinking in several areas -- food security, economic stability, and transportation (subjects that are seen anew from the relational perspective in the following chapter) – our interest here in visiting their city is focused on their built environment and its engagement with their ecosystem. As for the areas already considered in the previous chapters, on education and healthcare, we may assume that Relationton revamped its approach by adopting every single research discovery and successful model presented there. They are a remarkably thorough people.

Relationton is a Heartland city of about 100,000 inhabitants whose historical section is nestled in the bend of a sizable river. In the 1990s a consortium of civic organizations initiated a process of brainstorming, planning, and executing projects called Sustaining Relationton. With regard to community design and architecture, they divided their work into two sections: habitat (including landscaping) and buildings. In each area, their guiding, and interrelated, questions were these: "What does the community need for optimal dwelling and interrelationships?" "What does our ecosystem, including its flora and fauna, need from us?"

It was not difficult to convince the municipal government to require at least the minimal level of LEED certification for all new buildings and major renovations and, following the examples of several larger cities, to require at least the silver level of LEED certification for all municipal buildings. The coalition realized, however, that businesses and organizations needed reassurance that ecological design really works in the types of buildings they were planning to build for their particular uses. In response, a team of high school students worked with the reference librarians at the city's main library to create a database of successful green-designed and LEED-certified buildings. They gathered examples from all over the country in various categories: churches and retreat centers, apartment buildings, office and mixed-use buildings, conference centers and exhibition halls, museums, hospitals, schools and dormitories, restaurants, shopping arcades and sundry businesses, and residences. With these real-world examples at hand – and a list of experienced green architects and builders in the region – momentum grew.

This collective conversion experience was aided by Relationton's annual tour of green buildings and gardens. Drought-resistant landscaping plants around new buildings were mulched with pulverized wood scraps from the construction process. The green office buildings feature fixed solar fins above each row of windows (to allow solar heat gain during the winter and block solar heat gain during the summer), living green roofs of vegetation (to filter storm water and to insulate), solar panels for heating potable water, and much more. These buildings were found to lease more quickly than others, as their daylighting results in better productivity and less sick time, and their utility bills are lower. This fiscal boon led to an informal competition among businesses who were commissioning the design of new buildings to have them qualify for silver, gold, or even platinum levels of LEED certification. Eventually, the municipal government of Relationton, following that of London, required that any large-scale building must provide 10 percent of its energy needs from on-site renewable sources.

For owners of existing homes, the students also compiled information about high- and low-cost versions of green modifications in bathrooms, landscaping and irrigation, air-conditioning, energy consumption, and drawing in or closing out the sun.[296] One of the committees within the Sustaining Relationton project focused on water-wise ways to achieve flourishing gardens and farms while drawing less water from the underground water table, the major source of the city's water. In addition to encouraging xeriscaping (landscaping with plants that have a low water requirement, once the roots are established), the committee sought to avoid the vast amounts of storm water run-off that coursed through the city streets and storm channels to the river after heavy rains, leaving property owners to draw later on from the municipal water supply to keep the grass and garden green. They held workshops throughout the city to explain various techniques for harvesting rainwater: installing swales, pits, and diversion drains; catching roof water for later use, and channeling urban run-off to irrigate playing fields or create green parks and preserves. Following the model in Chicago, the city of Relationton repaved its alleys with porous materials that allow rain to seep into the soil and replenish the groundwater. In addition, the new pavement is made of recycled materials that reflect heat rather than absorbing it, helping to cool the city during the summer and reduce energy needs.[297]

From the outset the Sustaining Relationton process devoted equal attention to buildings and to improving the ecological quality of their urban habitat – in ways that would also deepen the city's relationship to its unique history and culture. An easy place to begin was the broad support for an urban tree-planting campaign, as lining the sidewalks with trees would help clean the air and keep the city cooler during summer. Inspired by the Million Trees LA initiative in Los Angeles, several native species were selected, along with some non-natives that require little water to thrive, once they are established. Around the perimeter of schoolyards, a variety of fruit trees – as well as some almond and walnut trees – were planted so that the children watch the progression from leafing out and blossoming through the growth and ripening of the fruit and nuts, harvested for the school cafeteria and summer programs. Residential neighborhoods were also encouraged to plant a fruit tree or two in each yard, so that neighbors could trade among themselves at harvest time. A subcommittee gathered information about the old-fashioned varieties, with far more flavor than their counterparts in industrial agriculture, and compiled a list of regional sources from which bare-root saplings could be bought (with financial assistance available for households that needed it). The entire city is now dotted with a wide variety of trees yielding exceptionally flavorful fruit and nuts. Every year the plethora of springtime blossoms delight Relationtonians and remind them of the civic effort that linked every neighborhood and district through the tree-planting initiative of the 1990s. Fruit and nuts from trees planted on public land, other than the schools, is harvested by local service organizations and distributed to the local food bank, assistance agencies, and churches with aid programs. Another source of food for low-income residents is the scores of community gardens that were established on vacant lots, following the example of Pittsburgh, which has more than 200.

Inspired by the miles of Midtown Greenway created in Minneapolis, the Sustaining Relationton project sought to create more green habitat within the city. Their solution was to form a public-private land trust that gradually, over the next dozen years, bought strategically located vacant lots and plots of land to create pocket parks and to link new and existing parks to form several green corridors for birds and other wildlife, as well as walkways and bike paths for humans. The citizens of Relationton learned to identify several species of the flora and fauna through nature walks, programs in the schools, and through posters created by local art students that were displayed around the city.

Yet the people involved with the Sustaining Relationton project felt there was more to really dwelling in place than paying greater attention to the creatures and water flow and land forms of the bioregion. They aspired to cultivate a sense of deep time with the land on which they lived, so a committee decided to research and design an experiential way in which citizens could learn about the time-developmental depth of their city's evolution. For a site, they decided on one of the green corridors that was created by linking small parks and vacant lots. This particular corridor meanders through the urban blocks to Municipal Park, a large plot of land with trees around the perimeter and an open lawn with a bandstand in the center.

Starting a quarter-mile out from the park, this green walkway has been designed as a stroll through the historical emergence of Relationton. In each area along the way one finds a pair of benches, informative plaques, appropriate plantings, and allusive sculptures and other artifacts relating to a particular period. Just inside the entrance of this walkway looms a large piece of bedrock that was uplifted around 245 million years ago, following the Permian Period of the Paleolithic Era. Erosion, weathering, and sedimentary layering followed. Moving into the Pleistocene Era, the next area along the walkway shows the course of the great preglacial Teays River, which flowed from headwaters in North Carolina northward across Virginia and West Virginia, entered Ohio at present-day Portsmouth, and flowed north into south-central Ohio; there it turned to the northwest and flowed across Indiana and Illinois to the ancestral Mississippi River. The Teays flowed near Relationton, whose own river eventually eases, south of the city, into part of the ancient Teays riverbed and makes it way down to the Ohio River.

The next area in the walkway shows the effects of the last major glaciation, the Wisconsin, which moved down from Canada during the Pleistocene Era, reaching its farthest point, near Relationton, some 18,000 years ago. Relationton's soil was formed of the high-lime deposits left behind in the till (ground moraine, sand, and gravel) as the Wisconsin glacier receded. The land north and west of Relationton was flattened by the glacier, but the land to the east and south rolls toward the bedrock hills of preglacial periods, forming the gradual approach to the ancient Appalachian Mountains.

Relationton's earliest residents are honored in the next section. Native American cultures have inhabited the area since the Paleoindian Period (13,000-7000 BCE). Later came the Adena and the Hopewell cultures, followed in the Later Prehistoric Period (1200-1650) and beyond by various cultures who were speakers of the Algonquian language: the Shawnee, the Delaware, the Wyandot, the Miami, and the Sauk, and others. Descendents of these Algonquian peoples still live in and near Relationton and participate annually in a regional Native American pow-wow.

Until they spent some time in the next area along the walkway, few people knew that the boundaries of three districts established shortly before and after the Revolutionary War converge at the north end of Relationton, where some of the roads still bear the names of those districts. In the final area of the walkway, the founding and incorporation of the Village of Relationton in 1798 is commemorated. From there one enters the open expanse of Municipal Park. The rather dilapidated bandstand and gazebo were rebuilt by the Sustaining Relationton project, with the addition of a mural around the circular base that depicts all the ethnic groups who have settled in the city – as well as all the local species who have been here all along. This area is the site of many concerts, the annual inter-faith picnic, and numerous civic events.

The tree-plantings, the local Walk through Time, and the many other green corridors meandering through the city, however, were only the beginning of what Sustaining Relationton hoped to achieve in deepening Relationtonians' sense of place and their connection with other species. They decided to create a number of programs and activities that would acquaint residents with the various stories of their bioregion: the story of the weather and climate, the story of the seasons, the story of their watershed, and the story of the wildlife – all of which unfold within the story of geologic, deep-time told in the Walk through Time.[298] These various programs were offered in parks and on school grounds once a month. Within a few years, most Relationtonians were well acquainted with the ways of the ecosystems in their area. Because they gradually came to notice so much that had never registered before, their sense of place has been deeply enriched. That is, they live more fully.

While the Sustaining Relationton project created its projects and proposals, the municipal government was experiencing the usual budgetary constraints so several good ideas had to be tabled. In 2009 through 2011, however, the steep decline in real estate prices allowed the city government to acquire a number of properties, sometimes by writing off part of the back property taxes owed as a term of agreement in the sale. The city bought two inner-city low-budget hotels and three apartment buildings and remodeled them to provide housing for homeless people. To do so, they incorporated recent research on what sort of buildings are psychologically comforting, rather than off-putting, for the homeless. For instance, many homeless people fear involuntary incarceration, so interviewing and counseling should not take place in a small, private office or cubicle but, rather, in a large room with desks around the perimeter and easy access to the door. Also, homeless people are more likely to enter a building and seek counseling or quarters if vibrant, cheerful color is present, in contrast with the unhappy associations they tend to have with the usual institutional color schemes.[299] The special needs of veterans were also taken into account, for in Relationton, as elsewhere in the United States, fully one-quarter of the homeless are veterans of all ages (though they constitute only 11 percent of the population).[300]

The city also bought four large three-story houses, each located next to or across the street from a police station, which were remodeled to become shelters for battered women and their children. In addition to installing emergency communication with the adjacent police personnel, numerous security measures were installed without making the house look different from the street from those around it. On both the first and second floors, a small room for emergency hiding, in case of a violent spouse at the door, was created with an entrance that is hidden from view. Sometimes new arrivals insist on spending the first several days and nights in the hidden room, before moving into one of the bedrooms. In all rooms of both the homeless housing and the women's shelters is at least one live, low-maintenance house plant. The city also convinced the county government to follow the lead of fifteen counties nationwide that (with a federal grant from the U.S. Department of Justice) had built a Family Justice Center to house under one roof a range of services needed by survivors of domestic violence: law enforcement, legal services, rape-crisis services, healthcare, educational services, job training, and spiritual services. The concept informing these centers is that the professionals should work around the victims, not the other way around.[301]

The municipal government also bought three small houses in various sectors of the city to serve as meeting places for foster children who were about to "age-out" of the foster care system, at age 18, to being "emancipated" on their own – or who had recently done so. A public employee from each of the agencies to which foster children and former foster children could apply for counseling and aid has a desk in the houses. Also, more plants! Citizens of Relationton were determined to do better for their "emancipated" foster-care children than let them end up as part of the tragic national statistics: fewer than half graduate from high school, fewer than 10 percent enroll in college and fewer than 1 percent graduate, and more than 25 percent of the males are incarcerated within two years of "aging out" of the system.[302] The foster-support houses include several small bedrooms upstairs for temporary stays by recently "emancipated" youth. Each house is decorated with colors to appeal to teenagers and to attract them to the support groups that begin with middle-schoolers and continue through high school and enrollment at the local community college or vocational programs. The garden in the backyard at each of the houses is a peaceful refuge with comfortable outdoor furniture.

Several green low-income apartment buildings, which include units for tenants with disabilities, were built to LEED standards by various public-private partnerships. Following the lead of the Dudley Street Neighborhood Initiative in Boston, a group of residents in a run-down area of Relationton created their own plan for revitalization and convinced the city to adopt it and to grant the group the power of eminent domain to acquire vacant lots for development by the neighborhood land trust.[303] Throughout the city, in all the multi-family dwellings of which the municipal government is a part owner, all public-service employees in Relationton – those who work in the hospitals, schools, fire and police departments, libraries, and other public-sector institutions – qualify for a subsidized rate of rent for their apartment, based on their income. Public-private consortiums also built several LEED-certified co-housing buildings, in which families can buy or rent a unit in a complex in which a large shared kitchen and other common rooms are at the center and a large backyard is enjoyed by all the residents.

In these new housing projects, as with new housing developments farther out from the center of the city (yet located on mass transit lines), recent breakthroughs in green building technology were incorporated throughout the design and construction phases. For instance, the plumbing directs water that has been used for bathing and washing to serve as the flushing water for the low-flow toilets. Other wastewater is piped to sewage treatment plants that clean the water biologically over a period of days as it moves through different tanks and ponds with water plants that thrive on devouring waste matter.

To reduce the level of carbon dioxide emissions released into the atmosphere by Relationton, a committee within the Sustaining Relationton project gathered information on best practices in green cities. Besides encouraging the city to continue planting leafy trees, which absorb carbon dioxide, along nearly all the streets of Relationton, the committee was able to put together a consortium of funders that made possible subsidized energy audits of the houses and buildings in the city, which identified sources of drafts, leaks, and wasted energy. Every audit includes a list of recommended changes, such as adding weather-stripping or caulking, as well as an estimate of how much the home or building owner's utility bill will go down if all the ameliorations are installed. Every spring and fall a "Relationton Home Repair Day" is held, on which service organizations provide volunteers to help elderly and low-income residents comply with the recommendations in their energy audits, as well as doing other repair projects and yard work as necessary. Intra-city connections are formed as energy efficiency is boosted.

One of the main concerns addressed in the Sustaining Relationton planning process was the need for a large building in which the main farmers market could be held no matter what the weather, half of which would be enclosed to house the Relationton Regional Emporium. The planning process was keen to avoid the fate of cities that had wisely established a permanent indoor array of stores, or stalls, selling locally and regionally grown or made products but had unwisely situated it within a privately owned building, with ever increasing rent. Everyone agreed that the emporium as well as the adjacent open area for farmers-market stalls had to be publicly owned by the City of Relationton. The solution was found in the old municipal bus yard and bus barn near the center of town. Those operations were moved to a different location, farther from the city center, and the bus barn, with huge overhead doors, became the farmers market area, as it is almost like being outdoors when all the doors are up. In addition, the roof was covered with an insulating green garden and skylights designed to control the inflow of heat and light from the sun seasonally. On a raised platform in the center, local musical groups perform each weekend. The old bus yard is now an ample parking lot, resurfaced with a permeable blacktop surface that allows rainwater to seep into the earth in place, instead of creating run-off. Several smaller farmers markets also take place farther from the city center.

In the rest of the old bus barn, as well as a spacious LEED-certified addition with a living green roof and daylighted design, are now housed the three sections of the Relationton Regional Emporium, which is open every day, unlike the adjacent farmers market. In the first section of the Emporium are food products (jams, honey, breads, cheeses), housewares, clothing, furniture, musical CDs, and other goods that are made in Relationton. In the second section, for locavores, are products grown or made within 100 miles of the city. In the third section are regional food and goods that are made in the adjacent states. The launching of the Emporium was, of course, accompanied by a public education program explaining the many ways in which food security and economic stability are enhanced when we all buy locally or regionally, keeping our money circulating largely within our town and region. (More about this orientation in chapter 5; imports from abroad are not disallowed but should not entirely replace a local and regional economy.) After the first five years, an annex to the Emporium had to built to accommodate the wares of thriving regional businesses.

In a park next to the Relationton Regional Emporium, children play on large, colorful sculptures of animals that live in the bioregion. It is in this park that the annual All Species Day parade forms, with children dressed in costumes replicating the shape and coloration of local animals. The parade winds through a walkway to a park in which a stream has been "liberated" from its underground culvert. This enstreamed park delivers them toward the river, where the children process along the frontage street that overlooks Riverside Park, the restored riparian habitat and walkway along the river. The parade ends in the Peace Park, a section of Riverside Park in which four pillars proclaim the names of each of Relationton's sister cities around the world, with whom they exchange information about ideas that have proven successful in the greening of their urban habitats and the reduction of their levels of carbon dioxide emissions.

Following Seattle's lead, the Sustaining Relationton project has gradually created several "urban villages," which cluster offices, stores, and homes in walkable communities that are adjacent to public transit lines. Those within the project who had dedicated their efforts to pushing for the developing of such clusters, or "villages," felt particularly validated when the report *Growing Cooler* came out in 2007: after analyzing scores of studies, researchers at Smart Growth America found that mixing housing and businesses in dense patterns, with walkable neighborhoods, could do as much to lower emissions as many of the more commonly promoted climate policies such as higher fuel standards for cars and trucks and cleaner fuels. (That is, if sprawling development continues to fuel growth in driving, the projected 48 percent increase in the total miles driven between 2005 and 2030 will overwhelm the expected gains from vehicle efficiency and low-carbon fuels.[304]) Moreover, Relationtonians who live in those "villages" have discovered that walking to work, to shopping, and to socializing has improved their health – and lowered the cost of their car insurance and gasoline usage. To make all residential streets and those business streets with considerable pedestrian traffic safer for walkers, they have been "calmed" with various techniques to slow drivers and keep them alert: curved streets, roundabouts with a tree planted in the middle, diverters, and protruding structures, such as large cement boxes in which a tree is planted.

Several of the city intersections in residential areas have been "repaired" with vibrant neighborhood décor arrived at by following the process established by the City Repair project in Portland. In the subdivisions near the periphery of Relationton, the zoning laws were amended to allow for the emergence of small islands of commerce and conviviality where possible, such as the corner of a park or adjacent empty lots near an intersection. These small businesses, including ice cream parlors and coffee shops, now draw considerable foot traffic from the surrounding homes.

In each neighborhood throughout the city, the elementary, middle, or high school has been retrofitted sufficiently to allow it to function as a community center in the evenings. In addition, the schools were partially remodeled to bring in more natural light, which resulted, as in other cities, in a significant improvement in the children's test scores. They were also repainted with nontoxic paints. Where appropriate, cubbyholes made of soy bean composite boards were installed, as were tiles made of recycled glass, carpets woven of nontoxic recycled material, and "hardwood" floors made of bamboo. In addition, the sizable school gardens provide not only fresh produce for the cafeteria but experiential lessons for the children about the relationships among soil, earthworms, water, seeds, sunlight, decomposing compost, and the ever ongoing energy of life – which they then take into their bodies as food.

Sustaining Relationton also addressed the problem of childhood obesity, which they noted was up to nine times higher in the lower-income neighborhoods than the more affluent parts of the city; rates of hypertension and diabetes were also higher among adults in the poorer neighborhoods. Following the model used in East Los Angeles, the city installed several "Fitness Zones" in pocket parks and in delineated sections of schoolyards and larger parks.[305] These small zones function as outdoor gyms, with steel elliptical and rowing machines, leg presses, and other exercise machines, all permanently installed into concrete. These fitness zones, which have become popular among working people before or after work and with retirees during the day, were partially paid for through grants from foundations furthering public health. Children come with their parents and "work out" playfully on the children's versions of the exercise machines. Exercise structures were also installed in many of the walkways throughout the city.

The citizens of Relationton were increasingly pleased with the cumulative effects of Greening their city, yet there was a general consensus that the built environment, even one dedicated to enhancing the ecosystem as well as the human habitat, is not enough to create an escape from the modern syndrome of overworking to fill our isolated homes with possessions. One response from the city council was to pass an ordinance that allows companies the "free speech" to advertize their products within city limits but only in ways that do not violate community standards: no manipulative billboards and posters designed to make people feel inadequate, no exploitation of children as selling agents, and no depictions of teenage girls and young women in sexually provocative "packaging" placed next to a product. As the momentum grew, Relationtonians sought to repair and create anew the social fabric, to melt the modern loneliness and alienation that weighs down so many busy lives today. Toward this end, a committee within Sustaining Relationton facilitated several block parties per year in the various "urban villages" and neighborhoods throughout the city, each of which applied for a permit to close off one block of a street.

One of these annual events is the Neighborhood Art Party, modeled on those in Minneapolis, at which residents knowledgeable about arts and crafts set up materials for a small-scale landscaping art project, such as creating molded "pavers" (stepping stones for gardens), making illuminaries that can be hung on porches, or making lovely and quirky Christmas wreathes for front doors. The installation of these art works sporadically throughout the neighborhood creates visual continuity as well as the remembrance of the community party that created them. One year the project in several neighborhoods was the construction of cedar doghouses and small playhouses that have living green roofs for insulation and bamboo drain spouts.[306] These block parties, like the others, include a potluck and activities for the children.

Sustaining Relationton also set up a centralized system for connecting volunteers with local organizations and institutions who need them. They then invigorated their homey Fourth of July parade by encouraging each of the urban villages to make a small float on which the neighborhood children ride; the design and construction of these projects around the various annual themes of the parade have often yielded memorable creations. The parade ends with all the floats parked around the perimeter of Municipal Park where a vast picnic spreads across the lawns. Afterwards, many people exit the park via the Walk through Time corridor, passing backwards from the incorporation of the Village of Relationton in 1798, through the formation of the soil following the last great glaciation, to the large upthrust chunk of bedrock from the Paleolithic Era... and out into the town.

V

THE RELATIONAL SHIFT
IN THE ECONOMY

A Snapshot of the Current Crises

In November 2008, as the global economic crisis continued to deepen, the financier George Soros wrote an essay for *The New York Review of Books* in which he asserted that the only way to understand what had caused the collapse was to shift our thinking to a relational analysis, toward perceiving what he calls financial "reflexivity." We must, he urged, abandon "the prevailing theory of financial markets, which ... holds that financial markets tend toward equilibrium and that derivations are random and can be attributed to external causes." This theory (which might be called mechanistic because it is based on the assumption that causal force occurs solely through random, external events) has been touted aggressively in recent decades to justify the belief that self-interest should be given free rein and that all markets should be deregulated. Soros rejects this "faulty logic" and the resultant "market fundamentalism." He observes,

> First, financial markets do not reflect prevailing conditions accurately; they provide a picture that is always biased or distorted in one way or another. Second, the distorted views held by market participants and expressed in market prices can, under certain circumstances, affect the so-called fundamentals that market prices are supposed to reflect. This two-way circular connection between market prices and the underlying reality I call reflexivity.[307]

Soros went on to note that while bubbles are not the only example of relational "reflexivity" in financial markets they are the most spectacular, always possessing two components: a trend that prevails in reality and a misperception related to that trend.

Nonetheless, the "free marketers" have always insisted that any "wealth creation," no matter how fast, vast, and bubble-like, must not be interfered with by government regulations because the expansion of wealth in a market economy delivers trickle-down benefits for society as a whole. Such an assumption, though, denies the relational reality involved: as is well known, the policies and tax breaks since the early1980s that favored the rich have resulted in vast disparity between the economic levels of the rich and those of the middle class and the working class not known in this country since the Great Depression. This is an destructive development because a strong correlation exists in all societies between income inequality and the prevalence of health problems, missed opportunities for education, depression, shortened life expectancy, infant mortality, criminality, mental illness, obesity, malnutrition, teenage pregnancy, illegal drug use, economic insecurity, personal indebtedness, and ongoing stress and anxiety. These social problems are far more marked in the United States and Britain than they are in the European social democracies or in Japan.

In fact, the relationship between income disparity and social problems, including widespread ill health, holds not only at the national level but also within states in our country, as demonstrated by Richard Wilkinson and Kate Pickett in *The Spirit Level: Why Greater Equality Makes Societies Stronger* (2009) and by Peter Corning in *The Fair Society* (2011). Levels of social trust also reflect the same relationship: in more equal countries, about two-thirds of the population trust others, while in the more unequal countries, fewer than one-fifth do. Within our country, social trust is high in the more equal states such as Vermont, New Hampshire, Wisconsin, and North Dakota, but it is lowest in the most unequal states such as New York and several Southern states. Also, children in the more unequal countries do less well on international tests in math and literacy, just as do children in the more unequal states when they take national tests.[308] The need to achieve greater social equality will remain a remote goal, however, until a relational analysis becomes more widely recognized.

The tragic – and maddening – economic collapse of 2008 was largely a function of the growing domination of market fundamentalism in recent decades, first promoted vigorously by both President Reagan and Prime Minister Thatcher as their guiding ideology during the 1980s. It has now proven hugely damaging to nations, communities, families, and individuals. Today in many quarters, however, that ideology being challenged by a more comprehensive, perceptive, and realistic view of economic theory. To begin with, what we know as "the economy" is a narrow band of economic activity, the part that involves monetary exchange, abstracted from a larger whole. Not counted is the huge "informal economy," in which goods and services (both legal and illegal) are bought and sold "off the books" or bartered – plus all the work done for no fee by family members, neighbors, and friends who help each other with needed services every day.

Moreover, the entire human sphere of economic activity is situated within the far larger Earth economy. The human economy could not exist without such "ecosystem services" as relatively inexpensive, or even free, water, food, fossil fuels, control of pests and pathogens, pollination, renewal of soil fertility, and flood control. Although taken for granted so thoroughly that they are absent from economists' standard flow charts, two-thirds of these "ecosystem services" are being degraded at unsustainable rates of use and will become costly or cease to be available in the future, thus transforming the operating environment of all businesses, according to the Millennium Ecosystem Assessment.[309]

The tightly proscribed focus of traditional modern economic theory, in contrast, helps to explain how economists, in both the public and private sectors, could have ignored so many essential relationships operating in the realm of the Real, denying the importance of resource depletion, ubiquitous pollution, and toxic poisoning long after the situation had become critical. Focusing solely on mathematically elegant conceptual models showing the through-put of resources into products and consumption, they blithely pronounced the modern economic system to be robust and dynamic – even though the planet was becoming severely degraded. Destructive effects of extraction and production were authoritatively labeled as "externalities," or more often "mere externalities," and set aside. In an attempt to remove economists' blinders regarding the actual relationships involved, Herman Daly, considered by many to be the father of ecological economics, became the first economist to reconceptualize economics as a life science, more like the science of ecology than the classical economics modeling based on Newtonian physics. Daly, while working as a senior economist at the World Bank, once observed that an illustration titled "The Relation of the Economy to the Environment," in the first draft of the 1992 World Development Report, merely replicated the classical, illusory graphic depiction of an economy: a rectangle with an input arrow entering and an output arrow exiting. Noting that the arrows actually come from somewhere and go to somewhere, Daly proposed that the rectangle be situated within a larger circle called Earth. The Bank's chief economist, who was then Lawrence Summers, nixed the idea. By the third draft, the illustration had been deleted entirely.[310]

As if leaving out the relationships with the entire natural world were not enough, still more essential considerations have been banished from the narrowly limited concept we call "the economy" through the ways in which it is measured by economists and governments. A country's Gross Domestic Product (GDP), or Gross National Product (GNP), for instance, is merely the total monetary value of the sale of all goods and services within a time period, usually one year. As ecosocial activists have noted for some 25 years, this rather crude system of national accounting does not tell us anything about whether a country is doing well or poorly because the results of even massive destruction and disintegration (such as clean-up services after a devastating toxic spill; fees to attorneys, real estate agents, and psychotherapists for a family during the process of a divorce; or medical services to treat epidemics of chronic disease) are simply counted along with all goods and services. In terms of GDP, as long as money is changing hands and the national total is higher than the year before, we're doin' fine!

The condition of the vast ecological and social spheres is ignored in the GDP – as is the careless depletion of our natural and human "resources."[311] Nonetheless, GDP became a touchstone for assessing national success in the post-World-War-II era because it fit well with the assumptions of modern economic theory, which had come to dominate our understanding of governance: that the chief role of a government is to bring about the (supposedly) unlimited benefits that (supposedly) follow from unqualified, unlimited economic expansion.

Similarly, it might seem odd that "per capita income" (average income per person, literally "per head," in a given year) became the other touchstone of measuring modern economic success. After all, narrowing the focus to the earnings of individuals conveys nothing about the condition of a society. This focus made sense, however, within the assumptions of modernity, which had enshrined since the late 18th century the abstract concept of the Autonomous Individual, unfettered by such premodern restraints as tradition, community, extended family, or religion and utterly free to serve his self-interest and thus maximize his status and net worth. In fact, no one exists in pure autonomy in this particular universe; rather, *everything emerges from, is constituted by, and is embedded in networks of dynamic relationships.* Economic decisions, then, are not made in a vacuum:

they often involve considerations of the well-being of one's family, friends, and community.[312]

Our modern sense of "the economy" is not only pathologically abstracted from the Real but is generally regarded as the very heart of the body politic.[313] Government in modern societies is seen to exist in service to the economy. From the perspective of this "economism" (the overarching frame of reference that places the economy at the center of society, viewing other endeavors and institutions as radiating outward from it), economic growth or expansion is both the overriding goal and the solution to the problems it causes. For 200 years theorists on both the left and the right sides of the modern political spectrum have adhered to this economist orientation, as if the economy were by its very nature a quasi-mystical ruling force of society. The market is, according to the 18th-century Scottish philosopher Adam Smith, the "invisible hand" that not only sets prices and distributes goods and services but also organizes society, via the mechanism of self-interest, into rational relations and structures – as long as the economy is free, that is, liberated, from the government to work its magic.[314]

Because modern economic theory is such a drastically reduced abstraction of all that really goes on in relation to economic activity, however, we have arrived today at the opposite of what Adam Smith had in mind.[315] (He specifically praised community-based economics with local ownership and abhorred the possibility of monopolies of companies.[316]) Far from elevating human existence to an ever-improving state of being, market dynamics, when largely unregulated, have delivered us to significant social breakdown, the slow poisoning of the world by industrial toxins, and the triple global crisis: catastrophic climate disruption, the end of the era of "cheap" fossil fuel, and global resource depletion.[317]

If the fallacy of supposedly self-regulating markets were not enough to silence the mantra of laissez-faire, neoliberal economics, 2008 was also a peak year for widespread food poisoning because the governmental regulatory agencies had been reduced, in both staff and allowable legal clout, to the largely powerless status desired by the big agribusiness producers. Neoliberal enthusiasts have tried their best to shred the social compact that had long assured the American people that they can feel confident to make purchases and loan agreements without being scammed, robbed, and poisoned. This confidence is comprised of relationships of trust that clearly must be protected by effective laws and strong enforcement at every level in every quarter of the economy. Instead, self-regulation by corporations failed in every sector with devastating results for people and places. The most urgent issues we now face – in addition to a shortage of good jobs – include reducing our level of carbon emissions, replacing fossil fuels, and restoring our gutted regulatory agencies.

Among the many other troubling aspects of modern economies that deserve attention, perhaps the most corrosive is the encroaching commercialization of nearly all spheres of human endeavor, that is, the ubiquitous intrusion of corporate marketing into our lives. When even young children can identify hundreds of corporate logos – which now surround them from infancy on—but know very few of the birds, trees, or plants in their area, we have allowed their precious formative years to become distorted by the rapacious goals of marketing. Adult life, as well, has become shaped, in both subtle and blatant ways, by the spreading presence of marketing dynamics as the normative model for society. Corporate advertising and other marketing tactics have invaded healthcare (inducements for doctors to prescribe certain brands of drugs); education (commercials in educational videos and television channels shown in classrooms); sports (a corporate name on every stadium, bowl game, and televised statistic); movies (product placement); and, of course, television (the content of programs being determined by what will best lure viewers to the commercials). As community and other relational ties have atrophied in modern America, people have become less connected and more isolated, often reduced to the Lone Consumer in front of the television, watching thousands of commercials that promise a happier life if the right product is purchased.

The commodification of modern life has intensified since the early 1980s when a plague of conspicuous consumption accompanied the falsely named "trickle-down" economics of the Reagan administration. His tax cuts for the rich and upper-middle class moved money upward very quickly, creating a slew of new millionaires and an expanded market for luxury goods, while increasing the burden of stagnant or falling wages, as well as reduced social services, for the middle class, the working poor, and various groups in need. Our society was changed during that decade of celebrating greed and flaunting wealth. Teenagers and young adults quickly came to accept that You Are What You Wear and *He who dies with the most toys wins*, as a bumpersticker from the 1980s proclaimed. The goal of living a healthy, vital, and even noble life was replaced by the newer model: a relentlessly driven consumption machine.

For the past twenty-five years, then, Americans have been

transformed more than ever into *Homo economicus*, an off-kilter version of our species who just can't seem to buy happiness and is oblivious to the destructive effects of our ever-expanding levels of conventional industrial production and consumption on our life-support systems, nature. As the economic situation worsened for working people after the presidential election in 2000, millions of Americans had to work longer to get by, often struggling without any health insurance, and very often feeling that there is scant time for living any sort of life beyond work. All the while, official reports on "the economy" are packaged for us with dispiriting sleight-of-hand manipulations, such as removing food and energy from the U.S. Consumer Price Index so that the numbers are more cheery than the truth would be. It is hardly possible to feel confidence in the macro-economic situation with all its bizarre abstractions, hidden information, and the high failure rate of its grand schemes.

Closer to the ground level, however, an entirely different, relational way to think about economic activity has been emerging throughout this same period. Its major distinction from both the liberal and conservative versions of modern economic thinking is that the economy is not seen as an end in itself, as the central focus of a society. Unlike the economism of both Adam Smith and Karl Marx, an ecosocial economy is understood to exist *in service to community*, to the creation of real wealth: the repair, cultivation, and flourishing of human communities embedded within healthy ecosystems ... the world over.

The Emerging Green, Relational Culture in Economics

When an economy is rooted in *place* – not the abstractions of modern economic theory but the very real capabilities and needs of both the people and the land in a particular bioregion (that is, the watershed in which they live) – a talent for caring and creativity is sparked. Beyond distributing goods and services, an ecosocial economy seeks to create wealth and ownership that is spread as broadly as possible (avoiding vast concentrations of either) and to help weave the social fabric of community. The goal is that everyone be able to live not only comfortably but well – rich in the relationships that a healthy human needs to have with community and with the more-than-human world. The business sector, and hence the tax base, is diversified so that there is far less danger of economic collapse or local recession than there would be if everything depended on one or two dominant corporations that might leave at any time. Moreover, money does not leave the area every time a purchase is made, sent directly to a distant corporate headquarters. Rather, *money circulates largely within the city and the region* because everyone is aware of the benefits to the community of patronizing locally and regionally owned enterprises. Regional trade is cultivated by connecting suppliers and customers within a region of neighboring states, as well as cultivating trade throughout adjacent regions. Long-distance trade occurs but not to the extent that it dominates a local economy. As for daily purchases, a common slogan is *Be a Local Hero: Buy Locally.*

This model of wisely relational community-based economics and regional trade has been around since the early 1980s, both in the platforms of Green parties around the world and in gradually emerging forms developed by grassroots groups not affiliated with any political party. Yet it took a very long time to go mainstream, especially in the United States. In the 1980s I gave many presentations on community-based economics and regional trade (as well as other Green ideas) to which the general response from the audience, whether inner-city or suburban, was generally "This is very interesting and would probably be good for our community – but where is it already in place, already working?" I could cite partial examples, in towns such as Arcata, California, and numerous isolated projects that were successful, but the overall model could not seem to get much traction. What we ecosocial activists back then could not seem to figure out was that one segment of the model had the potential to take root as a compelling attraction and then serve as a catalyst for the relational development of other aspects. As it turned out, the key was food! Throughout the late 1980s and the 1990s, farmers markets were established in thousands of cities and town across the country, delivering freshness, taste, and a growing recognition that local food production is a beneficial economic component for one's town or city. From there came the local food movement; analyses of local food security; new attention to the local economy; and a celebration of local treasures, both edible and cultural.

Elsewhere in the world, the path to community-based economics was sometimes rougher, when it necessarily followed the collapse of the dominant economy. The cause of the collapse was often disastrous neoliberal policies, as in Argentina in 2001, or the destructive effects on countless communities of the new "free trade" policies enforced by the World Trade Organization. In the wake of failed or sacrificial economic policies in place at the national level, local groups began to create their own connections and networks to build a sustaining community with a new sort of economic activity.[318]

The Relational Shift in the economy is far more extensive, though, than community-based economics and regional trade. Its focus on dynamic relationships and a systemic perspective continually brings forth new possibilities for qualitative growth and societal well-being, while solving the problems that were caused by the mechanistic version of economics. Within this new orientation, the field of ecological economics has arisen with the goal of developing a deeper scientific understanding of the complex linkages between human-made systems and nature's systems. Ecological economists share a focus on the complex interrelationship between ecological sustainability, social sustainability, and economic sustainability. Research in this field is particularly concerned with uncertainty, which is a fundamental characteristic of all complex, dynamic systems involving irreversible processes.[319]

One of the more widely recognizable examples of this emerging "reality-based economics" are the quality-of-life indices that many governments around the world now use to supplement the limited information conveyed by their GDP. Such indices include the Index of Sustainable Economic Welfare, the Human Development Index, the Genuine Progress Indicator, and the Happy Planet Index. In addition, numerous municipal and national governments utilize the Ecological Footprint analysis, which measures how much land and water area a human population requires to produce that which it consumes and to absorb its wastes, using prevailing technology.[320] In September 2009 the European Union announced that it will develop an indicator to measure environmental stress, which they will use along with GDP.

As this chapter will present, the Relational Shift is changing the ways in which business is done: the ways we design and manufacture products, the new thinking about transportation, the new ways in which we eliminate emissions and other toxins in our environment, the ways in which we use water, the ways in which we attain and use sources of energy, and the ways in which we reduce our accumulation of trash, as well as new thinking about international trade and "development" in the "Third World." First, though, let's begin with food.

Agriculture and Food Security

What keeps us grounded in *place* – not projected into cyberspace through our computers, not mesmerized by the distractions of television and other media, not caught up in the abstractions that delineate modern life? To be fully present to ourselves and in relationship to others, we need to pay attention to the very real conditions of the bioregion in which we live: the condition of the habitats; the quality of the air, water, and soil; and the subtle shifting of the seasons. If we take into our bodies honey made by local bees, for instance, we become less susceptible to allergies to local weeds and native plants. If we take in fruits and vegetables, milk and cheese, fish and meat, and jams and pies and, say, pear brandy – all from our immediate region – we *become place*. No longer living on top of nature, we, like the flora and the fauna around us, then live on the bounty of our home region. Its processes of taking in sun, water, and nutrients from the soil become our processes, enabling us to create new cells, self-heal, and flourish.

Like our bodies, the land regains integrity when its natural processes are allowed to function. With the agrarian approach, small- and medium-sized farms produce food for consumption locally and regionally by working as closely and wisely with nature's processes as possible. This type of agriculture preserves topsoil, soil fertility, and biodiversity as it beautifies the landscape – and is, foremost, *a culture*, an orientation that involves everyone who eats, everyone who wants to participate in the historic shift beyond the mechanistic, ham-fisted approach of industrial might that has brought us such a crises-laden version of progress.[321]

The cultivation of local food systems has proceeded through the cultivation of relationships in place. In communities where enough people buy locally produced food, directly from a local farmers market or other retail outlet, a greenbelt of family farms in the surrounding countryside is preserved and can flourish.[322] The owners of those viable farms buy goods and services from other local businesses, helping to fuel the growth of the local economy. The thousands of American communities that have begun to develop a regional food system, thereby lessening their dependence on the national grid of corporate food distribution, have vastly reduced their vulnerability to interruptions, distant natural disasters, and financial manipulations of that system. In addition, a revival of the Victory Gardens movement from the First and Second World Wars is underway. In 1943 over 20 million Victory Gardens were planted on municipal lawns, in schoolyards, and next to apartment buildings and houses household yards. Fully one-third of all the vegetables consumed in the United States that year were raised in those civic and home gardens (so that crops from commercial farms could be shipped to the troops at war). Today there is a resurgence of interest in planting home gardens because creating even partial levels of local and regional reliance increases a community's level of food security significantly.

Of course, the far more dominant system comprising industrial agribusiness still controls most of the production and distribution of food in the United States. It relentlessly advertises that it provides the most efficient means of producing food at the lowest prices, but that is so only if one ignores a broad array of costs that fall outside the models of modern economic theory, that is, if one ignores industrial agribusiness's costly destruction to the Real, those pesky "mere externalities." For example, Americans have to spend $200 million annually to treat water pollution from crop fertilizers and animal wastes from large-scale "animal factories."[323] The overuse of chemical additives and (oil-dependent) machines has produced a massive loss of topsoil. Pesticide residue on produce damages our health,[324] and airborne diseases such as salmonella have increased in frequency since the advent of factory farming. Since 70 percent of all antibiotics used in the United States end up in feed troughs, antibiotic-resistant "superbugs" have developed, which may be reaching humans.[325] A study at Iowa State University in 2003 found that locally grown produce had traveled an average of 56 miles to the point of sale, while conventionally grown and distributed produce had traveled an average of 1,494 miles; conventionally sourced broccoli had traveled 92 times as far as had the locally grown broccoli. In addition, transporting the conventionally sourced food had required far more fuel and had spewed five to 17 times more carbon dioxide emissions.[326]

Many American farmers have been reduced to contract work for the giant agribusiness corporations. As ownership has concentrated in megafarms, millions of family farms have been put out of business, causing rippling circles of damage to rural communities. A study of 200 farming communities by the U.S. Office of Technology Assessment found that as farm size increases so does poverty, and the faster farm size increases, the faster poverty increases.[327] Similarly, a study conducted at the University of California at Davis found that as farm size and absentee ownership increase, social conditions in the local community deteriorate (empty storefronts, increased poverty and crime, and social breakdown).[328]

That situation worsened in the second half of 2008 as Wall Street hedgefund managers and other speculators, seeking the next vulnerable sector of the economy following the subprime-mortgage-securities scam, moved in on agriculture and began buying thousands of farms in the United States, Britain, Brazil, and elsewhere. By "owning structure" (including grain elevators, fertilizer plants, ships and barges, and other property necessary to produce and market crops), the hedge funds are increasingly able to control commodity prices. If corn prices, for instance, do not hit their investors' target numbers, the funds can store the corn and force prices up; if the price for corn is down in the United States, the funds can ship the crop to Japan or wherever else might be more profitable.[329] All this global selling and transporting of food (for reasons other than where food aid is needed) drives up the level of carbon dioxide emissions in a ridiculous exchange of agricultural shipping: for instance, in 2005 the United States exported 37,238 tons of green beans but imported 31,328 tons; we exported 24,344 tons of blueberries but imported 26,319 tons; we exported 288,171 tons of potatoes but imported 357,378 tons.[330] Is this necessary?

Not only is agribusiness in the pocket of the large corporations and finance firms but the actual nutritive quality of the produce it yields is deficient, compared to organic crops, because industrialized crops that grow larger and faster are not necessarily able to acquire nutrients at that faster rate, whether by synthesis or by acquisition from the soil. This "dilution effect" on nutrient density was widely observed by agricultural scientists even thirty years ago – yet another organic and essential relationship ignored by the modern, industrialized agribusiness. As mentioned earlier, during the period from 1950 to 1999, levels of phosphorous, iron, calcium, riboflavin, and ascorbic acid (a precursor of Vitamin C) declined significantly in conventionally produced fruits and vegetables, according to data gathered by the U.S. Department of Agriculture.[331]

Moreover, the food-like substances produced by industrial agribusiness do not *taste* nearly as good as more naturally grown food. As one of the founders of the local food movement, the restaurateur Alice Waters, has observed, "When it comes to locally grown, organic food, the 'politically correct' choice is the delicious one."[332]

For all these reasons, a glorious revolution of taste, nutrition, and community well-being has arisen in recent decades – which has not been limited to middle-class consumers. In many cities, the municipal government, in partnership with state or federal agencies and nonprofit organizations, has established farmers markets in inner-city neighborhoods. These markets often give priority space to produce grown on farms owned, or rented, by farmers-of-color. San Francisco was one of the first city governments to establish such a market and make it possible for the vendors to accept federal food stamps and also coupons from the Women, Infants, and Children nutritional food program. Some city governments have issued vouchers to low-income senior citizens and pregnant women that can be redeemed at farmers markets for fresh produce. In addition, inner-city food activists nationwide have helped to create bountiful community gardens in vacant lots.[333] In New York City, for instance, a large number of community gardens flourish now in the Bronx and Brooklyn. In Oakland, three young food activists in 2003 founded the West Oakland People's Grocery, which operates from a converted postal truck powered by solar energy and bio-diesel fuel. They sell organic produce and other food at ten locations, including stops at senior centers and schools, where they teach young people about the health benefits of getting off fast food and onto a nutritious, fresh diet.[334]

Filling a niche between a food-bank and a food cooperative, SHARE (Self-Help and Resource Exchange) operates in more than 33 states, via a loosely knit chain of non-profit groups, to distribute good-quality groceries to people who spend at least two hours in community service. As Anna Wingate, the president of SHARE Northwest, sees it, "America is one of the loneliest places on earth. The idea is to get people participating. It doesn't have to be at SHARE. It can be mowing a neighbor's lawn or helping at a school."[335] In return, members can place a monthly food order for pick-up at a very substantial discount at a community center, a church, or a neighborhood garage.

Many communities have Community Supported Agriculture (CSA) options, whereby people pay ahead to local farmers during the winter for a part of the harvest that will come to market in the summer and fall. In that way, the farmers receive needed income during the off-season months, and they enjoy the security of having sold part of their harvest ahead of time. In Burlington, Vermont, for instance one 200-acre CSA project called the Intervale Community Farm, on a formerly industrial site, produces about 7 percent of all the fresh food consumed in that city: 500,000 pounds of salable produce, plus more than 30,000 pounds gleaned for the local food banks.[336]

Yet neither a farmers market nor CSA by themselves is sufficient to build a secure agricultural base for a town or city. What is key is that the local institutions – schools, colleges, hospitals, municipal and county buildings, and any publicly owned entity with a cafeteria, café, or sandwich shop – buy produce and other food from the local farms. In many areas, programs match up local producers with wholesale buyers in both the public and private sectors.[337] Also, as agribusiness moves further into the expanding market for organic food, it is essential for the economic health of their community that people continue to ask for and buy food produced by moderate-size, independently owned local and regional farms (rather than corporately owned behemoth organic industrial farms).

One of the fastest growing segments of the local food movement in the early 21st century is the farm-to-school (or farm-to-cafeteria) movement. Thousands of school districts, colleges, and universities are now participants. In many areas, projects such as the Food Corps in Montana help school districts to "localize" their menus. At the college level, numerous institutions now build their entire menus around fresh, locally grown ingredients – and tout their relationships with local food producers as one of their recruiting attractions. In the summer of 2005 the second annual National Farm to Cafeteria Conference was hosted by Kenyon College, in Gambier, Ohio, where the college president, Dr. S. Georgia Nugent, observed, "You support the local economy – and it's a way of teaching young people about their local environment and connecting it with what happens internationally." Even the very large-scale food-service companies have had to adapt to finding local suppliers. The representative for one of those large companies, at Kenyon College, Niles Gebele, experienced an "epiphany" when he met Alice Waters and was sent to work in her restaurant for a while: "Everything was bottom line and numbers before; now it's about the food." He has since become a consultant for the farm-to-cafeteria movement, asserting, "This is what we should be doing. The globalization of food, the hidden costs, the loss of nutrition – it's not healthy for the planet or for the human body."[338]

The defense of local food, local cuisine, and related customs has helped to achieve regional food security and self-reliance, while delivering the benefits of fresh, healthy food. Even more, the local food movement has energized communities around the world in their effort to stave off industrial standardization and agribusiness monopolies, now enforced by the neoliberal trade laws enforced by the World Trade Organization. A brilliantly successful catalyst for this defense and recovery is the Slow Food Movement, started by Carlo Petrini when a McDonald's attempted to open near the Spanish Steps in Rome in 1986. Slow Food celebrates the small-scale, organic farmer who sells varieties of produce and other food that have long been a central part of the lived culture in a particular place. The movement's projects include the Ark of Taste (a catalogue of threatened foods); the Slow Food Foundation for Biodiversity; and the University of Gastronomic Sciences in Parma, Italy, where "ecogastronomy" unites ethics and pleasure.

In October 2004, 5000 Slow Food members from 130 countries gathered for the first of the organization's biennial global conferences, "Terra Madre," in Turin. There Petrini put out a call for everyone to defend the rights, knowledge, and creativity of small producers all over the world and to regard ourselves (consumers) as "co-producers and a critical link in creating a sustainable, just, healthy, food system."[339] Vandana Shiva, a scientist who was a keynote speaker at the "Terra Madre" conference, praised farmers in many countries who, even without significant investment and in the face of official disapproval, switched from industrial methods to improved organic practices that have increased yields and outputs dramatically, according to a recent study by the UN Food and Agriculture Organization. In Bolivia potato yields were increased from 4 to 14 tons per hectare by going organic; in Cuba vegetable yields of urban gardens almost doubled; in Ethiopia sweet potato yields increased from 6 to 30 tons per hectare; in Kenya maize yields increased from 2.25 to 9 tons per hectare; and in Pakistan mango yields increased from 7.5 to 22 tons per hectare. Shiva concluded that globalized industrial agriculture's "externalized" costs – $400 billion in subsidies annually (including those for transport, environmental mitigation, and healthcare) – are far too great a burden for the Earth to bear. In contrast, she praised Terra Madre as a celebration of "honest agriculture," in which prices do not lie and neither the Earth nor her caretakers are exploited.[340] Similar themes were struck at Slow Food Nation 2008, a gathering in San Francisco of the Slow Food movement in the United States, including presentations by some 40 project leaders involved with Slow Food USA.

The increased yields of agroecological (that is, organic) methods – plus the fact that they require far less fossil fuel and water, while conserving and improving soil quality[341] – are among reasons that biotechnology's invention of genetically modified (GM) crops and food is now increasingly regarded as "a solution looking for a problem."[342] A study commissioned in 2009 by the Union of Concerned Scientists found that, contrary to industry claims, the widespread introduction in the United States over the past thirteen years of genetically engineered, or "genetically modified," corn and soybeans (most of which were grown from Monsanto's Roundup-Ready GM seeds, which are designed to withstand intensive spraying of Monsanto's highly toxic Roundup herbicide) has achieved very little increase in crop yield.[343] Moreover, GM crops have proven to be responsible for the accidental contamination of our food crops, such as the incident in Texas in 2008 when a quarter-ton of harvested, experimental GM cotton (containing a gene that produces a pesticide) was mistakenly mixed with non-GM cotton, from which cottonseed oil was processed for animal feed.[344] The most basic problem with genetically modified crops, though, is that the gene pool of plants is being blindly changed: the corporations pushing GM seeds proclaim one outcome, but they cannot know all the others that will take place in the ecosystem surrounding a cultivated field. For instance, herbicide-tolerant GM crops as well as GM crops that carry a pesticide toxin in each of their cells, merely cause nature to respond with the development of resistant weeds and insects.

While not increasing yields, GM seeds have proven highly profitable for the corporations that make them because they are sterile so must be bought anew by farmers worldwide every year, as opposed to the traditional means of seed-saving by farmers. Moreover, GM seeds and "superweeds" have begun to spread through ecosystems. In Europe the grassroots refusal to consume GM foods is strong, while in the United States the industry's success in blocking the labeling of GM crops in food makes it impossible for Americans to know what we are eating. On the other hand, nonprofit activist institutes successfully blocked the GM industry's attempt to get GM foods including in the federal standards to qualify as "organic." In addition, many law suits on behalf of farmers seeking the right to plant non-GM-contaminated crops have been filed and won by the Center for Food Safety in Washington, DC., which also furthers the cultivation of organic, locally grown "True Food."[345]

The growing success of organic agriculture, like the growing appreciation for local food communities and the relationships they foster, has begun to shift our attention toward deep issues of what we are and how we live. How we bring forth food from nature and what we take into ourselves reflects our deepest relation to the Earth community. Presently, modern society is only beginning to figure out how to reengage with nature's processes, not only through organic farming but also through a range of promising experiments such as Natural Systems Agriculture, which is "no-plough" agriculture that imitates the productivity of the prairie through the breeding of perennial wheat, rye, and sorghum, thereby reducing soil erosion and the use of fossil fuel.[346] Similarly, there is widespread interest in a wisely relational design approach to gardens, farms, structures, and communities that is called permaculture (short for "permanent agriculture" and hence "permanent culture"). Permaculture involves the study of relationships and the skills to perceive them. All placements, lay-outs, and procedures are modeled closely on the processes of nature, such that byproducts or "waste" that result while producing one thing supply the needs of another.[347] For example, the heat given off by chickens and their manure are exactly what is needed by a lean-to greenhouse that is attached to the chicken coop.

All the various types of ecologically intelligent horticulture, local food systems, and convivial farmers markets are expressions of the core principle that runs through the entire emerging relational, Green culture: the urgent revitalization of our communities and the mutually enhancing relationships between the human and the more-than-human world. Without theory or a master plan, millions of communities around the world have discovered the bountiful ramifications that sprout and flourish once there is a collective intention to cultivate a local food system.

Doing Business Differently

Why has the modern West neglected to accrue extensive knowledge about the subtle *processes* of the natural world and their complex, relational, and dynamic interactions (a focus that is common in most nonmodern, indigenous cultures)? Our attention was largely focused, instead, on substance, structure, and categorization (building on Aristotle) and on the predictability of mechanistic behavior (following from Newton's synthesis of the new discoveries in mechanistic science). Yet in recent decades the new science of complexity studies has revealed what the modern, mechanistic lens missed: the intricate and dynamic creativity of natural systems. Moreover, our biological and ecological knowledge is now rapidly expanding. We are truly in a re-birth of learning, a renaissance of knowledge of Relational Reality. This time, unlike at the birth of modernity, we grasp the true challenge: the human economy must fit well with the processes and relationships of the Earth's economy. Modernity sought, with catastrophic results, to defeat nature, but Green ingenuity seeks mutual enhancement.

The application of our deepening knowledge of nature to the challenges of human design is called by Janine Benyus *biomimicry* (*bios* meaning life, and *mimesis* meaning to imitate). A pioneering consultant in biological design, she notes that nature has already solved many of the problems with which we are grappling today. A spider, for instance, produces a biodegradable silk that is far stronger than Kevlar, a high-tech material used in flak jackets. Moreover, Kevlar is created by a high-heat, high-pressure industrial process that leaves toxic by-products – unlike the room-temperature, nontoxic processes of the spider. Similarly, the crystalline coating that self-assembles into perfect precision on protein templates to form the shell of an abalone is stronger than any hard coatings we can manufacture. In short, Benyus asserts, "doing it nature's way" has the potential to change the way we grow food, make materials, harness energy, heal ourselves, store information, and conduct business.

The best known example of biomimicry is the invention of velcro, inspired by the sticking power of burrs. Yet the list of successful examples is growing quickly. A midrise building in Harare, Zimbabwe, designed by the architect Mike Pearce, copies the convection cooling built into termite mounds to keep the building cool without mechanical air-conditioning. A new paint called lotusan for the surfaces of buildings mimics the rough surface of a lotus, allowing the building to be cleaned by the free kinetic energy in rain. A method of extracting water from humid air was devised by an English scientist by studying the ways in which trees comb moisture from fog. A quieter bullet train was designed in Japan by engineers who studied a kingfisher's beak. Similarly, new aircraft technology was inspired by the body design of falcons, eagles, hawks, and owls. A system of carpet tiles can now be laid seamlessly without adhesives because a manufacturer in Georgia studied systems of bird feathers. In addition, waterproof, biodegradable bandages for use on internal injuries and as surgical patches have been developed with a "biorubber" base that mimics the tiny hairs and foot pads that enable a gecko to scale smooth walls.

Benyus, who was named one of "Ten New Gurus You Should Know About" by *Fortune* magazine in November 2008, believes that the "biomimic revolution" involves more than merely designing to mimic natural forms, natural processes, and even natural systems. It also entails acknowledging nature as model, as measure, and as mentor. Through her design firm, the Biomimicry Guild, in Helena, Montana, Benyus and her team are "creating a way for biological ideas to get into human designs."[348] In this deepening shift from regarding the more-than-human world as a mere storehouse of resources for human projects, we have begun to see that, for the good of all, our designs must fit well with the larger context of the Earth community.

In fact, our entire approach to manufacturing products – and designing the factories in which that takes place – is being radically rethought with nature as the inspiration. Modern economic theory emerged when skilled labor was relatively scarce and natural resources were plentiful. Today the situation is the opposite, and it has become clear to businesses large and small that increased efficiency in their use of resources is the key to vastly improved productivity at lower costs.

Several of the most significant breakthroughs in this "new industrial revolution" have been achieved by the firm MBDC, the partnership of the ecological architect and designer William McDonough and the industrial chemist Michael Braungart, who was a founding member of the German Green Party in the 1970s.[349] When they considered the effects of modernity's anti-relational ways in which things are fabricated, they concluded, "Sweeping away, shutting out, and controlling nature's imperfect abundance are implicit features of modern design, ones rarely if ever questioned. *If brute force doesn't work, you're not using enough of it.*"[350]

In contrast, they have developed two guiding concepts, which have led them to successful solutions to extremely challenging problems. First, the widespread goal of "eco-efficiency" (doing "less bad," tweaking the current ways of manufacturing such that lower levels of damage are done) should be seen as an intermediary step, which can now be superceded by the goal of "eco-effectiveness." By eco-effectiveness, McDonough and Braungart mean that our thinking about human fabrication needs to expand from the primary purpose of a product or system to consider the larger context, or web of relationships. "What are its goals and potential effects, both immediate and wide-ranging, with respect to both time and place?" they ask in their book *Cradle to Cradle: Remaking the Way We Make Things.* "What is the entire system – cultural, commercial, ecological – of which this made thing, and way of making things, will be a part? Once you begin to consider the larger picture, the most familiar features of human fabrication begin to shape-shift."[351]

They cite the example of a roof. Conventional roofing systems are expensive to maintain because they bake under the sun, receiving ultraviolet degradation and thermal shock. In the larger context of the surrounding ecosystem, they are part of the growing landscape of impervious surfaces that contribute to flooding, the heating up of cities in summer, and the loss of habitat. Addressing those problems piecemeal would improve some conditions while making others worse. Instead, McDonough and Braungart have been working with a green kind of roofing that resolves all the concerns, including the economic: a light layer of soil, a growing matrix, covered with plants. This living roof maintains the roofing at a stable temperature (providing evaporative cooling in summer and insulation in winter), shields it from the sun's destructive rays, absorbs storm water, and even makes oxygen, sequesters carbon, captures particulates like soot. In addition, it looks more attractive and saves money that would otherwise go to regulatory fees for storm-drainage management and to flooding. Tens of millions of square feet of such roofing is already used in Europe. In this country, McDonough and Braungart have installed a living roof on City Hall in Chicago (a city that plans to install extensive green roofing) and in their reconfiguring of the Ford Motor Company's Rouge River plant in Detroit, which channels excess rain water from the living roof down to an adjacent, restored marshland where organisms clean the water before it is channeled into the Detroit River.

The second guiding principle contributed by McDonough and Braungart is that eco-effective industrial design depends on perceiving two streams of materials: biological nutrients and technological nutrients. The problem with most products now is that they mix the two streams in such ways that they cannot be separated after the life of the item; instead, they are "monstrous hybrids" that are hauled to landfills or incinerated, which emits harmful gases and particulate matter. Eco-effective products could be designed to decompose on the ground, providing food for plants and animals and nutrients for the soil – or, after a simple process of separation, could be returned to industrial cycles to supply high-quality raw materials for new products.

McDonough and Braungart applied their eco-effective redesigning at a textile factory in Switzerland whose fabric trimmings had been ruled too toxic to burn in Swiss incinerators (so the trimmings were routinely exported to Spain for burning). Working with a chemical company, Braungart's team eliminated from consideration almost 8,000 chemicals commonly used in the textile industry (thereby eliminating the need for additives and corrective processes). They then identified 38 ingredients that have positive qualities. In the end, they came up with a higher-quality product that was more economical to produce and emitted effluent water from the factory that was even cleaner than the water going in! Here as elsewhere, their goal is not only to refrain from depleting but to replenish the ecosystem in which the manufacturing process is embedded.

Eco-effective design, like permaculture, views "waste" as a nutrient (either biological or technological) for another organism or process. Moreover, this relational approach broadens the narrowly "efficient" focus on production and profit to questions about what is needed for life to flourish – the lives of plants, animals, and humans for generations to come in that particular place. McDonough and Braungart offer a vision of buildings that produce more energy than they consume, tires on cars that absorb polluting particulates from the air, and much more. They point out that the new technologies such as cybertechnology, biotechnology, and nanotechnology replace the chemical reactions and brute force but are simply hyperefficient engines driving the steamship of the first Industrial Revolution to new extremes.[352] In the emerging Green, relational culture, in contrast, human ingenuity is furthering both interrelationships and diversity, the integrity of life.

McDonough and Braungart are certainly not the only eco-designers in the manufacturing sector,[353] but they have pioneered new, more effectively relational ways of thinking about the issues involved. Moreover, they have devised a quantitative system by which products, as well as their production processes, can be evaluated: the MBDC Cradle-to-Cradle Certification. A material or product is assessed in five categories: materials, material reutilization/design for environment, energy, water, and social responsibility. If a candidate material or product is found to achieve the necessary standards, it is certified as a Silver, Gold, or Platinum product or is certified as a Technological/Biological Nutrient.[354]

Once a product is manufactured, it is time to ascertain the true price. That is, a move is afoot to reject the supposed lack of any relationship between production costs and environmental damage. Such "externalities" are actually costs created by industry but paid for by the taxpayers. In fact, companies have prospered by maximizing their "externalitites" in order to minimize their costs (also known as externalizing their costs).

Take for example the industrial production of currently cheap meat via factory farms. Most meat in the United States is produced at massive "confined animal feeding operations" (CAFOs) that house tens of thousands of cattle or hogs or chickens. These "animal factories" generate not only vast quantities of meat but also rivers of sewage, clouds of contaminated dust, and nearly a fifth of all greenhouse gases. The stench from a CAFO blankets farms for miles around, lowering property values. The crowded, often unsanitary, conditions promote *e coli* outbreaks and other disease, which has led to a class of superbugs that are resistant to antibiotics.[355] The price of meat is relatively low, however, only because the meat companies externalize the full costs of production onto the taxpayers, such as $4.1 billion annually for local public works departments to clean up livestock sewage leaks, and $2.5 billion annually to treat salmonella. According to the Union of Concerned Scientists, the cost to taxpayers of addressing the environmental damage and public health problems caused by CAFOs may be as much as $38 billion annually.[356] Moreover, the loss of diversity in the economy of rural America has damaged families and communities.

How did we arrive at such an irrational model? For the simple reason

that the plan was completely rational – irrefutable, even – as long as no
one was so "unsophisticated" as to mention the relationship between the
concept of CAFOs and the biological and ecological realities in which they
would be embedded, that is, the Real. The U.S. Secretary of Agriculture
in the 1950s, Ezra Taft Benson, firmly proclaimed the "rational" direction
modern American agriculture was to follow: "Get big or get out!" This
trajectory followed the mechanistic premises of modern economics:
"economy of scale" (bigger is always more efficient), centralization of
production (centralizing operations always yields higher productivity),
and besting nature with a technological fix (livestock, when fed antibiotics,
can grow 25 percent faster on the same amount of feed because no calories
are burnt fending off normal, low-grade infections). The emergence of
CAFOs was also driven by the underlying leitmotif of the post-World-
War-II American economy: sacrificing small businesses and communities
for greater corporate profits.

Until recently, numerous organizations bringing to bear an ecosocial,
Green analysis of the situation for the past two decades were marginalized
by the influence of corporate lobbyists over lawmakers. Now, however,
as more local and national governments are enforcing the Polluter Pays
principle and other modes of requiring corporate responsibility, the true
costs of producing food and products in environmentally damaging – and
hence costly – ways are becoming apparent.[357] Any costs to manufacturers
such as high-priced fossil fuels, governmental fees imposed for every ton
of carbon dioxide emitted (as is the law in San Francisco), clean-up costs,
or mitigating legal fees, for instance, must be factored in to arrive at "true
pricing." In this way, the "externalities" are internalized into the price, so
the relationship between actual costs and true price becomes clear. If true
pricing continues to gain ground, products made in ecologically wise ways
will be less expensive to consumers – or, as a slogan proclaims, "The cleanest
is the cheapest!" (In the case of re-decentralizing livestock production to
small- and medium-farms, which produce far less environmental damage
and disease, accelerated tax depreciation and tax credit could be granted,
which would cost taxpayers far less than the current system.[358])

Increasingly, economics is no longer seen to operate in a vacuum
as the classical through-put charts taught. Hazel Henderson suggests in
Ethical Markets: Growing the Green Economy that the new, more relational
ways of doing business can be grouped as (1) sustainable solutions in energy,
manufacturing, agriculture, and healthcare; (2) ecosocially responsible
investing; and (3) ecosocial corporate responsibility. All of these sectors

employ sustainability metrics, which measure success, wealth, progress, productivity, efficiency, overall quality of life, and ecological footprints and efficiency by using multidisciplinary systems approaches. In addition, "triple bottom line accounting," pioneered by the Amsterdam-based Global Reporting Initiative, is now used by over 600 global companies to report their social, environmental, and governance performance as well as profitability. Henderson asserts that these new statistical reforms constitute the greatest revolution in accounting since the invention of double-entry bookkeeping during the Renaissance. [359] Another way to frame the Green shift in business is called "the three Rs" by Jonathon Porritt, who served for nine years as chair of the British government's Sustainable Development Commission: Resilience (reducing vulnerability to global supply chains of materials); Resolarization (reducing dependency on fossil fuels); and Relocalization (strengthening local food supply systems and commerce).[360]

Relational thought has also begun to ripple through the ways in which businesses are organized and how they function. The mechanistic assumptions that shaped most businesses resulted in the familiar organizational chart, focused on structure and parts as well as the machine-based concept of "fit." Over the past fifteen years, these static models have been replaced in many enterprises by a more organic understanding that dynamic interrelationships and processes are more important to the understanding of what is really going on than are Newtonian notions of cause and effect. Margaret Wheatley, an organizational consultant who has applied the discoveries of the new physics and complexity studies in her work, observes that successful structures are those that facilitate relationship and that structure itself is created by an interweaving of processes.[361] (It should be noted that studies have shown that telecommuters are less likely to get promoted than are their peers in the office, who can form in-person relationships with co-workers and superiors.[362])

Another widely used post-mechanistic approach to organizational development draws on systems thinking, which grew out of the "organismic" insights of the biologist Ludwig von Bertalanffy in the 1920s, cybernetics in the 1940s and beyond, and complexity studies in science since the 1980s. Peter Senge, an organizational consultant, has helped numerous enterprises grasp that systems thinking allows people to see *processes* of change, rather than a "snapshot." Instead of using static charts denoting structure, Senge suggests "process mapping" of relational activity flows. *Systemic* structure becomes apparent after relational patterns have been identified, following events. Foremost, Senge and others like him who are introducing process-oriented, relational thinking (long familiar to women) into the business world have demonstrated that every enterprise can become a learning organization.[363] Moreover, the sense that every human organization is a potentially learning, changing, and unfolding *living system* – as is every person within it – is relevant not only to companies but also to communities.

Community-based Economics

"The world is coming to a beginning rather than an end. We have the knowledge, tools, creativity, and capital to proceed. Our challenge is merely to begin where we live, with whatever capabilities are at hand."[364] Such is the optimism of Paul Glover, who makes it look easy. In recent years, he helped to make Ithaca, New York, a leader in community-based economics by founding Ithaca Hours local currency (based on the local hourly wage and printed with local scenes and "In Ithaca We Trust"); the Ithaca Health Fund (now part of the Ithaca Health Alliance); and the concept of community investing known as the Whole Ithaca Stock Exchange (WISE). More recently, he has designed a system known as the Philadelphia Regional & Independent Stock Exchange (PRAISE). Another area with a successful local currency is the Berkshire region in western Massachusetts: the BerkShare, founded in 2006, has an exchange rate equal to $1 and is accepted by businesses and customers throughout the region. In Ashland, Oregon, citizens have initiated the Rogue Valley Resiliency Fund to attract local equity investment in ecosocially responsible regional businesses.

Such efforts contribute to the relocalizing of capital and investment. Another example is the "Move Your Money" campaign launched by Arianna Huffington and Rob Johnson on her Huffington Post website in 2009: in the wake of the Wall Street bailout following the banks' disastrous scams, Huffington urged Americans to move their bank accounts from the big banks to community banks and community credit unions, both of which avoid reckless schemes with depositors' funds. With well-established local flows of capital not only does the community become more secure economically but money then functions – and this is truly revolutionary – to connect people rather than dominate them. A community-based economy advances the repair, strengthening, and flourishing of the social fabric. The multifaceted results, which are at once convivial and broadly efficacious, comprise what has been called "the economics of neighborliness."[365] In a similar vein, an Italian economist who has studied the Slow Food movement and other examples of community-based economics observes that keeping money circulating mostly in the municipality and the surrounding region is "encouraging relationships of exchange among local actors," a dynamic he has labeled "relational relocalization."[366]

A largely localized economy provides its own growth without the insecurity of trying to attract a corporate factory, which could pull out at any time (even after the municipal government has spent large sums on putting in new roads, sewage lines, and water lines, plus offering tax write-offs as incentives). Through the "local multiplier effect," 45 cents of every dollar spent in locally owned businesses is subsequently spent, that is, reinvested, locally as the store buys needed business services locally. In contrast, every dollar spent in a chain store yields only 15 cents for the local economy. Increasing the amount of local spending by 50 to 80 percent over a few years more than doubles the local effect. Moreover, buying local goods minimizes a community's participation in fuel use and carbon dioxide production: most produce sold in chain supermarkets travels up to 92 times farther than does produce grown locally.[367] An example of a store achieving both of these aims is the thriving New Seasons Market produce and grocery stores in Portland, Oregon, which are locally owned and sell only locally produced food. Toward that end, they have introduced a "Pacific Village" label to denote foods from Northern California, Oregon, Washington, or British Columbia. Also in the Pacific Northwest, a regional chain of 39 quick-service restaurants called Burgerville buys the bulk of its ingredients from regional farmers and offers such regional specialities as blackberry milkshakes (only in season, of course) and Walla Walla onions rings.

Joining the goal of local ownership with that of regional "import substitution," Michael Schuman, author of *The Small-Mart Revolution*, suggests the acronym LOIS (Local Ownership and Import Substitution) for the model of community-based economics. LOIS, he asserts, is the woman with whom the future lies, while TINA (There Is No Alternative to the globalized economy) is not.[368] To cultivate LOIS, a community is well advised to measure the monetary "leakage" out of their local economy. A subsequent step involves creating an inventory of the assets available to the community, which should include the potential assets such as vacant land, unoccupied buildings, and currently unemployed people seeking work. The quest is to determine what products and services could be made and sold locally instead of importing them – which is merely one aspect of the fertile possibilities of a community-based economy. A range of pragmatic visionaries have created books, magazines, and institutes to further this vital field.[369] Any one of them will do your community far more good than listening to the long-dominant "Chicago school" of neoliberal economics.

Community-based economics was always a good idea in itself – even before distant corporations succeeded in acquiring every single department store, every television and radio station, and even the utility company in most American cities. Since 1995, however, when the renegotiated General Agreement on Tariffs and Trade (GATT) was ratified and the World Trade Organization (WTO) was created, community-based economics has been increasingly recognized as a large part of the solution to a desperately worsening crisis. In truth, economic globalization can be said to have "leveled the playing field" only in the sense of running over communities worldwide with a steamroller, disempowering them and making them dependent on the whims of the big players, the major banks and transnational corporations. The challenge is now roughly the same for St. Louis as it is for Mumbai, the same for Aberdeen as for Ulan Bator: to limit their vulnerability to the vagaries of the globalized market. While the false promises have soured, grassroots efforts in cities and towns all over the world are creating real economic security through sustainable, community-based economics and regional trade.[370] This is the rising counterforce, both potent and joyful. You can find it at colorful monthly gatherings like the "Market Days of Athens' Own," in Athens, Ohio, or at the annual convergence of Local Social Forums of the Southern Alps, or in the barrios of Mexico City that have been transformed into a community commons.

Transportation

As cities strive to create or extend their light-rail systems, new thinking is succeeding in bringing transit and passengers into better relationship. For instance, development is being shaped in the vicinity of mass-transit stations to favor clusters of high-density housing units mixed in with some businesses, which constitute "transit villages." In fact, some regional transit authorities are now making rezoning around the proposed stations a condition for cities to receive money for building the light-rail lines.[371] Cities are also receiving various incentives to include affordable housing in those new transit villages. In addition, they are creating Bus Rapid Transit networks with dedicated bus lanes and controlled traffic signals. Some cities are considering "transit-only" streets, which would be open only to buses, shuttles, taxis, delivery vans, and bicycles. In Boulder, Colorado, bus service was redesigned to use smaller buses running more often – with the result that ridership increased five-fold.[372]

In the state that epitomizes car culture and sprawl, the California State Assembly passed the first law in the United States, in 2008, that links traffic control with efforts to slow climate change: top priority in the allocation of local, state, and federal transportation subsidies must be given to existing and new high-density, mixed-use centers where people live, work, and shop. The idea is that such developments will not only check sprawl and ease commute traffic but will lower the amount of carbon dioxide emissions. By 2012 transportation subsidies in California will go almost entirely to projects that comply with the high-density, mixed-use criteria. This linkage of urban planning, transportation spending, and California's goal of reducing its greenhouse gas emissions by 25 percent from 1990 levels by 2020 provides a relational model of how to get Americans out of their cars.

Energy

As in other areas, pragmatic solutions have emerged in this area at local and state levels, while Washington remained either ineffectual or obstructionist. Lacking any substantive national leadership determined to lessen our dependence on foreign oil – because the American oil corporations were profiting handsomely from the status quo and did not want any change in efficiency standards or usage patterns – the portion of our oil we import increased from 40 percent at the time of the Arab Oil Embargo in 1973 to 60 percent in 2008![373] Moreover, almost one-third of the world's oil and gas production and more than one-third of its total oil and gas reserves are now controlled by state-owned energy companies in countries not always favorably disposed toward the United States: Aramco of Saudi Arabia, Gazprom of Russia, CNPC of China, NIOC of Iran, PDVSA of Venezuela, Petrobras of Brazil, and Petronas of Malaysia. These new giant companies dwarf the major Western oil corporations (ExxonMobil, Chevron, BP, and Royal Dutch Shell), which now produce about 10 percent of the world's oil and gas and hold just 3 percent of reserves.[374]

Fortunately, a green-energy future for the United States is finally being taken seriously in high places. This transformation will require economy-wide improvements in energy efficiency along with combinations of diverse renewable sources: solar thermal, solar photovoltaic, hydroelectric, wind, geothermal, and biomass – as well as improved integration of the electrical grid, including "smart grid" improvements. Additionally, plug-in electric cars, geothermal heat pumps to heat and cool houses and other buildings, and numerous other smarter solutions to our energy problems are rapidly moving into mainstream usage.

Unfortunately, the nuclear power industry has attempted to resuscitate itself by claiming to be part of the green energy scenario. In addition to the lethal dangers of nuclear power, demonstrated at Chernobyl and Fukushima Daiichi, it is an endless drain on the U.S. budget, requiring billions in research and development subsidies, tax breaks, and unlimited taxpayer-backed loan guarantees and insurance protection for reactors (all of which were granted, once again, in the federal energy act of 2005, which was orchestrated by the Bush administration). Even without all the federal subsidies, as Amory Lovins has pointed out, nuclear power is seven times less cost-effective at displacing carbon than is the cheapest, fastest alternative: energy efficiency. If the $2 billion that a nuclear power plant typically costs were spent instead to insulate drafty buildings, purchase hybrid cars, or install super-efficient lightbulbs and clothes dryers, it would make unnecessary seven times more carbon consumption than would the nuclear power plant.[375] This seemed unlikely to one particular electrical engineer until he spent a year conducting a full technical review of the nuclear-free *and* coal-free energy scenario for the United States and became a convert, resulting in the book *Carbon-Free and Nuclear-Free.*[376]

President Obama's economic stimulus package (The American Recovery and Reinvestment Act of 2009) allocated billions of dollars for green energy and transportation projects, but even before that infusion, the number of "green jobs" in the United States had been growing nearly 2.5 times as fast as the number of jobs in traditional sectors (between 1998 and 2007). Similarly, a study done in California found that green employment – from research scientists to wind-energy technicians and solar-panel installers – increased by 10 percent between 2005 and 2007.[377] For decades several grassroots groups, including the Green Party, had asserted that investing in the greening of our economy would not only solve numerous problems but would also provide new kinds of green jobs at all socioeconomic levels, as had occurred in Europe, especially Germany and Denmark. In short, the guiding vision was a relational, ecosocial solution. These ideas were also presented in an influential book by Van Jones in 2008, *The Green Collar Economy.*

The green transformation of our economy was pioneered in myriad locations by inventive minds that recognized new, fruitful relationships at hand. For instance, as other production plants have done, an oil refinery in Texas saved $100 million a year in its electricity bills by moving off the grid and recycling its own waste heat through a generator.[378] In Dalton, Georgia, the "Carpet Capital of the World," Shaw Industries constructed an adjacent power plant that will fuel the plant by burning the 16,000 tons of overruns, rejects, and remnants produced every year, as well as the 6,000 tons of sawdust the company produces annually in making wood flooring (creating the same amount of pollution as would natural gas); the $10 million power plant is expected to save the company $2.5 million annually in fuel oil. Competitors are watching these new efforts closely, not wanting to be left behind.[379] Clearly, an entirely new era of exploring the potential relationships between "waste" and "resource" has begun.

Greenhouse Gas Emissions

In spite of minimal progress in cutting the level of carbon dioxide emissions during the Clinton adminstration and then the almost complete blocking by the Bush adminstration of any responsible action on slowing global climate disruption, real progress has been made in recent years at state and local levels to become more responsible about emissions. This could not have occurred unless a very wide range of elected officials and their constituents had come to realize the essential relationship between their immediate actions to cut emissions and the fate of future generations. For instance, on the day that the Kyoto Protocol went into effect for the signatories (but not for the United States) – February 16, 2005 – Seattle's mayor, Greg Nickels, launched the U.S. Conference of Mayors Climate Protection Agreement, a pledge to meet the reduction levels specified in the Kyoto Protocol. By 2011 the mayors of 1049 American cities, representing more than 88 million citizens, had joined the Agreement. Under the leadership of the U.S. Conference of Mayors, the federal Energy Efficiency and Conservation Block Grant (EECBG) Program was conceived, making it possible for the first time in our history for cities, counties, and states to receive federal grants specifically to fund energy-efficiency projects. This program was a high priority of the Mayors' 10-Point Plan and the Mayors' MainStreet Recovery Program. As part of the Obama administration's economic stimulus package (the American Recovery and Reinvestment Act of 2009), $2.8 billion was allotted for the

EECBG program, amounting to block grants for hundreds of American cities. Each of the mayors who has signed the Agreement has worked with his or her municipal government and civic groups to design a plan by which their city will reduce the level of its emissions. The City of Berkeley municipal government, for instance, reduced its greenhouse emissions by 14 percent in two years, beginning in summer 2003, through conservation measures and running municipal vehicles on alternative fuels, primarily vegetable oil (biodiesel) but also electricity, natural gas, and hybrid combinations of electricity and gasoline.

Although the U.S. Environmental Protection Agency under the Bush administration held that regulation of carbon dioxide emissions was not covered by the federal Clean Air Act, several states wanted to be able to apply the same tough standards for auto tailpipe emissions that California had passed in 2002. Those states jointly sued the federal EPA in a case that was ultimately decided, in favor of the states, by the U.S. Supreme Court in 2007.[380] Finally, in April 2010 the federal EPA and the U.S. Department of Transportation, under the Obama administration, issued a greenhouse gas pollution standard for motor vehicles that brought the nation in line with California's 2002 Clean Cars law (also known as the Pavley law for the California Assemblywoman who proposed it). State governments also filled a void of inaction by the federal government when they formed the Climate Registry in 2007 to track greenhouse gas emissions by major industries. California also passed the nation's most sweeping legislation to reduce the state's carbon footprint by 15 percent by 2020.[381]

In an effort, once again, to wake up our country to the urgency of the situation, the atmospheric scientist James Hanson presented data to a meeting of the American Geophysical Union in December 2007 indicating that a level of 350 parts of carbon dioxide per million is the uppermost safe limit our biosphere could stand before the myriad natural systems begin to unravel – and he added that we are now at 385 parts per million in the atmosphere, an amount that continues to rise every year. That figure inspired the writer Bill McKibben and seven young alumni of Middlebury College, shortly after the UN Climate Change Conference in Bali, Indonesia, to mount the 350 Campaign, an energetic global grassroots effort to get that simple number recognized around the world as the threshold of life support, the goal of our common and most urgent imperative.

Still, the situation worsens. When, in September 2008, the figures on levels of carbon dioxide emissions in 2007 were released, scientists were shocked at that the global level had jumped 2.9 percent that year, which was the high end of the estimate made only a year earlier by the U.N. Intergovernmental Panel on Climate Change. In January 2010, NASA announced that the decade ending in 2009 had been the hottest on record. At this point, nearly all atmospheric scientists agree that it is too late to prevent the significant damage and suffering that lies ahead, but it is not too late to act to minimize its intensity. If only the United States, China, and India would emulate the several countries in the European Union that have mounted a multifaceted national effort to lower their emissions since the mid-1990s and, through it all, have enjoyed a robust economy. Those European governments have provided a model for other industrialized nations to follow – if they wish. Clearly, the major challenge of our time is to break through the deadly, entrenched politics of ecocide. The tragic shortcomings of the nonbinding Copenhagen Accord, which was the outcome of the UN Framework Convention on Climate Change in December 2009, however, demonstrated the tenacious grip of the political and economic status quo.

Other Toxins

In recent years, Sandra Steingraber, the scientist who wrote *Living Downstream* in 1997, has noticed three trends in the public consciousness about environmental toxins. First, people seem to be more aware of the relationship between their health and the presence of toxins in their environment. Second, they are particularly aware of toxins in certain consumer products, such as pesticides in strawberries, lead in lipstick and toys, and Bisphenol-A in plastic water bottles. Third, however, there seems to be a general "environmental amnesia" concerning hazardous wastes affecting our soil and water sources, such that very few people in the audiences she addresses today recognize the term "Superfund sites." (These are the 1,305 worst toxic-waste sites in the United States; the Superfund trust, established by Congress in 1980 to clean up these sites, went bankrupt in 2003.) Steingraber recommends that everyone take a look at what comes up when you enter your zipcode in the Toxics Release Inventory, made public by the U.S. Environmental Protection Agency via their website. There are now so many cancer-causing chemicals, reproductive toxicants, and brain-destroying poisons circulating in our surroundings that she predicts that chemical reform will be a cornerstone of an emerging "environmental human rights movement."[382]

In California, Commonweal, a nonprofit research group on health, began a campaign of public awareness about our chemical body burden to support passage of the Healthy Californians Biomonitoring Program Act, which made California the first state to establish a statewide, confidential, voluntary program designed to test for contaminants in people's bodies. The actor Peter Coyote he took part in a biomonitoring program in 2005 to test for one's "chemical body burden" and found that his body contains high levels of mercury, probably because he has eaten lots of certain kinds of fish for decades as part of his health-conscious diet.[383] Saying he was outraged at his test results, he asked, "Who gave anybody the right to poison the commons?" Corporate capitalism buying off lawmakers and hence regulatory agencies? The ideology of modernity (that we live on top of nature)? Modern economic theory (that nature is merely an externality)? The corruption of a government we thought was protecting us? The absence of relational wisdom?

They are jointly responsible not only for polluted oceans but also for the fact that thousands of synthetic chemical compounds generated by American industries are sold in products without testing them for harmful effects on humans because the "business-friendly" federal laws do not require it. At least 51 of those synthetic chemicals have been identified as hormone-disrupters, which cause infertility and fundamental disruption of cellular activity. Most of us have scores of industrial chemicals in our bodies, most commonly DDT, mercury, PBDE flame retardants in fabric, and the chemicals in hard plastic bottles, Gore-Tex, and Teflon. Tired of waiting for effective regulation from the federal government, California passed two laws in 2008 that launched the most comprehensive program of any state to date to regulate chemicals that have been linked to cancer, hormone disruption, and other deadly effects on human health.[384]

Waste

By now most Americans, one hopes, have realized that there is no "away" to which we throw our garbage. Rather, there is a very real relationship between one's own weekly accumulation of trash and the mountains of garbage filling up landfills at a relentless pace day by day, causing an ongoing struggle to find new dumping grounds and try to reduce the amount of the landfill flow. A former garbage commissioner of New York City once observed with resignation, "In the end, the garbage will win."[385] Even the oceans are gagging on our trash: a huge vortex of plastic items that were thrown "away" now swirls in the middle of the

Pacific, covering an area about the size of Texas and slowly killing the sea birds that feed there.

Although municipal pleas for residents to recycle more and amass less garbage have rarely achieved desired levels of cooperation, Upper Arlington, Ohio, a suburb of 30,000 people adjacent to Columbus, hit upon a winning pay-as-you-throw strategy in 1992: the city's sanitation department announced that, instead of paying a quarterly garbage fee, residents must affix to the rim of the lid of every garbage can they set out for pick-up a brightly colored, rectangular sticker that costs $1.45 to purchase from the city government (at least, that was the initial price when this pioneering program began; as of 2011, the charge was $2.90 per sticker, plus an annual fee of $40). Immediately and lastingly, the attention of residents became focused on reducing the amount of garbage they set out each week. Interestingly, even people who you might think would not be concerned about spending an extra $1.45 to put out their usual second can of garbage became determined to spend only one sticker per week (or two stickers in the cases where they had previously put out three cans). They suddenly developed an abiding interest in recycling cans, bottles, and newspapers (bins for recyclable materials require no sticker), and they sometimes left excess packaging on store counters, requesting the store's employee to tell the manufacturer not to over-package the product. In short, the sticker-per-can method effected a massive behavioral reform (in my home town). As the solid waste supervisor, William Holbrook, remarked rather poignantly, "For so long they didn't care. Now every time residents put out a can of trash to be picked up, they know what it costs them."[386] Indeed. So successful is this method that the city reduced its landfill-bound garbage by 35% and increased its recycling by 51%, all within a few months.[387] By the summer of 2008, 25 percent of American households were on some type of pay-as-you-throw system of trash pick-up.[388]

An even more impressive shift is taking place in the treatment of sewage, as ecological technologies are beginning to replace the industrial methods. Perhaps the foremost pioneer in this area is the biologist John Todd, who for over 25 years has designed a range of ecological treatment plants that move sewage and industrial wastewater through various stages of biological action by tiny organisms and plants (often beds of beautiful water-flowers), transforming it into clean, clear water of re-use quality that emerges from the structure. Todd has created, to cite only a few examples, a successful biological sewage-treatment plant for a ski resort, a septic waste tank for a town in Vermont, and wastewater treatment facilities for a factory in England, a food-processing plant in Australia, and a slaughter house in Maryland – as well as a toxic waste site in Tennessee. Employing their model of "eco-machines," Todd and his associates also designed a successful remediation system that ecologically cleaned a smelly, sewage-laden canal in Fughou, a city in southern China, transforming it to a sparkling waterway with a pleasant central walkway that is lined with large, lush plants. They have also designed major environmental clean-up projects in Eastern Europe.[389] Similar ecological treatment systems are now designed by numerous firms, yet governments here and abroad largely continue to rely on the modern "brute force" methods of chlorinating drinking water and dumping strong chemicals into sewage in hopes of killing all deleterious microorganisms before the treated water is released into our waterways.

Water

Throughout the known universe, water is rare. On our blue-green garden planet, only 2.5 percent of all the water is freshwater, and only .5 percent is accessible groundwater or surface water, constituting a finite lifeline for all terrestrial animals and plants. Yet consumption of freshwater has grown sixfold during the past 70 years. As of 2001, 2.1 billion people in 61 countries were receiving less than the internationally accepted "basic daily water requirement" of 13.2 gallons.[390] The shortage is expected to become especially acute in the many "water-stressed" countries whose population may well increase by as much as six fold in the next 30 years.[391] By 2050, the United Nations Development Program predicts, 40 percent of the global population will suffer shortages of water.[392]

Clearly, those societies that protect our essential relationship with water and use it efficiently will have the greatest security for the future. Through a new focus in the "developed" world on water conservation – eliminating water waste and using less water to accomplish the same goals – several American cities have successfully reduced their water use. Seattle has kept water usage constant despite population growth of 30 percent since 1975. Bostonians reduced water usage by 30 percent over the past fifteen years, eliminating the need for a new dam. The Metropolitan Water District of Southern California decreased water usage by 16 percent from 1990 to 2003 despite a 14 percent increase in population. Promoting more efficient household fixtures and appliances, modernizing industrial usage, improving processes in restaurants and hotels, and installing smarter irrigation for landscaping are among the successful techniques.[393] Landscaping methods that retain rainwater in the land on which it falls, rather than allowing it to drain away to the gutter or storm drain as run-off are becoming widely adopted. These include gentle barriers that block the escape of the rainwater, such as a pattern of low mounds (berms) planted over with low-thirst plants, stone-lined recessed swills, and below-surface catchment tanks that slowly filter and allow the rainwater to seep into the groundwater below.

International Trade

Trade among societies has been a part of human experience ever since the settlements of the neolithic era and can be mutually beneficial. Except in the case of an imperial invasion and colonial occupation, it has always been the case that the host society could expect their own laws to be obeyed by any foreign visitors who came to conduct trade. All such trade relationships changed following the renegotiation of the General Agreement on Tariffs and Trade (GATT) between 1988 and 1994, which resulted in the establishment of a new world order of supranational trade laws enforced by the World Trade Organization (WTO). The subsequent claim that economical globalization has finally made the "game" fair by flattening the world into a "level playing field" for all enterprising individuals and countries is a neoliberal smokescreen that obscures the reality of myriad communities worldwide. As the physicist, activist, and development and trade analyst Vandana Shiva has observed, "When you look only at the worldwide web of information technology and refuse to look at the web of life, the food web, the web of communities, the web of local economies and cultures that economic globalization is destroying, it is easy to make the false and fallacious arguments that the world is now flat."[394]

Every city and nation is now vulnerable in similar ways under the new laws of "free trade" – in which the transnational corporations and banks are free to do nearly anything they want, but no one else is. "Quicksilver" investment capital is now free to zip around the world, pulling out of an economy in a flash because national governments are no longer permitted under the WTO to restrict capital flows into or out of their own country. In addition, beginning with the loan requirements imposed by the World Bank and the International Monetary Fund (IMF) prior to the establishment of the WTO, entire nations were forced to sacrifice their traditional economy and shift to large-scale production of export crops, according to the premise of a "rationalized" modern economy: export what you produce and import what you need to consume. Neoliberal economic theory stubbornly ignores the fact that requiring countries to base their income primarily on the export market makes them vulnerable to all sorts of disruptions in distant markets – ecological, political, economic, or simply logistical. Just as the ecosocial analysts predicted prior to the passage of the renegotiated GATT, its version of international trade is colossally unstable and insecure. By 1999 a report at the World Bank, *The Simultaneous Evolution of Growth and Inequality*, concluded, "Globalization appears to increase poverty and inequality.... The costs of adjusting to greater openness are borne exclusively by the poor, regardless of how long the adjustment takes."[395]

Do Americans feel more secure now that 97% of our clothing is made abroad (with nearly half of it made in one country, China)? Do we realize – after the scandal broke in 2008 concerning lead in toys made in China – that much of American brand-name manufacturing, which consumers used to trust for quality control, is now meaningless as a protection because there are no long-term obligations regarding safe materials and processes between American companies and the thousands of outsourcing factories in China? Was it worth it to trade American jobs and stability – of communities, families, and the nation – for somewhat lower consumer prices and huge profits for our transnational corporations? Wasn't the unmentioned element in the corporate-driven changes to the international trade laws the fact that American wages and standard of living would, eventually, have to fall significantly for the whole scheme to work? And how were working families to fare once our manufacturing sector had been moved abroad?

Proposals for redesigning the rules of international trade to arrive at a sustainable, socially just, democratic, and accountable multilateral trading system have been put forth by several organizations such as the Our World Is Not for Sale network, Global Trade Watch, the International Forum on Globalization (IFG), the Institute for Policy Studies, the Citizens Trade Campaign, and the Third World Network. For example, a book by the IFG, *Alternatives to Economic Globalization* (2004) presents ten principles of sustainable societies that are relevant to a relational rethinking of the rules of economic globalization. The editors, Jerry Mander and John Cavanagh, also emphasize the relational principle of subsidiarity (situating as many governmental decisions as possible at the local level), and they present several "alternative operating systems" in such areas as agriculture, transportation, energy, and manufacturing.

Another source of corrective alternatives is Lori Wallach, director of Global Trade Watch, who has proposed that a first step would be to delete from GATT and the WTO's regulations all rules allowing the unregulated sale of services (that is, rules aiding the total privatizing of the service sector in every country) and TRIPs (Trade-Related Aspects of Intellectual Property Rights, which allow corporations to patent medicinal uses of plants, for instance, which are the result of indigenous knowledge); both focus less on "trade" than investment.[396] After protecting locally owned services and the local uses of plants, Wallach would replace what is missing from the WTO and subordinate the remaining economic rules to democratic principles of sustainability and justice. Indeed, that is the fundamental challenge: to design rules for an international trade system that would place issues of economic security for communities and nations at the center.

The issues of international trade are complex, but the key to solving the overarching crises following the economic collapse of late 2008 – food, finance, and climate change – is to realize that they are interrelated. Local food subsistence has been destroyed by trade policies; industrialized, globalized agriculture runs on fossil fuels so has worsened climate disruption; and speculation through futures trading of food commodities has driven up prices. Vandana Shiva, an advocate for localized food sovereignty, observed in 2009,

> The financial crisis, the food crisis, and the climate crisis have the same common roots: an economy based on debt – debt to Nature, the debt of farmers, the debt of citizens. It is an economy ruled by fictions -- the fiction of a corporation as a legal person, the fiction of derivatives and futures and collatoral debt obligations, the fiction that corporations like Monsanto "invent" seed which is their "intellectual property," the fiction that soil fertility comes from fertilizer factories, and the fiction that food as a commodity can nourish and feed people. The solution to all three crises is to live according to the laws of Nature. . . . Biodiverse ecological agriculture provides higher nutrition and food per acre than industrial agriculture. It reduces emissions and mitigates climate change, while helping to adapt to it. And it frees farmers of debt and suicides.

Shiva views these relational solutions as a shift from "fictitious finance to the real wealth of Nature."[397] Moreover, she has noted that any international, or national, food laws should be appropriate to the content of the level they address: "A law for all food systems is a law that privileges large-scale industrial and commercial establishments and discriminates against and criminalizes the small, the local, the diverse."[398] International trade laws concerning food should always be examined, then, for the effect they would have on local food security.

"Development" in the "Third World"

The billions of dollars in development aid that the industrialized countries have sent to nonindustrialized countries since World War II might well seem, on the surface, to be an inherently relational act of caring for and sharing with the less fortunate members of the human family. Those aid programs were designed, however, to serve certain political, economic, and ideological ends that, over time, became so dominant that it hardly seemed to register with the donor nations that the recipient nations were falling further and further into poverty and desperate conditions. The wealthy countries simply kept on using the same approach year after year, in spite of the dismal results. When a major change was imposed by the donor institutions onto the development process – such as the neoliberal Structural Adjustments Program in the mid-1980s or the "liberalized" "free trade" rules enforced after the WTO was established in 1994 – the critical situation in most "Third World" countries became far, far worse. By the late 1990s, the World Bank admitted that up to 60 percent of its development projects overall, including 75 percent in Africa, had failed to meet their objectives. Even after such shocking revelations, the World Bank continued its same general approach to development, with the result that between 2000 and 2005, only 40 percent of the countries receiving loans for World Bank projects actually experienced any annual increase in per capita income. That is, the living conditions of the poor were still not improving in the majority of "developing" countries.[399]

The *modern* model of development follows a particular trajectory. At the bottom of the ladder, in the eyes of the experts trained in the modern worldview, is the (failed) agrarian economy, written off as being premodern. Next come micro-loan programs for village women, which are viewed as merely the first step of a modern make-over for the country. Then comes the movement of village women to towns or cities for jobs in sweatshop factories. Then comes the move by their children to a job in a corporate customer-service call center or a high-tech factory. Finally, the entire country, but for the hapless rural poor, is projected to achieve full modernity with a high-consumption, unsustainable, industrialized life-style.

The assumption of the universal appeal of the modern, industrialized, consumerist model is where millions of people in the "Third World" part company with the Western experts on "development."[400] While it is true that American popular culture – which has now become the globalized monoculture – looks glamorous and tantalizingly modern to young people worldwide, many of the mature adults throughout the "developing world" look at the crises facing the industrialized, modern West today and wonder why their culture should mimic such a course. They ask, *"Do we want an economic system in which one-fifth of the national income goes to the richest one per cent of the society, like the United States? Do we want our air and waterways to be poisoned with toxic emissions in a 'pro-business regulatory climate'? Do we want the youth culture of modernity to undermine our traditional respect for elders? Do we want to focus on only the most modern part of our country, the cities, while abandoning the rural communities as backward? Do we really want to regard nature as a 'mere externality' in economic growth? Must the transnational corporations own so much in our country, with no requirements for joint ownership? Would our culture and spirituality survive in a modern, Westernized consumer society? It does not appear to us that nearly unregulated economic growth is 'value-free' at all, since it devalues and destroys all that cannot be measured and sold, which is often precious to us."*

The major shift that has occurred during the past 25 years throughout the "Third World" (post-colonial countries) and the Fourth World (indigenous peoples' nations, also called the First Nations) is the assertion that each of their cultures has a paradigm, or worldview, which has authenticity and dignity that is equal to that of the paradigm of modernity. That is, they are completely "developed" and not at all "under-developed" in religion, wise relationships to nature, cosmological embeddedness, coherent expressions of culture, patterns of socializing their young, family ties, and much more. As such, they need neither to reject everything about modernity nor to surrender their entire way of life to it.

In order to develop options for their societies other than surrendering to the *laissez-faire* assault of neoliberal economics, a counterforce has arisen at the grassroots level that is sometimes called the Global Civil Society movement, or the Global Justice movement, attracting thousands of people to the annual World Social Forum (generally held in January, when the largely neoliberal World Economic Forum meets in Davos, Switzerland). Regional Social Forums are also held on nearly every continent. At those gatherings and elsewhere throughout the "developing world," there is growing interest in various working models of community-based economics, regenerating and protecting the agrarian communities, building up regional trade in the South, and tailoring a market economy to the needs and desires of each culture. For instance, if a "developing" capitalist society wants to spread wealth as broadly as possible (to avoid undemocratic, extreme concentrations), why not require that a percentage of annual profits in businesses over a certain size be shared in the form of a bonus for all employees, not only management? To spread ownership to include productive workers, why not give a tax break to co-operatives and collectively owned businesses? Why not insist that a percentage of any foreign business in one's country must be owned by local investors (as was the law in many "developing" countries before the WTO)? A graduated system of income tax (in which the rich pay their fair share), and substantial public investment in K-16 schools (that honor traditional wisdom as well as modern knowledge) and health clinics (that include traditional herbal and other efficacious treatments) would make sense, as well as subsidies for fuel-cell shuttle buses and light-rail transit (to avoid a glut of cars).

The sad truth is that most of the community-based measures for a more relational, ecosocial, or Green, economy tailored to the needs and desires of each country are now illegal under the neoliberal ideology enforced by the WTO and various foreign aid policies. Even before the WTO was created, the community-based, culture-protecting, nature-protecting options for economic development were kept off the table by Western development experts and modernized elites in the "Third World" alike as quaint but irrelevant nonmodern ideas. The disallowing of highly effective alternatives to the dominant industrial model of economic development – plus the corporate sector's relentless selling of the neoliberal model as "a rising tide to lift all boats" – positioned their version as the only one. Consequently, in countless conversations with liberal friends over the years I've been asked, after I have critiqued the *modern* model of development, why I'm "against development and helping the Third World poor." At those moments I have realized, once again, how skillfully the corporate lobbyists, publicists, talking heads on television, and opinion piece writers have framed the public's thinking about development: *You're either on the bus or you're not. Either factory jobs for the Third World or starvation, either export plantations or struggling small farms, either call centers or collapse. Get with the modern program. What's not to understand?*

Actually, scores of thousands of officials at various governmental levels throughout the "Third World" understand extremely well what sort of development projects have really helped poor communities and families and what sort have caused destructive effects – even if the current situation does not allow them to act on this knowledge. For decades as the large-scale, anti-community, anti-nature, "official development" modernizing projects were built and failed to achieve their purposes, grassroots aid organizations like Oxfam, the Global Fund for Women, and scores of religious groups focused on co-creating with communities throughout the "Third World" thousands of small-scale, community-based projects that usually were usually successful and made positive, lasting impacts on people's lives. In 2008 Women to Women International, for instance, launched a Commercial Integrative Farming Initiative in Rwanda that will train 3,000 women to raise crops that can both be sold for profit in their local market and used to feed their families. Another successful example is the community-controlled forestry policy in Mexico, where more than half of the forests are under village tenure. As one participant noted, "With community forestry, we see it is possible to conserve our resources but at the same time be productive and competitive and to start rebuilding our local economy."[401]

Throughout the "developing" countries, it has been found that tangible benefits to society accrue quickly when self-help development projects put money into the hands of women. Numerous studies have found that women spend their money on their children's schooling and well-being and on their homes and communities, in contrast to men's widespread pattern of spending income on alcohol and prostitutes. For this reason, the Nobel Laureate Muhammad Yunus, for instance, designed his highly successful and influential Grameen Bank to grant micro-loans solely to women. (In some cases, as women become successful in a very small business through a series of micro-loans, their husbands begin to work in the business and help it thrive.)

Another key to success is the honoring of cultural and spiritual values. Wangari Maathai, for example, combined all of these elements when she founded the Green Belt Movement in Kenya, which empowered rural women to plant millions of trees to restore their environment, earn a small amount of money (which made a great deal of difference in their lives), and begin to think through the questions of how the environment had become so degraded (apportioning responsibility between both the government and the people), which in turn led to an "outbreak of democracy" that became part of a people's nonviolent revolt and, in this case, the electoral removal of their country's dictator.[402] Reflecting on this experience, Maathai has observed, "A new attitude toward nature provides a space for a new attitude toward culture and the role it plays in sustainable development."

The successful examples of relational, community-based economics anywhere are now of interest everywhere because every town and city needs to figure out how to create real security that is not attached to the "global roulette wheel" of economic globalization. Yet there are far deeper lessons to be drawn from the supposedly "under-developed" South, as many Americans have discovered when they have visited a "Third World" country, either as individuals or in a small group, and lived for a while among families, especially in a rural area, staying long enough to experience the sense of life, the joyful engagement, the implicit embeddedness. Often an American recently returned from such a stay recounts wistfully, "The families I knew had so little, yet they were so happy" – as he or she struggles with the impulse to get on a plane and "go back there." It is common for the returnee to undergo a shock of reentry to our frenetic consumer culture. A sense of privation sets in because that which the traveler had experienced in the "developing" country is not to be found here, or is drowned out, or pulled apart such that the returnee perceives a barrenness in many quarters.

We in the fast-paced, hypermodern societies do not have all the answers. We can barely form the questions anymore. It seems self-evident, at least, that productive activity should reflect the larger and deeper relational values of a culture. "The economy" in isolation is a false concept. "The economy" ruling all else is madness.

VI

STEPPING UP

Reassessing the "Field Dependence" of Women

We have now considered scores of examples of the discoveries and successful developments that together constitute the emergent Relational Shift. Yet the question remains of whether modern cultures, so accustomed to perceiving and thinking with mechanistic assumptions, can really change their deeply entrenched mental habits. Clearly, we need to cultivate an appreciation of relational, contextual thought wherever we see it. I wonder, though, whether modern societies will be able to shed old prejudices so as to take advantage of a vast pool of talent and experience with relational ways of thinking.

Through the lens of the mechanistic worldview, people, problems, and situations were considered without much attention to their context of (causal) interrelationships. For centuries our modern institutions rewarded and advanced individuals who saw the world with crisp, clear logic floating confidently above any contextual messiness. This educated perspective was nearly always associated with men, who were felt to possess a natural propensity for context-free reasoning and a seemingly inherent grasp of the "fact" that life is composed of isolate, separative entities. As a well-known scientific experiment demonstrated, that gender association may well be true. But is perception through a lens of separative, isolate thought that is oblivious to relational context really a mark of superiority?

Since the 1950s, people who tend to ignore contexts – either because they are unable to perceive them easily or because they have been educated to consider them inconsequential – have been labeled by psychologists as "field-independent." This is a positive, approving term connoting a person capable of strongly independent, objective perception and thought. The term was coined in 1954 by Herman Witkin and his associates in the course of conducting what became a highly influential experiment to investigate visual perception. He asked subjects to focus on a rod and then to manipulate the frame in which it was embedded until the rod looked vertical. Those who focused strongly on the rod and viewed the frame as instrumental but otherwise unimportant were labeled "field-independent" thinkers. Witkin also devised an embedded figures test. Those who perceived the figures and their surroundings – or the rod and frame – as integrated were assigned the less admirable label "field-dependent." The gender correlation with either the "field-independent" or "field-dependent" response was quite strong. This experiment has been replicated over the years, with the usual findings being that women are more "field-dependent" than are men and that children are more "field-dependent" than are adults.

I think of Witkin and other psychologists whose work subsequently derived from these two experiments concluded that women, who were found to be lacking since they are "field-dependent," have a "susceptibility to external influences." The ability to perceive and think contextually was considered by all the psychologists involved to be nothing more than the rather pathetic display of a weak and inferior mind. Within a decade of Witkin's experiment, psychologists extrapolated from his findings that women's cognitive style is "conforming," "child-like," and "global," being – as Witkin himself added in 1962 – similar to the (supposedly) undifferentiated thought processes found in "primitive" cultures. He added that women's field-dependence renders them unable to maintain a "sense of separate identity," unlike the field-independent males, whose cognitive style was seen as "analytical" and "self-reliant."[403]

I think of Witkin's experiments, especially the researchers' conceptual interpretation of the data, as one of the nadirs of modernity's bizarre, self-imposed exile from even recognizing the contextual, relational nature of the Real – that is, our physicality and its interrelatedness with our surroundings on Earth and in the universe. Those esteemed psychologists actually categorized the half of humanity who tend to correctly perceive that reality is inherently relational as being slightly sub-standard humans who muddle along with an immature and inadequate cognitive style! The social scientists' supposedly "value-free" deductions got the situation exactly backwards – and, of course, they became highly regarded in their profession for this work. In addition, their biased interpretations became widely accepted in many academic fields. After all, their extrapolations in the 1950s and early 1960s reflected with precision the prejudices of a patriarchal culture – and even "proved" those prejudices to be utterly scientific.

Do we still live there? Perhaps – but as the discoveries presented in this book about the relational nature of reality become better known, surely the following corollary will become self-evident: being able to perceive situations and developments with an awareness informed by relational sensibilities is a highly valuable skill. Neither sex has a lock on that skill, but it does not take an experimental psychologist to notice – as myriad teachers, parents, and just about everyone else could testify – that females tend to perceive existence as being deeply relational. That is why it has long seemed to many of us that the modern, mechanistic (and patriarchal) world is oddly skewed and rests on a fixed infrastructure of mistaken assumptions that are at odds with the wisdom of the natural world and the real needs of human beings. *Who thought this up?*, we wondered as girls. Speaking only for myself, it has felt at times like being a "stranger in a strange land" to step out the door of my home into the public world of modernity, with its extreme artificiality built on anti-relational concepts mistaken for sophisticated cultural responses to the "obvious" truth of being. This is why the historic emergence of the Relational Shift has a personal dimension for me and why I have been delighted to watch it gain momentum within so many mainstream areas: it is potentially a long-awaited deliverance for our society and ourselves, a chance to bring human systems of thinking in sync, at last, with the relational, dynamic nature of the Earth Community.

But let me state again that I do not feel that "relational intelligence," as Nina Simons, co-founder of the Bioneers conferences, has aptly termed it,[404] is the provenance of women alone. Sex differences are a matter of statistical averages, not absolutes. Besides, men involved in ecological study or ecological activism, to name only one large field, are commonly known to perceive various subjects with a relational analysis. Whether they were drawn to ecology because of that tendency or became increasingly skilled at relational analysis through immersing themselves in ecological thought is not clear. No doubt everyone can cultivate relational, contextual intelligence, which was once widespread in earlier cultures.

It was one of the challenges of early modernity to replace relational ways of seeing and being wherever it was deeply embedded: in agrarian "peasant" societies; in indigenous peoples' cultures; in the person of traditional spiritual leaders; and in perhaps the longest attempted conversion of all, the informal society of women. All those stubborn cases had to be assimilated over time into modern mechanistic thinking ... or suffer the consequences. (I believe that the suffering involved with being forced into a thoroughly unnatural system of thinking and being, by the way, is related to the sharp increase in rates of depression among women since World War I, noted in chapter 3. Through war or peace, through economic boom or bust, many women during the 20th century tended to feel increasingly "out of sorts" and depressed as the high-speed, anti-relational aspects of modernity colonized more and more of daily life.) Yet many relational thinkers were able to opt for strategic external conformity without surrendering their inner awareness of the relational nature of the Real. We are still here … and relationally so.

As this is a pragmatic book, it is fitting to include what I hope is the utterly obvious pragmatic application of Witkin's findings (though not his patriarchal labels and extrapolations) and the similar findings in hundreds of other experiments examining holistic, or gestalt, modes of perception. To wit, any civic committee, workplace group, board of directors, legislative body, or international negotiation that seriously seeks to achieve a lasting, contextually wise (that is, relationally informed) outcome would do well to make certain that at least one-half of their members are female. Quite simply, society badly needs the relational perceptions and cognitive skills of women in positions of leadership. We cannot bring into being the full implications of the new discoveries of relational reality if we as a society insist on clinging to and replicating the old ways of thinking.

By stiff-arming relational perception and thought, "tough-minded" modernity has, in fact, moved us further from our source. The implicit ideal in Western patriarchal culture of the competitive Autonomous Individual who elbows his way to power and control as a birthright has distorted many of the interpretations of evolutionary studies in recent decades regarding how we became human. Scientists agree that we effected our transition out of the primate community by developing a more extreme sociality (our comparatively "hypertrophied social intelligence") and a greater capacity for cooperative behavior. The dominant explanation for that development, however, is that we evolved in that way in order to better compete against other humans. In 2009, Sarah Blaffer Hrdy, a primatologist and sociobiologist, challenged that reigning assumption. She makes the case in *Mothers and Others: The Evolutionary Origins of Understanding* that human babies are so dependent on their elders for such a long period that our fledgling species would never have made it unless human mothers had left behind the primate model of childcare. That is, mother chimpanzees and gorillas hold tight to their infants for the first six months of life and never trust others to hold them; although they accept food from the fathers, they largely tend and raise the infant on their own. Human mothers, in contrast, evolved as "cooperative breeders," assisted by as-if mothers (or "allomothers"), individuals of either sex who help to care for and feed the young. Very early on, then, human mothers developed a willingness to share, to trust in others, and to relax one's guard in a joint endeavor.

Hrdy theorizes that our capacity to cooperate in groups, to empathize with others, and to wonder what they are thinking probably arose in response to being in a cooperatively breeding social group. In that situation, we developed the need to trust and to be trustworthy and reliable in return. She rejects the idea that the origins of our "hypersociality" can be found in warfare or that in-group amity arose in the interest of out-group enmity. Human population was sparse for a very long while, Hrdy points out, with the major focus being not war but staying alive and raising the next generation.[405] Our development of language, I would add, more likely occurred in these "cooperatively breeding social groups" and among the gatherers of roots and fruits than among the bands of silent hunters. Passing a baby around in such groups evoked responses from the adults and created social bonds. Additionally, our species' development of abstract thought, which constituted a grand leap away from the primate community, may well have begun when the human females realized that their bodily pattern of menses was related to something outside of themselves and quite apart from them: the cycles of the moon.[406] For many reasons, we are what we are because of foundational relationships. In fact, that realization sheds light on the current debate in our culture over what causes religion to manifest itself so ubiquitously.

An Example of Applying the Relational Perspective: The Debate over the Origins of Religion

Why does every human culture, past and present, have some sort of religion or spiritual orientation? A perception of the sacred seems to be a constant. Surrounding that perception, a complex of elaborated modes of engagement with the sacred evolve, which are usually regarded as holding the deepest meaning and collective identity of the nation, tribe, or group. It seems remarkable that such a constant would cut across the extreme variation among human social structures worldwide. There are many cross-cultural biological constants, of course, but religion is rather mysterious for being a cultural constant. Or is there a biological constant behind it?

In recent years several scientists and science journalists have written books that purport to reveal the mechanisms that cause religion to emerge in human societies. In general, these explanations fall into two categories. The first blends cognitive science and evolutionary psychology, an example of which is *Religion Explained: The Evolutionary Origins of Religious Thought* by Pascal Boyer, an anthropologist and a psychologist. He notes that natural selection has resulted in the predispositions in the human brain to perceive, feel, think, and act in distinctive ways that have shaped our mental functioning. Humans have "hypertrophied social intelligence" and are very good at spotting, for instance, the "purposeful activity of other creatures," which and whom he calls "agents." Because of our propensity for social cognition, he reasons, we tend to see dynamics in the world largely in terms of agency and volitional behavior. Religion, Boyer posits, is a case of a "false positive": our cognitive tendencies to identify agency, even where there is none, thereby misleading us to identify supernatural agents that do not really exist. Consequently, he concludes, the recurrent properties of religious concepts and norms in different cultures are "parasitic" upon standard cognitive systems that evolved outside of religion, such as agency-detection, moral intuition, coalitional psychology (the study of adaptive collective action), and contagion-avoidance. Religious concepts and norms can be explained, in his view, as a mistaken by-product of standard cognitive architecture.[407]

Another reductionist attempt to explain away religion with cognitive science is the book *How Religion Works: Towards a New Cognitive Science of Religion* by Ilkka Pyysiainen. He refutes anthropological and sociological explanations that have been put forward to account for the presence of religion because he feels that such approaches are ignorant of the psychological processes involved in religious belief, experience, and practice. Religion derives not from cultural or social forces, Pyysiainen asserts, but from our cognitive structures shaped by our evolutionary history. In essence, he posits that we tend to have strong emotional responses to "counterintuitive representations" such as the notion of a god, and he attributes mystical experiences to "abnormalities" that can occur in the neural "circuitry" of our brains. He sees religious experiences as merely emotional and having no adaptive value, as our brains evolved to solve practical problems related for the most part to survival and reproduction. Religious ideas arise "merely because they are possible" and have no substantial grounding outside of our cognitive tendencies.[408] There are dozens more such "exposés" based on extrapolations in cognitive psychology from recent studies in neuro-imaging.

The second category of science-based theories that seek to explain religion focuses on evolutionary pressures on human development. Arriving at the opposite conclusion from Pyysiainen's assertion that religion is not adaptive and served no practical purpose during our evolution, Nicholas Wade posits in *The Faith Instinct: How Religion Evolved and Why It Endures* that religion has "all the hallmarks of an evolved behavior, meaning it was favored by natural selection." He cites the example of the sequential archaeological discoveries by Joyce Marcus and Kent Flannery in the Oaxaca Valley of Mexico: "The archaeological record begins with a simple dance floor, the arena for the communal religious dances held by hunter-gatherers in about 7,000 B.C. It moves to the ancestor-cult shrines that appeared after the beginning of corn-based agriculture around 1,500 B.C., and ends in A.D. 30 with the sophisticated, astronomically oriented temples of an early archaic state." Wade, a science writer for the *New York Times*, asserts that religious behavior was "hard-wired" into our neural "circuitry" before the ancestral human population dispersed from its African homeland because religion conferred essential benefits, primarily by binding humans into cooperative groups. He concludes that religion is an evolved instinct that aided survival by furthering social cohesion in groups that thrived.[409]

In a similar vein, Robert Wright, also a science writer, posits in *The Evolution of God* that evolutionary dynamics explain the emergence and history of religion. Specifically, he presents what he calls a materialist account of religion by focusing on the adaptive strategies adopted by religions to changing conditions in the world such as economics, politics, and war. In addition to evolutionary theory, Wright employs a concept from game theory known as "non-zero-sum interactions," by which he means mutually enhancing relationships. He notes that various religions responded to cross-cultural contacts by becoming more tolerant of other religions when that tolerance aided economic or political interactions. In this way, the "moral circle" expanded beyond one's clan to ethnic groups, to nations, and eventually to the entire human race. Wright's theory of the origins of religion is limited by his focus on the interpretative assumptions of one scholar, Mircea Eliade, and his peers about the nature of "primitive religions." For example, Wright asserts that when shamans emerged, they were primarily concerned with the prosecution of war and intratribal politics. When society became more complex and social harmony became important, he notes, religion became concerned with enforcing morality.

This led to the evolution of "moral imagination," the ability to put oneself in another's shoes and act with empathy.

I would like to place onto the discussion table a possible explanation for the existence of religion that is sorely lacking in the contemporary debate – even though it should be obvious to evolutionary thinkers. The primary impetus for the emergence of religion, it seems to me, lies in the relational nature of our existence. From the birth of the universe emerged helium, hydrogen, stars, and all the elementary particles of the cosmos that would later form the Milky Way galaxy and our home planet – all the mountains, trees, rivers, and seas, as well as our own bodies. Everything in our life experience, then, is kin. Everything is not only inherently related but is held in the gravitational embrace of the cosmological unfolding. All the material forms that evolved through the eons and enabled our being here came into existence through the arising and maintaining of relationships. Our solar system began when a relationship formed between a cloud of hydrogen gas and some interstellar dust containing heavy-element particles. The mixture grew hot and then compressed under its own gravity. At its center a new star began to form, which became our sun, surrounded by a white-hot disk of the same material, which gave rise to the Earth and its kindred planets, all orbiting in relationship. The Earth ended up being exactly the right distance from the sun and being just the right size such that the water that eventually formed on our planet is neither entirely frozen nor vaporized. This relationship made possible the evolution of life on Earth.

Our roots lie in the birth of the universe but most particularly in the emergence of organic compounds and cells on Earth. Clearly, an entirely new flowering of consequential relationships then became possible, though the dynamic by which organic cells first appeared is, as yet, the subject of several theories.[410] Once the simple, single-celled prokaryotic bacteria formed, some of them cozied up to others by moving into them. From this novel two-in-one symbiosis evolved a new type of complex cell with organelles, genetic material, and a nucleus: the eukaryotic cells. Through countless new relationships that followed, all the fungi, plants, and animals then evolved. At some point, for reasons that scientists do not really understand, our proto-human ancestors in Africa were led from primate existence to become a new species when the proto-human female body began to bleed in rhythm with the cycles of the moon. Eventually the female body sloughed off the primate pattern of estrus entirely. We emerged through novelty and continuity, as do all life forms, but our species' unique origin lies in a bodily relationship with the moon.

After we evolved slowly into our humanness, our bodymind retained inherent interrelatedness with the cosmological dynamics in which we live. Eventually, people noticed that the changing seasons affect our moods, our metabolism, our need for sleep, and our sex drive. The amount of light we experience each day influences our resistance to disease, the degrees of hunger we feel, our sleep patterns, and moods. The phases of the moon influence our behavior, sleep patterns, and libido in both sexes. We also found that music – the descendent of the "surround sound" of primate languages, bird calls, insect hums, roaring waterfalls, high winds, rolling thunder, and rustling breezes amid which we evolved – affects us deeply. The truth of our being is that we emerged and exist now in an unimaginable array of relationships with the grand forces and subtle processes of the Earth and the cosmological whole.

Yet the destiny of each human is to go through life with a physical appearance unlike anyone else's, with a bodymind composition that does not exactly match anyone else's, with unique variations in the possible human relationships, and with life experience that is a singular accumulation. Whether one is born into a culture that emphasizes intensive togetherness and comprehensive group bonding or a culture that emphasizes a highly individualized way of life with "every man for himself," there is no escaping the fact that our particular life experiences, including formative impressions made by very early occurrences that we do not remember, render each of us into a unique ontological category with only one member.

Our mental functions, then, are occupied in every moment with our own unique life experiences, whether those are group-oriented or not – yet every cell in our bodymind is composed of relationships, emerged from relationships, and shares a plethora of ongoing relationships with the patterns and invisible processes of life on Earth and with the gravitational embrace, non-local causality, and kinship of all universe life. When our early ancestors chanted together, made rituals together, and danced in a circle around the fire, they experienced a bodily replication of the relational nature of their very being. When they perceived the abundant cycles of nature's bounty and the cosmological drama of the passage of the moon and the changing seasons as constituting some sort of grand whole surrounding them, some sort of Great Mysterious, their feelings of profound relatedness were in sync with the relational, nature of reality. When they saw that their own birth, maturation, and death were patterns common to all life forms in the pulsing whole of the Earth Community, they ritualized those passages as inherent events of the larger reality – which they are.

The various human cultures evolved numerous ways to respond to the deeply relational dynamics that surge through the heavens, the weather, the seasons, and their lives. All the specific cultural ways that were developed in order to relate to the Great Mysterious, or the totality that exceeds human grasp, were merely variations of the basic engagement between themselves and the relational nature of the whole, the larger reality. Whether the cultural perception took the form of a god or a goddess, or the Great Holy, or the Taoist sense of "The Way," or the Buddhist sense of the extraordinarily complex causal relationships lacing the universe that they call *karma*, or an animal or animated power seen to be the originator of the whole cosmos, the common ground was always the kindred, interrelated nature of everything. This is why singing and chanting have such a central role in many religions – and why it feels good to us to sing hymns in church, for instance. This is also why it feels good to sing or dance in any group and why secular participatory concerts or events or movements that resemble religious practices in communal ways are experienced as transporting one beyond the separative ego of the individual.

Religion, in short, manifests itself in every human culture because it counterbalances the fact that our conscious mind is shaped and occupied by our individual inheritance and experiences. Religious practices enable deep communion with the biological, ecological, cosmological nature of our inherently relational selves and surroundings. They provide a way to "touch base" with the larger reality, to feel immersed in it and one with it – as, indeed, we truly are. For this reason, religious practices tend to make people feel "whole," "complete," and expansively content. They are a living reminder of and experiential pathway to ultimate reality and ultimate value: our bodily dynamic interrelatedness with every plant, animal, landform, and star – the numinous dimension we rightly call the sacred.

I do not disagree with the evolutionary theorists who point out the many ways that religious practices have evolved culturally in partnership, whether harmonious or oppositional, with the emergence of economic, political, and social circumstances – and certainly humans in many cultures have demonstrated a narcissistic tendency to personify the forces of the Great Mysterious as looking like themselves – but such analyses are subsets of the larger reason religion emerged in the first place. It is most certainly not because some erroneous cognitive functioning or brain structure causes us to falsely perceive a deeply interrelated dimension of our reality. Rather, religion is the cultural result of the human mind's apprehending and responding to the depth and immensity of interrelatedness that constitutes reality and its evolutionary unfolding since the beginning. Consequently, the deeply evolutionary and material perspective I present here corrects Stephen J. Gould's assertion that science and religion are "nonoverlapping magisteria": in fact, evolutionary science reveals the inherent interrelatedness of all life, which yields the relational impulse resulting in religion. The two fields are, or should be, kissin' cousins. Moreover, it is not accurate to claim, as do the "social evolution" theorists of religion, that the notion of God today has obviously progressed because it has become more abstract than in "primitive" times. In fact, many premodern, or nonmodern, cultures and nonWestern cultures had and have a complex, abstract sense of the Great Mysterious, often along side personifications of various powers within it.

Finally, the field of cognitive science is not uniformly on the side of interpreting religious behavior as an error of our brains. Several researchers in that field have conducted imaging and other studies that have found that transcendent experience can be identified in the brain and measured. One response of the brain when a person goes into a deeply transcendent, unitive experience is that the parietal lobe, which orients us in space, decreases its activity as a stronger perception takes over. (Of course, there are numerous accounts of people in many cultures having such experiences unexpectedly, without cultivating them through any meditation, prayer, or other spiritual practices. I have written elsewhere about those experiences as moments of cosmological revelation.[411]) One indicator that the findings of several postmechanistic cognitive scientists investigating religious experiences, such as Andrew Newberg and Mario Beauregard, are making their way into public awareness was an opinion piece in the *New York Times* in 2008 by the journalist David Brooks, in which he wrote, "The mind seems to have the ability to transcend itself and merge with a larger presence that feels more real." He summarized the findings of several neuroscientists as follows:

> First, the self is not a fixed entity but a dynamic process of relationships. Second, underneath the patina of different religions, people around the world have common moral intuitions. Third, people are equipped to experience the sacred, to have moments of elevated experience when they transcend boundaries and overflow with love. Fourth, God can best be conceived as the nature one experiences at those moments, the unknowable total of all there is.[412]

This sort of flow of postmechanistic, relational thought from academic discovery into common awareness is part of the Relational Shift. As we have seen, however, the vast implications of the shift are far more significant than academic debates. Living in such unstable times, we are acutely aware that we do not know what lies ahead. We apparently are living through not one but several massive transitions simultaneously. Most of the worrisome problems we face are a result of denying the relationships inherent in various situations – including, above all, denying for far too long the relationship between producing excessive levels of greenhouse gases and experiencing global climate disruption. The cumulative effects of all those supposedly "rational" denials of interrelatedness are coalescing into an extremely worrisome future.

The Relational Calling

I have no doubt that countless more examples of the Relational Shift will continue to appear as the momentum continues to build. It is my hope that readers of this book will now be able to identify these disparate events and discoveries as part of a larger coherence. More than recognizing examples of the shift, though, what is desperately needed by the Earth Community is that we moderns learn how to perceive, to think, and to live in more relational ways. Many people have an inkling that reality is far more interrelated than our modern socialization lets on, but this tacit knowledge does not seem to have a place in the modern, mechanistic ways of the world. Every day – in our homes, at our jobs, in our community involvement – we design, or help to design, creative responses to problems that arise, tasks that must be completed, and goals that lie ahead. In the modern, mechanistic orientation, the best response to such challenges was thought to be solutions informed by crystalline rationality that was inherently objective, context-free, and value-free – deployed, of course, by an imagined self who is fundamentally separate from everyone and everything else. Since that anti-relational projection is a bad fit with the relational reality of the universe in which we actually live, however, it makes a lot more sense to consider a problem or a situation by using a context-rich, context-sensitive, dynamically relational approach.

If we are to take a fresh look at what has gone wrong, to think through relationally effective alternatives, and to take the necessary actions, the involvement of everyone is needed across all our institutions and our communities. What is required, according to the French sociologist

Edgar Morin, is "thorough thinking," a way of thinking that can grasp "both text and context, individual and environment, local and global, the multidimensional – in a word, the complex: the conditions of human behavior."[413] A more "thoroughly" relational perspective will help us to link the various issues and problems so that we can grasp the causes more accurately. Similarly, any proposed solutions must be examined for their relational effects – which always show up later but are too often ignored by policymakers. Then, too, attention to the relational qualities of the new must be matched with attention to restoration and to healing the damage that has been done by institutions and systems of knowledge that lack any relational wisdom.

"Thorough thinking" that is not linear but seeks to apprehend the gestalt would also help us resculpt our habitual mental habits regarding our responses to life's events. That is, the way we deliberate about moral choices and act responsibly has traditionally focused in Western socialization on the capability of an individual to deliberate independently, choose morally, and initiate action (while quite possibly remaining nearly oblivious to the realities of other persons involved). An alternative, however, is proposed by several relational thinkers in a collection of essays titled *Relational Responsibility: Resources for Sustainable Dialogue*, edited by Sheila McNamee and Kenneth J. Gergen. They explore the benefits of shifting our notion of responsibility from a focus on the individual to a focus on the *relational process* involved. As we have seen, the notion of the Autonomous Individual is central to Western legal theory and ethical codes, but in practice such an individualistic framing of responsibility can leave a person feeling isolated and alienated. To move out of such patterns and cultivate awareness of interrelatedness, the authors of these essays have found that cultivating skills of dialogue creates bridges and new meaning in a situation.[414] For those seeking a relational approach to the challenge of changing an entire system, the Center for Ecoliteracy's "Seven Lessons for Leaders in Systems Change" is a good place to start.[415]

Alas, we in the West hardly have the necessary vocabulary in our Indo-European languages to shift our thoughts and utterances to a more deeply relational orientation. In response, the Vietnamese monk and peace activist Thich Nhat Hanh has suggested that we think of existence as a matter of *interbeing*. We interare. They interare. Everyone interis. He is speaking of our inherent, organic interconnection, of course, not the electronic version. Our bodymind needs real connection with the embodied presence of other people and with nature. Electronic immersion throughout our waking hours gives us a circumscribed version of that connection, enough to make the experience somewhat addictive, yet it is a poor substitute. To declare that we intertype (on a keyboard or pad) is not at all the same as fully realizing – in an embodied, embedded, whole-organism mode of knowing – that we interare, that the very nature of our existence is interbeing.

The more widespread the Relational Shift becomes, the more deeply its profound correction will awaken us, engage us, and heal us. We humans, after all, have a biological tendency to nurture and cherish our relationships with other persons, other groups, other cultures, with our animal companions and all species, and with the exquisite delicacy and forceful rushings of the natural world. It is through communion with nature that we attain our full humanity. Yet so thorough is our socialization in the "post-nature" values of modernity that most of us do not even realize the damage suffered by our bodyminds when our relationship to the rest of the natural world is largely severed and replaced by a human-made environment.

Only in recent years have social scientists begun to examine the effects on our behavior that result from a multifaceted relationship with nature. A series of four studies conducted in 2009 at the University of Rochester, for instance, found that immersion in nature (even sitting in a room with several plants or simply viewing slides of nature photography) causes people to be more caring, to value interpersonal relationships and community more strongly, and to be more generous than before the (slight) immersion in nature. Viewing slides of entirely human-made environments, however, had the opposite effect on expressions of human character: after that slide show, participants rated the attainment of money, fame, or an image of power as having far greater value than interpersonal relationships or generosity. The researchers found that "living in modern, non-nature environments may have a powerful isolating and/or self-alienating effect on people." Conversely, they concluded, "full contact with nature can have humanizing effects, fostering greater authenticity and connectedness."[416]

Communion with nature, then, yields even greater benefits than the more widely documented restorative effects on our health: nature evokes in us the expression of our core potential as relational beings. It enables us to be our true, caring, generous, and expansive selves. It seems to free us of the psychological restrictions – self-absorption, disengagement, and diminished empathy – commonly imposed by modern, industrialized cultures, which are proudly devoted to progressing in opposition to nature. Yet more than half of all the people alive today know nothing but an urbanized existence of nature-deprivation. Since the modern city has largely considered itself to be beyond nature, almost no thought of enabling human communion with the natural world was built into the design of most buildings and most urban environments. Yet that situation is changing now, as the field of city planning has realized the benefits of having pocket parks, green corridors, and bike paths.

By evoking our full humanity in all fields of endeavor, the Relational Shift – which is truly a Relational Renewal – brings us into a deeper realization of our inherent relationship with the sacred whole, the entire creative presence, the divine mystery of it all. This deepening can be cultivated through religious practice – or through contemplative quiet time apart from the clatter and hype. What do we find there? With each of us a node in the living web that stretches to infinity, what is emerging at this moment of historic upheaval? At this time, on this planet, during the shattering of an old but destructive stability and the shaping of our best hopes for the new, what is required of each of us? What is the significance of a life when life itself is on the line? The old ideal of the Absolutely Autonomous Individual denied the relational reality of our selves and the world. The new – and very ancient – perception of the self in dynamic, relational context is far more healthy, creative, and responsible. This is the liberation the Earth Community has been waiting for us to achieve.

For All Our Relations

About the Author

Charlene Spretnak was born in Pittsburgh and raised in Columbus, Ohio. She is the author of several books on ecological and relational thought, cultural history, spirituality, feminism, and contemporary events. These include *Green Politics: The Global Promise* (principle coauthor); *The Spiritual Dimension of Green Politics*; *States of Grace: The Recovery of Meaning in the Postmodern Age*; *Missing Mary*; and *The Resurgence of the Real: Body, Nature, and Place in a Hypermodern World*. In 2006 she was named by the Environment Department of the British government one of the "100 Eco-Heroes of All Time." She resides in Ojai, California, with her husband. For further information about her books, see www.CharleneSpretnak.com.

Acknowledgements

Two people in particular prodded and encouraged me to write this book, a work that sounded simple enough at the outset but grew into a very large research project spanning several years as the subject continued to unfold in many fields simultaneously. I'm grateful to both for their initial nudge and their ongoing support as dear Green friends.

The first is Andrew Kimbrell, founding director of the Center for Food Safety and of the International Center for Technology Assessment, both in Washington, DC.

The second is Kelly McMenimen, a former student of mine who is passionately committed with the questing energy of the next generation to a Green future.

The Green Institute provided a generous research grant that made the initial phase of this work possible.

The California Institute of Integral Studies provided a stipend for a research assistant in the early stage of the work.

I thank my graduate students over the years at the California Institute of Integral Studies on whom I tried out new observations and reflections on the Relational Shift.

I also thank Zoe Murdock, Lissa Merkel, Daniel Moses, and David Moses for an abundance of assistance and encouragement in the final stages.

I am pleased that *Relational Reality* is a Green Horizon Book, published in association with the Green Horizon Foundation, because a relational analysis and vision have long been at the heart of Green thought and activism. Thanks there especially to John Rensenbrink.

Bibliography

Chapter 1: Relational Revelations

Brooks, David. *The Social Animal: The Hidden Sources of Love, Character, and Achievement.* New York: Random House, 2011.

Christakis, Nicholas A. and James H. Fowler. *Connected: The Surprising Power of Our Social Networks and How They Shape Our Lives.* Boston: Little, Brown, 2009.

Gergen, Kenneth J. *Relational Being: Beyond Self and Community.* New York: Oxford University Press, 2009.

Gladwell, Malcolm. *The Tipping Point: How Little Things Can Make a Big Difference.* Boston: Little, Brown, 2000.

_____. *Outliers: The Story of Success.* Boston: Little, Brown, 2008.

Rifkin, Jeremy. *The Empathic Civilization: The Race to Global Consciousness in a World in Crisis.* New York: Tarcher, 2009.

Chapter 2: The Relational Shift in Education and Parenting

Astin, Alexander W., Helen S. Astin, and Jennifer A. Lindholm. *Cultivating the Spirit: How College Can Enhance Students' Inner Lives.* San Francisco: Jossey-Bass, 2010.

Bowers, C. A. *Educating for Ecological Intelligence.* Portland, OR: Ecojustice Press, 2009 (available via free download from www.cabowers.net).

_____. *Perspectives on the Ideas of Gregory Bateson, Ecological Intelligence, and Educational Reforms.* Eugene, OR: Eco-Justice Press, 2011.

Capra, Fritjof. *The Hidden Connections: A Science for Sustainable Living.* New York: Anchor Books, 2004.

_____. *The Science of Leonardo: Inside the Mind of the Great Genius of the Renaissance.* New York: Doubleday, 2007.

Ferrer, Jorge N. and Jacob H. Sherman, editors. *The Participatory Turn: Spirituality, Mysticism, and Religious Studies.* Albany, NY: State University of New York Press, 2008.

Gergen, Kenneth J. *Relational Being: Beyond Self and Community.* New York: Oxford University Press, 2009.

Harding, Stephan. *Animate Earth: Science, Intuition, and Gaia.* White River Junction, VT: Chelsea Green, 1998.

Henderson, Nan, Editor, with Nancy Benard and Nancy Sharp-Light. *Resiliency in Action: Practical Ideas for Overcoming Risks and Building Strengths in*

Youth, Families, and Communities, Second Edition. Ojai, CA: Resiliency in Action, 2007.

Jordan, Judith V. *Relational-Cultural Therapy*. Washington, DC: American Psychological Association, 2009.

Liebreich, Karen, Jutta Wagner, and Annette Wendland. *The Family Kitchen Garden: How to Plant, Grow, and Cook Together*. Portland, OR: Timber Press, 2009.

Louv, Richard. *Last Child in the Woods: Saving Our Children from Nature-Deficit Disorder*. Chapel Hill, NC: Algonquin Books, 2004.

Margulis, Lynn. *Symbiotic Planet: A New Look At Evolution*. New York: Basic Books, 1999.

Mathews, Freya. *For Love of Matter: A Contemporary Panpsychism*. Albany, NY: SUNY Press, 2003.

Montessori, Maria. *To Educate the Human Potential*. Oxford, England: Clio Press, 1989.

Morin, Edgar. *Seven Complex Lessons in Education for the Future*. Paris: UNESCO, 1999.

Neufeld, Gordon and Gabor Maté. *Hold On to Your Kids: Why Parents Need to Matter More than Peers*. New York: Ballantine Books, 2005.

Newberg, Andrew. *Why We Believe What We Believe: Uncovering Our Biological Need for Meaning, Spirituality, and Truth*. New York: Free Press, 2006.

Orr, David W. *Earth in Mind: On Education, Environment, and the Human Prospect*. Washington, DC: Island Press, 2004.

O'Sullivan, Edmund. *Transformative Learning: Educational Vision for the 21st Century*. London: Zed Books, 1999.

O'Sullivan, Edmund, Amish Morrell, and Mary Ann O'Connor, Editors. *Expanding the Boundaries of Transformative Learning: Essays on Theory and Praxis*. New York: Palgrave Macmillan, 2002.

O'Sullivan, Edmund and Marilyn M. Taylor, Editors. *Learning Toward an Ecological Consciousness: Selected Transformative Practices*. New York: Palgrave Macmillan, 2004.

Phillips, Anne. *Holistic Education: Learning from Schumacher College*. Totnes, England: Green Books, 2008.

Robb, Christina. *This Changes Everything: The Relational Revolution in Psychology*. New York: Farrar, Straus and Giroux, 2006.

Seamon, David and Arthur Zajonc, editors. *Goethe's Way of Science: A Phenomenology of Nature*. Albany, NY: State University of New York Press, 1998.

Senge, Peter M., Nelda H. Cambron McCabe, Timothy Lucas, Art Kleiner, Janis Dutton, and Bryan Smith. *Schools That Learn: A Fifth Discipline Fieldbook for Educators, Parents, and Everyone Who Cares About Education*. New York: Broadway Business, 2000.

Shepherd, Linda Jean. *Lifting the Veil: The Feminine Face of Science*. Boston: Shambhala, 1993.

Siegel, Daniel J. *The Developing Mind: How Relationships and the Brain Interact to Shape Who We Are*. New York: Guilford Press, 1999.

Sobel, David. *Place-Based Education: Connecting Classrooms with Communities*, Nature Series #4. Great Barrington, MA: The Orion Society, 2004.

Stone, Michael and the Center for Ecoliteracy. *Smart by Nature: Schooling for Sustainability*. Healdsburg and Berkeley, CA: Watershed Media / University of California Press, 2009.

Stone, Michael and Zenobia Barlow, Editors. *Ecological Literacy: Educating Our Children for a Sustainable World*. San Francisco, CA: Sierra Club Books, 2005.

Swimme, Brian Thomas and Mary Evelyn Tucker. *Journey of the Universe*. New Haven: Yale University Press, 2011.

Taylor, Betsy and the Center for a New American Dream. *What Kids Really Want that Money Can't Buy: Tips for Parenting in a Commercial World*. New York: Grand Central Publishing, 2003.

Vitek, Bill and Wes Jackson, Editors. *The Virtues of Ignorance: Complexity, Sustainability, and the Limits of Knowledge*. Lexington, KY: University of Kentucky Press, 2008.

Whitehead, Alfred North. *Science and the Modern World*. New York: Free Press, 1967 (1925).

_____. *The Aims of Education*. New York: Free Press, 1970 (1929).

_____. *Process and Reality*. New York: Free Press, 1978 (1929).

_____. *The Function of Reason*. Boston, MA: Beacon Press, 1958 (1929).

_____. *Adventures in Ideas*. New York: Free Press, 1933.

Chapter 3: The Relational Shift in Health and Healthcare

Abram, David. *Becoming Animal: An Earthly Cosmology*. New York: Pantheon Books, 2010.

Baron-Cohen, Simon. *Zero Degrees of Empathy: A New Theory of Human Cruelty*. London: Allen Lane, 2011.

Buzzell, Linda and Craig Chalquist. *Ecotherapy: Healing with Nature in Mind*. San Francisco and Berkeley, CA: Sierra Club Books / Counterpoint, 2009.

Denby, David. *Snark*. New York: Simon & Schuster, 2009.

Doidge, Norman. *The Brain That Changes Itself: Stories of Personal Triumph from the Frontiers of Brain Science*. New York: Penguin Books, 2007.

Dossey, Larry M.D. *Healing Words: The Power of Prayer and the Practice of Medicine*. San Francisco, CA: HarperOne, 1997.

_____. *Reinventing Medicine: Beyond Mind-Body to a New Era of Healing*. San Francisco, CA: HarperOne, 2000.

Diamond, Jed. *The Irritable Male Syndrome: Managing the Four Key Causes of Depression and Aggression*. Emmaus, PA: Rodale Books, 2004.

Englander, Joan. *Joy in the Evening of Our Lives: Nurturing the Elderly Soul, A Practical Guide and Inspirational Journey*. Ojai, CA: Healing River Press, 2008.

Gavigan, Christopher. *Healthy Child, Healthy World: Creating a Cleaner, Greener, Safer Home*. New York: Dutton Adult, 2008.

Gibson, John W. and Judy Pigott. *Personal Safety Nets: Getting Ready for Life's Incalculable Changes and Challenges*. Seattle, WA: Safety Nets Unlimited, 2007.

Greenspan, Stanley I. and Serena Wieder. *Engaging Autism: Helping Children Relate, Communicate, and Think with the DIR Floortime Approach*. Cambridge, MA: Da Capo Lifelong Books, 2006.

The Health Benefits of Volunteering: A Review of Recent Research. Washington, DC: Corporation for National and Community Service, 2007.

Honoré, Carl. *In Praise of Slowness: How a Worldwide Movement Is Changing the Cult of Speed*. San Francisco, CA: HarperOne, 2005.

Jackson, Maggie. *Distracted: The Erosion of Attention and the Coming Dark Age*. Amherst, NY: Prometheus Books, 2008.

A Light in the Mist: The Journal of Hope. (www.healingenvironments.org/light)

Louv, Richard. *Last Child in the Woods: Saving Our Children from Nature-Deficit Disorder*. Chapel Hill, NC: Algonquin Books, 2005.

McCally, Michael, Editor. *Life Support: The Environment and Human Health* Cambridge, MA: MIT Press, 2002.

McKibben, Bill. *Enough: Staying Human in an Engineered Age*. New York: Times Books, 2003.

Plotkin, Bill. *Soulcraft: Crossing into the Mysteries of Nature and Psyche*. Novato, CA: New World Library, 2003.

_____. *Nature and the Human Soul: Cultivating Wholeness and Community in a Fragmented World*. Novato, CA: New World Library, 2008.

Pollan, Michael. *Food Rules: An Eater's Guide*. New York: Penguin, 2009.

Post, Stephen G., Editor. *Altruism and Health: Perspectives from Empirical Research*. New York: Oxford University Press, 2007.

Robinson, Ricki G. *Autism Solutions: How to Create a Healthy and Meaningful Life for Your Child*. Don Mills, Ontario, Canada: Harlequin, 2011.

Roszak, Theodore. *The Voice of the Earth: An Exploration of Ecopsychology*. Grand Rapids, MI: Phanes Press, 2001.

Roszak, Theodore, Mary E. Gomes, and Allen D. Kanner, Eds. *Ecopsychology: Restoring the Earth, Healing the Mind*. San Francisco: Sierra Club Books, 1995.

Schlitz, Marilyn and Tina Amorok, with Marc S. Micozzi. *Conscious Healing:*

Integral Approaches to Mind-Body Medicine. Marilyn Heights, MO: Elsevier Science, 2004.

Turkle, Sherry. *Alone Together: Why We Expect More from Technology and Less from Each Other.* New York: Basic Books, 2011.

White, Jerry. *I Will Not Be Broken: 5 Steps to Overcoming a Life Crisis.* New York: St. Martins Press, 2008.

Yeager, Selene and the Editors of *Prevention* Magazine. *The Doctors Book of Food Remedies.* Emmaus, PA: Rodale Books, 2007.

Chapter 4: The Relational Shift in Community Design and Architecture

Alexander, Christopher. *The Nature of Order – Book One: The Phenomenon of Life*; Book Two: *The Process of Creating Life*; Book Three: *A Vision of a Living World*; Book Four: *The Luminous Ground.* Berkeley, CA: Center for Environmental Structure, 2002-2004.

Architecture for Humanity (Kate Stohr and Cameron Sinclair, Editors). *Design Like You Give a Damn: Architectural Responses to Humanitarian Crises.* New York: Metropolis Books, 2006.

Chen, Karen. Rethinking Community Preparedness: A Relational Approach to Self-Reliance. San Francisco: California Institute of Integral Studies Doctoral Dissertation, 2011.

The City Repair Project's Placemaking Guidebook, Second Edition. Portland, OR: The City Repair Project, 2006.

Davis, Sam. *Designing for the Homeless: Architecture that Works.* Berkeley, CA: University of California Press, 2004.

Dean, Angela. *Green by Design: Creating a Home for Sustainable Living.* Layton, UT: Gibbs Smith, 2003.

Durrett, Charles. *The Senior Cohousing Handbook: A Community Approach to Independent Living*, 2nd Edition. Gabriola Island, BC, Canada: New Society Publishers, 2009.

E / The Environmental Magazine (www.emagazine.com)

Environmental and Architectural Phenomenology Newsletter (www.arch.ksu.edu/seamon/EAP)

Flores, Heather Coburn. *Food Not Lawns: How to Turn Your Yard into a Garden and Your Neighborhood into a Community.* White River Junction, VT: Chelsea Green, 2006.

Frank, Lawrence D., Peter O. Engelke, and Thomas Schmid. *Health and Community Design: The Impact Of The Built Environment On Physical Activity.* Washington, DC: Island Press, 2003.

Hallsmith, Gwendolyn. *The Key to Sustainable Cities: Meeting Human Needs, Transforming Community Systems.* Gabriola Island, BC, Canada: New Society Publishers, 2003.

Hayden, Dolores. *Redesigning the American Dream: Gender, Housing, and Family*

Life, Second Edition. New York: W. W. Norton, 2002.

Hemenway, Toby. *Gaia's Garden: A Guide to Home-Scale Permaculture*, Second Edition. White River Junction, VT, 2009.

Jencks, Charles. *The Universe in the Landscape: Landforms by Charles Jencks.* London: Francis Lincoln, 2011.

Johnson, Catherine J., Susan McDiarmid, and Edward R. Turner. *Welcoming Wildlife to the Garden: Creating Backyard and Balcony Habitats for Wildlife.* Vancouver, BC, Canada: Hartley & Marks, 2004.

Kellert, Stephen R., *Building for Life: Designing and Understanding the Human-Nature Connection.* Washington, DC: Island Presss, 2005.

Kennedy, Joseph F., Editor. *Building without Borders: Sustainable Construction for the Global Village.* Gabriola Island, BC, Canada: New Society Publishers, 2004.

Lawlor, Anthony. *A Home for the Soul: A Guide for Dwelling wtih Spirit and Imagination.* New York: Clarkson Potter / Crown Publishing, 1997.

Mazmanian, David A. and Michael E. Kraft, Editors. *Toward Sustainable Communities: Transition and Transformations in Environmental Policy*, Second Edition. Cambridge, MA: MIT Press, 2009.

McHarg, Ian. *Design with Nature.* New York: John Wiley & Sons, 1992.

Mendler, Sandra F., William Odell, and Mary Ann Lazarus. *The HOK Guidebook to Sustainable Design*, Second Edition. New York: Wiley, 2005.

Neal, Peter, Editor. *Urban Villages and the Making of Communities.* London and New York: Taylor & Francis, 2003.

Newman, Peter and Isabella Jennings. *Cities as Sustainable Ecosystems: Principles and Practices.* Washington, DC: Island Press, 2008.

Orr, David W. *The Nature of Design: Ecology, Culture, and Human Intention.* New York: Oxford University Press, 2004.

Papanek, Victor. *The Green Imperative: Ecology and Ethics in Design and Architecture.* London: Thames & Hudson, 1995.

Pearson, David. *New Organic Architecture: The Breaking Wave.* Berkeley, CA: University of California, 2001.

Roberts, Jennifer. *Good Green Homes: Creating Better Homes for a Healthier Planet.* Layton, UT: Gibbs Smith, 2003.

Scotthanson, Kelly and Chris Scotthanson. *The Cohousing Handbook: Building a Place for Community.* Gabriola Island, BC, Canada: New Society Publishers, 2004.

Starhawk (Miriam Simos). *The Earth Path: Grounding Your Spirit in the Rhythms of Nature.* San Francisco: HarperOne, 2004.

Stoner, Tom and Carolyn Rapp. *Open Spaces Sacred Places: Stories of How Nature Heals and Unifies.* Annapolis, MD: TKF Foundation, 2008.

Taylor, Nancy H. *Go Green: How to Build an Earth-Friendly Community.* Layton, UT: Gibbs Smith, 2008.

Todd, Nancy Jack. *A Safe and Sustainable World: The Promise Of Ecological Design.* Washington, DC: Island Press, 2004.

Todd, Nancy Jack and John Todd. *From Eco-Cities to Living Machines: Principles of Ecological Design.* Berkeley, CA: North Atlantic Books, 1994.

Van der Ryn, Sim and Stuart Cowan. *Ecological Design,* Tenth Anniversary Edition. Washington, DC: Island Press, 2007.

Walljasper, Jay. *All That We Share: How to Save the Economy, the Environment, the Internet, Democracy, Our Communities and Everything Else that Belongs to All of Us.* New York: The New Press, 2010.

Walljasper, Jay and the Project for Public Spaces. *The Great Neighborhood Book: A Do-It-Yourself Guide to Placemaking.* Gabriola Island, BC, Canada: New Society Publishers, 2007.

Wann, Dave and Dan Chiras. *Superbia! 31 Ways to Create Sustainable Neighborhoods.*

Wilhide, Elizabeth. *Eco: An Essential Sourcebook for Environmentally Friendly Design and Decoration.* London: Quadrille Publishing Ltd., 2001.

Wines, James. *Green Architecture.* Cologne, Germany: Taschen, 2000.

Yudelson, Jerry. *Green Building A to Z: Understanding the Language of Green Building* Gabriola Island, BC, Canada: New Society Publishers, 2007.

Chapter 5: The Relational Shift in the Economy

Andrews, Geoff. *The Slow Food Story: Politics and Pleasure.* Montreal: McGill-Queen's University Press, 2008.

Ausubel, Kenny with J. P. Harpgnies, Editors. *Nature's Operating Instructions: The True Biotechnologies.* San Francisco: Sierra Club Books, 2004.

Bendrick, Lou. *Eat Where You Live: How to Find and Enjoy Fantastic Local and Sustainable Food No Matter Where You Live.* Hastings, England: Skipstone Press, 2008.

Benyus, Janine M. *Bimimicry: Innovation Inspired by Nature.* New York: William Morrow, 1997.

Berry, Wendell. *Bringing It to the Table: On Farming and Food.* Berkeley, CA: Counterpoint Press, 2009.

Broad, Robin and John Cavanagh. *Redevelopment Redefined: How the Market Met Its Match.* Boulder, CO: Paradigm Publishers, 2008.

Brown, Peter G. and Geoffrey Garver. *Right Relationship: Building a Whole Earth Economy.* San Francisco: Berrett-Koehler, 2009.

Cavanagh, John and Jerry Mander, Editors. *Alternatives to Economic Globalization: A Better World Is Possible,* Second Edition. San Francisco, CA: Berrett-Koehler, 2004.

Center for Food Safety and Institute for Responsible Technology. *Non-GMO Shopping Guide.* Washington, DC: Center for Food Safety and Institute for

Responsible Technology, 2008.

Conroy, Michael E. *Branded!: How the "Certification Revolution" Is Transforming Global Corporations.* Cambridge, MA: South End Press, 2007.

Cullinan, Cormac. *Wild Law :Protecting Biological and Cultural Diversity.* Totnes, England: Green Books, 2003.

Cummings, Clare Hope. *Uncertain Peril: Genetic Engineering and the Future of Seeds.* Boston: Beacon Press, 2008.

Danaher, Kevin, Shannon Biggs, and Jason Mark. *Building the Green Economy: Success Stories from the Grassroots.* Sausalito, CA: PoliPoint Press, 2007.

The Ecologist Magazine (www.theecologist.org)

Edwards, Andres R. and David W Orr. *The Sustainability Revolution: Portrait of a Paradigm Shift.* Gabiola Island, B.C., Canada: New Society Publishers, 2005.

Eisler, Riane. *The Power of Partnership: Seven Relationships That Will Change Your Life.* Novato, CA: New World Library, 2002.

Falk, Richard. *Predatory Globalization: A Critique.* London: Polity Press, 1999.

Fowler, Charles W. *Systemic Management: Sustainable Human Interactions with Ecosystems and the Biosphere.* New York: Oxford University Press, 2009.

GEO: Grassroots Economics Organizing Newsletter (www.geonewsletter.org)

Halweil, Brian. *Eat Here: Reclaiming Homegrown Pleasures in a Global Supermarket.* New York: Worldwatch Institute / W. W. Norton, 2004.

Hawken, Paul. *The Sustainability Revolution: Portrait of a Paradigm Shift.* New York: Viking Penguin, 2007.

_____. *The Ecology of Commerce* by Paul Hawken (1993 ?)

Hawken, Paul, Amory Lovins, and L. Hunter Lovins. *Natural Capitalism: Creating the Next Industrial Revolution.* Boston: Little, Brown, 1999.

Henderson, Hazel. *Beyond Globalization: Shaping a Sustainable Global Economy.* Sterling, VA: Kumarian Press, 1999.

Henderson, Hazel with Simran Sethi. *Ethical Markets: Growing the Green Economy.* White River Junction, VT: Chelsea Green, 2006.

Henderson, Hazel, Jon Lickerman, and Patrice Flynn, Editors. *Calvert-Henderson Quality of Life Indicators.* Bethesda, MD: Calvert Group, 2000.

Hill, Steven. *Europe's Promise: Why the European Way Is the Best Hope in an Insecure Age.* Berkeley: University of California Press, 2010.

_____. *10 Steps to Repair American Democracy.* Sausalito, CA: Polipoint Press, 2006.

Hopkins, Rob and Richard Heinberg. *The Transition Handbook.* White River Junction, VT: Chelsea Green, 2008.

House, Freeman. *Totem Salmon : Life Lessons from Another Species.* Boston: Beacon Press, 1999.

Howard, Patricia L., Editor. *Women and Plants: Gender Relations in Biodiversity Management and Conservation.* London: Zed Books, 2003.

Hunt, Constance Elizabeth. *Thirsty Planet: Strategies for Sustainable Water Management* London: Zed Books, 2004.

Jackson, Wes. *Consulting the Genius of the Place: An Ecological Approach to a New Agriculture.* Berkeley, CA: Counterpoint, 2010.

Jones, Van. *The Green Collar Economy: How One Solution Can Fix Our Two Biggest Problems.* San Francisco: HarperOne, 2008.

Kent, Deirdre. *Healthy Money, Healthy Planet: Developing Sustainability through New Money Systems.* Nelson, New Zealand: Craig Potton, 2005.

Kimbrell, Andrew. *Your Right to Know: Genetic Engineering and the Secret Changes in Your Food.* San Rafael, CA: Earth Aware Editions, 2007.

Kimbrell, Andew, Editor. *Fatal Harvest: The Tragedy Of Industrial Agriculture.* San Francisco: Foundation for Deep Ecology, 2002.

Kinsey, Michael J. *Economic Renewal Guide: A Collaborative Process for Sustainable Community Development, Third Edition.* Snowmass, CO: Rocky Mountain Institute, 1997.

Korten, David C. *Agenda for a New Economy: From Phantom Wealth to Real Wealth.* San Francisco: Berrett-Koehler, 2009.

_____. *The Great Turning: From Empire to Earth Community.* San Francisco: Berrett-Koehler, 2006.

Lappé, Anna. *Diet for a Hot Planet: The Climate Crisis at the End of Your Fork and What You Can Do About It.* New York: Bloomsbury USA, 2010.

Lappé, Anna and Bryant Terry. *Grub: Ideas for an Urban Organic Kitchen.* New York: Tarcher/Penguin, 2006.

Lappé, Frances Moore and Anna Lappé. *Hope's Edge: The Next Diet for a Small Planet.* New York: Tarcher/Putnam, 2003.

Lovins, Amory and E. Kyle Datta. *Winning the Oil Endgame.* Snowmass, CO: Rocky Mountain Institute, 2005.

Mander, Jerry and Victoria Tauli-Corpuz, Editors. *Paradigm War: Indigenous Peoples' Resistance to Economic Globalization.* San Francisco: Sierra Club Books, 2006.

McDonough, William and Michael Braungart. *Cradle to Cradle: Remaking the Way We Make Things.* New York: North Point Press, 2002.

McKibben, Bill. *Eaarth: Making a Life on a Tough New Planet.* New York: Times Books, 2010.

_____. *Deep Economy: The Wealth of Communities and the Durable Future.* New York: Holt, 2007.

_____. *Fight Global Warming Now: The Handbook for Taking Action in Your Community.* New York: Times Books / Holt, 2007.

_____. *Wandering Home: A Long Walk Across America's Most Hopeful Landscape: Vermont's Champlain Valley and New York's Adirondacks* New York: Crown, 2005.

_____. *Hope, Human and Wild: True Stories of Living Lightly on the Earth.*

Boston: Little, Brown, 1995.

Murphy, Pat. *Plan C: Community Survival Strategies for Peak Oil and Climate Change*. Gabriola Island, B.C., Canada: New Society Publishers, 2008.

Norberg-Hodge, Helena, Todd Merrifield, and Steven Gorelik. *Bringing the Food Economy Home: Local Alternatives to Global Agribusiness*. London: Zed Books, 2002.

Petrini, Carlo. *Slow Food Nation: Why Our Food Should Be Good, Clean, And Fair*. New York: Rizzoli Ex Libris, 2007.

Petrini, Carlo in conversation with Gigi Padovani. *Slow Food Revolution: A New Culture or Eating and Living*. New York: Rizzoli, 2006.

Porritt, Jonathon. *Capitalism as If the World Matters*, Updated Edition. London: Earthscan Publications, 2007.

Ransom, David and Vanessa Baird, Editors. *People-First Economics: Making a Clean Start for Jobs, Justice and Climate*. Oxford, England: New Internationalist / World Changing, 2009.

Read, Donna and Starhawk. *The Growing Edge: Beyond Sustainability to Regeneration*. DVD. San Francisco: Belli Productions, 2010.

Rushkoff, Douglas. *Life Inc.: How the World Became a Corporation and How to Take It Back*. New York: Random House, 2009.

Sachs, Wolfgang, Editor. *The Development Dictionary: A Guide to Knowledge as Power*, Second Edition. London: Zed Books, 2010.

Schor, Juliet. *Plenitude: The New Economics of True Wealth*. New York: PenguinPress, 2010.

Senge, Peter M. *The Fifth Discipline: The Art & Practice of the Learning Organization*, Updated Edition. New York: Doubleday, 2006.

Senge, Peter M., Charlotte Roberts, Richard B. Ross, Bryan J. Smith, and Art Kleiner. *The Fifth Discipline Fieldbook: Strategies and Tools for Building a Learning Organization*. New York: Broadway Business, 1994.

Shirk, Martha and Anna S. Wadi. *Kitchen Table Entrepreneurs: How Eleven Women Escaped Poverty and Become Their Own Bosses*. New York: Basic Books, 2002.

Shiva, Vandana. *Soil Not Oil: Environmental Justice in an Age of Climate Crisis*. Cambridge, MA: South End Press, 2008.

_____. *Earth Democracy: Justice, Sustainability, and Peace*. Cambridge, MA: South End Press, 2005.

_____. *Water Wars: Privatization, Pollution, and Profit*. Cambridge, MA: South End Press, 2002.

Shiva, Vandana, Editor. *Manifestos on the Future of Food and Seed*. Cambridge, MA: South End Press, 2007.

Shuman, Michael H. *Going Local: Creating Self-Reliant Communities in a Global Age*. New York: Free Press, 1998.

_____. *The Small-Mart Revolution: How Local Businesses Are Beating the Global Competition.* San Francisco: Berrett-Koehler, 2006. *Solutions* Journal (www.thesolutionsjournal.com)

Soros, George. *The New Paradigm for Financial Markets: The Credit Crisis of 2008 and What It Means.* Washington, DC: Public Affairs, 2008.

Speth, James Gustave. *The Bridge to the Edge of the World: Capitalism, the Environment, and Crossing from Crises to Sustainability.* New Haven, CT: Yale University Press, 2009.

Spratt, Stephen, Andrew Simms, Eva Neitzert, and Josh Ryan-Collins. *The Great Transition: A Tale of How It Turned Out Right.* London: New Economics Foundation, 2009.

Stoyke, Godo. *The Carbon Buster's Home Energy Handbook: Slowing Climate Change and Saving Money.* Gabriola Island, B.C., Canada: New Society Publishers, 2006.

Vitek, William and Wes Jackson, Editors. *Rooted in the Land: Essays on Community and Place.* New Haven, CT: Yale University Press, 1996.

Whitefield, Patrick. *Permaculture in a Nutshell,* Second Edition. Totnes, England: Green Books, 1993.

Wilkinson, Richard and Kate Pickett. *The Spirit Level: Why Greater Equality Makes Societies Stronger.* New York: Bloomsbury Press, 2009.

Wirzba, Norman, Editor. *The Essential Agrarian Reader: The Future of Culture, Community, and the Land.* Lexington, KY: University of Kentucky Press, 2003.

Yunus, Mohammad. *A World without Poverty: Social Business and the Future of Capitalism.* Washington, DC: Public Affairs, 2008.

Chapter 6: Stepping Up

Atlee, Tom. *The Tao of Democracy: Using Co-Intelligence to Create a World that Works for All,* Revised Edition. Cranston, R.I.: Writers' Collective, 2003.

Beauregard, Mario and Denyse O'Leary. *The Spiritual Brain: A Neuroscientist's Case for the Existence of the Soul.* San Francisco: HarperOne, 2007.

Berry, Thomas. *The Sacred Universe: Earth, Spirituality, and Religion in the Twenty-first Century.* Edited by Mary Evelyn Tucker. New York: Columbia University Press, 2009.

Center for Ecozoic Studies, *The Ecozoic Reader* (quarterly) and *CES Musings* (monthly), Chapel Hill, NC: Center for Ecozoic Studies (www.ecozoicstudies.org).

Ehrenreich, Barbara. *Dancing in the Streets: A History of Collective Joy.* New York: Metropolitan Books, 2007.

Hart, William. *The Art of Living: Vipassana Meditation as Taught by S. N. Goenka.* San Francisco: HarperOne, 1987.

Kaza, Stephanie. *Mindfully Green: A Personal and Spiritual Guide to Whole Earth*

Thinking. Boston: Shambhala Publications, 2005.

Lappé, Frances Moore. *Liberation Ecology: Reframing Six Disempowering Messages that Keep Us from Aligning with Nature – Even Our Own*. Cambridge, MA: Small Planet Media, 2010.

_____. *Getting a Grip: Clarity, Creativity and Courage in a World Gone Mad*. Cambridge, MA: Small Planet Media, 2007.

Lappé, Frances Moore and Jeffrey Perkins. *You Have the Power: Choosing Courage in a Culture of Fear*. New York: Tarcher/Penguin, 2004.

Macy, Joanna and Molly Young Brown. *Coming Back to Life: Practices to Reconnect Our Lives, Our World*. Gabriola Island, BC: New Society Publishers, 1998.

Marshall, Judi, Gill Coleman, and Peter Reason. *Leadership for Sustainability: An Action Research Approach*. Sheffield, UK: Greenleaf Publishing, 2011.

McNamee, Sheila and Kenneth J. Gergen, editors. *Relational Responsibility: Resources for Sustainable Dialogue*. Thousand Oaks, CA: Sage Publications, 1998.

Meadows, Donella. *Thinking in Systems: A Primer*. White River, VT: Chelsea Green, 2008.

Nagler, Michael N. *The Search for a Nonviolent Future: A Promise of Peace for Ourselves, Our Families, and Our World*. Novato, CA: New World Library, 2004.

Simons, Nina, editor. *Moonrise: The Power of Women Leading from the Heart*. Rochester, VT: Park Street Press, 2010.

Spring, Cindy and Anthony Manousos, editors. *Earthlight: Spiritual Wisdom for an Ecological Age*. Torrance, CA: Friends Bulletin, 2007.

Tucker, Mary Evelyn. *Worldly Wonder: Religions Enter Their Ecological Phase*. Peru, IL: Open Court, 2003.

Wheatley, Margaret J. *Leadership and the New Science: Discovering Order in a Chaotic World*, Second Edition. San Francisco: Berrett-Koehler, 1999.

_____. *Finding Our Way: Leadership for an Uncertain Time*. San Francisco: Berrett-Koehler, 2005, 2007.

General

Bateson, Gregory. *Steps to an Ecology of Mind*. Chicago: University of Chicago Press, 2000 (1972).

_____. *Sacred Unity: Further Steps to an Ecology of Mind*. Edited by Rodney E. Donaldson. San Francisco: HarperOne, 1991.

Berry, Thomas. *The Dream of the Earth*. San Francisco: Sierra Club Books, 1988.

_____. *The Sacred Universe: Earth, Spirituality, and Religion in the Twenty-first Century*, edited by Mary Evelyn Tucker. New York: Columbia University Press, 2009.

Berry, Thomas and Brian Swimme. *The Universe Story: From the Primordial*

Flaring Forth to the Ecozoic Era -- A Celebration of the Unfolding of the Cosmos. San Francisco: HarperSanFrancisco, 1992.

Capra, Fritjof and Luigi Luisi. *The Systems View of Life: A Unifying Vision.* Forthcoming from Cambridge University Press.

Chen, Karen. *Rethinking Community Preparedness: A Relational Approach to Self-Reliance.* Doctoral dissertation. San Francisco: California Institute of Integral Studies, 2011.

Corning, Peter. *The Fair Society: The Science of Human Nature and the Pursuit of Social Justice* (Chicago: University of Chicago Press, 2011).

Green Horizon Magazine (www.green-horizon.org)

LaConte, Ellen. *Life Rules: Why So Much Is Going Wrong Everywhere at Once and How Life Teaches Us to Fix It.* Topsham, ME: Green Horizon Books, 2010.

Lerner, Michael. *Spirit Matters.* Charlottesville, VA: Hampton Roads, 2000.

McConnell, Carolyn and Sarah Ruth van Gelder, Editors. *Making Peace: Healing a Violent World.* Bainbridge Island, WA: Positive Futures Network, 2003.

Orion Magazine (www.orionline.org)

Realistic Living Newsletter (www.realisticliving.org)

Resurgence Magazine (resurgence.gn.apc.org)

Schor, Juliet and Betsy Taylor. *Sustainable Planet: Solutions for the Twenty-first Century.* Boston: Beacon Press, 2002.

Sharp, Gene. *Waging Nonviolent Struggle: 20st-Century Practice and 21st-Century Potential.* Manchester, NH: Extending Horizons Books, 2005.

Steffen, Alex, Editor. *Worldchanging: A User's Guide for the 21st Century.* New York: Harry N. Abrams, 2008.

Suzuki, David with Amanda McConnell. *Earth in Balance: Rediscovering Our Place in Nature,* 2nd Edition. Vancouver, BC: Greystone Books, 2006.

Williams, Terry Tempest. *The Open Space of Democracy.* Great Barrington, MA: Orion Society, 2004.

Williamson, Marianne. *Healing the Soul of America.* New York: Simon & Schuster, 2000.

Yes! A Journal of Positive Futures (www.yesmagazine.com)

Endnotes

[1] The sources for the studies cited in the opening paragraph are as follows:

a. Laura Fratiglioni, Hui-Xin Wang, Kjerstin Ericsson, Margaret Maytan, Bengt Winblad, "Influence of Social Network on Ocurrences of Dementia: A Community-Based Longitudinal Study," *The Lancet*, 2000; vol. 355, no. 9212, Apr. 15, 2000, pp. 1315-19. Also see Hui-Xin Wang, Anita Karp, Bengt Winblad, and Laura Fratiglioni, "Late-Life Engagement in Social and Leisure Activities Is Associated with a Decreased Risk of Dementia: A Longitudinal Study from the Kungsholmen Project," *American Journal of Epidemiology*, vol. 155, no. 12, 2002, pp. 1081-1087. Retrieved from http://aje.oxfordjournals.org/cgi/content/abstrac155/12/1081 on July 7, 2009.

b. Susan Brink, "Idle Chatter? Hardly," *Los Angeles Times*, Nov. 5, 2007. These discoveries were made by a team of psychologists at the University of Michigan led by Oscar Ybarra and were published in the *Personality and Social Psychology Bulletin* in February 2008. They surveyed 3,500 people from ages 24 to 96. In addition, they found that a group of 25 college students who had a ten-minute group discussion did equally as well on follow-up cognitive tests as did a group who had spent ten solitary minutes doing intellectual exercises (reading comprehension); both groups did better than the group who had spent the ten minutes in isolation watching *Seinfeld*.

c. Aron S. Buchman, MD; Patricia A. Boyle, PhD; Robert S. Wilson, PhD; Debra A. Fleischman, PhD; Sue Leurgans, PhD; and David A. Bennett, MD, "Association Between Late-Life Social Activity and Motor Decline in Older Adults," *Archives of Internal Medicine*, vol. 169, no. 12, June 22, 2009, pp. 1139-1146. This was a cohort study of 906 persons without stroke, Parkinson disease, or dementia who were participants in the Rush Memory and Aging Project.

d. Regarding the correlation between volunteering and better health and longevity, see *The Health Benefits of Volunteering: A Review of Recent Research* (Washington, DC: Corporation for National and Community Service, 2007; nationalservice.gov). Also see, Stephen G. Post, editor, *Altruism and Health: Perspectives from Empirical Research* (New York: Oxford University Press, 2007).

[2] Benedict Cary, "Research Finds Firstborns Gain the Higher I.Q.," *New York Times*, June 22, 2007; the research was based on an analysis of the military records of 241,310 young men in Norway aged 18 or 19. (Of course, any discussion of IQ points must include the critique of the ways in which the unavoidable cultural bias of the tests disadvantages some groups, plus other concerns.) Earlier studies in other countries, such as the work of Robert Zajonc at Stanford University, had established the correlation between birth order and IQ, but the Norwegian study

found that the correlation holds even if a younger child becomes the eldest after the death of an older sibling or two.

Also see Richard E. Nisbett, *Intelligence and How to Get It: Why Schools and Culture Count* (W. W. Norton & Co., 2009) for studies on other relationships that stimulate the development of intelligence.

[3] Shari Roan, "Spanking lowers a child's IQ, researcher suggests," *Los Angles Times*, www.latimes.com, Sept. 24, 2009. This article reports on a study conducted by Dr. Murray Straus, a sociologist and co-director of the Family Research Laboratory at the University of New Hampshire, which he presented at the 14th International Conference on Violence, Abuse, and Trauma in San Diego. According to a summary posted by the UNH Media website (www. unh.edu/news) on Sept. 25, 2009, Straus and Mallie Paschall, senior research scientist at the Pacific Institute for Research and Evaluation, studied nationally representative samples of 806 children ages 2 to 4, and 704 ages 5 to 9. Both groups were retested four years later. IQs of children ages 2 to 4 who were not spanked were 5 points higher four years later than the IQs of those who were spanked. The IQs of children ages 5 to 9 years old who were not spanked were 2.8 points higher four years later than the IQs of children the same age who were spanked. "How often parents spanked made a difference. The more spanking the slower the development of the child's mental ability. But even small amounts of spanking made a difference," Straus noted.

Internationally, Straus also found a lower national average IQ in nations in which spanking was more prevalent. His analysis indicates the strongest link between corporal punishment and IQ was for those whose parents continued to use corporal punishment even when they were teenagers. Straus and colleagues in 32 nations used data on corporal punishment experienced by 17,404 university students when they were children. According to Straus, there are two explanations for the relation of corporal punishment to lower IQ. First, corporal punishment is extremely stressful and can become a chronic stressor for young children, who typically experience corporal punishment three or more times a week. For many it continues for years. The research found that the stress of corporal punishment shows up as an increase in post-traumatic stress symptoms such as being fearful that terrible things are about to happen and being easily startled. These symptoms are associated with lower IQ. Second, a higher national level of economic development underlies both fewer parents using corporal punishment and a higher national IQ. The good news is that the use of corporal punishment has been decreasing worldwide, which may signal future gains in IQ across the globe. "The worldwide trend away from corporal punishment is most clearly reflected in the 24 nations that legally banned corporal punishment by 2009. Both the European Union and the United Nations have called on all member nations to prohibit corporal punishment by parents. Some of the 24 nations that prohibit corporal punishment by parents have made vigorous efforts to inform the public and assist parents in managing their children. In others little has been done to implement the prohibition," Straus observed. "Nevertheless, there is evidence that attitudes favoring corporal punishment and actual use of corporal punishment have been declining even in nations that have done little to implement the law and in nations which have not prohibited corporal punishment."

[4] See Lisa Berlin et al., "Correlates and Consequences of Spanking and Verbal Punishment for Low-Income White, African American, and Mexican American Toddlers, *Child Development*, vol. 80, issue 5, Sept./Oct. 2009, pp. 1403-1420. This study examined the prevalence, predictors, and outcomes of spanking and verbal punishment in 2,573 low-income white, African American, and Mexican American toddlers at ages 1, 2, and 3. Both spanking and verbal punishment varied by maternal race/ethnicity. Child fussiness at age 1 predicted spanking and verbal punishment at all three ages. Cross-lagged path analyses indicated that spanking (but not verbal punishment) at age 1 predicted child aggressive behavior problems at age 2 and lower Bayley mental development scores at age 3. Berlin is a researcher with the Center for Child and Family Policy at Duke University.

[5] Clive Thompson, "Is Happiness Catching?," *New York Times Magazine*, Sept. 13, 2009, pp. 28, 30-35, and 42. Thompson focused on the extrapolations conducted by Nicholas Christakis and James Fowler from data gathered in the Framingham Heart Study, a long-term study begun in 1948 by the National Heart Institute and still going on, following more than 15,000 Framingham residents and their descendents. One of the questions on an updating page of information asks the participant to list a friend, as well as next of kin, so Christakis and Fowler were able to map connections among participants in their social networks and then to correlate for mimicked (or "contagious") behavior. Not surprisingly for our narcissistic human selves, the correlation of influence was much stronger between a participant and someone s/he considered a close friend; in contrast, if the other person did not feel the participant to be a close friend, there was no mimicking behavior by that person. This phenomenon is called "directionality." In other words, we are far less affected by other people's feelings of attachment than our own. Thompson cites critics of the work of Christakis and Fowler who note that they have demonstrated correlation but not causality. Two other possible causes for, say, weight gain within a group of friends might be environmental (a McDonald's moved into their neighborhood, for example) and "homophily," the tendency of people to gravitate towards others who are like them. A fuller presentation of the work of Christakis and Fowler on connectivity can be found in their book, *Connectivity: The Surprising Power of Our Social Networks and How They Shape Our Lives* (Boston: Little, Brown & Co., 2009). Earlier, related studies have been done on "emotional contagion" by several social scientists as well.

[6] To separate "body" from "mind" is a mechanistic projection that no longer makes sense in light of numerous discoveries in physiology and biology in recent decades. Perception, memory, and creative response occur throughout the bodymind.

[7] Shakti Maira, "The *Ananda* Experience," *Resurgence* Magazine, No. 256, Sept.-Oct. 2009, p. 63.

[8] "A New Kind of Criminal Justice," *Parade* Magazine, Oct. 25, 2009, p. 6. The article cites findings from Scott Wood, director of the Center for Restorative Justice at Loyola Law School in Los Angeles; Beverly Title, who runs a program of restorative justice in Longwood, Colorado; and Lawrence Sherman, director of the Jerry Lee Center of Criminology at the University of Pennsylvania. They recidivism rate of only 10 percent was stated by Ms. Title. Mr. Sherman added, "Every $1 spent on restorative justice may save $8 in the criminal justice system."

[9] See the Guide to the European Social Survey (http://www.esds.ac.uk/International/access/I4732.asp [accessed on Jan. 8, 2010]), a section within the website for Economic and Social Data Service in the U.K.

[10] The World Database of Happiness: Continuous Register of Scientific Research on Subjective Appreciation of Life is directed by Ruut Venhoven of Erasmus University Rotterdam. The website is http://worlddatabaseofhappiness.eur.nl/index.

[11] The Happy Planet Index is a project of the New Economics Foundation in London (www.happyplanetindex.org).

[12] Dorothy Foltz-Gray, "What Really Makes Us Happy," *Prevention* magazine, Feb. 2006, p. 158. Foltz-Gray cites a survey of 5,000 people conducted by Martin Seligman's research group at the Center for Positive Psychology at the University of Pennsylvania in which five core "heart strengths" emerged as key traits associated with happiness: the ability to love and to be loved, gratitude, hope, and zest.

Also see Jen Angel, "10 Things Science Says Will Make You Happy, *Yes!* Magazine, Winter 2009, p. 22. Drawing on the research conducted by Ed Diener, Robert Biswas-Diener, Sonja Lyubomirsky, and Stephen Post, Angel compiled the following list: (1) savor everyday moments; (2) avoid comparisons; (3) put money low on the list; (4) have meaningful goals; (5) take initiative at work; (6) make friends, treasure family; (7) smile even when you don't feel like it; (8) say thank you like you mean it; (9) get out and exercise; and (10) give it away, give it away now!

Also see "Spend Yourself Happy," *AARP* Magazine, Nov./Dec. 2008, p. 20. Elizabeth Dunn, of the University of British Columbia led a survey of 632 Americans of various income levels; she found significantly higher levels of happiness when money given subjects was spent on other people, as gifts or to charity, rather than on themselves. She found that the good feeling can last from six to eight weeks.

[13] Carol Graham, "The Economics of Happiness," in *The New Palgrave Dictionary of Economics*, 2nd edition (New York: Palgrave Macmillan, 2008). On individuals' experiencing loss more deeply and lastingly than gain, Graham cites the findings of three psychologists, D. Kahneman, A. Krueger, and N. Schwartz, in their

coauthored book, *The Foundations of Hedonic Psychology* (New York: Russell Sage, 1999). On the relative weight of loss in one's life, Graham cites the work of R. Easterlin showing that individuals adapt better to loss in the financial realm than in the relational, emotional realm; see his pioneering article "Does economic growth improve the human lot? Some empirical evidence," in *Nations and Households in Economic Growth*, ed. by David A. Paul and Melvin W. Reder (New York: Academic Press, 1974) and his later article "Explaining happiness," in *Proceedings of the National Academy of Sciences* 100 (19), 11176-83.

[14] George Soros, *The New Paradigm for Financial Markets: The Credit Crisis of 2008 and What It Means* (New York: PublicAffairs, 2008).

[15] Thomas Friedman, "The New Red, White and Blue," *New York Times*, Jan. 6, 2006. Also see his then-surprising column "Seeds for a Geo-Green Party," *New York Times*, June 16, 2006. Shortly before Earth Day in the following year, Friedman wrote a long article, "The Power of Green" (*New York Times*, April 15, 2007), that is remarkable for its opening declaration. After noting that "In the world of ideas, to name something is to own it," Friedman announces that he is hereby renaming "green" to mean something positive. Specifically, he asserts, as if it is a new idea, that "living, working, designing, manufacturing, and projecting America is a green way" would be a wisely strategic direction in which to go. Again, allow me to note that he wrote that in 2007!

Even Newt Gingrich, one of the Republican co-authors of the "Contract on America" (as horrified onlookers called the GOP's draconian agenda in their "Contract for America" in 1994), jumped on the Green express train then with a book titled *A Contract with the Earth*, co-authored with Terry L. Maple (Johns Hopkins University Press, 2007).

Sigh. All late conversions are welcome.

[16] Early in 2007, even the intensely pro-Republican Fox News television network expressed concern over global climate change and our high levels of carbon emissions. By summer, though, they reverted to type, as did the rightwing talk-radio stars: global warming was emphatically and relentlessly declared to be a hoax, merely "Gore's pet project" and a scam by scientists to get research funding for themselves. The polar ice caps were literally melting, yet a highly strategic rightwing media onslaught convinced millions of Americans that such things were not important. It was a morally criminal response. Still, by November 2007, a major television network's coverage of a Monday Night Football game included the insertion during half-time of a correspondent's report from a part of the melting polar icecap, as the words *Green Is Universal* flashed at the top of the screen. After the year ended, with ads urging us to celebrate "A Green Holiday," the momentum continued. By spring 2008 ubiquitous ad campaigns by several of the major retail chains and other corporations proudly declared the numerous greening steps they had taken, such as converting all their stores to solar power, using far more

post-consumer recycled materials in their packaging, reducing their use of water, replacing toxins in their building and cleaning materials, and producing a trimmed down stream of waste materials. Along with this (temporary) sea change in the attitudes of American corporations came a new corporate staff position – the environmental director (or coordinator, or officer) – to drive the greening process and oversee these new ways of doing business. For months it seemed that almost the entire country was of one mind, a mind awakened by the ecological crises and energized by the creativity of figuring out solutions.

[17] The underlying impetus for that widespread shift was grassroots common sense: 79 percent of the American public had told pollsters annually since the 1970s that they wanted to see stronger action on environmental issues. People had known for a long time that things were going badly wrong for the natural world and the health of their children, but those concerns were continually sidelined by big business and their associates in media and government. In addition to the public's dis-ease with the environmental crises, some credit for the Green Awakening goes to the 4000 church groups who showed *An Inconvenient Truth* to their members during the first year of the film's release. Moreover, heroes spoke up in every sector of society, where they were usually in the minority, in order to strengthen the emergent green shift in thinking.

One example of the public's shift in attitude was manifested in the congressional elections in November 2006, when, because of concerns about the wars in Iraq and Afghanistan, they gave control of both houses of Congress to the Democrats. The new leadership immediately pledged serious action on reducing our country's level of carbon emissions, but the follow-through on this new focus was extremely disappointing, as usual.

[18] "Benchmarking Humanities in America," *Religious Studies News*, American Academy of Religion, March 2009, p. 3.

[19] See James L. Heckman and Paul A. LaFontaine, "The Declining American High School Graduation Rate: Evidence, Sources, and Consequences," *National Bureau of Economic Research Reporter*, no. 1, 2008, retrieved from www.nber.org/reporter/2008number1/heckman on Dec. 28, 2008. The authors challenge the commonly heard U.S. high school graduation rate of 88%, arguing that it is really around 75%.

Also see Ben DuBose, "Urban vs. suburban: the high school graduation gap," *Los Angeles Times*, April 2, 2008.

[20] See Sam Dillon, "U.S. Students Achieve Mixed Results on Writing Test," *New York Times*, April 4, 2008.

To teach students how to structure an essay (and do well on the sections on writing and reading proficiency in the state test), many school districts have adopted the Jane Schaffer Writing Program, which imposes a rigid structure of paragraph construction in the beginning that can be relaxed once students demonstrate that they are able to design a cogent exposition with a coherent structure.

[21] See Richard Arum and Josipa Roksa, *Academically Adrift: Limited Learning on College Campuses* (Chicago: University of Chicago Press, 2011). The study presented is available at highered.ssrc.org.

[22] Sam Dillon, "Literacy Falls for Graduates from College, Testing Finds," *New York Times*, Dec. 16, 2005. When the National Assessment of Adult Literacy (administered by the US Dept. of Education) was first given, in 1992, 40 percent of college graduates scored at the proficient level, meaning that they were able to read lengthy, complex texts in English and draw complicated inferences. By 2003 only 31 percent of college graduates read at that level, 53 percent scored at the intermediate level, and fully 14 percent could read and understand only short, simple examples of prose texts.

[23] See Raymond A. Schroth, "A world without books," *National Catholic Reporter*, Jan. 25, 2008, p. 33. Fr. Schroth reports in this article on both *Reading at Risk*, a survey of 17,000 adults conducted by the National Education Association (Research Division Report No. 46, Nov. 2004) and the follow-up study, *To Read or Not to Read* (National Education Association, Research Division Report No. 47, Nov. 2007), from which the data is cited.

[24] See Richard Arum and Josipa Roska, *Academically Adrift: Limited Learning on College Campuses* (Chicago: University of Chicago Press, 2011).

[25] See Hilary Stout, "Antisocial Networking?," *New York Times*, May 2, 2010; the statistic cited is from the Pew Research Center's "Internet and American Life Project" (www.pewinternet.org/Reports/2010/Teens-and-Mobile-Phones).

[26] Susan Douglas, cited in Tom Abate, "Generation M: Are we so immersed in media brine that it's become an environmental health hazard?," *San Francisco Chronicle Magazine*, Jan. 1, 2006.

[27] See David Elkind, "Playtime Is Over," opinion piece, *New York Times*, March 27, 2010.

[28] Hilary Stout, "Antisocial Networking?," *New York Times*, May 2, 2010; the article cites several studies, including the Pew Research Center's study released by their Internet and American Life Project. The journalist notes, "The question on researchers' minds is whether all that texting, instant messaging, and online social networking allows children to become more connected and supportive of their friends – or whether the quality of their interactions is being diminished without the intimacy and emotional give and take of regular, extended face-to-face time. It is far too soon to know the answer." Also see The Impact of Social Media on Children, Adolescents and Families, a clinical report from the American Academy

of Pediatrics, *Pediatrics* journal, published online on March 28, 2011.

[29] See Tara Parker-Pope, "A One-Eyed Invader in the Bedroom," *New York Times*, March 4, 2008. Also see "One more reason to get kids to turn off the TV," *Los Angeles Times*, Oct. 3, 2006. This article cites the following study of middle school children, comparing their scores on school tests among the group who watched television or played video games on school nights and those who did not: Iman Sharif, MD, MPH and James D. Sargent, MD, "Association Between Television, Movie, and Video Game Exposure and School Performance," *Pediatrics*, vol. 118, no. 4, Oct. 2006: pp. e1061-e1070.

[30] Lisa Belkin, "Can TV Make Your Teen Pregnant?," *New York Times*, Nov. 3, 2008; the article reports on a study conducted by the Rand Corporation of 700 girls aged 12 through 17 for three years. Of the half who watched sex scenes the far more often, 25 percent became pregnant, compared with 12 percent in the half who watched few such programs. See Anita Chandra, Steven Martino, Rebecca L. Collins, Marc N. Elliott, Sandra H. Berry, David E. Kanouse, and Angela Miu, *Exposure to Sex on TV May Increase the Chance of Teen Pregnancy* (www.rand. org/pubs/research_briefs/RB9398).

[31] See Mark Bauerlein, *The Dumbest Generation: How the Digital Age Stupifies Young Americans and Jeopardizes Our Future, or Don't Trust Anyone Under 30* (Los Angeles, CA: Tarcher/Penguin, 2008).

[32] See Alana Semuels, "Little avatars behaving badly: Parents find it takes a village to keep kids from preying on each other in virtual worlds," *Los Angeles Times*, July 2, 2008; the study was conducted by two researchers at UCLA and published in the proceedings of the third international conference of the Digital Games Research Association.

[33] See Rachel Abramowitz, "The X/Y factor," *Los Angeles Times*, Dec. 30, 2007. The article presents findings of Jane Buckingham on "the next-generation zeitgeist."

Demographically the age group most likely to say that lying is acceptable is the 18-29 group; see Jocelyn Noveck, "Hedging Truth Not Bad," *San Francisco Chronicle*, July 12, 2006.

[34] See the study "Egos Inflating over Time: A Cross-Temporal Meta-Analysis of the Narcissistic Personality Inventory," conducted by Jean Twenge et al. of San Diego State University, *Journal of Personality*, vol. 76, issue 4, July 2008, pp. 875-902, plus discussion on pp. 903-28. In early 2007 the authors of the study reviewed the results of Narcissistic Personality Inventory, a survey taken by 16,475 college students between 1982 and 2006; the data indicate that students today are significantly more narcissistic, self-absorbed, and self-centered than a generation ago.

[35] Julie Albright, a digital sociologist at the University of Southern California, cited in Mark Milian, "People act differently on Twitter," *Los Angeles Times*, 14 May

2010.

[36] See Elizabeth Olson, "Killings Prompt Efforts to Spot and Reduce Abuse of Teenagers in Dating," *New York Times*, Jan. 4, 2009. The article cites several studies that found that significant, and growing, percentages of teenage girls have been verbally assaulted or physically violated by a romantic partner. The National Teen Dating Abuse Hotline operates a website: www.loveisrespect.org.

On the effects of young males' growing up on violent video games: Chris Magnus, chief of police in Richmond, CA, notes, "There's a mentality among some people that they are living in a really violent video game…. We seem to be dealing with an awful lot of people who have zero conflict-resolution skills"; cited in Kate Zernike, "Violent Crime in Cities Shows Sharp Surge, Reversing Trend," *New York Times*, March 9, 2007.

On the disappearance of the socialization for boys that dating traditionally provided, Michael Kimmel, author of *Guyland: The Perilous World Where Boys Become Men* (New York: HarperCollins, 2008), notes: "When I tell moms about the gender asymmetry of the oral sex 'epidemic' [girls give to boys, never the other way around], for example, or what the hooking-up culture is like, they seem shocked at how predatory it is, how the sex seems so disconnected from anything resembling even liking the other person. The fathers, though, get jealous."

[37] N. A. Daniels, L. MacKinno, S. M. Rowe, N. H. Bean, P. M. Griffin, and P. S. Mead, "Foodborne disease outbreaks in United States schools," *Pediatric Infectious Disease Journal*, vol. 21, no. 7, 2002, pp. 623–8; outbreaks of food-borne illness were found to have increased by 10 percent each year throughout the 1990s.

[38] Eryn Brown, "Study links teen bullying to social status," *Los Angeles Times*, February 8, 2011; the article reports on a study headed by Robert Faris, of UC Davis, that was published in the February 2011 issue of the *American Sociological Review*.

[39] Rosalind Wiseman, "How to fight the new bullies," *Parade* Magazine, Feb. 25, 2007, p. 6-8.

[40] Jaron Lanier, *You Are Not a Gadget: A Manifesto* (New York: Alfred A. Knopf, 2010).

[41] Umair Haque, quoted in Jessica Guynn, "People-rating site a danger, critics warn," *Los Angeles Times*, April 2, 2010.

[42] Melissa Healy, "My pal, my bully," *Los Angeles Times*, Jan. 26, 2009; the article describes the United States Attorneys General 2009 task force report, *Enhancing Child Safety and Online Technologies* (http://cyber.law.harvard.edu/pubrelease/isttf) and cites several concurring observations by school psychologists.

[43] "Keeping an eye on 'sexting,'" editorial, *Los Angeles Times*, June 1, 2009; the

editorial discusses the findings of a recent survey conducted by the National Campaign to Prevent Teen and Unplanned Pregnancy (www.thenationalcampaign. org/sextech).

[44] Melissa Healy, "My pal, my bully," *Los Angeles Times*, Jan. 26, 2009.

[45] I am grateful to Amanda Tomei, a clinical psychologist, for research assistance on the ill effects of young people's use of online social networking sites. See, for instance, M. Ybarra, C. Alexander, and K. Mitchell, "Depressive symptomatology, youth Internet use, and online interactions: a national survey," *Journal of Adolescent Health*, vol. 36, no. 1, 2003, pp. 9-18. Also see L. Buffardi and W. K. Campbell, "Narcissism and social networking sites," *Personality and Social Psychology Bulletin*, vol. 34, no. 10, 2008, pp. 1303-1314.

Also see Steve Lopez, "Unwiring and reconnecting," *Los Angeles Times*, April 29, 2009, and "The rigors of life unplugged," *Los Angeles Times*, May 6, 2009; Lopez reports on a class of high school sophomores who undertook a one-week total media fast, as the urging of one of their teachers. After the painful beginning of the week of electronic silence, students "felt as though they were more in touch with themselves and the world around them." Also, their teacher noted that their homework was significantly better than their usual performance.

[46] Maureen O'Connor and Jacob Savage, "Facebook never forgets," *Los Angeles Times*, July 14, 2008, Opinion Piece.

[47] See *The Importance of Family Dinners V*, a report released in Sept. 2009 by the National Center on Addiction and Substance Abuse at Columbia University (www. casacolumbia.org). The Center first began studying the effects of family dinners in 1996. Their 2009 study found that, compared to teens who have frequent family dinners (five to seven family dinners per week), those who have infrequent family dinners (fewer than three per week) are twice as likely to have used tobacco or marijuana, and more than one and a half times likelier to have used alcohol. The relationship between the frequency of family dinners and substance use is especially strong among the youngest teens in the survey. As frequency of family dinners increases, reported drinking, smoking and drug use decreases.

[48] Neal Gabler, "The attack of the louts: Meet the new male role model. It's a boy!," *Los Angeles Times*, February 13, 2011.

[49] See, for instance, the website for Attachment Parenting International (www. attachmentparenting.org), founded by Barbara Nicholson and Lysa Parker. The are coauthors of *Attached at the Heart: 8 Proven Parenting Principles for Raising Connected and Compassionate Children*, which is available through the website.

[50] Gordon Neufeld, PhD and Gabor Maté MD, *Hold On to Your Kids: Why Parents Need to Matter More than Peers* (Toronto: Alfred A. Knopf Canada, 2004; New York: Ballantine Books, 2005). Dr. Neufeld is clearly the principle coauthor of this

extremely significant book, as Dr. Maté explains in his "Note to the Reader": "Dr. Neufeld's background and experience as a psychologist and his brilliantly original work are the source of the central thesis we present and the advice we offer. In that sense he is the sole author of the book.... I am proud to help bring Gordon Neufeld's transformative ideas to a much broader public."

For another good book on the relational perspective on parenting, see Becky A. Bailey, Ph.D., *Easy to Love, Difficult to Discipline: The 7 Basic Skills for Turning Conflict into Cooperation* by (New York: Wm. Morrow, 2000).

[51] Sandy Banks, "A younger view of feminism," *Los Angeles Times*, April 10, 2009.

[52] See Edith Cobb, *The Ecology of Imagination in Childhood* (Dallas, TX: Spring Publications, 1993 [1977]), pp. 16-17, 20. Cobb appreciated Kenneth Clark's 1954 Romanes lecture at Oxford, "The Moment of Vision," which he later noted might well have been titled "The Moment of Intensified Physical Perception"; Clark asserts that "the sense of wonder in childhood can be synthesized in adult imagination only after further intercourse with literature or art" (p. 93).

[53] Rachel Carson, "Help Your Child to Wonder," *Woman's Home Companion*, July 1956. This essay was published as a short book with photographs as *The Sense of Wonder* in 1965 by Harper & Row, who issued a new edition in 1998.

[54] The report by the Accountability Committee of the Broader, Bolder Approach to Education (BBA) Campaign (www.boldapproach.org) was led by BBA co-chair Thomas Payzant and Committee co-chairs Christopher Cross, Susan Neuman, and Richard Rothstein. Payzant, Cross, and Neuman are all former Assistant Secretaries of Education, Payzant in a Democratic and Cross and Neuman in Republican administrations. Cross noted in the press release announcing the report, which was released on June 25, 2009: "We must not lose sight of the larger, more important picture that educating our youth is a coordinated effort. We must insist upon coordination between schools and other community institutions that provide early childhood care and education, parent education and support, physical and mental health care, and high-quality out-of-school time programs."

[55] See Anthony Bryk and Barbara Schneider, *Trust in Schools: A Core Resource for Improvement* (Chicago: University of Chicago Press, 2002).

Also see Patrick B. Forsyth, Laura L.B. Barnes, and Curt M. Adams, "Trust-effectiveness patterns in schools," *Journal of Educational Administration*, vol. 44, issue 2, 2006, pp. 122-141.

[56] Alan B. Krueger and Diane M. Whitmore, "The Effect of Attending a Small Class in the Early Grades on College-Test Taking and Middle School Test Results: Evidence from Project STAR," *The Economic Journal*, vol. 111, no. 468 (Jan. 2001).

[57] "Marnell Jameson, "C'mon, get happy," *Los Angeles Times*, Sept. 8, 2008; the article

cites, among others, Martin Seligman, past president of the American Psychology Association and founder of the positive psychology movement: "We've learned in 10 years that happy people are more productive at work, learn more at school, get promoted more, are more creative, and are more liked."

Also see Rosemary Clandos, "Too stressed out to learn?," *Los Angeles Times*, Sept. 1, 2008; the article discusses research on the detrimental effects on learning of habitual fear and stress often experienced by children in poverty. A program called "Enriching the Brains of Poverty," designed by Eric Jensen, is summarized.

[58] "College kids lacking empathy, study says," *U.S. News & World Report*, May 28, 2010. The article reports on a study presented by Sara Konrath, an assistant research professor at the University of Michigan, at the annual meeting of the Association for Psychological Science in Boston. The meta-analysis studied data about empathy in 14,000 college students over thirty years. The pull-quote in this article was "'Generation Me' tends to be self-centered, competitive, U.S. research shows." Also see Pamela Paul, "From Students, Less Kindness For Strangers?," *New York Times*, June 27, 2010.

[59] Daniel Goleman, *Emotional Intelligence* (New York: Bantam, 1996); *Social Intelligence* (New York: Bantam, 2006); and *Working with Emotional Intelligence* (New York: Bantam, 1998). According to Goleman, the fundamentals of emotional intelligence include self-awareness, handling emotions, self-motivation, empathy, and social skills. See the author's website: www.DanielGoleman.info.

[60] See the Center for Nonviolent Communication (www.cnvc.org) for information, materials, and how to find a local nvc group or the schedule of presentations by Marshall Rosenberg and other teachers.

[61] See Nan Henderson's website: www.resiliency.com. The student's definition cited in Ch. 4 of this book is on the website. Also see, for example, the publications and projects of the Resilience Solutions Group at Arizona State University (resilience. asu.edu).

[62] Teresa Watanabe, "Listen, Hear," *Los Angeles Times*, Nov. 27, 2010; the article reports on the program whereby the Ojai Foundation, of Ojai, CA, introduced the practice of council to many schools in the Los Angeles Unified School District. Through the Ojai Foundation (www.ojaifoundation.org/council), the practice of council is now used by more than 12,000 students via 600 trained teachers in more than 60 schools.

[63] Michael O'Shea, "Fit Kids Get Better Grades," *Parade*, Jan. 11, 2009; the article reports on studies commissioned by the California Department of Education and by Centers for Disease Control. Also see Lori Nudo, "Born to Walk," *Prevention*, April 2005, p. 115; a study of elementary school students conducted by researchers at the University of Illinois also found a high correlation between those who scored

well on a physical assessment scale and on state achievement tests.

[64] Research conducted by Thomas N. Robinson at Stanford University School of Medicine in 1999 found that children who cut down their television time gained less weight than their peers. See Thomas N. Robinson, "Reducing Children's Television to Prevent Obesity: A Randomized Controlled Trial," *Journal of the American Medical Association*, vol. 282, no. 16, 1999, pp. 1561-1567.

[65] Peg Tyre, "Coaching Students to Stay in School," *Parade* Magazine, June 7, 2009, pp.10, 12-13. The article describes a successful program of graduation coaches in South Atlanta schools.

[66] Karen Ann Cullotta, "The Parent-Teacher Talk Gains a New Participant," *New York Times*, Dec. 28, 2008.

[67] Ulysses Torassa, "Kids Less Violent After Cutting Back on TV," *San Francisco Chronicle*, Jan. 15, 2001; a study published on that date in the *Archives of Pediatric and Adolescent Medicine* found that after a 21-week curriculum in which students were urged to watch no television the first week and only 7 hours per week thereafter, and to cut back on time spent playing videogames, there was a 50 percent reduction in the level of verbal aggression and a 40 percent reduction in physical aggression seen on the playground. The children who were the most aggressive at the beginning of the study showed the most benefit. See Thomas N. Robinson, Marta L. Wilde, Lisa C. Navracruz, K. Farish Haydel, and Ann Varady, "*Effects of Reducing Children's Television and Video Game Use on Aggressive Behavior: A Randomized Controlled Trial,*" *Archives of Pediatric and Adolescent Medicine*, 2001, Issue 155, pp. 17-23.

[68] Winnie Hu, "Seeing No Progress, Some Schools Drop Laptops," *New York Times*, May 4, 2007. The article reports on one of the largest ongoing studies, in which the Texas Center for Educational Research found no overall difference on state test scores between 21 middle schools where students received laptops in 2004 and 21 schools where they did not. (For the final report on this study, see *Evaluation of the Texas Technology Immersion Pilot Final Outcomes for a Four-Year Study(2004-05 to 2007-08)*, available at www.tcer.org/research/etxtip/documents/y4_etxtip_final. pdf.) The *New York Times* article also noted that the president of the school board in Liverpool, New York, which decided to phase out its laptops, said, "After seven years, there was literally no evidence it had any impact on student achievement – none." Moreover, teachers had come to see that "the box" was "a distraction in the educational process."

[69] Lowell Monke, "Charlotte's Webpage," *Orion* Magazine, Sept./Oct. 2005, pp. 24-31. The essay was supported by *Orion*'s Thoughts on America Fund.

Other recommended works on the losses to children from computer-based education are the many books by Chet Bowers, and the classic essay by Theodore

Roszak, "Computers in the Schools: Nineteen NeoLuddite Rules" (*The New Internationalist*, no. 286, 1996). Also see Jane Healy, *Failure to Connect: How Computers Affect Our Children's Minds – and What We Can Do About It* (New York: Simon & Schuster, 1999); Mark Bauerlein, *The Dumbest Generation: How the Digital Age Stupifies Young Americans and Jeopardizes Our Future, or Don't Trust Anyone Under 30* (Tarcher/Penguin, 2008); and Maggie Jackson, *Distracted: The Erosion of Attention and the Coming Dark Age* (Amherst, NY: Prometheus Books, 2008).

[70] Kaiser Family Foundation, "A Teacher in the Living Room? Educational Media for Babies, Toddlers, and Pre-schoolers," Dec. 14, 2004 (see www.kff.org/entmedia/7427.cfm).

[71] Edith Cobb, *The Ecology of Imagination in Childhood* (Dallas, TX: Spring Books, 1993 [1977]), pp. 70, 105, 51, and 30. Cobb wrote this book from the 1950s (when correcting the Freudian grip on the thinking about child development struck her as imperative) through the mid-1970s.

[72] Ron Matus, "Cultivating Young Gardeners, *St. Petersburg Times* (www.tampabay.com), Feb. 7, 2009. The garden described is a joint project of the students at Lakewood Elementary School and assisting students from nearby Eckerd College. Also see Carla Rivera, "Green thumbs sprouting early," *Los Angeles Times*, Dec. 25, 2010; the article reports on the Nature Explore program, which operates programs in hundreds of preschools, child care centers, churches, and libraries.

[73] The Center for Ecoliteracy (www.ecoliteracy.org) was cofounded by Fritjof Capra, Peter Buckley, and Zenobia Barlow; she serves as Executive Director. I highly recommend their online monthly newsletter and the many resources available on their website. In addition, among their many substantive publications is an anthology titled *Ecological Literacy: Educating Our Children for a Sustainable World* (San Francisco, CA: Sierra Club Books, 2005) and a guide for educators titled *Smart by Nature: Schooling for Sustainability* (Healdsburg, CA: Watershed Media, 2009).

[74] This point was originally made by Edith Cobb (see her book, *The Ecology of Imagination in Childhood*). It is further developed by Louise Chawla. See her article "Spots of Time: Manifold Ways of Being in Nature in Childhood," in *Children and Nature: Psychological, Sociological and Evolutionary Investigations*, ed. By P. Kahn Jr. and Stephen Kellert (Cambridge, MA: MIT Press, 2002). Also see Louise Chawla, *In the First Country of Places: Nature, Poetry, and Childhood Memory* (Albany, NY: SUNY Press, 1994).

[75] Richard Louv, "Leave No Child Inside," *Sierra* Magazine, July/Aug. 2006 (www.sierraclub.org/sierra/200607/child.asp).

[76] Liz Bowie, "Getting scientific about arts education," *Los Angeles Times*, May

24, 2009; the article reports on various studies and the new interdisciplinary field that is forming at the convergence of neuroscience, education, and music, such as the research conducted through the Neuro-Education Initiative at Johns Hopkins University. Also see *The Music Instinct: Science and Song*, a two-hour PBS documentary, which first aired on various PBS stations during June 2009; available on DVD from www.PBS.org.

[77] Randy Kennedy, "Guggenheim Study Suggests Arts Education Benefits Literacy Skills," *New York Times*, July 27, 2006.

[78] See Maja Djikic, Keith Oatley, Sara Zoeterman, and Jordan B. Peterson, *"On Being Moved by Art: How Reading Fiction Transforms the Self," Creativity Research Journal*, vol. 21, issue 1, 2009, pp. 24-29. Also, looking back on his reading of fiction in high school, a journalist, Mark Schurman, relates, "I'm not sure if it really ever made me any more intelligent. Yet it did ease the loneliness. It did broaden my perspective on people and the world. I found it easier to live with my problems and in my own skin. I discovered that from a literary perspective, there really is no such thing as not fitting in" (*Los Angeles Times*, Jan. 10, 2006, Opinion Piece).

[79] See John Henry Newman, *The Idea of a University* (Notre Dame, IN: Notre Dame University Press, 1990 [1854]).

[80] Alfred North Whitehead, *The Aims of Education* (New York: The Free Press, 1970 [1929], pp. 50-51. For Whitehead's concept of "misplaced concreteness," see Alfred North Whitehead, *Science and the Modern World* (New York: The Free Press, 1953 [1925], p. 51.

[81] The annual College Sustainability Report Card is conducted by Green Report Card (greenreportcard.org). In 2009, 91 percent of the colleges and universities surveyed bought food from local farms; 64 percent serve fair-trade coffee; 65 percent have high-performance building standards for new buildings; 54 percent have cut their carbon dioxide emissions; 42 percent use hybrid vehicles; and 37 percent buy renewable energy – with 30 percent producing some of their own via wind- or solar-powered generators.

[82] Margulis, Lynn, *Symbiotic Planet: A New Look At Evolution* (New York: Basic Books, 1999), pp. 5-9. "Endosymbiosis" is the name Margulis gave to her discovery that simple cells evolved into complex ones via the relational dynamic of symbiosis"; she published this theory in *The Origin of Eukaryotic Cells* (Yale University Press, 1971)."Symbiogenesis" is the name for her theory that species originated largely through symbiosis. "The Gaia Theory" is the explanation she co-developed with the atmospheric chemist James Lovelock to identify and describe the self-regulating dynamics of Earth's atmosphere and biomass, which together achieve and maintain a life-sustaining, dynamic balance in the atmospheric mix of gases.

[83] Sally J. Goerner, *After the Clockwork Universe: The Emerging Science and Culture of Integral Society* (Chapel Hill, NC: Triangle Center for Complexity Studies, 2007 [1999]). Also see Sally J. Goerner, *The New Science of Sustainability: Building a Foundation for a Great Change* (Gabiola, BC, Canada: New Society Publishers, 2008).

[84] Russell Shorto, "Breath of Thought," a review of *The Invention of Air: A Story of Science, Faith, Revolution, and the Birth of America* by Steven Johnson, *New York Times Book Review*, Jan. 25, 2009, p. 13.

[85] Jan Fuhse and Sophie Mützel, descriptive statement on Relational Sociology for the international symposium on Relational Sociology in Berlin on Sept. 25-26, 2008.

[86] See Wesley J. Wildman, "An Introduction to Relational Ontology," Boston University, May 15, 2006, for an overview of relational ontology and his explication of causal theories of relation (retrieved from people.bu.edu/wwildman/WeirdWildWeb/media/docs on April 28, 2009). Wildman notes in his abstract that, rather than siding with relational ontology over substantivist ontology, he takes the position that "the best philosophical approaches are causal theories of relation in which both relations and entities take their rise from an ontologically fundamental causal flux. The causal theories of relations and entities discussed are Neoplatonist participation metaphysics, Buddhist *pratītya-samutpāda* metaphysics, Whitehead's process metaphysics, Peirce's semiotic metaphysics, and Bohm's implicate-order metaphysics, all of which require an approach to causation that extends far beyond commonsense concepts of causation. The paper illustrates the explanatory virtues of causal theories of relations and entities in relation to the realms of fundamental physics, ordinary life, and theology—particularly the metaphysics of causation at the root of Trinitarian concepts within Christian theology such as generation, procession, and perichoresis."

[87] Examples of recent scholarly works that reveal, or further our understanding of, interrelationships among fields, entities, or areas include *The Shape of Ancient Thought: Comparative Studies in Greek and Indian Philosophy* by Thomas McEvilley; *When Asia Was the World* by Stewart Gordon; and a case for scholarly humility before the unimaginably complex interrelationships that constitute reality: *The Virtues of Ignorance: Complexity, Sustainability, and the Limits of Knowledge*, edited by Bill Vitek and Wes Jackson.

[88] See the Forum on Religion and Ecology, founded and directed by two professors of religion at Yale University, Mary Evelyn Tucker and John Grim (www.yale.edu/religionandecology).

[89] The Center for Process Studies (CPS) is a research center within Claremont Graduate School of Theology and is affiliated with Claremont Graduate University.

CPS (www.center4process.org) seeks to promote the common good by means of the relational approach found in process thought, which is based on the work of philosophers Alfred North Whitehead and Charles Hartshorne. An example of their public lectures was "The Emerging Relational Worldview" by Stephen Rowe on May 13, 2009.

An example of a fully accredited, independent graduate institute that has pioneered an approach to the various disciplines that incorporates the relational perspective and honors the spiritual dimension of intellectual life is the California Institute of Integral Studies, in San Francisco (www.ciis.edu).

[90] See, for example, Jorge N. Ferrer and Jacob H. Sherman, editors, *The Participatory Turn: Spirituality, Mysticism, and Religious Studies* (Albany, NY: SUNY Press, 2008).

[91] Mihaly Csikszentmihalyi, "More Ways Than One to Be Good," a review of *Mapping the Moral Domain: A Contribution of Women's Thinking to Psychological Theory and Education* by Carol Gilligan, Janie Victoria Ward, and Jill McLean Taylor, with Betty Bardige, *New York Times Book Review*, May 18, 1989.

Also see the website for the Jean Baker Miller Training Institute at Wellesley College (http://www.jbmti.org) concerning Relational-Cultural Theory, including a history of the emergence of this orientation in the late 1970s and early 1980s at the Stone Center at Wellesley and a list of over 50 publications on relational psychology. Also see Christina Robb's history of the pioneering work in relational psychology, *This Changes Everything: The Relational Revolution in Psychology* (New York: Farrar, Straus and Giroux, 2006).

[92] Lisa L. Frey, Denise Beesley, and Merle R. Hiller, "Relational Health, Attachment, and Psychological Distress in College Women and Men," *Psychology of Women Quarterly*, vol. 30, no. 3, Sept. 2005, pp. 303-311.

[93] See, for instance, the following books by or about these deeply relational thinkers: Fritjof Capra, *The Science of Leonardo: Inside the Mind of the Great Genius of the Renaissance* (New York: Doubleday, 2007; see especially the Epilogue for a summary of Leonardo's organic approach and his close attention to nature); David Seamon and Arthur Zajonc, editors, *Goethe's Way of Science: A Phenomenology of Nature* (Albany, NY: State University of New York Press, 1998); John Ruskin, "The Nature of Gothic," in *Stones of Venice* (Cambridge, MA: Da Capo Press, 1985); collections of Darwin's lively and sensitive writings about animals he observed; all writings by John Muir, plus the wise and poignant study of his work by Michael P. Cohen, *The Pathless Way* (Madison, WI: University of Wisconsin Press, 1986); Maria Montessori, *To Educate the Human Potential* (Oxford, England: Clio Press, 1989); and several works by Alfred North Whitehead: *The Aims of Education* (New York: Free Press, 1970 [1929]), *Adventures in Ideas* (New York: Free Press, 1933), *Science and the Modern World* (New York: Free Press, 1967 [1925]), *The Function*

of Reason (Boston, MA: Beacon Press, 1958 [1929]), and *Process and Reality* (New York: Free Press, 1978 [1929]; for most students, this book requires a study guide).

In "The Impact of Faith on Relational Thought" by Martin J. Buss (*Consensus*, vol. 31, no. 2, 2006, pp. 75-85), he notes that a relational view of reality "had been important in theology but had not been well represented in Western philosophy after the Presocratics." Instead, the major ongoing philosophical debate was between "particularism" (only the particular is real; categories are merely ideas, or names [hence they are dismissed as mere "nominalism," which was a reaction against Platonism]) versus the position that categories are as real as are particulars. In the 19th century, Charles Sanders Peirce held that relationships are the fundamental reality. He was influenced initially by his first wife's (Melusina Fay) social, feminist interpretation of Trinitarian doctrine, in 1859, and also by the relational ontology framed by Catherine Beecher in 1860. Peirce became intrigued with a triadic relational structure, which he felt was a basic structure of reality, as a triad cannot be derived from a simpler pattern but can be the basis for complex structures; he furnished a mathematical explication of that theory. Peirce's semiotic relational philosophy influenced William James and John Dewey, among others. Another stream of (abstract) relational thought emerged in the early 20th century in Europe and took as its basis the three "persons" of language (I, you, it) and focused on a "grammatical-dialogical" approach. The work of Hermann Cohen influenced Mikhail Bakhtin and others; the work of Ferdinand Ebner influenced Martin Buber and Ludwig Wittgenstein.

[94] See the website for Schumacher College, one of the pioneering institutions in Green-relational-activist adult education: www.SchumacherCollege.org.uk. Also see Anne Phillips, *Holistic Education: Learning from Schumacher College* (Totnes, England: Green Books, 2008). I taught at Schumacher College, in beautiful Devon, as a Scholar-in-Residence in 1992, 1997, and 2003 and highly recommend this noble institution, which attracts extremely interesting students from around the world.

[95] According to a study conducted by the Kaiser Foundation Research Institute that was released in Nov. 2009, BPA is present in 93 percent of Americans tested; see "BPA linked to erectile problems," *Los Angeles Times*, Nov. 11, 2009. For the study itself, see De-Kun Li et al., "Occupational Exposure to Bisphenol-A (BPA) and the risk of Self-Reported Male Sexual Dysfunction," *Human Reproduction*, vol. 25, no. 2, pp. 519-527. Researchers followed 634 male workers exposed to BPA at four Chinese factories. Over the course of five years, those men were four times as likely to have erectile dysfunction and seven times more likely to have difficulty with ejaculation. BPA, the primary component of hard and clear polycarbonate plastics — including water bottles, baby bottles, and the linings of canned foods — appears to adversely alter the hormonal balance in humans. As of early 2011,

only the EU and Canada (plus a few states within the USA) ban plastic baby bottles containing BPA.

[96] "Scientists note dramatic decline in sperm count," *San Francisco Chronicle*, March 8, 1992; one study showed a decrease of 50 percent in the sperm count in industrialized Western countries between 1940 and 1990, due largely to long-term exposure to environmental toxins; other studies since 1940 have found similar results. Also see, Dr. Isidore Rosenfeld, "Fumes Take a Toll on Sperm," on the detrimental effects of breathing car exhaust among toll takers and others living near auto fumes on highways in Italy, *Parade Magazine*, Dec. 7, 2003. Also, sexual problems in males, including erectile dysfunction, have been linked to exposure to high levels of bisphenol A (BPA), which has been widely used in thousands of consumer products, including dental sealants and canned food can-linings. According to a study conducted by the Kaiser Foundation Research Institute that was released in November 2009, BPA is present in 93 percent of Americans tested; see "BPA linked to erectile problems," *Los Angeles Times*, Nov. 11, 2009.

[97] Sandra Steingraber, "Living Downstream," *Orion*, Summer 1997, pp. 64-75. Rates of childhood cancer, and also testicular cancer in young men, have soared since World War II, as has the rate of breast cancer. American women born between 1947 and 1957 now have nearly three times the risk of breast cancer as their great-grandmothers had at the same age.

Heart disease is the leading cause of death in the United States, and cancer is second, each accounting for about one-quarter of American deaths annually. All other diseases account for much smaller portions of the total.

Sarah Burd-Sharps, Kristen Lewis, and Eduardo Borges Martins, *The Measure of America: American Human Development Report 2008-2009*, Social Science Research Council (New York: Columbia University Press, 2008); this study applies the Human Development Index (HDI), which was designed by the Nobel Laureate economist Amartya Sen and published in 2007 by the United Nations Development Programme (UNDP) to the United States. The United States slipped from 2nd place in 1990 to 12th place in 2008. All of the 11 countries that rank higher than the United States in human development has a lower per-capita income.

[98] Thomas Maugh II, "Diet soda linked to key heart risk," *Los Angeles Times*, July 24, 2007. The study was published online in *Circulation: Journal of the American Heart Association* (July 24, 2007), and the part related to diet soda was summarized in the "Journal Report" posted on the website of the American Heart Association on July 23, 2007, "Diet and regular soft drinks linked to increase in risk factors for heart disease" (www.americanheart.org/presenter.jhtml?identifier=3049074). The study found that people who drink one can of diet soda per day were found to have 44 percent greater risk of developing metabolic syndrome than people who did not. They also had a 31 percent greater risk of becoming obese, a 30 percent greater risk of having a larger waistline, a 25 percent greater risk of developing

high levels of blood triglycerides or high blood sugar, a 32 percent greater risk of having low levels of good cholesterol, and a trend toward increased risk of high blood pressure. Also see Jill U. Adams, "Rats may get fat, but we may get lucky," *Los Angeles Times*, March 17, 2008, for studies in the debate over the effects of diet sodas.

[99] Jennifer 8. Lee, "Child Obesity Is Linked to Chemicals in Plastics," *New York Times*, April 17, 2009. The article reports on a study done in East Harlem of 400 girls ages 9 to 11 by researchers who presented the results at Mount Sinai Medical Center on April 16, 2009. The heaviest girls had the highest levels of phthalates metabolites in their urine.

Regarding findings that obesity may be a less important factor increasing the risk of diabetes than is exposure to "persistent organic pollutants" (POPs, which include certain chemical byproducts, PCBs, and certain insecticides), see Duk-Hee Lee et al., "A Strong Dose-Response Relation Between Serum Concentrations of Persistent Organic Pollutants and Diabetes: Results from the National Health and Examination Survey 1999–2002," *Diabetes Care*, July 2006, vol. 29, no. 7, pp. 1638-1644. Also see Ji-Sun Lim, Duk-Hee Lee, and David R. Jacobs, Jr., "Association of Brominated Flame Retardants With Diabetes and Metabolic Syndrome in the U.S. Population, 2003–2004," *Diabetes Care*, vol. 31, no. 7, Sept. 2008, pp. 1802-1807. Also see Duk-Hee Lee, In-Kyu Lee, Michael Steffes, and David R. Jacobs, Jr., "Extended Analyses of the Association Between Serum Concentrations of Persistent Organic Pollutants and Diabetes." *Diabetes Care*, vol. 30, no. 6, June 2007, pp. 1596-1598.

[100] Stephanie Saul, "Weight Drives the Young to Adult Pills, Data Says," *New York Times*, July 26, 2008. One contributing cause to the childhood obesity epidemic might be a drop-off in breastfeeding, which (if done for four to six months) significantly cuts the risk of childhood obesity; see Sally Squires, "Hey, parents, time to take charge," *Los Angeles Times*, Sept. 25, 2006; also recommended is eating meals with one's children and exercising with them from an early age.

[101] These results from a study in 1988 were cited in "Veggies Take the Plunge," *Garden Design*, Oct. 2000, p. 22-23. Also see Donald R. Davis, "Trade-Offs in Agriculture and Nutrition," *Food Technology*, March 2005, vol. 59, no. 3; Davis found that between 1950 and 1999 the levels of phosphorous, calcium, and iron declined between 9 and 16 percent; riboflavin declined by 38 percent, and ascorbic acid declined by 15 percent. Also see Anne-Marie Mayer, "Historical Changes in the Mineral Content of Fruits and Vegetables," *British Food Journal*, vol. 99, no. 6, 1997, pp. 207-211; Mayer found significantly lower levels of nutrients in 1980, compared to those of 1930. Also see Deborah Rich, "Not All Apples Are Created Equal," *Earth Island Journal*, Spring 2008, pp. 26-30.

Several studies have found similar decreases, for which the major cause is that the hybrid crops used in industrial agriculture today grow larger and faster but cannot acquire nutrients from the soil at that same rate; in addition, synthetic fertilizers block the plants' ability to synthesize and to absorb nutrients (see Donald R. Davis article, above).

[102] Amina Khan, "Warming overload," *Los Angeles Times*, 15 May 2010. The article reports on a study by Arnold J. Bloom, Martin Burger, Jose Salvador Rubio Asensio, and Asaph B. Cousins, "Carbon Dioxide Enrichment Inhibits Nitrate Assimilation in Wheat and Arabidopsis," *Science*, vol. 328, no. 5980, pp. 899 – 903, published online in May 14, 2010.

[103] "The Winner: Organic," *Prevention* magazine, March 2009, p. 48.

[104] Siobhan McDonough, "Survey finds sleep woes affect most Americans," *San Francisco Chronicle*, March 29, 2005; Benjamin Pimentel, "E-mail addles the brain," *San Francisco Chronicle*, May 4, 2005.

[105] Siobhan McDonough, "Survey finds sleep woes affect most Americans," *San Francisco Chronicle*, March 29, 2005.

[106] Karyn Maier, "Painless Vision Quest," *Energy Times*, June 2005, p. 18.

[107] Shari Roan, "Distance vision is all a blur to more of us," *Los Angeles Times*, Dec. 15, 2009. The journalist cites Susan Vitale, the lead author of the study at the National Eye Institute, a part of the National Institutes of Health.

[108] See, for example, David Perlman, "Early aging tied to chronic stress," *San Francisco Chronicle*, Nov. 30, 2001.

[109] William R. Mattox, Jr., "The Great (Clinical) Depression," *San Francisco Chronicle*, April 8, 1999.

[110] Also see Gregg Easterbrook, *The Progress Paradox* (Random House, 2003) on the increasing levels of depression in the United States even as the levels of living conditions improved. Also see *American Mania: When More Is Not Enough* by Peter C. Whybrow (New York: Norton & Co., 2005).

[111] Roni Caryn Rabin, "What Happy People Don't Do," *New York Times*, Nov. 20, 2008; this article reports on a study conducted by John Robinson, a sociologist at the University of Maryland, which was published in the journal *Social Indicators Research* (vol. 89, no. 3, 2008, pp. 565-571).

Also see Karen Kaplan, "The dark side of watching to much TV," *Los Angeles Times*, Feb. 3, 2009; this article reports on a study conducted by researchers at the University of Pittsburgh and Harvard University covering the period between 1995 and 2002, in which they found that excessive television time as an adolescent increases the risk for depression as an adult; see Brian A. Primack, Brandi Swanier, Anna M. Georgiopoulos, Stephanie R. Land, and Michael J. Fine, "Association Between Media Use in Adolescence and Depression in Young Adulthood: A

Longitudinal Study," *Archives of General Psychology*, vol. 66, no. 2, Feb. 2009, pp.181-188.

[112] Marla Cone, "Scientists issue group warning on plastic chemical's hazards," *Los Angeles Times*, Aug. 3, 2007, reporting on a statement published online by the journal *Reproductive Toxicology*.

[113] See, for example, Robert H. Lustig, "Childhood obesity: behavioral aberration or biochemical drive? Reinterpreting the First Law of Thermodynamics," *Nature Clinical Practice Endocrinology & Metabolism*, vol. 2, no. 8, Aug. 2006, pp. 447-458. Lustig, a pediatric neuroendocrinologist at the University of California at San Francisco, has determined that a key reason for the epidemic of pediatric obesity, now the most commonly diagnosed childhood ailment, is that high-calorie, low-fiber Western diets promote hormonal imbalances that encourage children to overeat. After conducting a comprehensive review of obesity research, he concluded that food manufacturing practices have created a "toxic environment" that dooms children to being overweight. Our current Western food environment has become highly insulinogenic, Lustig notes, as demonstrated by its increased energy density, high-fat content, high glycemic index, increased fructose composition, decreased fiber, and decreased dairy content. He concludes, in particular, that fructose (too much) and fiber (not enough) appear to be cornerstones of the obesity epidemic through their effects on insulin. It has long been known that the hormone insulin acts on the brain to encourage eating through two separate mechanisms. First, it blocks the signals that travel from the body's fat stores to the brain by suppressing the effectiveness of the hormone leptin, resulting in increased food intake and decreased activity. Second, insulin promotes the signal that seeks the reward of eating carried by the chemical dopamine, which makes a person want to eat to get the pleasurable dopamine "rush." Calorie intake and expenditure normally are regulated by leptin. When leptin is functioning properly, it increases physical activity, decreases appetite, and increases feelings of well-being. Conversely, when leptin is suppressed, feelings of well-being and activity decrease and appetite increases - a state called "leptin resistance." Changes in food processing during the past 30 years, particularly the addition of sugar to a wide variety of foods that once never included sugar and the removal of fiber, both of which promote insulin production, have created an environment in which our foods are essentially addictive.

[114] "Toxic Chemicals by the Hundred Found in Blood of Newborns," Environmental News Service, July 14, 2005; the study, "Body Burden: The Pollution in Newborns," by the Environmental Working Group is available on-line at www.ewg.org/reports/bodyburden2.

[115] Sandra Steingraber, "The Story about the One: Pro-life and pro-choice can find common ground over toxins," *Orion*, July-Aug. 2009, p. 17.

[116] See Nicholas D. Kristof, "It's Time to Learn from Frogs," *New York Times*, June 28, 2009; Kristof reports in this column on a 50-page statement released in June 2009 by the Endocrine Society, a group of researchers, who stated: "We present the evidence that endocrine disruptors have effects on male and female reproduction, breast development and cancer, prostate cancer, neuroendocrinology, thyroid, metabolism and obesity, and cardiovascular endocrinology." Sadly, such evidence was presented twelve years earlier – but largely ignored – in *Our Stolen Future: Are We Threatening Our Fertility, Intelligence, and Security? – A Scientific Detective Story* by Theo Colburn, Dianne Dumanoski, and John Peter Meyers (New York: Plume, 1997). Kristof notes that federal Environmental Protection Agency "is moving toward screening endocrine disrupting chemicals, but at a glacial pace."

[117] Lindsey Tanner, "Anti-psychotics' use for kids skyrockets," *San Francisco Chronicle*, March 17, 2006.

[118] Benedict Carey, "Psychosis drugs on the rise for children," *San Francisco Chronicle*, June 6, 2006.

[119] Denise Gellene, "Side Effects of Ritalin Greater in Preschool," *Los Angeles Times*, Oct. 17, 2006.

[120] Katherine Seligman, "Scientists baffled as autism cases soar in state, with no relief in sight," *San Francisco Chronicle*, February 4, 2005. In California the number of new autism cases increased by 13 percent in 2004 over the previous year, with 26,000 autistic people getting treatment at regional centers operated by the state's Department of Developmental Services in 2004, compared to 5,000 people in 1993.

[121] "Study puts autism rate at 1 in 150," *Los Angeles Times*, Feb. 9, 2007. Also see Benedict Carey, "Study Increases Prevalence of Autism Disorders," *New York Times*, Dec. 19, 2009; also see Trine Tsouderos, "1% of 8-year-olds diagnosed as autistic," *Los Angeles Times*, Oct. 5, 2009, which also reports on the 2009 study conducted by the CDC. Also, see the CDC website (www.cdc.gov/ncbddd/autism/index.html); the rate of 1 in 110 was current as of the updating of the site on Dec. 29, 2010.

Also see Marla Cone, "Pesticide link to autism suspected," *Los Angeles Times*, July 30, 2007; two organochlorine pesticides remaining in use long after others were banned, dicofol and endosulfan, correlated with a high incidence of autism in babies whose mothers lived near agricultural fields duringpregnancy where the two were applied and were airborn in probable pesticide drift. Also see A note on the history of autism: prior to 1964 the general medical view on autism (thanks to the grip of Freudian theory in the postwar years, I would surmise) was that this mental disorder was the psychological byproduct of "refrigerator mothers," cold, unfeeling women who forced their children to withdraw into a protective shell of indifference! This blame-the-mother theory (rather like another Freud-influenced theory then that inconsistent mothering was the cause of schizophrenia) was dislodged by Bernard Rimland in his book *Infantile Autism: The Syndrome and Its Implications for a Neural Theory of Behavior* (New York: Appleton-Century-Crofts, 1964). In fact, altering the brain chemistry of people with Asperger's syndrome, by increasing their level of the social-bonding hormone called oxytocin, was found in a study in 2010 to dramatically increase their social learning skills, feelings of trust, and interest in looking at faces; see Elissar Andari, Jean-René Duhamel, Tiziana Zalla, Evelyn Herbrecht, Marion Leboyer, and Angela Sirigu, "Promoting social behavior with oxytocin in high functioning autism spectrum disorders," *Proceedings of the National Academy of Science*, Vol. 107, No. 7, published online before print on February 16, 2010.

[122] See Philip J. Landrigan, "What causes autism? Exploring the environmental contribution," *Current Opinion in Pediatrics*, published online-ahead-of-print on 16 January 2010. Dr. Landrigan, a professor of pediatrics and chair of the department of preventive medicine at the Mount Sinai School of Medicine in New York notes that indirect evidence for an environmental contribution to autism comes from studies demonstrating the sensitivity of the developing brain to external exposures such as lead, ethyl alcohol and methyl mercury, but the most powerful proof-of-concept evidence derives from studies specifically linking autism to exposures in early pregnancy – thalidomide, misoprostol, and valproic acid; maternal rubella infection; and the organophosphate insecticide, chlorpyrifos. He asserts, "Expanded research is needed into environmental causation of autism. Children today are surrounded by thousands of synthetic chemicals. Two hundred of them are neurotoxic in adult humans, and 1000 more in laboratory models. Yet fewer than 20 percent of high-volume chemicals have been tested for neurodevelopmental toxicity. I propose a targeted discovery strategy focused on suspect chemicals, which combines expanded toxicological screening, neurobiological research and prospective epidemiological studies." Also see Nicholas D. Kristof, "Do Toxins Cause Autism?," *New York Times*, Feb. 26, 2010; in writing about Dr. Landrigan's study, Kristof concludes, "The precautionary principle suggests that we should be wary of personal products like fragrances unless they are marked phthalate-free. And it makes sense — particularly for children and pregnant women — to avoid most plastics marked at the bottom as 3, 6 and 7 because they are the ones associated with potentially harmful toxins."

[123] Shari Roan, "Proximity to freeways may raise autism risk," *Los Angeles Times*, Dec. 17, 2010. The article reports on a study published in journal *Environmental Health Perspectives*; the lead author was Heather Volk, who notes that pollution is merely one of the contributing factors.

[124] Thomas Maugh II, "Studies link autism to two genetic defects," *Los Angeles Times*, Jan. 12, 2008. The results of two studies were announced by the Autism Consortium in New England.

Also see a study on the role of pesticide exposure in the womb as a causal factor in the increased rates of autism: mothers who were within 500 meters of fields sprayed with organochlorine pesticides during their first trimester of pregnancy were six times higher to have children with autism compared to mothers who did not live near the fields; see Eric M. Roberts, Paul B. English, Judith K. Grether, Gayle C. Windham, Lucia Somberg, and Craig Wolff, "Maternal Residence Near Agricultural Pesticide Applications and Autism Spectrum Disorders among Children in the California Central Valley," *Environmental Health Perspectives*, vol. 115, no. 10, Oct. 2007 (for a summary, "Autism and Agricultural Pesticides: Integrating Data to Track Trends," see http://www.ehponline.org/docs/2007/115-10/ss.html#auti).

Also see "Birth spacing, autism linked," *Los Angeles Times*, Jan. 10, 2011; the article reports on a study published in the journal *Pediatrics*.

Also see Lindsey Tanner, "Paternity by men in 40s or older linked to possibility of autism in their offspring," *San Francisco Chronicle*, Sept. 5, 2006. (Regarding the link between lower IQ and paternity after the early 40s, see Roni Caryn Rabin, "IQ scores fall for children of older dads study finds," *The Sacramento Bee*, March 10, 2009 (reprinted from the *New York Times*, March 9, 2009).

Also, a Swedish study of 1,227 children with autism who were born between 1977 and 2003 found higher rates than normal of depression and personality disorders among the mothers; see "Parental ills are linked to autism," *Los Angeles Times*, May 5, 2008; for the study, see Julie L. Daniels, Ulla Forssen, Christina M. Hultman, Sven Cnattingius, David A. Savitz, Maria Feychting, and Par Sparen, "Parental Psychiatric Disorders Associated With Autism Spectrum Disorders in the Offspring," *Pediatrics*, vol. 121, no. 5, May 2008, pp. 1357-1362.

Also see "Premature births linked to autism," *Los Angeles Times*, April 5, 2008; for the study, see Catherine Limperopoulos, Haim Bassan, Nancy R. Sullivan, Janet S. Soul, Richard L. Robertson, Jr, Marianne Moore, Steven A. Ringer, Joseph J. Volpe, and Adré J. du Plessis, "Positive Screening for Autism in Ex-preterm Infants: Prevalence and Risk Factors," *Pediatrics*, vol. 121, no. 4, April 2008, pp. 758-765.

[125] Mary Engel, "Autism higher for kids in rainy climes," *Los Angeles Times*, Nov. 4, 2008; see Michael Waldman, Sean Nicholson, Nodir Adilov, and John Williams, "Autism Prevalence and Precipitation Rates in California, Oregon, and Washington Counties," *Archives of Pediatric Adolescent Medicine*, vol. 162, no 11, Nov. 2008, pp. 1026-1034.

[126] See Amy M. Branum and Susan L. Lukacs, "Food Allergy Among Children in the United States," *Pediatrics*, vol. 124, no. 6, Dec. 2009, pp. 1549-1555. This study, conducted by the National Center for Health Statistics at the Centers for Disease Control and Prevention in Hyattsville, MD, looked at several surveys from recent years of subjects under 18 years of age and found a sharp increase in the number of self-reported allergic reactions to foods, doctor visits because of allergic reactions,

and hospitalizations; fully 9 percent of American children tested positive for Immunoglobulin E antibodies to peanuts.

[127] See *F Is for Fat 2009: How Obesity Policies Are Failing in America*, an annual report issued by the Trust for America's Health and the Robert Wood Johnson Foundation, July 2009; childhood obesity rates are highest in the South (Alabama, Mississippi, Tennessee, and West Virginia), and they are lowest in Colorado – but they are over 30 percent in 30 states! Also see Jamie Stengle, "More than 10% of kids ages 2 to 5 overweight," *San Francisco Chronicle*, Dec. 31, 2004. Also see Lee Bowman, "Heavy data: 1 in 10 tots are overweight," *San Francisco Chronicle*, Aug. 10, 2006. Also see Sally Squires, "Kids fill up on sugary TV ads," *Los Angeles Times*, April 9, 2007.

[128] Lindsey Tanner, "2 million U.S. children seen as diabetes risks," *San Francisco Chronicle*, Nov. 7, 2005; Jamie Stengle, "More than 10% of kids ages 2-5 overweight."

[129] Lindsey Tanner, "Many teens are so unfit they'd fail a treadmill test," *San Francisco Chronicle*, Dec. 21, 2005; this national survey was conducted at Northwestern University.

[130] Matea Gold, "Kids' eyes are glued to TV," *Los Angeles Times*, Oct. 27, 2009. The article discusses the study, "TV Viewing Among Kids at an 8-Year High," conducted by Patricia McDonough of the Nielsen Company and released on Oct. 26, 2009 on their website, blog.nielsen.com/nielsenwire. American children aged 2-11 are watching more and more television than they have in years. New findings from the Nielsen Company show kids aged 2-5 now spend more than 32 hours a week on average in front of a TV screen. The older segment of that group (ages 6-11) spend a little less time, about 28 hours per week watching TV, due in part that they are more likely to be attending school for longer hours.

[131] See Joseph Chilton Pierce, *Evolution's End: Claiming the Potential of Our Intelligence* (New York: HarperCollins, 1992).

Also see "France aims against TV for toddlers," *Los Angeles Times*, Aug. 21, 2008; France's broadcast authority has banned French channels from airing TV shows aimed at children under three years of age to shield them from developmental risks.

Also see Carl Erik Landhuis, Richie Poulton, David Welch, and Robert John Hancox, "Does Childhood Television Viewing Lead to Attention Problems in Adolescence? Results From a Prospective Longitudinal Study," *Pediatrics*, vol. 120, no. 9, Sept. 2007, pp. 532 - 537.

[132] Kaiser Family Foundation, Program for the Study of Media and Health, *Generation M2: Media in the Lives of 8-to-18-Year-Olds*, Jan. 20, 2010 (www.kff.org/entmedia/mh012010pkg.cfm).

[133] Kaiser Family Foundation, Program for the Study of Media and Health, *A Teacher in the Living Room? Educational Media for Babies, Toddlers, and Pre-schoolers*, Dec. 14, 2004 (www.kff.org/entmedia/7427.cfm). Also see, Lauran Neergaard, " Many parents introduce tots to television right away," AP wire story, *Columbus Dispatch*, May 25, 2006. Also see the website of BabyFirstTV, a 24-hour-a-day network that debuted in 2006 and features scores of programs that are supposedly "specifically tailored to meet the needs of infants and toddlers" and was broadcasting in seven countries by 2010 (wwwbabyfirsttv.com [accessed on Feb. 10, 2010]).

[134] Tamar Lewin, "Explosion of computer games, videos for toddlers, study says," *San Francisco Chronicle*, Oct. 29, 2003; Lindsey Tanner, "TV hobbles learning, studies find," *San Francisco Chronicle*, July 5, 2005.

[135] Marianne McGinnis, "Breaking News: Skip the soda, turn off the TV – Modern life is bad for kids' bones," *Prevention*, June 2004, p. 146.

[136] "ADHD again tied to pesticides," *Los Angeles Times*, Aug. 21, 2010; the article reports on a study of Mexican-American children in the Salinas Valley in California, which was published in the journal *Environmental Health Perspectives*.

[137] Chelsea Martinez, "They may snooze in class but …," *Los Angeles Times*, Aug. 6, 2007. For the findings cited in this article, see Sasko D. Stojanovski, Rafia S. Rasu, Rajesh Balkrishnan, and Milap C. Nahata, "Trends in Medication Prescribing for Pediatric Sleep Difficulties in US Outpatient Settings," *Sleep*, vol. 30, no. 8, pp. 1013-1017. The article by Martinez also cites a drug-trend report published by Medco that found a 14.6 percent rise in 2006 in prescription-drug usage prescribed for children with sleep problems.

[138] Madeline Levine, "What Price, Privilege?," *San Francisco Chronicle Magazine*, June 25, 2006.

[139] Lindsey Tanner, "Study finds many at 2 top schools who cut, burn themselves," *San Francisco Chronicle*, June 5, 2006.

[140] Larry Gordon, "UCLA stabbing puts renewed focus on mental health," *Los Angeles Times*, Oct. 25, 2009. The article cites results of the 2009 *National Survey of Counseling Center Directors*, sponsored by the American College Counseling Association. Among the results of the survey, 93.4 percent of the directors reported that the recent trend toward greater number of students with severe psychological problems continues to be true on their campuses. Directors reported that 48.4% of their clients have severe psychological problems.

[141] Erica Goode, "Students' emotional health worsens," *San Francisco Chronicle*, Feb. 3, 2003.

[142] Sheldon Cohen, "The Pittsburgh Common Cold Studies: Psychosocial Predictors of Susceptibility to Respiratory Infectious Illness," *International Journal*

of Behavioral Medicine, vol. 12, no. 3, Sept. 2005, pp. 123-131; this overview article covers twenty years of research at Carnegie Mellon University have resulted in the findings that social integration is associated with reduced risk irrespective of stress levels and that social support protects persons from the pathogenic influences of stress. Also see an earlier study: Sheldon Cohen et al., "Social Ties and Susceptibility to the Common Cold," *Journal of the American Medical Association*, vol. 277, no. 24, June 25, 1997, pp. 1940-1944. Participants were 276 healthy volunteers, aged 18 to 55 years. In response to two viruses, those with more types of social ties were less susceptible to common colds. Susceptibility to colds decreased in a dose-response manner with increased diversity of the social network. There was an adjusted relative risk of 4.2 comparing persons with fewest (1 to 3) to those with most (6 or more) types of social ties. Although smoking, poor sleep quality, alcohol abstinence, low dietary intake of vitamin C, elevated catecholamine levels, and being introverted were all associated with greater susceptibility to colds, they could only partially account for the relation between social network diversity and incidence of colds.

[143] Linda K. Russek and Gary E. Schwartz, "Feeling of Parental Caring Predict Health Status in Midlife: A 35-Year Follow-up of the Harvard Mastery of Stress Study," *Journal of Behavioral Medicine*, vol. 20, no. 1, Feb. 1997, pp. 1-13. In the early 1950s, multiple-choice scores reflecting feelings of warmth and closeness with parents were obtained from a sample of healthy, undergraduate Harvard men who participated in the Harvard Mastery of Stress Study. Thirty-five years later, detailed medical and psychological histories and medical records were obtained. Ninety-one percent of participants who did not perceive themselves to have had a warm relationship with their mothers (assessed during college) had diagnosed diseases in midlife (including coronary artery disease, hypertension, duodenal ulcer, and alcoholism), as compared to 45 percent of participants who perceived themselves to have had a warm relationship with their mothers. A similar association between perceived warmth and closeness and future illness was obtained for fathers. Since parents are usually the most meaningful source of social support in early life, the perception of parental love and caring may have important effects on biological and psychological health and illness throughout life. Note: The lead researcher in the follow-up study, Dr. Linda Russek, is the daughter of one of the original researchers who collaborated on the Harvard Mastery of Stress Study in the early 1950s, Dr. Henry I. Russek. Her follow-up study of her father's work has contributed significantly to our emerging understanding of relational physiology.

[144] Both the empirical and the intangible benefits of having a doula present during childbirth are summarized in "What is a doula?" by Lauri Smit (www.storknet. com/cubbies/childbirth/doula.htm).

Also see Grace Manning-Orenstein, "A birth intervention: the therapeutic effects of Doula support versus Lamaze preparation on first-time mothers' working models of caregiving," *Alternative Therapies in Health and Medicine*, vol. 4, no. 4, July 1998, pp. 73-81. Also see Martin T. Stein, John H. Kennell, and Ann Fulcher, "Benefits of a Doula Present at the Birth of a Child," *Pediatrics*, vol. 114, no. 5, Nov. 2004, pp. 1488-1491.

[145] See Melissa Bartick and Arnold Reinhold, "The Burden of Suboptimal Breastfeeding in the United States: A Pediatric Cost Analysis," *Pediatrics*, April 5, 2010 (online); their study determined that the relationship between breastfeeding and infant health is so strong that the lives of nearly 900 babies would be saved each year, along with billions of dollars, if 90 percent of U.S. mothers breastfed their babies for the first six months of life.

[146] "Breast-fed babies smarter, say studies," *San Francisco Chronicle*, 8 May 2002, reporting on an overview article in the *Journal of the American Medical Association*. Also see Lindsey Tanner, "Breast-feeding found to help moms fend off type 2 diabetes," *San Francisco Chronicle*, Nov. 23, 2005. Also see Devon Schuyler, "Breast or bottle? No final answer yet," *Los Angeles Times*, Dec. 3, 2007; breastfed babies are 64 percent less likely to develop gastrointestinal infections, 72 percent less likely to be hospitalized for lower respiratory tract disease, 36 percent less likely to die from Sudden Infant Death syndrome, 27 to 40 percent less likely to develop early-childhood asthma, and 39 percent less likely to develop Type II diabetes as adults. Unfortunately, most breastfeeding mothers are weaning their babies before the maximal benefits can occur. Nearly 75 percent of new mothers in the USA breastfeed currently (the highest rate in at least twenty years), but only about 30 percent are still doing so at three months, and only 11 percent at six months; see "Breast-feeding at a high, but tapers fast," *Los Angeles Times*, Aug. 3, 2007.

[147] Denise Gellene, "Study links IQs, breastfeeding," *Los Angeles Times*, May 6, 2008; see Michael S. Kramer et al., "Breastfeeding and Child Cognitive Development: New Evidence From a Large Randomized Trial," *Archives of General Psychiatry*, vol. 65, no. 5, May 2008, pp. 578-584. In this study, a total of 17,046 healthy, breastfeeding infants were enrolled, of whom 13,889 (81.5 percent) were followed up at age 6.5 years. The experimental intervention led to a large increase in exclusive breastfeeding at age 3 months (43.3 percent for the experimental group vs 6.4 percent for the control group) and a significantly higher prevalence of any breastfeeding at all ages up to and including 12 months. At age 6.5, the experimental group had higher means on all of the Wechsler Abbreviated Scales of Intelligence measures; in addition, teachers' academic ratings were significantly higher in the experimental group for both reading and writing. The children who had been breastfed scored an average of 7.5 points higher on a verbal IQ test.

[148] Lindsey Tanner, "Study sees hope for brain-damaged preemies," *San Francisco Chronicle*, Feb. 12, 2003.

[149] Ellen Michaud, "Reconnect," *Prevention* magazine, December 2000, p. 124. Also

see Edward M. Hallowell, *Connect: 12 Vital Ties That Open Your Heart, Lengthen Your Life, and Deepen Your Soul* (New York: Pantheon, 1999). Also see Lynne C. Giles, Gary F. V. Glonek, Mary A. Luszcz, and Gary R. Andrews, "Effect of social networks on 10 year survival in very old Australians: the Australian longitudinal study of aging," *Journal of Epidemiology and Community Health* 2005; 59:574-579.

[150] Shari Roan, "Maybe nostalgia's gotten a bad rap," *Los Angeles Times*, Dec. 22, 2008. The article summarizes a study conducted by researchers in China; see Xinyue Zhou, Constantine Sedikides, Tim Wildschut, and Ding-Guo Gao (Sun Yat-Sen University and University of Southampton), "Counteracting Loneliness: On the Restorative Function of Nostalgia," *Psychological Science*, vol. 19, no. 10, Oct. 2008, pp.1023-1029.

[151] Denise Gellene, "'Cold and lonely' go together – literally," *Los Angeles Times*, Sept. 20, 2008.

[152] Denise Gellene, "Is that a hot cup of coffee or are you just glad to see me?," *Los Angeles Times*, Oct. 24, 2008.

[153] Denise Gellene, "Loneliness often precedes elder dementia, study finds," *Los Angeles Times*, Feb. 10, 2007. Also see Krister Håkansson, Suvi Rovio, Eeva-Liisa Helkala, Anna-Riitta Vilska, Bengt Winblad, Hilkka Soininen, Aulikki Nissinen, Abdul H Mohammed, and Miia Kivipelto, "Association between mid-life marital status and cognitive function in later life: population based cohort study," *British Medical Journal*, issue 339, July 2009, p. 2462; the study found that people cohabiting with a partner in mid-life (mean age 50.4) were less likely than all other categories (single, separated, or widowed) to show cognitive impairment later in life at ages 65-79. Those widowed or divorced in mid-life and still so at follow-up had three times the risk compared with married or cohabiting people.

[154] Pam Belluck, "Giving Alzheimer's Patients Their Way, Even Doses of Chocolate," *New York Times*, January 1, 2011.

[155] Jeannine Stein, "Toll of loneliness," *Los Angeles Times*, March 22, 2010; the article reports on the Chicago Health, Aging and Social Relations Study, which was published in the journal *Psychology and Aging* and which found that people who ranked as feeling the most lonely had blood pressure levels 14.4 points higher than those who felt the least lonely.

Regarding loneliness and genetic expression, see Marnell Jameson, "Stress Hurts: The bright side of life," *Los Angeles Times*, Dec. 1, 2008; this article cites a study done at UCLA in 2007, published in the journal *Genome Biology*, which found that the immune system's inflammatory response was much higher in cells from people who felt socially isolated and lonely. Also see J. Bradley Williams et al., "A Model of Gene-Environment Interaction Reveals Altered Mammary Gland

Gene Expression and Increased Tumor Growth following Social Isolation," *Cancer Prevention Research*, vol. 2, no. 10, Oct. 2009, pp. 850-861. Also see Gretchen L. Hermes, Bertha Delgado, Maria Tretiakova, Sonia A. Cavigelli, Thomas Krausz, Suzanne D. Conzen, and Martha K. McClintock, "Social isolation dysregulates endocrine and behavioral stress while increasing malignant burden of spontaneous mammary tumors," *Proceedings of the National Academy of Sciences*, vol. 106, no. 52, Dec. 2009, pp. 22393-22398; the study found that lonely, stressed rats were at a much higher risk to develop naturally occurring breast tumors than were rats living in a social group.

[156] Brian C. Trainor, Colleen Sweeny, and Robert Cardiff, "Isolating the Effects of Social Interactions on Cancer Biology," *Cancer Prevention Research*, vol. 2, no. 10, Oct. 2009, pp. 843-846.

[157] Dr. Sheldon Cohen, cited in "Buddies Are Good for You," *AARP Bulletin*, Oct. 2007, p. 16.

[158] Gregory Rodriguez, "Feeling lonely is a real pain," *Los Angeles Times*, Feb. 23, 2009; the journalist does not cite the study but does cite the book *Loneliness: Human Nature and the Need for Social Connection* by John Cacioppo, a neuroscientist at the University of Chicago (New York: W. W. Norton & Co., 2009).

[159] Shari Roan, "Happy with deep discussions," *Los Angeles Times*, March 22, 2010; the study was conducted by researchers from Washington University and the University of Arizona and was published online in the journal *Psychological Science*.

[160] Lynn Schnurnberger, "The Truth about Family Dinners," *Parade* Magazine, Nov. 11, 2007, p. 10.

[161] Lisa F. Berkman and Lester Breslow, *Health and Ways of Living: The Alameda County Study* (Oxford University Press, 1983).

[162] See Ben Harder, "Here's to good buddies, good health," *Los Angeles Times*, Oct. 16, 2006; the article reports on a study of 12,000 male employees in their 40s and 50s at a French gas and electricity company, which tracked deaths among them for ten years and found that those who felt least socially integrated were three times more likely to die during that period. See Lisa F. Berkman, Maria Melchior, Jean-François Chastang, Isabelle Niedhammer, Annette Leclerc, and Marcel Goldberg, "Social Integration and Mortality: A Prospective Study of French Employees of Electricity of France–Gas of France: The GAZEL Cohort," *American Journal of Epidemiology*, vol. 159, no. 2, Jan. 15, 2004, pp. 167-174.

[163] Kristina Orth-Gomer, Annika Rosengren, and Lars Whilhelmsen, "Lack of social support and incidence of coronary heart disease in middle-aged Swedish men," *Psychomatic Medicine*, vol. 55, no. 1, 1993, pp. 37-43.

[164] Edward M. Hallowell, M.D., quoted in Ellen Michaud, "Reconnect," *Prevention* magazine, Dec. 2000, pp. 126-127. Also see Stephen Post and Jill Neimark, *Why Good Things Happen to Good People* (New York: Broadway Books, 2007).

[165] Deborah Halter, "Many learn forgiveness transforms," *National Catholic Reporter*, Dec. 15, 2005. Studies are beginning to show that those who are able to forgive enjoy better interpersonal and social support, as well as lower cardiovascular risks and increased rates of survival rates from several types of cancer. Unforgiving persons, on the other hand, are shown to suffer anxiety, paranoia, heart disease, depression, and other psychosomatic symptoms.

[166] Eileen Mitchell, "Just what the doctor ordered," *San Francisco Chronicle*, Sept. 20, 2003. See Marty Becker, *The Healing Power of Pets* (New York: Hyperion, 2002); also see studies cited by the Delta Society (www.deltasociety.org).

[167] For a study finding a strong correlation between the well-being, happiness, health, and longevity of people who are "emotionally and behaviorally compassionate" (so long as they are not overwhelmed by helping tasks), see Stephen G. Post, "Altuism, Happiness, and Health: It's Good to Be Good," *International Journal of Behaviorial Medicine*, Volume 12, no. 2, June 2005, pp. 66-77. Also see Terry Y. Lum and Elizabeth Lightfoot, "The Effects of Volunteering on the Physical and Mental Health of Older People," *Research on Aging*, vol. 27, no. 1, 2005, pp. 31-55. This study found empirical support for earlier claims that volunteering slows the decline in self-reported health and functioning levels, slows the increase in depression levels, and improves mortality rates for those who volunteer at least 100 hours per year.

[168] Keay Davidson, "Scientists discover how the brain feels others' pain," *San Francisco Chronicle*, Feb. 20, 2004.

[169] Shankar Vedantam, "If It Feels Good to Be Good, It Might Be Only Natural," *Washington Post*, May 28, 2007. The term "healthy-helper syndrome" was coined by two psychologists, Allan Luks and Howard Andrews, who collected surveys from more than 3,000 student volunteers; reported in *The Lark Letter*, April 2004, p. 2.

[170] All of the findings cited in this paragraph (except those with their own footnote) were noted by Erin Middlewood, "Social Medicine," *Orion*, Sept.-Oct. 2005, p. 70.

[171] Susan Weiner, "Don't Go Breaking Your Heart," *Energy Times*, Feb. 2005, p. 35; the data cited was published in *Depression and Anxiety*, 1998. Also see

[172] Karen Kaplan, "People who feel wronged can really take it to heart," *Los Angeles Times*, May 15, 2007. See Roberto De Vogli, Jane E Ferrie, Tarani Chandola, Mika Kivimäki, and Michael G Marmot, "Unfairness and health: evidence from the Whitehall II Study," *Journal of Epidemiology and Community Health*, vol. 61, pp.

513-518; the study found that unfairness is an independent predictor of increased coronary events and impaired health functioning.

[173] Ulysses Torassa, "Taking lumps more seriously," *San Francisco Chronicle*, July 14, 2002; the study was conducted by Dr. William Goodson, a breast surgeon at California Pacific Medical Center in San Francisco.

[174] Janet Cromley, "Meet, greet, then treat," *Los Angeles Times*, June 18, 2007. The accrediting association is the Accreditation Council on Graduate Medical Education.

[175] Columbia University's School of Education, advertisement announcing the new M.S. in Narrative Medicine, *The New Yorker*, April 6, 2009, p. 37.

[176] Janet Quinn, "Holding sacred space: The nurse as healing environment," *Holistic Nursing Practice*, vol. 6, no. 4, 1992, pp. 26-36.

[177] See, for example, Dr. Marianne Legato, *Eve's Rib: The New Science of Gender-Specific Medicine and How It Can Save Your Life* (New York: Harmony Books, 2002). Also see Carol Ann Rinzler, *Why Eve Doesn't Have an Adam's Apple: A Dictionary of Sex Differences* (New York: Facts on File, 1996).

[178] Shelley E. Taylor, L. C. Klein, B. P. Lewis, T. L. Gruenewald, R. A. R. Gurung, and J. A. Updegraff, "Female Responses to Stress: Tend-and-Befriend, Not Fight-or-Flight," *Psychological Review*, vol. 107, no. 3, 2000, pp. 411-429.

[179] "Contact High," an article on a study conducted by Kathleen C. Light at the University of North Carolina in Chapel Hill, *Allure*, July 2005.

[180] Denise Gellene, "A wife's silence isn't golden in marital spats," *Los Angeles Times*, Sept. 24. 2007.

[181] Rebecca C. Thurston and Laura D. Kubzansky, "Women, Loneliness, and Incident Coronary Heart Disease," *Psychosomatic Medicine*, vol. 71, no. 8, Oct. 2009, pp. 836-842.

[182] Bob Young, "Learning to Listen: Truly hearing what is being said can improve health, relationships," *Los Angeles Times*, Living Well supplement, Oct. 14, 2008.

[183] Gerard Karsenty, quoted in Natalie Angier, "Bone, A Masterpiece of Elastic Strength," *New York Times*, April 28, 2009.

[184] Melissa Healy, "An alarming side effect: thoughts of suicide," *Los Angeles Times*, April 14, 2008.

[185] Deborah L. Shelton, "Study questions removal of ovaries," *Los Angeles Times*, April 21, 2009. The study was conducted by researchers from Harvard University who mined the data in the national Nurses' Health Study, which has analyzed the health of 122,700 female registered nurses ages 30 to 55 since 1976; the study

focused on health effects of the removal of the ovaries before age 50. See William H. Parker, Michael S. Broder, Eunice Chang, Diane Feskanich, Cindy Farquhar, Zhimae Liu, Donna Shoupe, Jonathan S. Berek, Susan Hankinson, and JoAnn E. Manson, "Ovarian Conservation at the Time of Hysterectomy and Long-Term Health Outcomes in the Nurses' Health Study," *Obstetrics & Gynecology*, vol. 113, no. 5, May 2009, pp. 1027-1037.

[186] It could be concluded that within American medicine the mechanistic model of the (female) body merely provided a means of regularizing an irrepressible urge in patriarchal cultures to violate female bodies and that this dynamic combined with the American Medical Association's postwar dominance of the health insurance in our country to allow millions of surgeons to become wealthy through myriad unnecessary surgical removals of the female organs – and even, less often, the frontal lobes of the female brain.

Moreover, biomechanical medicine simply does not grasp the complex and dynamic functions of various bodily "parts." For instance, removal of a woman's ovary (which is sometimes done solely to prevent possible disease in the future) has been found be associated later in life with increased risk of developing cognitive impairment or dementia, especially if a woman had both ovaries removed before age 46 or one ovary removed before age 38; see "Ovary removal linked to increased risk of dementia," *Mayo Clinic Health Letter*, Aug. 2006, p. 4.

[187] Emily Sohn, "The power of potassium," *Los Angeles Times*, February 23, 2009. The article reports on studies that found the subjects who had consumed a high amount of potassium and a low level of sodium (about twice as much potassium as sodium) were 50 percent less likely to die of cardiovascular disease than those who ate the most sodium and the least potassium. Most importantly, the ratio of the two nutrients mattered more than the amount of either one when it came to predicting cardiovascular disease. Concentrations of potassium are found in bananas, potatoes, spinach, raisins, and orange juice.

Also, the relationship, or ratio, between copper and zinc (normally 1:1 in humans) is out of balance in violent, aggressive boys, according to research conducted by William Walsh and his colleagues at the Health Research Institute in Skokie, IL; see "Violence Linked to Imbalance of Cooper, Zinc," *San Francisco Chronicle*, Nov. 25, 1994. Dr. Walsh notes that "most violent criminals have a metal metabolism disorder or an imbalance of histamine," a body chemical released during an allergic reaction.

[188] Candace B. Pert, Henry E. Dreher, and Michael R. Ruff, "The Psychosomatic Network: Foundations of Mind-Body Medicine," *Consciousness and Healing: Integral Approaches to Mind-Body Medicine*, edited by Marilyn Schlitz and Tina Amorok with Marc S. Micozzi (St. Louis: Elsevier Churchill Livingstone, 2005), pp. 61-78.

[189] See Michael Gerson, *The Second Brain: The Scientific Basis of Gut Instinct and a Groundbreaking New Understanding of Nervous Disorders of the Stomach and Intestines* (New York: HarperCollins, 1998). Also see "The Brain-Gut Connection," Alternative Medical Angel website on holistic medicine (http://altmedangel.com and then "Gutbrain").

[190] Carl T. Hall, "UCSF Researchers Unscramble Nerve Cell Growth," *San Francisco Chronicle*, March 11, 2001.

[191] James C. Grotta, MD; Elizabeth A. Noser, MD; Tony Ro, PhD; Corwin Boake, PhD; Harvey Levin, PhD; Jarek Aronowski, PhD Timothy Schallert, PhD, "Constraint-Induced Movement Therapy," *Stroke*, vol. 35, Nov. 2004, pp. 2699-2701.

[192] Denise Gellene, "Pricier pills are seen as better," *Los Angeles Times*, March 5, 2008.

[193] Many studies in epigenetics have demonstrated that our inherited genome and our environmental experience are inherently interrelated, causing changes in our epigenome. See, for example, the PBS website that accompanies the NOVA program *Ghost in Your Genes* (www.pbs.org/nova/genes), which was originally broadcast in October 2007. Also see Natalie Angier, "Not Just Genes: Moving Beyond Nature vs. Nurture," *New York Times*, Feb. 25, 2003.

[194] Sandra Steingraber, "Ecological Inheritance," *Orion* Magazine, Nov./Dec. 2009, pp. 12-13.

[195] A biologist's Question and Answer session on the PBS website for the program *Ghost in Your Genes* (see footnote above) notes that rat studies show that maternal nurturing of the offspring after birth reduces their reaction to stress by altering the epigenome in the brain; see, for example, Moshe Szyf, Ian Weaver, and Michael Meaney, "Maternal care, the epigenome and phenotypic differences in behavior," *Reproductive Toxicology*, vol. 24, no. 1, July 2007, pp. 9-19. There is also evidence in humans that prenatal exposure to maternal stress induced by war can increase the risk of subsequently developing schizophrenia; see, for example, J. van Os and J. P. Selten, "Prenatal exposure to maternal stress and subsequent schizophrenia: The May 1940 invasion of The Netherlands," *British Journal of Psychiatry*, vol. 172, 1998, pp. 324-326.

[196] See especially Art Brownstein, MD, *Extraordinary Healing* (Emmaus, PA: Rodale Press, 2006) for numerous examples of patients who were faced with a serious disease or chronic condition and whose bodymind's own healing capabilities, once supported, achieved full cures. Also see Julie K. Silver, MD, *Super Healing* (Emmaus, PA: Rodale Press, 2007. Also see Andrew Weil, MD, *Spontaneous Healing* (New York: Knopf, 1995); Christiane Northrup, MD, *Women's Bodies, Women's Wisdom* (New York: Bantam Books, 1994); and books by Bernie Siegel,

MD and Larry Dossey, MD.

[197] Susan Weiner, "Don't Go Breaking Your Heart," *Energy Times*, Feb. 2005, p. 36.

[198] See, for instance, studies cited in Paul Pearsall, *The Heart's Code: Tapping the Wisdom and Power of Our Heart Energy* (New York: Broadway Books, 1998.

[199] Thomas H. Maugh II, "Same-sex heart recipients fare better," *Los Angeles Times*, Nov. 13, 2008; this article cites a study presented at a meeting of the American Heart Association in New Orleans in 2008. The journalist notes, "The results surprised experts because, for most types of transplants, sex differences are irrelevant as long as a good immunocompatability is achieved." Eric Weiss of Johns Hopkins University, who headed the study, noted, "We hypothesized that we would see a big difference in the short-term survival – which we did, most likely because of heart-size issues – but what was interesting was the substantial difference in the long term, as well." See Eric Weiss, Nishant D. Patel, Stuart D. Russell, William A. Baumgartner, Ashish S. Shah, and John V. Conte, "Gender Matching Aids Long-term Survival After Heart Transplants," American Heart Association's Scientific Sessions, 2008.

[200] M. L. Lyke, "Vet becomes crusader for victims of soldier rape," *Seattle Post-Intelligencer*, April 11, 2006.

[201] See Joshua M. Smyth, Arthur A. Stone, Adam Hurewitz, and Alan Kaell, "Effects of Writing About Stressful Experiences on Symptom Reduction in Patients With Asthma or Rheumatoid Arthritis: A Randomized Trial," *Journal of the American Medical Association*, vol. 281, no. 14, April 14, 1999, pp. 1304-1309.

[202] See the many articles by Gary E. Schwartz and Linda G. Russek on "dynamical energy systems" and "cardiac energetics"; he is the director of the Laboratory for Advances in Consciousness and Healing at the University of Arizona.

[203] "Pre-surgery hypnosis may help reduce pain," *Los Angeles Times*, Aug. 29, 2007. The article reports on a randomized clinical trial of 200 patients; see Guy H. Montgomery et al., "A Randomized Clinical Trial of a Brief Hypnosis Intervention to Control Side Effects in Breast Surgery Patients," *Journal of the National Cancer Institute*, vol. 99, Sept. 5, 2007, pp. 1304-1312.

[204] The research on the efficacy of relaxing before surgery explains to me the witty banter of the anesthesiologist just before my daughter's surgery in 1999. When I encountered him in the hallway later, it turned out that he is actually a grouchy misanthrope, but in service to his patients, he transforms himself into a gently convivial comedian in that last conversation preceding the surgery.

[205] From an article on guided imagery on the American Psychological Association's website, Psychology Matters (www.psychologymatters.org/guidedimagery): "Research on psychoeducational care is confirming that the mind's workings can

indeed influence the body's health. 'Psychoeducational care' includes teaching patients such techniques as guided imagery, relaxation exercises, and hypnosis, as well as providing patients with information about procedures, pain, and recovery. One of the first psychooeducational techniques to show health-promoting potential is guided imagery. During guided imagery, patients think about what is happening to their bodies, and how their bodies should respond in order to be healthy....

Blue Shield of California was the first health plan in the U.S. to offer a guided imagery program to its surgical patients, and the results of a recent study of its effects are impressive. Blue Shield's program combines self-care, pre-surgical guided imagery exercises (via video and CD recordings) with one-on-one telephone support from a Blue Shield nurse health coach. According to Blue Shield, of 3500 patients sent guided imagery tapes before surgery, 75% listened to them. Patients who used the guided imagery tapes experienced less anxiety before surgery and less pain after surgery than did patients who did not use the guided imagery tapes. A full 20% of those who listened to the tapes chose to listen to them after surgery as well. From this study, a subsample of hysterectomy patients who listened to the tapes was compared with hysterectomy patients who did not use guided imagery. Those using guided imagery had hospital bills that were an average of 4.5% lower--an average savings of $654 per patient."

The 36-minute-long guided imagery tape used by Blue Shield of California was developed by Bellaruth Naparstek; it is now widely used. Also see Joseph Casey, *Surgery Preparation for Faster healing and Recovery through Coaching and Hypnosis* (Charleston, SC: BookSurge Publishing, 2004); www.wellnesscoaching. net/surgery_recovery.

[206] Andrea R. Vaucher, "Doctor's orders: Cross your legs and say 'Om,'" *Los Angeles Times*, Oct. 29, 2007. [Note: The glib title affixed to this article by an editor is the opposite of the content: mindfulness-based stress reduction" practices are described as "Buddhist meditation without the Buddhism," not that Om is even a Buddhist concept, of course.] See, for example, the randomized, controlled clinical trial of older patients with lower-back pain that was conducted by Natalia E. Morone, Cheryl S. Lynch, Cartol M. Greco, Hilary A. Tindle, and Debra K. Weiner, "I Felt Like a New Person: The Effects of Mindfulness Meditation on Older Adults With Chronic Pain: Qualitative Narrative Analysis of Diary Entries," *Journal of Pain*, vol. 9, issue 9, Sept. 2008, pp. 841-848.

[207] See Daniel Goleman, *Destructive Emotions: A Scientific Dialogue with the Dalai Lama* (New York: Bantam, 2004); also see, in that volume, "The Protean Brain," by Richard J. Davidson, director of the Laboratory for Affective Neuroscience at the University of Wisconsin.

[208] There are many teachers and meditation centers for mindfulness meditation in the United States today. One I can recommend from experience is the Vipassana Meditation Center in Shelburne Falls, MA, which has many affiliated centers in

the United States and around the world (always owned by a local non-profit trust, not by the founding teacher, S. N. Goenka). I also recommend my old friends Joseph Goldstein and Sharon Salzberg, two renowned Vipassana teachers who are based at the Insight Mediation Center in Barre, MA.

[209] Julie C. Lumeng, Deepak Somashekar, Danielle Appugliese, Niko Kaciroti, Robert F. Corwyn, and Robert H. Bradley, "Shorter Sleep Duration Is Associated With Increased Risk for Being Overweight at Ages 9 to 12 Years," *Pediatrics*, vol. 120, Nov. 2007, pp. 1020-1029.

[210] Chelsea Martinez, "They may snooze in class but … many sleepless kids get meds," *Los Angeles Times*, Aug. 6, 2007. For an overview of behavior therapies, see J. D. Whitworth et al., "Clinical Inquiry: Which nondrug alternatives can help with insomnia?," *Journal of Family Practice*, vol. 56, no. 10, Oct. 2007, pp. 836-7 and 840. Also see C. M. Morin et al., "Psychological and behavioral treatment of insomnia: update of the recent evidence," *Sleep*, vol. 29, no. 11, Nov. 1, 2007, pp. 1398-1414.

Besides the behavioral therapy patients are not offered, they are also not offered highly effective herbal therapies. See Hilary E. MacGregor, "Dozing off without a prescription," *Los Angeles Times*, Aug. 25, 2006; a report published in the *Archives of Internal Medicine* the previous week found that many people with sleep problems found relief with complementary therapies (self-hypnosis, guided imagery, or other relaxing techniques), biological therapies (such as the herbs valerian, kava kava, or melatonin), or amino acids therapy (such as tryptophan and theanine). According to one of the researchers, the most effective herb for sleep is valerian because it "doesn't overly sedate, and over time it helps restore normal 'sleep architecture.'" She added that it is best for those who fall into a deep sleep but wake up not feeling rested.

[211] Susan Brink, "A nap may give your heart a rest," *Los Angeles Times*, Oct. 22, 2007. A study of 23,000 people in Greece published in the Feb. 12, 2007 edition of *Archives of Internal Medicine* found a 37% reduction in heart attacks among people who napped at least three times a week for a minimum of 30 minutes; this was the first such Mediterranean study to weed out sick and sedentary nappers and to control for physical activity and diet. See Androniki Naska et al., "Siesta in Healthy Adults and Coronary Mortality in the General Population," *Archives of Internal Medicine*, vol. 167, no. 3, Feb. 12, 2007, pp. 296-301.

A study published in the Oct. 15, 2007 online edition of the *Journal of Applied Physiology* found a significant drop in blood pressure when the nine volunteers slept, but not when they merely relaxed; see Mohammad Zaregarizi et al., "Acute changes in cardiovascular function during the onset period of daytime sleep: comparison to lying awake and standing," *Journal of Applied Physiology*, vol. 103, 2007, pp. 1332-1338.

[212] Erin Verkler, "Fit kids are smart kids," *Prevention* magazine, April 2005, p. 41.

[213] Susan Brink, "On par with Zoloft," *Los Angeles Times*, Sept. 17, 2007.

[214] Julia M. Klein, "Simply Happy," *AARP* Magazine, Nov. & Dec. 2007, pp. 42 and 44.

[215] Elisabeth Rosenthal, "Research Suggests Exercise May Keep Senility at Bay," *New York Times*, Oct. 11, 2005. Also see Greg Miller, "Brainpower: Think upkeep," *Los Angeles Times*, Oct. 16, 2006; people who were physically active at age 36 (and kept it up) were far less likely to have dementia later in life.

[216] "Brain exercises pay off," *Los Angeles Times*, Dec. 25, 2006. More than 2,800 people with an average age of 73 were given 10 to 12 hours of training in such skills as mnemonics (remembering by using acronyms and rhymes) in 1998 and were observed through 2004; see Sherry L. Willis et al. for the ACTIVE Study Group, "Long-term Effects of Cognitive Training on Everyday Functional Outcomes in Older Adults," *Journal of the American Medical Association,* vol. 296, Dec. 2006, pp. 2805-2814.

[217] Katharine Greider and Roberta Yared, "One, Two, Three, One, Two, Three...," *AARP Bulletin*, Jan. 2007, p. 17.

[218] Benedict Carey, "Child Studies May Ease Fears on Misbehavior," *New York Times*, Nov. 12, 2007; also see Denise Gellene, "ADHD may be temporary, study suggests," *Los Angeles Times*, Nov. 13, 2007.

[219] See Marianne J. Legato, *Eve's Rib: The New Science of Gender-Specific Medicine and How It Can Save Your Life* (New York: Harmony Books, 2002), p. 185.

[220] Amanda Schaffer, "In Diabetes, a Complex of Causes," *New York Times*, 16 Oct. 2007.

[221] See the Institute for Functional Medicine (www.ifm.org). Also see *Textbook of Functional Medicine* by Sidney MacDonald Baker, Peter Bennett, Jeffrey S. Bland, and Leo Galland (Gig Harbor, WA: Institute for Functional Medicine, 2005).

[222] Judy Foreman, "All those birthdays may be making you happy," *Los Angeles Times*, July 16, 2007; this article reports on a study done in Australia in 2006 on the centers in the brain, as well as on other studies.

[223] Shari Roan, "Going for golden," *Los Angeles Times*, Oct. 15, 2007. Also see Shari Roan, "Happy with deep discussions," *Los Angeles Times*, March 22, 2010; the article discusses a study published in *Psychological Science* the findings of which "demonstrated that the happy life is social rather than solitary and conversationally deep rather then superficial;" although this study was done with college students, it may be relevant to happy elders because many older people tend to have little patience for endless small talk, preferring significant conversation.

[224] Carl T. Hall, "Secret to body's 24-hour time clock is in the eye," *San Francisco Chronicle*, Feb. 4, 2002. Also see "Light sensors controlling body clock are discovered," *Los Angeles Times*, June 14, 2008; scientists at the Regulatory Biology Laboratory of the Salk Institute discovered a light-sensitive molecule called melaonpsin; see M. Hatori et al., Temasek Life Sciences Laboratory, Singapore, "Inducible Ablation of Melanopsin-Expressing Retinal Ganglion Cells Reveals Their Central Role in Non-Image Forming Visual Responses," *PLoS ONE*, vol. 3 no. 6, June 11, 2008, p. e2451.

[225] "Sleep hormone deficit tied to breast cancer," *San Francisco Chronicle*, July 25, 2005; the article reports on a study conducted at Brigham and Women's Hospital in Boston; see Eva S. Schernhammer, Francine Laden, Frank E. Speizer, Walter C. Willett, David J. Hunter, Ichiro Kawachi, and Graham A. Colditz, "Rotating Night Shifts and Risk of Breast Cancer in Women Participating in the Nurses' Health Study," *Journal of the National Cancer Institute*, vol. 93, no. 20, October 17, 2001 , p. 1563-1568. Also see Scott Davis, Dana K. Mirick, and Richard G. Stevens, "Night Shift Work, Light at Night, and Risk of Breast Cancer," *Journal of the National Cancer Institute*, vol. 93, no. 20, Oct. 17, 2001, pp. 1557-1562.

[226] "Suffering Less from Late Hours," *Energy Times*, Jan. 2004; see John Axelsson, Torbjörn Åkerstedt, Göran Kecklund, Anne Lindqvist, and Reine Attefors, "Hormonal changes in satisfied and dissatisfied shift workers across a shift cycle," *Journal of Applied Physiology*, vol. 95, July 25, 2003, pp. 2099-2105. Also see Shari Roan, "Cheating Sleep," *Los Angeles Times*, March 24, 2008.

[227] "When Health Is Tethered to the Weather," *Prevention* magazine. Also see Eric Nagourney, "Tanning could put a smile on your face," *San Francisco Chronicle*, July 13, 2004; in a study 14 volunteers (13 women, 1 man) came twice a week to a lounge containing two seemingly identical tanning beds; one of the beds was equipped with a UV filter, and the other was not. In mood assessments given afterward, those who had not been shielded from the UV light consistently seemed more content and more relaxed; when given a chance on a subsequent visit to choose which tanning bed they wanted to lie in, 11 out of 12 people headed straight for the bed that provided ultraviolet light. See Steven R. Feldman, Anthony Liguori, Michael Kucenic, et.al., "Ultraviolet exposure is a reinforcing stimulus in frequent indoor tanners," *Journal of the American Academy of Dermatology*, vol. 51, issue 1, July 2004, pp. 45-51.

[228] "Seasonal variations in cholesterol," *San Francisco Chronicle*, April 27, 2004.

[229] Art Brownstein, M.D., *Extraordinary Healing* (Emmaus, PA: Rodale Press, 2006), pp. 101-103.

[230] Elena Conis, "Call it tropic of less cancer," *Los Angeles Times*, May, 26, 2008.

[231] Amanda Leigh Mascarelli, "Kids' time outside may lower myopia risk," *Los*

Angeles Times, February 13, 2011; the article reports on a study published in 2008 in the journal *Opthalmology*.

[232] UCLA Health System advertisement, *Los Angeles Times*, Sept. 14, 2008.

[233] Bruce Taylor Seeman, "City dwellers suffer as the tree canopy declines," *San Francisco Chronicle*, April 5, 2006. This article reports on the studies regarding the benefits of having trees outside hospital windows, trees in a public housing project, and other locations.

[234] Judy Foreman, "Music soothes and awes – and may help heal us," *Los Angeles Times*, Nov. 5, 2007. Also see the website of the American Music Therapy Association (www.musictherapy.org). Also see David L. Chandler, "Music Through the Years and Ears: Scientists say a taste for melody crosses the lines of time and species," *San Francisco Chronicle*, Nov. 5, 2007.

[235] Sari Harrar, "Try the Music Cure," *Prevention* magazine, August 1999, p. 102. Also see "Music to Your Heart," *Prevention* magazine, Oct. 2008, p. 23; a study at the University of Florence, in Italy, found that among 28 adults who were already taking hypertension medication and listened to soothing classical, Celtic, or Indian music for 30 minutes daily while breathing slowly the following results were measured after only one week: the average systolic reading had dropped by 3.2 points. One month later the average systolic reading had dropped by 4.4 points. See Pietro A. Modesti et al., "Daily sessions of music can reduce 24-hour ambulatory blood pressure in mild hypertension," American Society of Hypertension's Twenty-Third Annual Scientific Meeting and Exposition, 2008: Abstract 230.

Also see the CDs (*Calming, Uplifting, Energy,* and *Sound Asleep*) recorded by the concert pianist Lisa Spector for a psychoacoustics series that draws solely from the classical repertoire, available from Essential Sound (www.EssentialSoundSeries. com). They are highly effective.

[236] Dan Whipple, "A Wilderness Tonic," *Orion*, May/June 2005, p. 70.

[237] See, for instance, *Advanced Aromatherapy: The Science of Essential Oil Therapy* by Kurt Schnaubelt, Ph.D. (Rochester, VT: Healing Arts Press, 1998. Also see Benedict Carey, "Study Uncovers Memory Aid: A Scent During Sleep," *New York Times*, March 9, 2007.

[238] Nissa Simon, "The Scent of Roses for Rosy Dreams," *AARP Bulletin*, Nov. 2008, p. 26. The article reports findings from a German study; see Boris Stuck and Pamela Dalton, presentation, American Academy of Otolaryngology -- Head and Neck Surgery Foundation annual meeting, Chicago, Sept. 21, 2008.

On a related topic, our unconscious relationship with color, see Pam Belluck, "Need a Creative Boost? Find the Blue Room," *New York Times*, Feb. 6, 2009.

[239] "Flower power!," *Prevention* magazine, April 2004, p. 33. Also see, "To Spark

Creativity," *Prevention*, April 2008, p. 176; the article describes research conducted at Texas A & M University, in which women in a room with two blooming potted plants and a bouquet of flowers generated 13 percent more ideas than did women in a room with abstract sculptures. Also see Amanda Macmillan, "Homegrown Healing," *Prevention*, March 2006, p. 117; she cites a study done at Kansas State University in which researchers used brain scans to analyze 90 male and female typists while some typed next to plants and others typed at bare desks: women exposed to flowers were less stressed (though men typing next to flowers did not experience the same benefit as did the women typing next to flowers).

[240] Melissa Healy, "Perks of office plants," *Los Angeles Times*, May 26, 2008.

[241] "Nature Outings May Help Ease Kids' Hyperactive Disorders," *Wall Street Journal*, Aug. 31, 2004. Re garden therapy for traumatized children, see Anne Raver, "A child grows to health in a doctor's garden," *San Francisco Chronicle*, Jan. 18, 2005. Also see especially Sebastiano Santostefano, MD, *Child Therapy in the Great Outdoors* (Analytic Press, 2004).

[242] See J. Maas, R. A. Verheij, S. de Vries, P. Spreeuwenberg, F. G. Schellevis, and P. P. Groenewegen, "Morbidity is related to a green living environment," *Journal of Epidemiology and Community Health*, vol. 63, no. 12, Dec. 2009, pp. 967-973. The annual prevalence rate of 15 of the 24 disease clusters was lower in living environments with more green space in a 1 km radius. The relation was strongest for anxiety disorder and depression. The relation was stronger for children and people with a lower socioeconomic status. Furthermore, the relation was strongest in slightly urban areas and not apparent in very strongly urban areas. The study stresses the importance of green space close to home for children and lower socioeconomic groups.

[243] Danny C. Flanders, "Horticulture therapy takes root in diverse treatment, rehab," *San Francisco Chronicle*, Dec. 1, 2004.

[244] Jules Pretty, "Green Care," *Resurgence*, No. 234, Jan./Feb. 2006, p. 9

[245] "Hort for Your Health," *Garden Design*, Feb./March 2001, p. 15; the article reports on a study that was conducted by researchers at the University of North Carolina at Chapel Hill.

[246] Malcolm Ritter, "Diet may affect brain health, study shows," *San Francisco Chronicle*, April 20, 2006. Also see Dr. Idadore Rosenfeld, "The Latest News about Alzheimer's," *Parade* magazine, Nov. 25, 2007, pp. 19-19. Also see "How Caffeine Helps," *Parade* Magazine, May 4, 2008, p. 24; researchers working with rabbits at the University of North Dakota found that caffeine protects the "blood-brain barrier," which can otherwise be weakened by cholesterol; once weakened, harmful substances from the bloodstream can enter the brain, a process that is thought to lead to Alzheimer's Disease. See X. Chen, J. W. Gawryluk, J. F. Wagener, O,

Ghribi, and J. D. Geiger J. D., "Caffeine blocks disruption of blood brain barrier in a rabbit model of Alzheimer's disease," *Journal of Neuroinflammation*, Vol. 5, April 2008, 12. Also, studies have shown that a deficiency in carotenoids (especially (1) zeaxanthin, found in dark green, leafy vegetables and in yellow and orange fruits and vegetables, and (2) lycopene, found in tomatoes and watermelon) correlates with diminished levels of cognitive functioning in people in their 70s. Also see Nicholas Bakalar, "Coffee Linked to Lower Dementia Risk," *New York Times*, Jan. 24, 2009; the article reports on a study of 1,409 middle-aged men and women in Sweden; see Marjo H. Eskelinen, Tiia Ngandu, Jaakko Tuomilehto, Hilkka Soininen, Miia Kivipelto, "Midlife Coffee and Tea Drinking and the Risk of Late-Life Dementia: A Population-Based *CAIDE* Study," *The Journal of Alzheimer's Disease*, Jan. 2009, pp. 85-91. Also, several studies have found that drinking green, black, or oolong tea boosts mental neural activity and concentration because of the effect of the amino acid theanine paired with the caffeine.

[247] Leah Garchik, "Ravings From a Dehydrated Brain," *San Francisco Chronicle*, April 18, 1999.

[248] Janet Cromley, "Eating away at illness," *Los Angeles Times*, May 12, 2008. This article reports on a number of tailored food plans that have proven successful in treating disease.

[249] Thomas H. Maugh II, "Adverse drug reactions rise sharply, study finds," *Los Angeles Times*, Sept. 11, 2007. Also see Thomas H. Maugh II, "Side effects of prescribed drugs reach record," *Los Angeles Times*, Oct. 23, 2008.

[250] Thomas H. Maugh II, "Acid inhibitors may raise risk of developing dementia," *Los Angeles Times*, Aug. 4, 2007.

[251] Thomas H. Maugh II, "Cancer chemotherapy is shown to impair the brain," *Los Angeles Times*, Dec. 1, 2006.

[252] Andrew Pollack, "Genetic Tests Offer Promise of Personalized Medicine," *New York Times*, Dec. 30, 2008.

[253] Claudia Dreifus, "Saving Lives With Tailor-Made Medication," *New York Times*, Aug. 29, 2006.

[254] Lee Bowman, "Aspirin found to benefit the two sexes differently," *San Francisco Chronicle*, Jan. 18, 2006.

[255] Nigel Hawkes, "Pollutant Found in Blood Is Linked to Sperm Damage," *TimesOnline* (London), Oct. 13, 2005; "Shift in Sex Ratio: Male Numbers Sink in Great Lakes Community," *Environmental Health Prospectives*, Oct. 2005. Also see Paula Baillie-Hamilton, MD, *Toxic Overload* (New York: Penquin Group/Avery, 2005), in which she suggests that taking a good multivitamin/mineral supplement, added vitamin C, magnesium, amino acids, omega-3 fatty acids, probiotics, and

fiber can help to counter environmental toxins.

In addition, long-term exposure to low-level ozone pollution in our air can be lethal in both sexes, increasing the risk of death by up to 50 percent in cities with very polluted air, such as Los Angeles and Riverside, California; see Michael Jerrett, et al., "Long-Term Ozone Exposure and Mortality," *New England Journal of Medicine*, vol. 360, no. 11, March 12, 2009, pp. 1085-1095. Also see Jill U. Adams, "Spewing out some more bad news," *Los Angeles Times*, Oct. 12, 2009; the article cites two studies correlating increases in air pollution with disease. The first was a study by Gillad G. Kaplan et al., "Effect of Ambient Air Pollution on the Incidence of Appendicitis," *Canadian Medical Association Journal*, vol. 181, no. 9, Oct. 2009, pp. 591-597; males were more likely to be affected. The second study was presented at the annual meeting of the American Academy of Otolaryngology-Head and Neck Surgery in San Diego in October 2009 by Nina Kaplan and Neil Bhattacharyya, presenting data that indicates that the reduction in cases of ear infection in children correlates with improvement in air quality over the last decade.

[256] Shankar Vedantam, "Research Links Lead Exposure, Criminal Activity," *Washington Post*, July 8, 2007. The article reports on research by the economist Rick Nevin, who asserts that lead poisoning accounts for much of the variation (change in rates over different periods) of violent crime in the United States and in nine other countries as well. See Rick Nevin, "Understanding international crime trends: The legacy of preschool lead exposure," *Environmental Research*, vol. 104, issue 3, July 2007, pp. 315-336.

[257] "Sharp increase in pre-teen signs of puberty," *The Copenhagen Post*, April 28, 2009. This online article reports on a study in Denmark of 2,000 girls between ages 5 and 20 who were examined in 1992-1993 and in 2006-2008. See Lise Aksglaede, Kaspar Sørensen, Jørgen H. Petersen, Niels E. Skakkebæk, and Anders Juul, "Recent Decline in Age at Breast Development: The Copenhagen Puberty Study," *Pediatrics*, vol. 123, May 2009, pp. e932-e939.

[258] Susan Brink, "Modern Puberty: Early development is the new normal," *Los Angeles Times*, Jan. _ 2008.

[259] Tuna is not the only type of fish with "potentially harmful levels of mercury and other chemicals": they are found in the fish in about half of the lakes and reservoirs in the United States, according to a three-year study released by the EPA in Nov. 2009; see Bloomberg News Release, "Fish have high levels of mercury," *Los Angeles Times*, Nov. 11, 2009. Also see Shari Roan, "Living for Two" and "Poor nutrition in utero, heavy child tomorrow?," *Los Angeles Times,* Nov. 12, 2007. Also see Jill U. Adams, "Alcohol, coffee and baby," *Los Angeles Times*, Nov. 10, 2008; coffee has been found to cause a lower birth weight than would occur without the presence of caffeine in the pregnant mother; the risk of miscarriage also increases if caffeine

is consumed.

[260] Susan Brink, "Birth of the blues?," *Los Angeles Times*, 12 March 2007. A study at Duke University School of Medicine of 700 girls between age 9 and 16 found that 8 percent of the girls of normal birth weight and 38 percent of the girls of low birth weight developed depression during adolescence. Adding two stressful events to the teens' lives, such as poverty or a traumatic event, caused depression to rise to about 15 percent among the girls of normal birth weight but to 80 percent among the girls of low birth weight. See Elizabeth Jane Costello, Carol Worthman, Alaattin Erkanli, and Adrian Angold, "Prediction From Low Birth Weight to Female Adolescent Depression A Test of Competing Hypotheses," *Archives of General Psychiatry*, vol. 64, 2007, pp. 338-344. Also see the website "Mind, Disrupted" (minddisrupted.org) for information on the effects of toxins on our brains.

[261] Shari Roan, "Living for Two," *Los Angeles Times*, Nov. 12, 2007; Charlotte Brody, "Gender Sensitive," *Orion*, March-April 2005, pp. 70-71.

[262] Marla Cone, "Study finds DDT, breast cancer link," *Los Angeles Times*, Sept. 30, 2007.

[263] Charlotte Brody, "Gender Sensitive," *Orion*, March-April 2005, pp. 79-71; like many other women who have examined the situation of female sensitivity to toxins, Brody makes a strong case for revising allowable levels of toxins, which are currently set at a level that sacrifices women and children.

[264] Stress, in the enveloping sense of "hard times," has also been found to cause a drop in the number of male babies born. See "Fewer boys are born in tough times," *Los Angeles Times*, Aug. 25, 2008. During stressful times, such as war and environmental disasters, pregnant mothers' bodies often increase early release of hormones causing premature labor. Most miscarriages, premature births, and stillbirths routinely occur in male fetuses, and during stressful times, more of those occur. It is also thought that stress affects male fertility in that it may well slow the motility of sperm, which might result in fewer X-Y-chromosome-carrying sperm (usually the faster moving sperm) reaching the egg.

[265] Jerry Heindel, a biochemist and scientific program administrator at the National Institute of Environmental Health Sciences, quoted by Shari Roan in "Living for Two," *Los Angeles Times*, Nov. 12, 2007.

[266] "Ecological Medicine: A Call for Inquiry and Action," in *Ecological Medicine: Healing the Earth, Healing Ourselves*, ed. by Kenny Ausubel with J. P. Harpignies (San Francisco: Sierra Club Books, 2004).

[267] Lee Silver, "A Quandary that Isn't," *Time*, Sept. 21, 1998; cited in Bill McKibben, *Enough: Staying Human in an Engineered World* (New York: Henry Holt, 2003), p. 22.

[268] Gregory Stock, "The Prospects for Human Germline Engineering," *Telepolis*, Jan. 29, 1999; cited in Bill McKibben, *Enough: Staying Human in an Engineered World* (New York: Henry Holt, 2003), p. 34.

[269] Ashlee Vance, "Merely Human? So Yesterday," *New York Times*, 13 June 2010.

[270] Ibid.

[271] Ibid.

[272] "Environmental, social factors in suicide," *San Francisco Chronicle*, April 28, 2003; the article reports on a Danish study conducted by Ping Qin, Esben Agerbo, and Preben Bo Mortensen, "Suicide Risk in Relation to Socioeconomic, Demographic, Psychiatric, and Familial Factors: A National Register–Based Study of All Suicides in Denmark, 1981–1997," *American Journal of Psychiatry*, April 2003, issue 160, pp. 765-772.

[273] Phillipe Thiebaut, *Gaudí: Visionary Architect* (New York: Abrams, 2002), p. 41.

[274] "Modernism" is a term used within the arts to refer to a body of work, in all fields, that was created approximately between 1905 and 1939. It is distinct from the larger, overarching phenomenon called modernity, or the modern era (15th century to the present). There are two types of modernism: the organic (exemplified by Gaudí) and the pro-modernity, machine-inspired (exemplified by Le Corbusier). For a discussion of these two branches of modernism, especially the organic, please see chapter 4 in my earlier book *The Resurgence of the Real: Body, Nature, and Place in a Hypermodern World*.

[275] Mindy Thompson Fullilove, *Root Shock: How Tearing up City Neighborhoods Hurts America, and What We Can Do About It* (New York: Ballantine Books, 2004), pp. 121-3; cited by Eva-Maria Simms in "Urban Renewal and the Destruction of African-American Neighborhoods," *Environmental & Architectural Phenomenology*, vol. 16, no. 1, Winter 2005, pp. 3-6.

[276] Stephen Silha, "Street-Corner Revolution," *Yes!: A Journal of Positive Futures*, Summer 2004, p. 19.

[277] Stephen Silha, "Street-Corner Revolution," 2004, p. 19.

[278] This system was used for a time by the city government of Austin, Texas, for instance, to analyze proposed development projects; see Gary Gardner and Erik Assadourian, "Rethinking the Good Life," *State of the World, 2004* (Worldwatch Institute, 2004), p. 176. The Smart Growth program is still in effect in Austin (see www.ci.austin.tx.us/smartgrowth), but analyses are now done without the Matrix method.

[279] *Noisette: The New American City*, Noisette Company, North Charleston, SC; also see their website: www.noisettesc.com.

[280] John Knott, presentation at the University of California ecological conference at Zaca Lake, Santa Barbara, CA, May 30, 2005.

[281] Dana Perrigan, "A Trust in Housing: The pioneering effort is by public and private sectors," *San Francisco Chronicle*, Aug. 14, 2005, p. J-1.

[282] A broadside available from the Ecological Design Institute, 245 Gate Five Road, Sausalito, CA 94965. Also see their website: www.ecodesign.org.

[283] Esther M. Sternberg, *Healing Spaces: The Science of Place and Well-Being* (Cambridge, MA: Belknap Press/Harvard University Press, 2009). Sternberg, a physician, divides the book into chapters on vision (the difference to our healing process of looking out a window at a brick wall or a tree, for instance); sound; touch; smell; and other parameters such as stress and memory.

[284] Rachel McCann, "On the Hither Side of Depth: An Architectural Pedagogy of Engagement," *Environmental & Architectural Phenomenology*, vol. 16, no. 3, Fall 2005, pp. 8-19; this essay was originally published in *Writings in Architectural Education* (Copenhagen: EAAE, 2005). I highly recommend the journal *Environmental & Architectural Phenomenology*, which is edited by Professor David Seamon at Kansas State University. It is one of the essential nodes of the Relational Shift within the architectural profession.

[285] Robert Gay, "The Nature of Order," a review of *The Nature of Order, Book One: The Phenomenon of Life* by Christopher Alexander (Oxford: Oxford University Press, 2000), in *Whole Earth*, Winter 2001, p. 73; also see *The Structurist*, no. 45/46, 2005-2006, Double Issue on Regenerating Art and Architecture in Nature's Landscape, pp. 4-47, for an interview with Christopher Alexander and reviews of the four volumes of *The Nature of Order*. For essays by Christopher Alexander written after *The Nature of Order* about this subject, see the websites www.natureoforder.com and www.patternlanguage.com. Also see Christopher Alexander, "Sustainability and Morphogenesis: The Rebirth of a Living World," *The Structurist*, no. 47, Art and Architecture in the Biological Century, 2007/2008. *The Structurist*, an extremely impressive journal, has been edited for decades by Eli Bornstein at the University of Saskatchewan.

[286] The building is the Bachenheimer Building in Berkeley, California, completed in 2008. The architect is Kirk Peterson. His firm's website (www.kpaarch.com) includes a few photos of the Bachenheimer Building, but they cannot convey the feeling of seeing the building in person. Try to approach it first, whether on foot or by car, by traveling south on Shattuck Avenue to where it intersects with University Avenue; there sets the Bachenheimer Building, an mixed-use apartment building of low-income and market-rate apartments.

[287] William McDonough, "Toward a Sustaining Architecture for the 21st Century," available at www.mcdonough.com. Also see several of his other essays on his

website, including "A New Geography of Hope: Landscape, Design, and the Renewal of Ecological Intelligence."

[288] The National Design Award is presented by the Smithsonian Institution's Cooper Hewitt National Design Museum (see http://ndm.si.edu/NDA/2004/ENVIRONMENT/mcdonough).

[289] "If a Building Could Be Like a Tree: An Interview with Architect William McDonough," *Orion Afield*, vol. 5, no. 2, Spring 2001, p. 21.

[290] Information on the U.S. Green Building Council's website: www.usgbc.org. In spite of its widespread acceptance, some criticism has arisen about the program's cost, complexity, bureaucratic requirements, and what some charge is a disconnection between the point system and actual environmental benefit.

[291] U.S. Green Building Council's website: www.usgbc.org; see Public Policies [retrieved on Feb. 19, 2011].

Also see Margot Roosevelt, "Going green may be L.A. law," *Los Angeles Times*, Feb., 16, 2008. As of early 2008, more than 120 municipal governments require LEED certification for any proposed public-sector building, more than a dozen cities had extended the requirement for LEED certification to buildings in the private sector, beginning with large-scale buildings.

[292] Dana Abbott, "San Francisco Builds Green," *E Magazine*, Jan./Feb. 2005, p. 11.

[293] See www.aia.org/cote for information about the American Institute of Architects' Committee on the Environment and the "Top Green Projects" of the year.

[294] Margot Roosevelt, "New anti-warming tool: white roofs," *Los Angles Times*, Sept. 10, 2008; see Hashem Akbari, Surabi Menon, and Arthur Rosenfeld, "Global Cooling: Increasing World-wide Urban Albedos to Offset $CO2$," *Climatic Change*, vol. 95, no. 3-4, June 2009; this study was presented at California's annual Climate Change Research Conference in Sacramento on Sept. 9, 2008. Since 2005 California has required that new flat-roofed commercial buildings have a white roof; as of 2009, heat-reflective roofing will be required of all new and retrofitted buildings, whether they have flat or sloping roofs, whether commercial or residential.

[295] Guy Dauncey, "What We Can Do About Buildings," *Yes!* Magazine, Spring 2008, p. 30.

[296] Abigail Goldman, "Living green, by design," *Los Angeles Times*, July 29, 2007.

[297] Lea Hartog, "Up Your Alley," *Sierra* magazine, Bold Strokes, March/April 2008; available online at http://www.sierraclub.org/sierra/200803/lol.asp [retrieved on July 17, 2009].

[298] See Karen Harwell and Joanna Reynolds, *Exploring a Sense of Place: How to Create Your Own Local Program for Reconnecting with Nature*, preface by Thomas

Berry (Palo Alto, CA: Conexions: Partnerships for a Sustainable Future, 2008).

[299] Kevin Fagan, "More than a shelter, home," *San Francisco Chronicle*, Feb. 21, 2005; this article reports on the work of Sam Davis, author of *Designing for the Homeless: Architecture that Works* (Berkeley, CA: University of California Press, 2004).

[300] "Vets make up a quarter of U.S. homeless, report says," *Los Angeles Times*, Nov. 8, 2007.

[301] This observation was made by Nancy O'Malley, chief assistant district attorney of Alameda County, California, who led the effort to get a County Family Justice Center in Oakland; see Kelly St. John, "New center opens for domestic-violence victims," *San Francisco Chronicle*, Sept. 1, 2005.

[302] The source is the U.S. Department of Health and Human Services; cited in "Foster Care Reform Efforts Gain Momentum," editorial on bills in the California State Assembly effecting foster children, *San Francisco Chronicle*, Dec. 12, 2005. This article was part of a series that began on Sept. 11, 2005, one of the "Chronicle Campaigns" featured occasionally on the editorial page in that newspaper.

[303] Holly Sklar, "No Foreclosures Here," *Yes!* Magazine, Winter 2009, pp. 51-54.

[304] Reid Ewing, Steve Winkelman, Keith Bartholomew, Jerry Walters, et al., *Growing Cooler: The Evidence on Urban Development and Climate Change*, Smart Growth America, The Urban Land Institute, 2008.

[305] Mary Engel, "Disparity seen in children's obesity rates," *Los Angeles Times*, Nov. 10, 2007; also see Paloma Esquivel, "Outdoor gyms aim to reduce health woes," *Los Angeles Times*, Dec. 28, 2007.

[306] See www.sustainablepet.com for design ideas for green doghouses.

[307] George Soros, "The Crisis & What to Do about It," *The New York Review of Books*, Dec. 4, 2008; this essay is drawn from his book *The New Paradigm for Financial Markets: The Credit Crisis of 2008 and What It Means* (New York: PublicAffairs, 2008).

[308] Kate Pickett and Richard Wilkinson, transcript of the Bill Moyers interview with them about their book *The Spirit Level: Why Greater Equality Makes Societies Stronger* (New York: Bloomsbury Press, 2009), program on April 2, 2010, titled "American Inequality," *Bill Moyers Journal* (www.pbs.org/moyers/journal; then click on Archives).

[309] Polly Ghazi, "When natural capital runs low….," *Green Futures*, no. 54, Sept./Oct. 2005, p. 15; see the Millennium Ecosystem Assessment, "a high-level international initiative involving 1,360 experts worldwide, with partners including the United Nations and the World Bank": www.MAWeb.org; also see World Resources

Institute (www.wri.org). It should also be noted that birds provide numerous "services" needed by "the economy" such as controlling rats, mice, and insects and dispersing seeds and pollen; however, it is estimated that over 1200 species of birds will be driven into extinction in the next 90 years (see Jane Kay, "Where are all the birds?," *San Francisco Chronicle*, July 4, 2006.) Also see the work of the Global Footprint Network (www.footprintnetwork.org) on the ecological deficit, or state of "overshoot," in which the planet now exists. In Oct. 2006, for instance, they determined that it now takes the Earth 15 months to regenerate what we use in a year.

[310] Paul Hawken, "Natural Capitalism," *Mother Jones*, March/April 1997, p. 42; Hawken relates the story about Herman Daly and the classical chart illustrating an economy. Daly himself has written about it in "Economics blind spot is a disaster for the planet," *New Scientist*, Issue 2678, Oct. 15, 2008.

[311] See Jonathan Rowe, "Our Phony Economy," *Harper's*, June 2008, p. 17- 20 and 22-24 for a pithy overview of the problems with our current sense of "the economy"; on p. 24 Rowe cites from Simon Kuznets' article in *The New Republic* in 1962. Kuznet was the economist who was charged with devising the first set of national accounts during the Great Depression, when he warned against equating a nation's capacity for monetized exchange with its economic success as a society. In evaluating the economy, he subsequently warned in 1962, "distinctions must be kept in mind between quantity and quality, between its costs and returns, and between the short and the long run.... Goals for 'more' growth should specify more growth of what and for what."

[312] This objection to the concept of a supposedly Purely Autonomous Man Who Makes All Economic Decisions on the Basis of Maximizing His Own Wealth was critiqued by John Ruskin, and others, in the mid-19th century. Yet this core assumption of liberal economic theory has lived on.

[313] The stock market itself is seen to have a delicate constitution, reflected in such common observations as "The market is nervous when there is instability"; "The market shuddered after the latest reports were released"; or "The market breathed a sigh of relief today." Such animism at the core of such a supposedly tough-minded, rational system!

[314] Smith's theory was called "liberal" because it argued that the market system must be absolutely free, or liberated, to operate without government regulation (a policy of *laissez-faire*, or "leave alone") in order for a market economy's beneficial results to accrue for society. Consequently, the label "liberal economics" or, more recently, "neoliberal economics" refers to the *laissez-faire* model of unregulated capitalism (championed by the right wing of conservative parties, such as the Republican Party) – even though the political term "liberal" came to mean a system of governance that safeguards individual and collective rights but also regulates

some of the activities of capitalism (championed by liberal parties such as the Democratic Party). In the modern era, then, the following paradoxical labeling prevails: political "liberals" oppose "liberalized [or neoliberal] economics." The political liberals feel that capitalism requires some boundaries to prevent excessive and destructive practices.

The philosophers of Adam Smith's day saw society not as an organic whole but an "atomized" aggregate of unconnected individuals; that is, they were influenced by Newton's expressions of the modern physics in which the world is understood to be composed of small bits of unrelated atoms. Smith declared that individuals (the fragmented, unrelated "atoms" of society) are effectively organized by the dynamics of the market. Modern economic theory, then, had is beginnings as a very Newtonian *apologia* for the central position that the forces related to monetary exchange had come to occupy in people's lives. Viewed through the lens of modern economic theory, the workings of "the economy" replaced the relationships of religion, kinship, and community as the essential organizing dynamic of society.

[315] Regarding modern economics' irrational relationship with nature, again the mechanistic worldview of the 18th century has colored modern thinking. Because that perspective held that the natural world is merely a mechanism by which inert matter is acted upon by physical laws of action and reaction, nature was historically regarded as mere raw material for the wonder of industrial production. As industrialization proceeded, modern humans increasingly felt that they lived on top of nature. Most modern economists failed to see that nature provides the human economy with a vast range of absolutely necessary processes, or "business services," as Paul Hawken calls them in his influential books on "natural capitalism."

[316] In spite of the elegant theory, the actual practice of *laissez-faire* economics quickly created a living hell in the British midlands for the factory workers (many as young as eight years old) in the "dark Satanic mills," as the poet William Blake described them. The workers, recently displaced from agricultural work when the commons were enclosed and privatized, toiled for long hours six days a week in unhealthy conditions. The air they breathed in the clattering mills and in their nearby crowded housing was thick with pollution. They were paid only subsistence wages, an act that was theorized by David Ricardo for the mill owners as an utterly rational response to the Invisible Hand of the Market: if demand for a product indicated that more workers would be needed, increase the wages enough that worker families can afford to buy some extra food, which will lead to worker-babies being born, who in a mere eight years will fill the factories as a new wave of workers. Conversely, if fewer workers were desired, one should reduce the (already low) wages so that worker families could barely afford enough food to stay alive and would not tend to reproduce. (For good reason this new economic system was not called laborism; rather, it was capital that was always protected.)

The appalling levels of suffering that "rational" liberal economics caused were eventually addressed by the British government, by public demand, with reforms and protective regulations beginning in the 1820s. After the rise of the Labour Party in the early years of the 20th century, workers gained further protections and eventually a universal healthcare system.

In the United States the raw, largely unregulated period of industrialized capitalism stretched from 1865 to the 1890s as the "Robber Barons" grabbed whatever they could, intimidated and crushed whomever they wished to, deftly manipulated markets, ruthlessly exploited workers, and squelched any political attempts at regulation that might have thwarted their expansionist schemes. Only through the long struggles of the labor movement and the progressive movement was child labor finally outlawed, working conditions made safer, and unions established, in the decade after 1900.

[317] For an excellent analysis and proposals for ways to address the interlocking crises, see *Manifesto on Global Economic Transitions* (www.ifg.org/pdf/manifesto. pdf), jointly produced by the International Forum on Globalization and by the Institute for Policy Studies and the Global Project on Economic Transitions, Sept. 2007.

[318] Many of these efforts are presented in the book *Blessed Unrest: How the Largest Movement in the World Came into Being and Why No One Saw It Coming* by Paul Hawken (New York: Viking Press, 2007).

[319] See Robert Costanza, "Ecological Economics Is Post-Autistic," *Post-Autistic Economics Review*, issue 20, June 3, 2003, article 2 (www.paer.net/PAEReview/ ecologicaleconomics/Costanza20). Also see Robert Costanza, John H Cumberland, Herman Daly, Robert Goodland and Richard B. Norgaard, *An Introduction to Ecological Economics*, Second Edition (New York: CRC Press, 2010). Also see Robert Costanza, *Ecological Economics: The Science and Management of Sustainability* (New York: Columbia University Press, 1991). Also see Herman E. Daly and Joshua Farley, *Ecological Economics: Principles and Applications* (Washington, DC: Island Press, 2003. Also see Joshua Farley, Jon Erickson, and Herman E. Daly, *Ecological Economics: A Workbook for Problem-Based Learning* (Washington, DC: Island Press, 2005). Also see Herman E. Daly, *Ecological Economics and Sustainable Development: Selected Essays of Herman Daly (Advances in Ecological Economics)* (Cheltenham, England: Edward Elgar Publishing, 2007).

[320] See the website for the Global Footprint Network: www.footprintnetwork.org.

[321] To grasp the striking aesthetic contrast between agrarian and industrial agriculture with all its ramifications, see the photo essays in *Fatal Harvest: The Tragedy Of Industrial Agriculture* (Sausalito, CA: Foundation for Deep Ecology, 2002), edited by Andrew Kimbrell.

An example of local culture inspired by the development of a local food system is the chain of Edible Communities magazines, such as *Edible Brooklyn, Edible Memphis, Edible Twin Cities, Edible Austin,* and *Edible Missoula.* This idea began with *Edible Ojai,* in Ojai, California, and then spread across the country. Each issue of the various local versions contains articles on local food, cooking, and related matters. See www.ediblecommunities.com.

[322] The farmers market complex at the Embarcadero area in San Francisco includes outdoor markets and indoor restaurants and stores featuring only regional foodstuffs. The beams in the corridors are painted with the names of all the agricultural communities in the surrounding seven counties. However, because this complex is not owned by the city or non-profit groups, it serves as a cautionary tale: when a private developer controls the (high) rents on such stores, the regional producers are forced to charge high prices and the potential of the entire enterprise is compromised.

[323] George Pyle, "Stalin's Revenge," *Orion,* May/June 2005, p. 11.

[324] According to the Environmental Working Group (www.ewg.org), a nonprofit organization in Washington, DC, the following fruits and vegetables are those with the highest levels of pesticides when gown industrially: apples, cherries, imported grapes, nectarines, peaches, pears, raspberries, strawberries, bell peppers, celery, hot peppers, potatoes, and spinach. The EWG suggests that the organic version of this produce be consumed.

[325] "Moo-ving Antibiotics Out of Animal Feed," *Energy Times,* June 2005, p. 6.

[326] Rich Pirog and Andrew Benjamin, *Checking the Food Odometer: Comparing the Food Miles for Local versus Conventional Produce Sales to Iowa Institutions,* Leopold Center for Sustainable Agriculture, Iowa State University, 2003. The study that also included a calculation of the fuel usage and carbon dioxide emissions in long-distance produce travel is *Food, Fuel and Freeways: An Iowa perspective on how far food travels, fuel usage, and greenhouse gas emissions* (2001).

[327] "The Myth of Efficiency," #2 in the Series on Industrial Agriculture, Turning Point Project (www.turningpoint.org).

[328] "The Myth of Efficiency," #2 in the Series on Industrial Agriculture, Turning Point Project (www.turningpoint.org).

[329] Jim Hightower and Phillip Frazer, "Speculators and Our Food: EIEIO!," *The Hightower Lowdown,* July 2008, p. 3.

[330] Figures are from the UN Food and Agriculture Organization; see www.faostat. fao.org/site/537.

[331] See Deborah K. Rich, "Organic fruits and vegetables work harder for their nutrients," *San Francisco Chronicle,* March 25, 2006; Donald R. Davis, a research

associate at the Biochemical Institute at the University of Texas, Austin, conducted a study in 2005-06 in which he analyzed data gathered by the US Dept. of Agriculture on nutrient content in 1950 and 1999. He found that over the 50-year period three minerals – phosphorous, iron, and calcium – had declined between 9 and 16 percent; riboflavin had declined 38 percent; and ascorbic acid (a precursor of Vitamin C) had declined 15 percent; see Donald R. Davis, Melvin D. Epp, and Hugh D. Riordan, "Changes in USDA Food Composition Data for 43 Garden Crops, 1950 to 1999," *Journal of the American College of Nutrition*, vol. 23, no. 6, 2004, pp. 669-682.

Another study, at the University of California at Davis found that organic broccoli and tomatoes had more significantly more Vitamin C and heart-protective bioflavonoids than did their industrially raised counterparts ("Organic Edge," *Prevention*, Jan. 2005, p. 70).

[332] "Think Globally, Taste Locally: An Interview with Alice Waters," *Inquiring Mind*, vol. 20, no. 2, Spring 2004.

What is not in organic food? According to *The Organic Foods Sourcebook* by Elaine Marie Lipson and the "OTA Fact Sheet: Sewage Sludge" (www.ota.com), food products that are certified organic have been produced without any of the following substances: persistent synthetic herbicides and pesticides, sewage sludge (containing dangerous toxins), genetically modified organisms, irradiated materials, and growth hormones and antibiotics. While lobbyists for the agribusiness corporations have fought relentlessly to dilute the legal definition of "organic," activists groups such as the Center for Food Safety in Washington, DC, have largely managed to hold the line on behalf of consumer protection.

[333] The farmers market that opened in the Bayview-Hunters Point neighborhood of San Francisco in May 2005 was a joint project of the San Francisco Department of the Environment, the Pacific Coast Farmers' Market Association, Literacy for Environmental Justice, and Girls 2000; see "Farmers' market to open in Bayview," *San Francisco Chronicle*, May 21, 2005; also see "Farmers' market premieres in Bayview," *San Francisco Chronicle*, May 22, 2005.

[334] "The Jefferson Award: Malaika Edwards, grocery founder," *San Francisco Chronicle*, March 26, 2005. Also see City Slicker Farms (www.city-slickerfarms.org), a non-profit project established in West Oakland by Willow Rosenthal. Also see Just Food, a non-profit organization working in New York City (www.justfood.org). The largest community farm plots in New York City are flourishing in Brooklyn and the Bronx. Also see the Community Food Security Coalition (www.foodsecurity.org), a national coalition of almost 300 organizations from social and economic justice, anti-hunger, environmental, community development, sustainable agriculture, community gardening and other fields.

[335] "Generous Helpings," *AARP* Magazine, Jan. & Feb. 2007, p. 16.

[336] Sue Halpern and Bill McKibben, " Eating Locally and Organically," *House & Garden*, May 2006, p. 114 and 116.

[337] "No Chipped Beef on Toast," *Sierra* Magazine, May/June 2005, p. 14. Even large-scale private-sector food suppliers have had to respond to requests from the public for fresh, locally grown food. One of the first large companies to do so was the Bon Appetit Management Company, which serves 55 million cafeteria meals to 148 university and corporate clients; its mission statement now emphasizes sustainable agriculture, with a focus on locally available organic produce, meat without hormones or antibiotics, and seafood caught according to the guidelines set by the Monterey Bay Aquarium.

[338] Marian Burros, "Fresh Gets Invited to the Cool Table," *New York Times*, Aug. 24, 2005.

[339] Vandana Shiva, "Celebrating Food Economies," *Resurgence*, No. 229, March/April 2005, p. 49. Also see Deborah Madison, "Grace before Dinner," *Orion*, March/April 2005.

[340] Vandana Shiva, "Celebrating Food Economies," *Resurgence*, No. 229, March/April 2005, p. 49.

[341] "Organic: The Same for Less," *Earth Island Journal*, Winter 2006, p. 9; this article reports on a study done at Cornell University comparing an organic animal-based farm, an organic legume-based farm, and a conventional farm that applied industrial pesticides and fertilizers at the rates recommended by the manufacturer; the study was initially described in *Science Daily*, July 14, 2008. See David Pimentel, Paul Hepoperly, James Hanson, David Douds, and Rita Seidel, "Environmental, Energetic, and Economic Comparisons of Organic and Conventional Farming Systems," *BioScience*, vol.55, issue 7, July 2005, pp. 573-582.

[342] Kathleen McAfee, "Food biotechnology – A solution looking for a problem," *San Francisco Chronicle*, June 6, 2004. She is the executive director of Food First / Institute for Food and Development Policy (www.foodfirst.org).

[343] Doug Gurian-Sherman, *Failure to Yield: Evaluating the Performance of Genetically Engineered Crops*. Cambridge, MA: Union of Concerned Scientists, March 2009. This was the first report to analyze nearly two decades worth of peer-reviewed research on the yield of genetically engineered food/feed crops in the United States and to arrive at new yield values for those crops. The report reveals that only one major GE food/feed crop—Bt corn, a variety engineered with a gene from the bacterium *Bacillus thuringiensis*, which produces toxins to protect the plant from several insects—has achieved any significant yield increase in the United States. The 3–4 percent yield increase achieved by Bt corn over the 13 years that it has been grown commercially is much less than what has been achieved over that time by other methods, including conventional breeding. Over the past

several decades, corn yields have increased about one percent per year, or about 14 percent (due to the compounding property of yield gain) over the 13 years since *Bt* was first commercialized. Therefore, by this rough calculation, *Bt* has contributed only 21–28 percent of yield gain in corn, with other approaches contributing 72–79 percent. The report contrasts this small yield increase achieved by engineered *Bt* corn with the yield of a suite of alternatives including organic, low-external-input methods, conventional breeding, and modern breeding methods that use technological advances to speed up the selection process for desired traits without actually inserting new genes. Collectively, such methods are capable of increasing crop yields far more than GE has yet managed to do (see *Failure to Yield*, Chapter 4). However, the public funding deck has been stacked against these other methods to date, as resources have been channeled toward GE research and development.

[344] "Biotech crop gets into food chain," *Los Angeles Times*, Dec. 6, 2008.

[345] One of the leading institutes fighting the encroachment of genetically modified foods is the Center for Food Safety in Washington, DC, directed by Andrew Kimbrell (www.centerforfoodsafety.org). One project of the Center, the True Food Network (www.TrueFoodNow.org) is a grassroots network with, as of early 2010, over 90,000 members across the country "saying no to industrial agriculture and yes to True Food!"

[346] See Wes Jackson's Land Institute (www.landinstitute.org) for pioneering work in no-till agriculture.

[347] Permaculture was developed in Australia in the 1970s by Bill Mollison and David Holmgren; they coined the term in their book *Permaculture One* (Bath, U.K.: eco-logic books, 1978). Also see *Permaculture in a Nutshell* by Patrick Whitefield (Glastonbury, UK: Unique Publications, 1992). Also see the website for the Regenerative Design Institute (**www.regenerativedesign.org),** founded by Penny Livingston Stark and James Stark.

[348] Janine Benyus, "Mother Nature's School of Design," *Yes! A Journal of Positive Futures*, Fall 2001.

[349] Their partnership is McDonough Braungart Design Chemistry, known as MBDC (www.mbdc.com), a product and systems design firm assisting client companies in implementing their unique sustaining design protocol.

[350] William McDonough and Michael Braungart, *Cradle to Cradle* (New York: North Point Press, 2002), p. 86.

[351] William McDonough and Michael Braungart, *Cradle to Cradle*, p. 82.

[352] William McDonough and Michael Braungart, *Cradle to Cradle*, p. 155.

[353] For example, Cooper-Hewitt National Design Museum in New York featured an

exhibition in summer 2007 on "Design for the Other 90%," featuring such devices as the Bamboo Treadle Pump, which allows farmers to irrigate their fields by using their feet, and the Q Drum, which can be filled with water and then rolled home, even by a child, using a pull-rope instead of carrying it.

Valerie Casey, named by *Fortune* magazine (online at http://money.cnn.com) on Nov. 11, 2008 as one of "Ten New Gurus You Should Know About," wrote the *Designers Accord* (www.designersaccord.org/index.php?title=Guidelines), a set of guidelines that commits its signatories to support sustainable design and requires them to track their own carbon footprint. It struck a chord: More than 100,000 people and organizations - including Johnson & Johnson Consumer Products, and Autodesk - have signed on. Her goal was to get designers - and their clients - to think about sustainability before, not after, they create.

Also see John Barrie's non-profit organization, Appropriate Technology Collaborative (apptechdesign.org), which designs low-tech, effective devices in Ann Arbor, MI, to be used in villages in the mountains of Central America.

[354] See the website for MBDC (www.mbdc.com/certified) for information on their Cradle-to-Cradle certification program.

[355] Paul Roberts, "The cost of steak," opinion piece, *Los Angeles Times*, Aug. 23, 2008; Roberts is author of *The End of Food* (Boston, MA: Houghton Mifflin Harcourt, 2008).

[356] Paul Roberts (above). Also see Marla Cone, "Foul state of affairs found in feedlots," *Los Angeles Times*, Nov. 17, 2006; a series of scientific studies found that the quality of life in agricultural regions in the United States and Europe is deteriorating and that damage to human health and the ecosystems often goes unmonitored.

Also see Daniel Imhoff, editor, *CAFO: The Tragedy of Industrial Animal Factories* (San Rafael, CA: Earth Aware / Foundation for Deep Ecology, 2010). This is the best book I have encountered on CAFOs.

[357] The process of internalizing costs is also beginning to result in a major shift in corporate planning, regarding the ability to generate revenue, manage risks, and sustain competitive advantage, according to Al Gore and David Blood; see their opinion piece "For people and planet" (*San Francisco Chronicle*, April 3, 2006. They note that organizations such as the World Resources Institute, Transparency International, the Coalition for Environmentally Responsible Economies (CERES), and AccountAbility are "helping companies explore how best to align corporate responsibility with business strategy."

[358] This suggestion is made in a report released on April 29, 2008, by the Pew Commission on Industrial Farm Animal Production, a group of prominent scientists, lawmakers, and experts in agriculture who conducted a 2.5-year study (www.ncifap.org/reports); also cited by Paul Roberts in "The cost of steak," opinion

piece, *Los Angeles Times*, Aug. 22, 2008. The report addresses the effects of "confined animal feeding operations" (COFAs) in four areas (Public Health, Environment, Animal Welfare, and Rural America) and recommends several changes.

[359] Hazel Henderson, " Chicago Boys' Curse Comes Home to Wall Street," carried during the week of Sept. 15, 2008 by CSR Wire and Radio, InterPress Service, and GreenBiz; also posted on Ms. Henderson's website: www.ethicalmarkets.com. Her organization, Ethical Markets Media, in partnership with the Climate Prosperity Alliance, has created the Global Climate Prosperity Scoreboard, which tracks private investment in companies growing the green economy globally. They announced in December 2009 that since 2007 nearly $1.25 trillion in total investment was made, indicating that investors and entrepreneurs are leading governments in promoting sustainable growth. The scoreboard totals investments in solar, wind, geothermal, ocean/hydro, energy efficiency and storage, and agriculture.

[360] Jonathon Porritt, "The Three R's," *Resurgence*, no. 257, Nov.-Dec. 2009.

[361] Margaret J. Wheatley, *Leadership and the New Science* (San Francisco: Berrett-Kohler, 1992), p. 118.

[362] See Molly Selvin, "Telecommuters may go nowhere – careerwise," *Los Angeles Times*, Jan. 17, 2007.

[363] See Peter M. Senge, *The Fifth Discipline: The Art & Practice of the Learning Organization* (New York: Doubleday, 1990); also see *The Fifth Discipline Fieldbook: Strategies and Tools for Building a Learning Organization* by Peter M. Senge, Charlotte Roberts, Richard B. Ross, Bryan J. Smith, and Art Kleiner (New York: Doubleday, 1994). Senge's "fifth discipline" is systems thinking.

[364] An elusive citation! In an e-mail from Paul Glover on July 31, 2009, he confirmed that the statement attributed to him in this text is, indeed, something he has, and does say; he thinks it appeared in an article he write for *Communities* magazine, the Winter 2004 issue. Glover coordinates an e-mail network of local currency groups using the Hour model and sells a *Hometown Money Starter Kit* (www.lightlink.com/hours/ithacahours/starterkit). Also see Glover's website: www.paulglover.org. For information about local currencies, also see the E. F. Schumacher Society's website (www.smallisbeautiful.org/local_currencies.htm). For information about BerkShares, see www.berkshares.org.

[365] The phrase was coined by Bill McKibben; see Bill McKibben, *Deep Economy: The Wealth of Communities and the Durable Future* (New York: Times Books, 2007). Also see Bill McKibben, *Wandering Home* (New York: Crown, 2005).

[366] Gianluca Brunori, "Relocation, Relocation, Relocation," *Resurgence* Magazine, no. 254, May/June 2009, pp 36-37; Dr. Brunori is a professor of agrarian economics at the University of Pisa.

[367] See "The Local Multiplier Effect," *Yes!* Magazine, Winter 2007, p. 35. The study in which it was found that $100 spent in a national retailer yields a return of about $15 to the local economy, where as the same $100 spent with a locally owned retailer yields $45 circulating in the local economy, was commissioned by Reclaim Democracy (www.reclaimdemocracy.org).

Typical elements of a community-based economy commonly include non-profit community development corporations and business "incubator" programs (to help new small-scale businesses get a solid start); some sort of profit-sharing, or worker-ownership (though this ideal does not exclude from the diversified model a range of privately owned and publicly owned businesses, as well); and producer-consumer associations, which can play a role in establishing new business initiatives that benefit the community. Ways to finance community-oriented businesses include micro-credit programs; community-development financing systems that use local banks as administrators; and self-financing programs that avoid loans (such as a business selling scrip, or "notes," to raise additional capital for a remodeling or an expansion). Community land trusts have made land available for farming and businesses, preserving the land from both urban and rural speculators. Energy conservation programs have stopped large amounts of local money from flowing outside the community. Many towns have established re-use centers or online versions, where thrown-away objects find new users. Those are the basics. A few more ideas from Paul Glover include a bioregional food center (a market that also has facilities in which crops can be processed into food products); edible public parks; and insulation co-ops (pooling money to manufacture or buy insulation for homes and buildings).

Also see the website for the Institute for Local Self-Reliance (www.ilsr.org) and their New Rules Project: Designing Rules As If Community Matters.

[368] Michael Schuman, *The Small-Mart Revolution: How Local Businesses Are Beating the Global Competition* (San Francisco: Berrett-Koehler Publishers, 2006) and *Going Local: Creating Self-Reliant Communities in the Global Age* (New York: Free Press, 1998). Also see *Going Local: New Opportunities for Community Economics*, a lecture presented by Michael Schuman to the annual meeting of the Community Land Trust of the Southern Berkshires in January 2002, published by the E. F. Schumacher Society of America (www.smallisbeautiful.org).

[369] See, for example, Hazel Henderson, *Ethical Markets: Growing the Green Economy* (White River Junction, VT: Chelsea Green, 2006), based on the PBS series of the same name; David Korten, *The Great Turning: From Empire to Earth Community* (San Francisco: Berrett-Koehler Publishers, 2006); the Business Alliance for Local Living Economies (BALLE); *Yes!* Magazine; and the Institute for Local Self-Reliance (www.ilsr.org), to name only a few.

Two of the oldest institutes for community-based economics were founded in the late 1970s, as America watched many of its local stores go under because of the chains, its land and housing stock manipulated by speculators, and its urban neighborhoods decay further. The E. F. Schumacher Society of America (www. smallisbeautiful.org), named for the author of *Small Is Beautiful*, has operated pilot projects such as the Self-Help Association for a Regional Economy (SHARE), by which citizens can invest their savings in making micro-credit loans to businesses that are often considered "high risk" by traditional lenders. During the twelve years the Society ran the program in the Berkshires area of western Massachusetts, the 23 collateralized loans had a 100% rate of repayment. Over the years the Society has hosted numerous lectures (such as the Annual E. F. Schumacher Lecture), symposia (such as "Building Sustainable Local Economies"), and conferences (such as "Local Currencies in the 21st Century: Understanding Money, Building Local Economies, Renewing Community.")[370] They have also assisted community land trusts around the country.

Another esteemed elder has a decidedly more urban focus: the Center for Neighborhood Technology (www.cnt.org). Located in Chicago, they have sought to define and create community-scale programs that meet human needs by creating environmentally sound, long-term investment opportunities the directly benefit lower-income communities. In 1993 they launched a Campaign for a Sustainable Chicago, a goal that was eventually adopted by City Hall. In particular, the Center has furthered community-scaled technologies that meet needs, rebuild neighborhoods, and create jobs. They began by building community solar greenhouses and facilitating the retrofitting of numerous run-down homes and have gone on to influence policy at all levels, often through original reporting in their newsletter, *The Neighborhood Works*.

For the record: community-based economics and regional trade has always been the economic platform of the Green Parties around the world, since the 1970s, with the addition that all foreign trade should be structured in just and sustainable ways.

[371] See Colin Hines, *Localization: A Global Manifesto* (London: Earthscan, 2000).

[372] Michael Cabanatuan, "Plan to link housing to transit," *San Francisco Chronicle*, July 9, 2005.

[373] Guy Dauncey, "What We Can Do About Transportation," *Yes! A Journal of Positive Futures*, Spring 2008, p. 36.

[374] "Energy Insecurity," an interview with General Jim Jones (USMC, Ret.), who heads the U.S. Chamber of Commerce's Institute for 21st-Century Energy, *Parade*, Aug. 22, 2008, p. 7.

[375] See Carola Hoyos, "The new seven sisters: Oil and gas giants that dwarf the West's top producers," *Financial Times*, London, March 12, 2007. Even though the largest four Western oil corporations hold only 10 percent of the oil and gas reserves, their integrated status (which means they sell not only oil and gas, but

also gasoline, diesel, heating oil, and petrochemicals) pushes their revenues notably higher than those of the newcomers – for now.

[376] Amory Lovins quoted in Mark Hertsgaard, "Nuclear energy can't solve global warming," *San Francisco Chronicle*, Aug. 7, 2005; also see Rebecca Solnit, "Dirty Bombs and Dirty Secrets," *Orion*, May/June 2004, p. 12-13, about the plans to transport high-level nuclear waste through nearly every state in the union to the underground federal repository in Yucca Mountain, Nevada.

[377] Ted Nace, "Stopping Coal in Its Tracks, *Orien*, Jan.-Feb. 2008, pp. 68-69; the book is *Carbon-Free and Nuclear-Free: A Roadmap for U.S. Energy Policy* by Arjun Makhijani (Muskegon, MI: RDR Books, 2007).

Hydrogen fuel cells hold some promise as well, although there are problematic aspects to their widespread usage. Since electricity is needed to produce them, the only "clean" hydrogen fuel cells are those made by using electricity from renewable sources. (See "Future Power," *National Geographic*, Aug. 2005, p. 23.)

[378] Ron Scherer, "Report: 'Green' jobs outpacing traditional ones," *Christian Science Monitor*, June 10, 2009; the article reports on a study conducted by Pew Charitable Trusts' Pew Center for the States. Also see Marla Dickerson, "'Green' growth is key to state, report shows," *Los Angeles Times*, Jan. 26, 2009; the article reports on a study conducted by Collaborative Economics for the nonprofit research group Next 10 (www.next10.org), located in Palo Alto, CA. Also see "Green jobs outpace overall employment growth in California," *International Business Times* (online), Jan. 20, 2011.

[379] Ana Campoy, "Valero Harnesses Wind Energy to Fuel Its Oil-Refining Process," *Wall Street Journal*, June 29, 2009.

[380] Greg Bluestein, "Carpet diem: Rug scraps turned into an energy source," *San Francisco Chronicle*, July 11, 2005.

[381] The story behind the landmark U.S. Supreme Court case *Massachusetts v EPA* involved the California laws and their offspring in many states, but it began when a crucial legal petition and then a lawsuit were filed by the Center for Technology Assessment in Washington, DC – specifically by Joseph Mendelson, ICTA Legal Director and Andrew Kimbrell, ICTA Director. Using the science behind the Second Assessment report of the 1995 Intergovernmental Panel on Climate Change (IPCC), the ICTA filed, in 2000, an administrative legal petition – essentially a legal request – demanding that the EPA regulate the release of carbon dioxide and other greenhouse gases because, under the US Clean Air Act, they were 'air pollutants' that were "reasonably anticipated to harm public health and welfare." The petition languished in the halls of the Bush EPA. For the petition to have any meaningful impact, the ICTA knew the issue would have to be forced. In 2002, the ICTA, joined by the Sierra Club and Greenpeace, filed a lawsuit that compelled

the Bush Administration to respond to the petition. As the groups expected, the ultimate agency response was to reject the petition's demands to regulate GHG emissions from cars. In answering the petition, the EPA cited an array of disjointed legal and policy reasons including the need to maintain President Bush's ability to negotiate international agreements and the uncertainty of the science that surrounds climate change. The petition's denial was the galvanizing moment that ICTA and others had long anticipated. In denying the petition, the EPA had opened itself up to a formal legal challenge. A diverse number of groups joined together to make that challenge. With the State of Massachusetts taking the lead, joined by 10 other state governments, three cities, and 12 other environmental groups, ICTA again marched into federal court, in October 2006, attacking the legal bases of the EPA's petition denial. What had been an administrative law dispute with the EPA transformed into a legal showdown with the Bush Administration over its refusal to tackle global warming, ending finally in the U.S. Supreme Court. (This account is taken from Joseph Mendelson, "The Path to Climate Change," *The Ecologist*, April 12, 2007.)

[382] Margot Roosevelt, "Rules will limit auto emissions," *Los Angeles Times*, April 2, 2010.

[383] Sandra Steingraber, "Environmental Amnesia," *Orien*, May-June 2008, pp. 16-17.

To check the findings of the US EPA's Toxics Release Inventory (TRI) in your area, go to www.epa.gov/tri; on the right side of the home page is a column titled Quick Links, at the bottom of which is the box in which you can enter a zipcode. The data on (reported) releases will then be brought up for that area. For her thoughts on an emerging environmental human rights movement, see Sandra Steingraber, "3 Bets: On Ecology, Economy, and Human Wealth," *Orion*, May-June 2009, pp. 20-23.

[384] Jane Kay, "What's inside some noted Californians," *San Francisco Chronicle*, Aug. 31, 2005. Also see the website for Commonweal in Bolinas, California, founded by Michael Lerner, MD, for information about their biomonitoring program to ascertain chemical body burden (www.commonweal.org).

[385] Margot Roosevelt, "Chemical regulation broadens," *Los Angeles Times*, Sept. 30, 2008. The first of the two laws, AB 1879 in the California Assembly, 2007-08 Session, lays out a framework to regulate toxics over their life cycle; the second law, SB 509 in the California Senate, 2007-08 Session, creates a scientific clearinghouse for information on the effects of specific chemicals.

[386] See Elizabeth Royte, *Garbage Land: On the Secret Trail of Trash* (New York: Back Bay Books, 2006).

[387] Emily Caldwell, "Arlington's pioneering trash program," *Columbus Monthly*,

Oct. 1992, p. 75.

[388] See the website for the City of Upper Arlington, Ohio (www.ua-ohio.net/reservices/cityservices/trash) regarding their pioneering Trash Sticker Program, which has now been combined with the charge of an annual flat fee for garbage services.

[389] Lyric Wallwork Winik and Mark Naymik, "Should You Pay for Your Garbage?," *Parade* Magazine, Aug. 24, 2008, p. 6.

[390] See Todd Ecological Design (www.toddecological.com). Also see Ocean Arks International (www.oceanarks.org), which includes information about the periodical *Annals of Earth*, edited by Nancy Jack Todd, co-founder of OAI. Also see Nancy Jack Todd, *A Safe and Sustainable World: The Promise of Ecological Design* (Washington, DC: Island Books, 2005). Also see John Todd, "Living Technologies: Wedding Human Ingenuity to the Wisdom of the Wild," in *Nature's Operating Instructions*, ed. by Kenny Ausubel with J. P. Harpignies (San Francisco: Sierra Club Books, 2004).

[391] Joan Lowry, "Water supply won't meet world's needs," *San Francisco Chronicle*, Nov. 11, 2001. This article summarizes the Worldwatch Institute report titled *Pillar of Sand: Can the Irrigation Miracle Last?* by Sandra Postel.

[392] See Sandra Postel, *Last Oasis: Facing Water Scarcity* (New York: Norton, 1997).

[393] Leslie Crawford, "Water crisis looms worldwide," *Los Angles Times*, April 16, 2007.

[394] Jenna Olsen, "More conservation, not capacity," *San Francisco Chronicle*, Aug. 5, 2005.

[395] Vandana Shiva, "Flat Vision," *Resurgence*, No. 232, Sept.-Oct. 2005, p. 61.

[396] *The Simultaneous Evolution of Growth and Inequality*, a World Bank report, 1999; cited in *Does Globalization Help the Poor?* (San Francisco: International Forum on Globalization, 2001).

[397] Lori Wallach, presentation at "The Global Political Moment: Transition and Opportunity," an associates meeting of the International Forum on Globalization, held in San Francisco, CA, January 6-8, 2006. Also see Lori Wallach, "About Global Trade Watch," April 2008, on the website of Public Citizen, of which GTW is a division (www.citizen.org/trade/about). She suggests the removal of rules covering both services and "intellectual property" rights. More and more, she notes, the so-called "trade" agreements have shifted focus onto investment: "These new international commercial agreements encompass 'everything that you cannot drop on your foot,' and include services such as banking, telecommunications, postal services, tourism, transportation, waste disposal, oil and gas production,

and electricity. They also cover those services universally considered to be essential to human health and development, like healthcare, education, and drinking water. Services make up about 70% of the U.S. economy and more than 60% of the global economy."

[398] Vandana Shiva, "Wealth of Nature," *Resurgence*, no. 253, March/April 2009, No. 253, p. 51.

[399] Vandana Shiva, *Earth Democracy: Justice, Sustainability, and Peace* (Cambridge, MA: South End Press, 2005), p. 159. Also see her subsequent book, *Soil not Oil: Environmental Justice in an Age of Climate Crisis* (London: Zed Books, 2008).

[400] Report of the International Financial Institutions Advisory Commission (also known as the Melzer Commission), March 2000. The Commission was established by Congress as part of the 1998 funding for the International Monetary Fund to examine the efficacy of existing aid programs and to propose any needed reforms. Among their findings were the following: "The World Bank's evaluation of its own performance in Africa found a 73% failure rate"; "Reviews of performance are subjective, but even the World Bank's self-audited evaluations reveal an astonishing 55-60% failure rate to achieve sustainable results." Several years later, little had improved, as the World Bank's own auditing arm, the Independent Evaluation Group, found in its *Annual Review of Development Effectiveness 2006*: only 40 percent of "developing" countries participating in World Bank programs, which emphasize economic growth (usually through large-scale projects), had actually succeeded in raising per capita income during the period of the projects: "Only two in five borrowing countries have recorded continuous per capita income growth over the 5 years ending in 2005, and just one in five did so for a full 10 years…. Strategies aimed only at boosting overall growth may miss opportunities to reduce poverty more effectively." In short, the living conditions of the poor were still not improving, even after all the assessments of failure of the World Bank's approach and preferences in development.

[401] See, for instance, Charlene Spretnak, "Questioning Modernity," *Resurgence*, No. 215, Nov.-Dec. 2002.

[402] Mario Zavaleta Perez, cited in Benjamin Hodgdon, "A Future with Forestry," *Earth Island Journal*, Winter 2009, pp. 44-47; Zavaleta Perez is quoted on p. 45.

[403] For more information, see Professor Wangari Maathai's website: www. wangarimaathai.or.ke. Also see her books, including *Replenishing the Earth: Spiritual Values for Healing Ourselves and the World* (New York: Doubleday, 2010).

[404] See the discussion of Witkin's two experiments, the Rod and Frame Test and the Embedded Figures Test and the extrapolation from the data about cognitive styles in Diane F. Halpern, *Sex Differences in Cognitive Abilities*, 3rd edition (Mahweh, NJ

and London: Lawrence Erlbaum Associates, 2000), pp. 110-111; Halpern includes citations for the statements by Witkin and other psychologists that are mentioned in Ch. 6 of *Relational Reality*.

[405] Nina Simons, "Relational Intelligence," *Earthlight: Spiritual Wisdom for an Ecological Age*, edited by Cindy Spring and Anthony Manousos (Torrance, CA: Friends Bulletin, 2007). I came across this essay when I was nearly finished writing this book. Nina Simons, the co-founder and co-director of the Bioneers annual conference and national network of ecosocial activists, has written several articles, as I learned from doing a web search, on the subject of relational intelligence in ecosocial work. Needless to say, I heartily concur!

Also see an ecosocial activist's article that cites brain research about the human need to be in relationship: David Korten, "We Are Hard-Wired to Care and Connect," *Yes!* Magazine, Fall 2008, pp. 48-51. Korten is the author, most recently, of *Agenda for a New Economy: From Phantom Wealth to Real Wealth* (San Francisco: Berrett-Koehler Publishers, 2009) and *The Great Turning: From Empire to Earth Community* (San Francisco: Berrett-Koehler Publishers, 2007).

[406] Sarah Blaffer Hrdy is quoted from an interview by Natalie Angier, "In a Helpless Baby, the Roots of Our Social Glue," *New York Times*, March 3, 2009. Also see Sarah Blaffer Hrdy, *Mothers and Others: The Evolutionary Evolution of Mutual Understanding* (Cambridge, MA: Harvard University Press, 2009) and *Mother Nature: Maternal Instincts and How They Shape the Human Species* (New York: Ballantine Books, 2000). Hrdy notes that, unlike primate mothers, human mothers in virtually every culture studied allow other people to hold, pass around, and commune with their infants, to a greater or lesser degree depending on their culture. Among the !Kung foragers of the Kalahari, for instance, babies are held by a father, grandmother, older sibling, or other allomother about 25 percent of the time. Among the Efe foragers of Central Africa babies are carried around by someone other than their mothers for 60 percent of every day.

Blaffer Hrdy also synthesizes new research in anthropology, genetics, infant development, and comparative biology, which has overturned the long-standing assumption in scientific quarters that our species is naturally patrilocal (with young mothers moving away from their birth family to join that of the baby's father). Instead, it seems likely that mothers in most traditional societies had their mothers and other female relatives close at hand and available to serve as allomothers.

[407] See Judy Grahn, *Blood, Bread, and Roses: How Menstruation Created the World* (Boston: Beacon Press, 1993). Grahn traces not only the origin of abstract thought but also the invention of numerous rituals and ritual objects to the cultural responses to menses, especially to menarche. Many of the practices devised to be observed by the menstruant, such as seclusion, were later adopted as rituals for hunters prior to the hunt. Earlier, the psychologist Bruno Bettelheim had reached similar conclusions about the mimicking menses rites in male rites; see

his *Symbolic Wounds: Puberty Rites and the Envious Male* (Glencoe, IL: The Free Press, 1954).

[408] See Pascal Boyer, *Religion Explained: The Evolutionary Origins of Religious Thought* (New York: Basic Books, 2001).

[409] Ilkka Pyysiainen, *How Religion Works: Towards a New Cognitive Science of Religion* (Brill Academic Publishers, 2001); the terms cited in quotation marks are on pp. 131, 142, 164, and 229.

[410] Nicholas Wade, "The Evolution of the God Gene," *New York Times*, Nov. 15, 2009. In this article he presents the thesis of his book *The Faith Instinct: How Religion Evolved and Why It Endures* (New York: Penguin Press, 2009). Also see Nicholas Wade, "Is 'Do Unto Others' Written Into Our Genes?," *New York Times*, Sept. 18, 2007; Wade discusses the "Happiness Hypothesis" of Jonathan Haidt, a moral philosopher at the University of Virginia who holds that religion played an important role in human evolution by strengthening and extending the cohesion provided by moral systems.

[411] One theory holds that organic materials were delivered to Earth from an extraterrestrial source via meteorites, such as the one fell near Murchison, Australia on Sept. 28, 1969 and was found to contain a variety of organic molecules. Other theories hold that after the oceans and land masses had formed, relationships between basic elements created compounds such as hydrogen sulfide, methane, and ammonia, in and around primordial tidal pools as well as the sea. Through the catalyst of electrical discharges from lightening, or heat from hydrothermal vents or volcanoes in oceans, or intense ultraviolet radiation, complex organic molecules formed. Such a transformation from inorganic to organic material was replicated in a laboratory experiment conducted by Stanley Miller and Harold Urey in 1953. With regard to the evolution of early organic matter, endiosymbiotic theory is now widely accepted as an explanatory model; it emphasizes the interdependent and cooperative existence of multiple prokaryotic organisms in which one organism engulfed another, though both survived and evolved eventually into a eukaryotic cell. This theory was proposed by Lynn Margulis in her book *Origin of Eukaryotic Cells* in 1970.

[412] Charlene Spretnak, *States of Grace: The Recovery of Meaning in the Postmodern World* (San Francisco: HarperSanFrancisco, 1991), chapter 6.

[413] David Brooks, "The Neural Buddhists," *New York Times*, May 13, 2008. In this op-ed piece he is summarizing the findings of the following neuroscientists: Andrew Newberg, Daniel J. Siegel, Michael S. Gazzaniga, Jonathan Haidt, Antonio Damasio, and Marc D. Hauser. I would also add Mario Beauregard, author with Denise O'Leary of *The Spiritual Brain: The Case for the Existence of the Soul* (New York: HarperOne, 2007).

[414] Edgar Morin, *Seven Complex Lessons in Education for the Future* (Paris: UNESCO, 1999), p. 53. Also see Edgar Morin and Anne Brigitte Kern, *Homeland Earth: A Manifesto for the New Millennium* (Cresskill, NJ: Hampton Press, 1999).

[415] Sheila McNamee and Kenneth J. Gergen, editors, *Relational Responsibility: Resources for Responsibility* (Thousand Oaks, CA: Sage Publications, 1999).

[416] See the website for the Center for Ecoliteracy (www.ecoliteracy.org). "Seven Lessons for Leaders in Systems Change" was posted in the March 10, 2011 issue of their online newsletter.

[417] Netta Weinstein, Andrew K. Przybylski, and Richard M. Ryan, "Can Nature Make Us More Caring? Effects of Immersion in Nature on Intrinsic Aspirations and Generosity," *Personality and Social Psychology Bulletin*, vol. 35, no. 10, Oct. 2009, pp. 1315-1329. Four studies examined the effects of nature on valuing intrinsic and extrinsic aspirations. Intrinsic aspirations reflected prosocial and other-focused value orientations, and extrinsic aspirations predicted self-focused value orientations. Participants immersed in natural environments reported higher valuing of intrinsic aspirations and lower valuing of extrinsic aspirations, whereas those immersed in non-natural environments reported increased valuing of extrinsic aspirations and no change of intrinsic aspirations. Three studies explored experiences of nature relatedness and autonomy [defined here as "being in touch with oneself"] as underlying mechanisms of these effects, showing that nature immersion elicited these processes whereas non-nature immersion thwarted them and that they in turn predicted higher intrinsic and lower extrinsic aspirations. Studies 3 and 4 also extended the paradigm by testing these effects on generous decision-making indicative of valuing intrinsic versus extrinsic aspirations. Note: the researchers' statements cited in chapter 6 of this book appear on the last two pages of the article, which are pp. 13 and 14 in the PDF; the page numbering in the journal are different.

Index

Made in the USA
Las Vegas, NV
09 November 2022

59078827R00171